The Broadview Guide to Writing
4/e

The Broadview Guide to Writing
4/e

Doug Babington, Don LePan,
and Maureen Okun

broadview press

Library and Archives Canada Cataloguing in Publication

Babington, Doug
    The Broadview guide to writing / Doug Babington, Don LePan, and Maureen Okun. — 4/e

Includes bibliographical references and index.
ISBN 978-1-55111-969-4

    1. English language—Rhetoric—Handbooks, manuals, etc. 2. English language—Grammar—Handbooks, manuals, etc. 3. Report writing—Handbooks, manuals, etc. I. LePan, Don, 1954- II. Okun, Maureen Jeannette, 1961- III. Title. IV. Title: Guide to writing.

LB2369.B23 2009   808'.042   C2009-900953-6

Broadview Press is an independent, international publishing house, incorporated in 1985. We welcome comments and suggestions regarding any aspect of our publications—please feel free to contact us at the addresses below or at broadview@broadviewpress.com.

North America	PO Box 1243, Peterborough, Ontario, Canada K9J 7H5
	2215 Kenmore Ave., Buffalo, New York, USA 14207
	Tel: (705) 743-8990; Fax: (705) 743-8353
	email: customerservice@broadviewpress.com
UK, Ireland, and continental Europe	NBN International, Estover Road, Plymouth, UK PL6 7PY
	Tel: 44 (0) 1752 202300; Fax: 44 (0) 1752 202330
	email: enquiries@nbninternational.com
Australia and New Zealand	UNIREPS, University of New South Wales
	Sydney, NSW, Australia 2052
	Tel: 61 2 9664 0999; Fax: 61 2 9664 5420
	email: info.press@unsw.edu.au

www.broadviewpress.com

Broadview Press acknowledges the financial support of the Government of Canada through the Book Publishing Industry Development Program (BPIDP) for our publishing activities.

The publishers wish to acknowledge One Below for the design of the previous edition of this book, most of the elements of which have been incorporated into the design of the present edition.

This book is printed on paper containing 30% post-consumer fibre.

PRINTED IN CANADA

◎ CONTENTS

◎ HOW TO USE THIS BOOK

The goal of *The Broadview Guide* is to provide a comprehensive yet concise writing reference that is easy to use in every respect. We've made the book easy to carry around, and easy to use lying flat on a desk. We've also built in several features that we hope will make the book easy for you to find your way around in:

> **section dividers**: Flip to the section you want using the tabs on the section dividers. Here you'll find the contents of that section.

> **page headers**: Flip through the book with your eye on the page headers; these list section headings on the left, chapter headings on the right.

> **index**: Go to the index at the back of the book to find the location in the book for any topic, large or small.

> **table of contents**: The detailed table of contents at the beginning of the book sets out the sections, chapters, and topics within chapters.

The book opens with a substantial discussion of the writing process, focusing in particular on what is involved in writing essays at the university level. Like the rest of the book, this part has headers provided for ready reference, but we recommend reading it in its entirety.

If you are using this book as a reference for essay writing, two other sorts of links may be useful:

- the sample essay reproduced on pages 85–106 is provided as an example of essay style and structure, as well as format and referencing style; the essay is continually referred to as an example during the discussion of the essay-writing process (pages 15–83).

- additional essays, providing further examples of essay style and structure, as well as examples of different referencing styles (APA, Chicago, and CSE, as well as MLA), are available through the Broadview Press website; go to www.broadviewpress.com, and click on links.

This book does not provide one feature that you will find in many other writing reference books: highlights in blue or red or green throughout the book. Largely because the text is printed in one colour, however, the publisher is able to offer *The Broadview Guide* at a very substantially lower price than most other texts; this is one other respect in which we hope the new *Broadview Guide* will be a truly student-friendly text.

◎ PREFACE TO THE 4th EDITION

This latest edition includes a new chapter on sentence combining by Professor Maureen Okun, who has also made all the necessary revisions to bring this edition into line with the changes to MLA Style announced in 2008—not only to the section on MLA Style, but also to the sample essay and elsewhere. Beyond that, small revisions and updates have been made throughout.

As with the third edition, the exercises accompanying the guide are available online rather than in a separate bound book of exercises.

We are grateful to all those who have made suggestions for the new edition. Special thanks must go to Professor Robert M. Martin of Dalhousie University, who provided numerous pages of suggestions; many have been incorporated into the new edition.

◉ INTRODUCTION

Open any book to no page in particular. Turn it upside down. What appears is a strange pattern of black marks and white spaces—the essential stuff of any writer's efforts. Reading that pattern, different on every page of text, means (for most of us North Americans) moving from left to right and from top to bottom. With the page right side up, those black marks become symbols of a sound (*s*) or an image (*door*) or a concept (*oppression*) or even an emotion (*!*)—while the white ones run the necessary interference, establishing the spaces and divisions that help writers make their meanings.

Selecting symbols and arranging them (left to right, top to bottom) so that they communicate sensibly is every writer's occupation. Nothing more, in the end. But at the beginning, and every step along the way, the experiences of writers can be very frustrating and uncertain, whether they work in journalism, business, the performing arts, advertising, sports, politics, or—where so many really get their start—at a university, writing essays.

Because it deals with writing, *The Broadview Guide* looks at ways of handling frustration and uncertainty. But a grim primer on pain-survival it certainly is not. Satisfaction, discovery—and even playfulness—are all part of the demanding and worthwhile experience shared by capable writers in every field of professional endeavour; we hope we have succeeded in reflecting at least something of all of these.

Part One of *The Broadview Guide* discusses the four essentials that every essay-writer must develop: voice, ideas, fluency, and collaboration. From there on, the book moves on to cover grammar, usage, and a range of other mechanical and stylistic issues. We aim for a common-sense approach; the emphasis throughout is on showing through example. The repeated use of a "needs checking" and "revised" structure in the presentation of these examples is designed to encourage students to focus on the process of revising and improving their writing. And, by choosing examples from highly respected writers as well as from student writing, we attempt to underscore the point that *everyone's* writing can benefit from careful checking and revision; no student should be demoralized by the presence of imperfections in a final draft—let alone a first one. The process of working towards better writing is a continual one; it may never be easy, but it can be truly rewarding.

Reprinted following the book's long first section is the complete text of a university essay: "What Limits to Freedom?" We refer to this essay frequently, as an important part of *The Broadview Guide's* system of cross-references.

◎ THE WRITING PROCESS

⊙ Voice Work

Academic writing is easy to spot, even when it appears well beyond the academic world. Take, for instance, "The Brain of Brawn," a baseball article written by the late Stephen Jay Gould of Harvard University. Gould presents a thoughtful analysis of second baseman Chuck Knoblauch's difficulty in making accurate throws to his New York Yankee teammate over at first base. The writer asserts that "one of the most intriguing, and undeniable, properties of great athletic performance lies in the impossibility of regulating certain central skills by overt mental deliberation: the required action simply doesn't grant sufficient time for the sequential processing of conscious decisions" (17). He goes on to point out that "one form of unwanted, conscious mentality may be intruding upon a different and required style of unconscious cognition."

Knoblauch's manager and coaches wouldn't express themselves in quite the same manner, even if they agreed with Gould. Their voices would probably be much less formal, less abstract, less rigorous in distinguishing between, say, *mentality* and *cognition*. In other words, their voices would be less academic.

Formal phrasing, abstract language, and logical rigour certainly contribute to a recognizably academic *voice*. In writing university essays, however, it is tempting to rely excessively on these characteristics: you may end up using plenty of fancy words without presenting a clear argument; or you may create a magnificent deductive path that carries the reader far, far away from the announced topic.

Another challenge in establishing an appropriate voice is, of course, the fact that reading and writing are predominantly silent endeavours. A speaking voice has little in common with a writing voice, as Louis Menand explains:

In fact, speech is characterized by all the things writing teachers tell students to eliminate from their prose in the interest of clarity: repetition, contradiction, exaggeration, run-ons, fragments, and clichés, plus an array of tonal and physical inflections—drawls, grunts, shrugs, winks, hand gestures—unreproducible in written form. People talk for hours without uttering a single topic sentence. (94)

By contrast, essay-writers must always deal with the necessity of topic sentences, not to mention the impossibility of winking or grunting in the middle of a paragraph.

Such pressure can drain the voice of a good writer, just as pressure drains the throw of a good second baseman: "Knoblauch's problem takes the same form as many excruciating impediments in purely mental enterprises with writer's block as the most obvious example, when obsession with learned rules of style and grammar impedes the flow of good prose." Gould is a successful writer who knows better than to become obsessed by learned rules of style and grammar. Important as those rules are, it is far better—at the outset of the writing process—to approach your essay as an opportunity for clear and fluent expression of independent, informed thinking. In other words, concentrate on developing a *voice* that will enhance your own ideas, acknowledge the position of your readers, and make clear the main reason for the essay's existence.

O Attitude

The key to enhancing your own ideas is a mental *attitude* of self-confidence and self-assertion. A competent writer's voice is born from a position of power over the assignment at hand, the resources at hand, and the deadline that looms ahead. If no real power is felt to exist, then it must be manufactured:

"Three-thousand words in five days? Not a problem."
"There are definitely ways in which Milton's verse disappoints me."

"This professor of mine is about to really learn something."

Of course, establishing full control at the outset of the writing process is impossible. "How do I know what I think," wrote E.M. Forster, "until I see what I have to say?" The point is that writers see what they have to say—they start writing—only by believing in themselves. Some manufactured power at the outset will lead to real power along the way.

Weak writing, then, can often be traced to an attitude problem. The passive writer-in-waiting views his or her blank pages like some ominous battlefield whose land mines will commence exploding with the first timid step forward. Passiveness and timidity combine to abort the writer's fledgling voice. But **active** confrontation with an assignment, however tough that assignment may first appear, allows the voice to grow. As one sociology professor advises (in notes distributed to all her students),

> In writing the work, do not be afraid to give your own views. It is of considerable interest to the tutor to know what students think about the material, and especially what they think they have learned from the exercise. If you find material obscure or unconvincing say so, but always give the reasons.

O *Audience*

Attention to attitude, which gives birth to a writer's voice, is often followed by attention to audience, which modifies that voice. Competent writers realize the folly of locking themselves in to any set formulas of style or organization—because these things often change, depending upon the demands or expectations of a given audience. "Avoid the passive voice," cautions one professor of English literature. "Reports must be written in the third person, passive voice, and past tense," announces the professor of chemistry. What's a writer to do? Listen carefully, for one thing, and ask questions. Look over past essays written for similar audiences.

Conformity to reasonable audience expectations—such as writing in English instead of Urdu—does not mean slavish imitation. Ideas can be strong and original, and evidence can be compelling, even as a writer writes to please, say, the grammatical or bibliographical preferences of his or her reader-to-be.

Two examples from the world of academic publishing illustrate the sort of concessions good writers make to their audiences—and point up something important about the matter of writing introductions to essays. Here are introductory paragraphs from two articles, both of which appeared in publications that are aimed at a general academic audience. The first appeared in the Canadian journal *Queen's Quarterly*, the second in *The New York Review of Books*. First, from Susan P.C. Cole's "The Legacy of Terry Fox":

> More than nine years have elapsed since Terry Fox began his run across Canada to raise money for cancer research and eight years have passed since his death from the disease he sought to conquer. The events of the early 1980s surrounding Terry's Marathon of Hope can now be viewed with some perspective, and one might begin to answer a number of questions. Could the medical profession do more for Terry if he were alive today than they were able to do when he was first stricken with cancer? How has the money raised been spent? What has been the impact of his run on the efforts of the cancer research community in Canada? Has Terry's dream been kept alive? This article will address these questions and discuss the influence of Terry Fox and his Marathon of Hope on cancer research in Canada. (253)

Second, from Garry Wills's "The Negro President" (an article summarizing for a wider readership the argument of a book on the same topic he was about to publish):

> I have admired Jefferson all my life, and still do.... But I have now devoted an entire book to one deadly part of his legacy— the protection and extension of slavery through the three-fifths

clause in the Constitution. That work depends on the general and growing labour of modern historians to grasp the pervasiveness of slavery's effects on early American history. I don't mean to join an unfortunate recent trend toward Jefferson-bashing. I disagree with those who would diminish his great achievement, the Declaration of Independence (Maier 1997). Or those who call him more a friend to despotism than to freedom (Cruise O'Brien 1996). Or those who would reduce his whole life to an affair with a slave. My Jefferson is a giant, but a giant trammeled in a net, and obliged, he thought, to keep repairing and strengthening the coils of that net. (45)

Cole is a pharmacologist, used to writing for other scientists, while Wills is a historian, used to writing for other humanists. Not surprisingly, given this background, their approaches to writing introductory paragraphs differ. After clearly announcing her topic, the scientist poses a series of relevant questions and then confirms for her readers what the article will accomplish. (She would be in trouble with the English professor who instructs his students to "avoid telling the reader about your writing; stick to your topic instead. Cut phrases such as *We will examine* and *This paper will show that*.") The humanist also begins with a clear announcement of his topic, but that is where the similarity ends. He immediately carves out the argumentative territory of his essay, stating his topic in his second sentence, and then summarizing a range of opposing views before presenting his own thesis statement (19) in the final sentence of the paragraph. (Wills would find more favour with the English professor: "I consider it conventional, and therefore essential, that your thesis be stated in the last sentence of paragraph one.")

Like most scientific writers, Susan Cole saves her argumentative assertions—the answers to questions posed in the introductory paragraph—for the "Conclusion" of her article. Again, this bottom-heavy approach, which contrasts with the top-heavy approach of Wills, is related to the discipline the writer works in. Yet neither Cole nor Wills ignores the wider profile of the

Queen's Quarterly and *New York Review of Books* readership; both publications are intended to appeal to a broad, interdisciplinary readership.

Certainly, the more diverse the audience, the more freedom a writer may enjoy in decisions of organization and style. Many university essay-writers tend to err, however, in the other direction: by envisioning an audience of one—namely, the professor responsible for the assignment. Even if she may, in fact, be the only one who will read the paper, it is better to write not only for the professor but also for one's peers, for the other people in the lecture hall or classroom, so as to avoid unnaturally stilted language and overly grandiose assertions. In writers' worlds, the most successful voices are the least strained.

O *Purpose*

But even with diligent attention to attitude and audience, some very important voice work remains to be done. No writer can get on with the business of filling up pages and sorting out paragraphs unless some compelling purpose for it all exists. "What's it all about?" "Why am I sitting here losing sleep and working myself into a state of anxious indigestion?" Such questions must be raised and must be answered—at least partially: "I don't believe the writer should know too much where he's going," says James Thurber. "If he does, he runs into old man blueprint—old man propaganda." Certainly no good journalist follows an editor's blueprint. But each writer requires a purpose, one that is more than the mere desire to earn this month's salary or this term's B+ in history.

The stated assignment is an obvious place to begin. "Discuss the rise to power of Francisco Franco." Or "Thoroughly explain the advances in medical imaging since the 1980s." Or "Analyse the connections between Margaret Atwood's poetry and her novels." Very few writers are absolutely free to devise their own purposes. Most receive orders or commands (*Discuss, Explain, Analyse*), either from some external figure of authority or from inside their own writerly consciences. Such commands are usually quite vague and open-ended, though. It's enough to make an honest writer quiver and squirm:

> How am I supposed to discuss the rise to power of Francisco Franco? That could take years! And what is "Discuss" supposed to mean? Do I tell the story of the Spanish Civil War? Do I try to ascertain Franco's psychological makeup, or to analyse socio-economic influences at work at the time? How does my professor feel; what exactly is she expecting with this paper, anyway?

If she's a professor who really cares about writing, she's expecting some tension to be located and resolved. Purpose in writing comes from tension, from the writer's personal sense of things out of kilter, in conflict:

> This clash engenders puzzlement, curiosity, a sense of enigma, sometimes of wonder, a pressure to restore equilibrium. While some people suppress such tension, the inquirer, the learner, strives to resolve it by searching for new understanding, by going beyond the known. (Lauer 90)

What Janice Lauer is actually recommending here is an attitude of risk; "the inquirer, the learner" confronts the essay topic in much the same way that King Lear confronts his stormy heath or Alice confronts her Wonderland. Worthy purposes are often a little off-beat, a little idiosyncratic. They turn otherwise formulaic, encyclopedia-entry essays into essays of personally distinct intellect. Competent writers can write personally without being subjective and intellectually without being pretentious or false.

What if (returning to Francisco Franco) a prospective writer is bothered by the whole notion of "power" in the world of Spanish politics and warfare? Ignoring that abstract and difficult word might very well short-circuit her ability to handle the assignment—whereas grappling with its definition (see page 39) might be sufficient purpose to set her writing in gear. Rather than halfheartedly narrate a string of events from the 1930s or merely list the political parties of that era, she would be motivated to write by the tension and ambiguity surrounding a single word in the assignment. Focusing on the nature of power might lead the writer to her thesis statement:

- Like most fascists, Franco saw power as an end in itself, not merely as a means to achieving other ends.

Unlike the topic, the thesis statement expresses an argumentative purpose and a point of view. It should be meaningful, clear, and concise—a sentence, two at the most. It need not declare anything earth-shattering, but it should not be trivial or self-evident. Effective thesis statements are moulded to fit both the length of the essay and the expertise of their writers. There is no logical sense in asserting, at the outset of a 3,000-word history paper, that *every military leader since Attila the Hun has repeated his mistakes* or that *all politicians who have supported scandal-prone companies such as Enron and Countrywide are morally corrupt.* The vocabulary of absolutes (*every, all, best, only,* etc.) always commits a writer to universal coverage—and authoritative knowledge—of the topic. Chances are the student writer will have neither time and space for the former nor sufficient education for the latter. Strength in argumentative writing often comes from willingness to qualify assertions and to acknowledge that contrary points of view are, if not convincing, at least intelligent and comprehensible. Words such as *often, usually,* and *largely,* and phrases such as *for the most part,* and *to a great extent* are not necessarily signs that the writer lacks the courage of her convictions; more frequently they are indications that she is careful.

All of the above rests on one important presupposition—that the writing assignment is clear to the student. What if you are uncertain not only about what the professor wants, but also about what she means? After all, the language of assignments, like academic language generally, is often difficult. Here, for example, is the gloss to an assignment provided by a sociology professor:

Thesis Statement: Some Examples

needs checking   Art is important to society in many ways, and I will talk about them in this essay. One of the artists I will focus on is Robert Mapplethorpe, the subject of much controversy over many years.

(Yawn. The statement is too general and too vague to have significance.)

revised   The art of Robert Mapplethorpe deserves to be exhibited—and at public expense—even if most people find it abhorrent.

(This statement is more precise, more limited, more interesting.)

needs checking   In this paper I will examine various reasons for launching the war in Kosovo in 1999.

(This is a statement of topic rather than of thesis. It's also wordy.)

revised   The moral case for the US and its allies to wage a bombing-only war against Yugoslavia in 1999 was stronger than the strategic one; air attacks alone had never before been enough to win a war.

(Suddenly an argument is being made.)

needs checking   The purpose of this essay is to explore the interplay between poetry and the novel. I will demonstrate that good poets don't usually write good novels and vice versa.

(Full points for ambition, but it's the subject for a book, not a term paper. At most, a short paper might justifiably speculate about such a large question in its conclusion; the main focus should be much narrower. Also, the statement is far too bold in its generalization. "What about Thomas Hardy?" the professor will ask. "What about Boris Pasternak?")

revised   Ondaatje's characters seem thin and unreal to the reader—alternately brittle and transparent. Paradoxically, however, it may be precisely these qualities that allow the poetic power of his prose—at once brutal and fragile—to strike the reader with full force.

(A much narrower but still controversial thesis exploring the connections between poetry and prose.)

The assignment involves learning to think sociologically and to present a sociological argument. The process involved is analogous to "inductive" reasoning (or what some sociologists refer to as "grounded theory") in that the object is to start from where you are and refine your thinking such that you develop general statements that represent the character of human social activity and that are capable of being treated with reference to empirical reality.

No student should be ashamed of asking for clarification here. In fact, it would be far worse to plunge blindly ahead, hoping against hope that your professor might not notice how much your sentences squirm. The language of intellectual discourse involves concepts, all of which are made up of abstract nouns—words representing things that cannot be seen or heard or appreciated by any physical sense. Consequently, concepts are difficult to grasp, especially when the abstract noun is preceded by an equally abstract adjective: *empirical reality,* for example, or *sociological argument,* or (turning to this very paragraph) *intellectual discourse.* Grappling independently with difficult concepts is central to anyone's higher education. Nevertheless, uncertainty and confusion may strike even the most experienced of writers. So always keep your lines of communication open. Talk over the assignment with fellow students, writing tutors, and teaching assistants, as well as with professors.

◉ ◉ ◉

Each and every university assignment could be distilled to a single imperative: "Respond!" Conscientious voice work ensures that your response will be worthy of the subject matter at hand. Once lethargy and timidity are shunned (attitude), and once the eventual readers are clearly in mind (audience), then any writer who is not brain-dead will be able to locate tension in the course material or in the statement of topic. To resolve that tension becomes the essay's purpose, one that may well change or expand or contract during the writing process but without which no writer's voice can ever be called complete.

⊙ Essential Activities

Something's been bothering Melissa Davis, ever since she received her "Effective Writing" essay assignment: "Discuss and examine a case that raises issues of social or cultural importance in North America. Include in your essay references to both popular and scholarly discussions of the issue." Selecting a general topic wasn't a problem; she had always been interested in the issue of censorship and freedom of expression. But what specific case should she focus on? She remembered hearing of a highly controversial episode involving a painting of the Virgin Mary that had incorporated feces into the artwork—had it been in the New York area? Much as she believed in freedom of speech and of expression, the more she tried to imagine a "painting" of this sort the more unsettled she felt. She Googled "New York feces art exhibit" and immediately found many references to Chris Ofili and the notorious 1999 "Sensation" exhibit at the Brooklyn Museum. Clearly this was an issue that had inspired heated debate, with spirited defences of free speech on one side, and on the other side heated condemnations of art galleries "feeding from the public trough to finance ... hate art targeting Christians" (Schlafly). Melissa didn't find the idea of this sort of art to be very appealing, but nor did she find the polemical attacks on it convincing. She began, then, with a desire to sort out her own gut reaction. In other words, Melissa Davis had a purpose in writing. Exactly how she would sort out either her own feelings or the various arguments was initially far from clear.

The final draft of Melissa's essay on freedom of expression (pages 85–106) is exactly that: the *final* residue of an intense thinking process, during which the purpose in her gut found articulate expression in a thesis and in the material supporting it. This mental refinement—from purpose to ideas—is usually the most mysterious and satisfying phase of the writing process: "The initial delight is in the discovery of something I didn't know I knew," the poet Robert Frost once said, realizing from long experience how completely writing and thinking grow together—mutually supportive and absolutely bound.

O Reading and Note-taking

First among activities that assist writers in discovering their own thoughts is *reading*. According to another celebrated American poet, Walt Whitman, it requires no less self-confidence and self-assertion than writing itself:

> Books are to be call'd for, and supplied, on the assumption that the process of reading is not a half-sleep, but, in the highest sense, an exercise, a gymnast's struggle; that the reader is to do something for himself, must be on the alert, must himself or herself construct indeed the poem, argument, history, metaphysical essay—the text furnishing the hints, the clue, the start or framework. Not the book needs so much to be the complete thing, but the reader of the book does. (par. 129)

The question of *what* to read is discussed below under "Collaboration and Research." Just as important is *how* to read. As Whitman's remarks imply, it is essential to be able to read actively rather than passively—to be prepared to make connections, be able to extend the ideas you are presented with, and to be able to question those ideas. In the case of Melissa Davis's research, it was important to be able to discern the underlying assumptions both of those who wrote of Ofili's work as an "assault on religion" and of those who condemned any limits to government funding for the arts as censorship. It was important as well, of course, to weigh the arguments presented by all sides against the evidence. Through this sort of reading it becomes clear that there is no such thing as a frozen, immutable text whose message can be unlocked only by a single, privileged reading. Rather, each reader has the opportunity to construct the text anew, provided that he or she is paying close attention to the words on the page. Even when faced with assigned chapters by renowned scholars, the reader must be ready to respond independently. Whitman is right: reading is valuable because it provides "the hints, the clue, the start or framework" of the reader's own text.

In practice, this means taking notes. As work begins for many a writer, paper and pencil are nearby. Or paper and pen, or laptop computer. Thoughts and insights can strike at any time, but they also have a way of evaporating quickly—so it's wise to be prepared. From the word "*Go!*", writing things down is central to the writing process. Some reading writers favour the pencil-in-the-margin approach, which yields brief and pointed reactions (such as "Bad logic" or "?" or "!" or "Yes!" or "Ho hum"). Others keep sheets of paper handy, to work up some preliminary sentences—or even paragraphs. Either way, the objective is to use reading as a catalyst in the discovery of ideas on the mind. (Another important function of note-taking— namely, as a research tool—will be discussed later in the book, on page 69.)

For many people who are reading to survive at universities, though, note-taking seems like a utopian luxury enjoyed in some distant time warp. There are simply too many pages of too many books and articles to plough through. Among such burdened readers, the most fortunate and effective are those who hang on to their pens by forfeiting some text: they *do* take notes, but they read selectively. Before ploughing through anything in an assigned reading, they skim over the introduction, the lead sentences of paragraphs, and the conclusion. In other words, they conduct a reconnaissance mission, based on strategic knowledge of most essays' terrains. The likely result is an accurate sense of the essay's thesis, key terminology, range of evidence, and logical organization. Such readers will then select passages for sustained and thorough surveillance, according to the purposes developed in their own voice work.

O *Mapping*

In the beginning, when the task at hand is choosing a topic or developing material for a thesis, an essay-writer's thinking may be quite unstructured. Indeed, it's beneficial to play with ideas, to think freely, and to take rough notes based on whatever comes to mind. Rather than sit for hours mulling over an assignment sheet, better to see what can be discovered by putting pen to paper—or fingers to keyboard.

As the topic comes into focus, though, a bit more structure is needed; the writer begins working on the details of his argument. Of course, those very details may change as the writing process moves forward, but a solid foundation can still be achieved through the essential activity of *mapping*.

Return to the example of Melissa Davis. As her "Works Cited" list shows (pages 104–106), she read numerous articles, consulted several books, searched the Internet, and sought out reproductions of the Ofili work itself in order to sort out her gut reaction to the issues raised by the "Sensation" exhibit controversy. With notes from this research she was able to map out an essay yet to be written (see page 29).

Several times while reading, Melissa had come upon the phrase *freedom of expression* and jotted down in her notes "need to clarify" or "define." As one of the commands in her mapping reveals, the essay will certainly strive to explain that term. Definition will be one of her key writing strategies.

The identification of such strategies, whose shared aim is to support the thesis, is yet another dividend of mapping. Every writer uses them because they are natural modes of human thought: not only does **definition** appear in Melissa's mapping out, but so do **narration** ("history of Ofili's work and the 'Sensation' exhibit"), **classification** ("is it art?"), and **comparison contrast** ("discuss moral/legal distinction"). We will return to these modes of thought and writing shortly (pages 37–49).

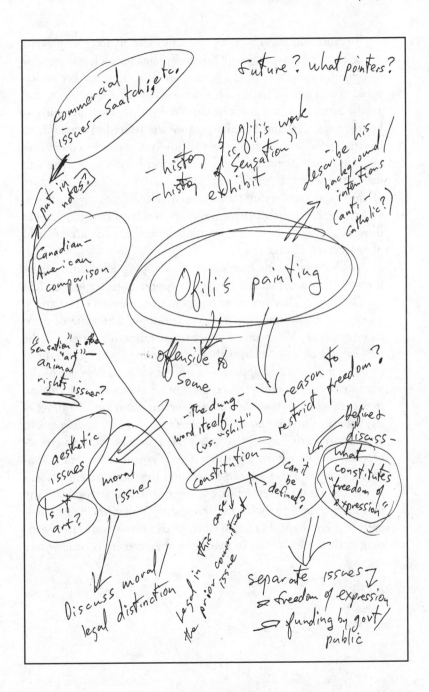

Because Melissa's mapping happens to be an accurate preview of the eventual essay (this will not always be the case), it is possible to pinpoint sentences in the final draft that represent her anticipated strategies. In paragraph 6 and again in paragraphs 9 and 10 she articulates one **contrast** that emerged through mapping—between the legal and moral aspects of the issue. In paragraph 10 **contrast** flows into example, just as fluidly as **narration** flows into **argument** in paragraph 5—where Melissa begins to analyse and take issue with Mayor Giuliani's views after outlining the story of the "Sensation" exhibit controversy. Fluidity, overlap, merger, and convergence are all characteristic of writing strategies, because those strategies represent a miraculously complex and kinetic field of energy: the human mind.

As Melissa's work demonstrates, mapping allows the many threads of an argumentative essay to appear together for the first time on paper. They may take the form of a question ("is it art?"), a key image (the dung itself), or a sub-topic (the issue of prior commitment). All of them, however, connect ultimately to the biggest idea of all—Melissa's thesis concerning freedom of expression. Its two-pronged appearance on the map carries over to the final draft (at the end of paragraph one): *Along the way cultural conservatives have raised legitimate concerns about the obligation of any society to provide funding for activities of which it disapproves; a greater concern, however, is that a free society continue to provide opportunities for the free expression both of artistic vision and controversial thought.* This sentence constitutes the thesis statement, and its strategy is **argument**. But the argumentative strength of any thesis depends entirely on its strategic accompaniment, which—even in a relatively short essay such as this one—is diverse. Mapping is an invaluable aid in managing the diversity of any writer's text.

O *Writer's Block*

Of course, not even the most thorough of essay-maps can guarantee a smooth journey; always lurking on the horizon are the frustrations of writer's block. Almost all of us know the experience of sitting down to write, notes and outlines and books close at hand. Then uncertainty strikes: "Perhaps my plan needs a bit more tinkering. What was it again that Smith and Sapsucker said about all this? Maybe I should go back and reread that passage. Maybe I should get a new pen to write with—or delete some of the stuff on this disk so I'll be sure to have enough space for the essay. Actually, a coffee might help." Students aren't the only ones susceptible to writer's block. Many's the time that a professor will say, "I'm working on a paper dealing with such and such. It's pretty much done; all I have to do is write it up." The prof knows as well as the student that this is a convenient fiction—that the writing is the main business, not merely an afterthought. Sometimes, though, the task just seems too daunting.

How can the affliction of writer's block be avoided? As mentioned at the outset of this section, the free play of ideas is one antidote. Just force that pen to move across the paper (or those keyboard keys to start clicking), quite literally writing anything that comes to mind, whether coherent or not, whether on or off topic. After ten or fifteen minutes, usable material will have turned up. The writing won't, of course, display perfect grammar, spelling, or punctuation—nor will it be organized into coherent paragraphs. But at this stage none of that matters.

Once a writer has begun writing fluidly on the topic, it does *not* pay to pause when she hits a point in the argument that requires an example or a reference that's not handy. Instead, she should jot down a note in the margin ("find example—Taylor's book?" or "support this with quotation—gravediggers' scene?") and keep on going. There will be plenty of time later to check for the required item, and chances are that doing so now will mean losing the flow of the argument.

Eventually the moment comes to set down the pen for a few minutes and take stock of the words on the page or the screen: to decide how much fits in, and where, what needs fleshing out, what should be scrapped. It may be the time to start revising the map in the light of what's been discovered while writing. For, as every experienced writer knows, writing is *not* simply a process of putting down on paper what is already known in the writer's mind. The very act of writing forces the writer, inevitably (but often quite unexpectedly), to see things differently, to combine ideas in unanticipated ways.

O *Dialogue*

Reading and mapping are two essential activities for the essay writer; dialogue with others is a third. Its importance is continually demonstrated these days by the success and rapid growth of writing centres at universities throughout North America. Here are a few impressions from Queen's University students, following one-to-one sessions with writing tutors:

- "I had a chance to explain what I wanted to convey. My tutor had a chance to look at my essay and then <u>together</u> we made progress based on her suggestions."

- "I liked the fact that I wasn't told what to do—it was more a discussion about possibilities. But I was also given excellent suggestions and advice on things that I was concerned about, such as my paragraph transitions."

- "I appreciate having someone new look over my work to give me a fresh perspective. Her helpful, clear comments will really aid me when I go back to revise my work."

Such dialogue is immediately encouraging for a serious essay-writer, who can step away from his solitary turbulence and benefit from an attentive eye and sympathetic heart (writing centre tutors tend to be writers themselves!). As the Queen's students express, dialogue can be a truly collaborative exercise, one that places a text in a new light and allows two readers to inform each other about where that text is headed. Sometimes the simplest of gestures—such as hearing your paper read aloud by another person—will lead to revisions that might never have occurred otherwise.

Certainly a writing tutor may clarify the proper use of the semicolon or answer some other question of English usage (such as those discussed elsewhere in this book). But productive dialogue goes far beyond the details of proofreading; its real value lies in the mutual encouragement of two writers' minds. Together they can travel further than either one alone.

Often, though, it may not be possible to see someone at a writing centre about each essay. One should also be ready and willing to show one's writing to friends, classmates—and of course instructors—at any stage. Too often we look at our work as sacrosanct; we are embarrassed by its weaknesses, shy of showing it to others before it's what we like to think of as perfect. And if at that late stage others see imperfections, we are too easily hurt. Ironically, the more experienced and confident a writer is, the more she is usually willing and eager to seek out dialogue—and criticism—from others. She has developed even within herself a critical stance towards her work; she knows it is not and will never be perfect, but she knows as well that dialogue with others is always a way to improvement, and is in itself a stimulating and enjoyable activity.

⊙ Double Fluency

Smooth, easy flow. Effortless movement. In a word, fluency—something that we aim for in any finished piece of writing. As all experienced writers know, however, the appearance of effortlessness and ease is superficial; the final draft of an essay is an opaque surface, showing readers none of the turbulence that is so much a part of the writing process. Transforming such turbulence into fluency depends on key components of logic and style, which no successful writer can afford to ignore.

O *Logical Fluency*

Because most university essays are argumentative, their strength depends greatly on logical fluency. Assertions need to be clearly supported by reasons, and those reasons need to be convincing. "Try to be more clear, convincing, and logical in future papers," advises many a well-meaning professor. Easier said than done. Fortunately, experience has taught competent writers some useful approaches—and some specific cautions.

A first step towards logical fluency is to be aware of the premises that guide your thought process. Most writing starts with certain conscious premises: Melissa Davis, for example, begins mapping out her essay by assuming that freedom of expression is a fundamental good. With this premise in mind she seeks to build a logical argument concerning the Ofili piece—why it has created controversy, and to what extent the objections to it may be justified. Along the way she also works from the premise that "moral obligations may often exceed legal ones." Consciously held premises such as these are useful and indeed necessary steps in building an argument.

Watch out, though, for the power of unconscious premises— general beliefs and automatic assumptions that may covertly direct your critical thinking. *I cannot possibly have anything worthwhile to say on this topic* is an example; if allowed to lurk in the back of the mind, this premise—this crisis of attitude (page 16)—will paralyse an essay's development. *Children over five years of age are just mini- ature adults* is a premise that could lead an editorialist to call for a return to corporal punishment in our schools. *Capitalism is in all circumstances the best system* is a premise that would certainly cloud a writer's judgement and reduce her capacity for understanding if she were writing an essay on the economic system of medieval

Europe, or that of traditional Inuit society. *Something I find offensive could never be a work of art* is perhaps another premise capable of clouding a writer's judgement. Premises, be they strong or weak, do not always appear in the text of an essay. All the more reason, then, for every writer to examine hers attentively, so that the essay's logic will be intentional, not inadvertent.

● *Elaboration and Repetition*

Even a clear and manageable thesis will be ineffective unless every one of its parts is clearly elaborated. When moving from paragraph to paragraph, it is all too easy to omit steps in the argument that you, the writer, feel are obvious. The problem is that readers may not feel the same way. Deliberate writers always ask themselves one key question: "Am I making everything clear for someone who has not done the research I have and who does not know anything of my argument beyond what I've told him?" In conversation, it's easy enough for the other person to interrupt by saying, "I can't follow your reasoning there." Readers don't have the same luxury. In Melissa Davis's essay paragraphs 5 and 6 include a good deal of elaboration, as the writer clearly lays out the legal limitations to freedom of expression, and the principles behind government support of the arts.

The space that is devoted to the ideas that appear is of as much importance as the order in which they appear. For this reason it is important to avoid long discussions of matters you consider to be of less importance—or else to relegate them to a note outside the main body of the text. (Notice how Melissa Davis has relegated several interesting points to the notes of her essay.) Similarly, it is wise to provide enough elaboration of your main idea, whether through extending the argument itself or through providing numerous examples, to signal your sense of the relative importance of the various ideas you are presenting. A good essay typically gives the most space to the ideas that the writer considers most important. (Obviously you may also signal this through the use of words and phrases such as *most important*, *crucially*, and so on.)

The amount of space devoted to an idea is one way of signalling its importance; another is to return more than once to an essay's most important points. Mere repetitiveness within the same paragraph is obviously off-putting to the reader—but repetition of key points over the course of an essay can greatly enhance its argumentative focus. At the end of Melissa's eighth paragraph, for example, she reiterates her thesis from her essay's introduction: *We value a society in which a wide range of free expression is supported— and we have come to expect that governments will provide a good deal of that support.* This statement not only repeats her position but also places it clearly in the context of public funding obligations. Similarly, in the essay's final paragraph, Melissa reiterates the central point of her thesis. Rather than merely repeat familiar material, she broadens the context of the argument significantly by referring to the change in attitudes toward freedom of expression that was prompted by the terrorist attacks of September 11, 2001. Without slipping into repetitiveness, then, she has managed to strengthen the argumentative crux of her essay.

Of course, methods of repetition can be as varied as writers' purposes. Appearing in the issue of *Queen's Quarterly* quoted earlier (18) is an article by Sylvia Ostry entitled "New Developments in Trade Policy." Its thesis, a vision of the world's economic future, foresees "a gradual, largely invisible transformation of the world trading system, a transformation that is unplanned and therefore essentially unpredictable" (216). (Some of the most compelling and clear thesis statements, by the way, can be those that express uncertainty or limited knowledge.) Because her logical focus is the future, Ms. Ostry begins the essay's conclusion with a question: *So what are the policy options?* After briefly identifying two such options, she returns to the interrogative mode: *Can or will the US exercise leadership without hegemony? And if not the US, then who?* (225). End of article. The posing of thoughtful questions, while consistent with the essay's thesis (*a transformation that is ... essentially unpredictable*), is not mere repetitiveness; a specific factor is introduced (US leadership) that keeps readers thinking.

Logical fluency is, essentially, a writer's ability to keep thinking so that his readers will too. To let the meaning choose the word and not the other way round. To resist work-saving formulas and, instead, to be independently responsible for a composition of language whose logical coherence is unique. After all, the pieces of no two essays come together in precisely the same way, so every writer must make good sense—every time out—as if for the very first time.

● *Modes of Thought/Modes of Writing*

Traditionally, essays tend to be grouped into categories such as descriptive, narrative, expository, or argumentative. In practice, such distinctions are overly simplistic; very few papers are written purely in one mode. Since college and university essays are usually organized around thesis statements, they tend to be primarily argumentative: the writer's paramount concern is the presentation of an informed point of view on her topic. Along the way, however, most argumentative essays employ several other modes of thought.

Melissa Davis's essay "What Limits to Freedom?", for example, is typical of university essays in the Humanities or Social Sciences in that it is primarily argumentative. But at two significant points Davis employs a narrative mode—first in Paragraph 2 (in summarizing the background of the exhibition coming to Brooklyn) and then again in Paragraph 13 (in summarizing the story of the court verdict and its aftermath). Narration is the first of four modes of writing whose academic purposes deserve detailed consideration.

○ NARRATION

The basic mode of thought involved in narration is a very simple one: one thing happens, and then another thing happens, and then another thing happens. For example, the "Methods" section of a scientific lab report is usually organized around a narrative sequence of events:

> A sugar maple leaf was collected from an area close to the trunk. This leaf was cut so as to cover the surface area of a leaf chamber, which was attached to a sensor. Carbon dioxide was flushed into the chamber and the oxygen production per minute was measured using a serial interface and computer. The average per cent oxygen output per minute was then calculated, as was the standard deviation.

Considering its linkage of events through time, narration is the most straightforward mode of thinking and of writing. Nevertheless, it should be used sparingly in academic essays. Professors of literature often warn students to "assume your reader has read the work," realizing that if an argumentative essay merely retells a novelist's story, it's not much of an argumentative essay. Remember that any plot summary included in your paper must support a point—not substitute for one. You should always ask yourself the question your marker is sure to ask: "Why is this important?" If a writer is discussing the violence that broke out in the Sudanese region of Darfur in 2004, the narrative mode may well be the best one to adopt; the sequence of events is a complex one, and getting it straight is crucial to any argument as to the guilt or innocence of those involved. But in most academic arguments narration should be introduced only in support of the writer's own argument; it should not be allowed to take the place of that argument.

O CLASSIFICATION

Classification is the process of sorting into groups. The mental act of classifying can be enormously complex, but it can also be enormously satisfying to our sense of order. And how well we learn to do it will make a real difference to the logical fluency of our writing.

Classification is particularly important to essays that make comparisons or draw contrasts. If the writer is comparing the Canadian economy with that of the United States, for example, she will sort the data or other evidence she has assembled into various classes: sizes of the two economies; strengths of particular economic sectors (manufacturing, services, government, etc.); trade; banking and interest rates; geographical and climatic inputs; and so on. In doing so she will need to make a number of choices. The boundary lines between groups are often fragile or give trouble; what should be grouped with what? What will go in and what will be left out? In large part this will be dictated by the thrust of her argument. (Essays of comparison and contrast, like other essays, must have a purpose; they should never be mere lists.) She must be careful, certainly, not to make the selection on a random or arbitrary basis.

Then there are questions of where given topics should appear in the paper. Should the essay deal with all aspects of one country's economy first, and then turn to the economy of the other country? Usually this approach weakens structural unity; it would be better to compare Canadian manufacturing with American manufacturing, Canadian banking with American banking, et cetera.

Classification is of equal importance if the essayist is writing in a descriptive mode: telling what something looks like or how it works. (This mode of writing is particularly common in the sciences.) If the writer is describing the behaviour patterns of the beaver, for example, he may decide to group them into headings such as feeding, dam- and lodge-building, and breeding habits. He will probably also want to discuss how the anatomy of the animal and its behaviours are adapted to each other—perhaps pausing after each category of behaviour has been described to relate it to particular anatomical features.

Classification is also vital to another mode of writing—definition. Sometimes an entire essay may have a question of definition as its focus:

- Definitions of "Liberalism" from the Nineteenth to the Twenty-first Century

- The Concept of Metonymy in Sixteenth-century Rhetoric and in Deconstructionist Criticism
- "Making Love" from the 1950s to the 2000s

In such cases the writer describes or analyses the ways in which a term or concept has been understood differently in different eras. How did the term *liberal,* which in the nineteenth century implied firm opposition to government intervention in the economy, come to imply the very opposite a hundred years later? How did *making love,* once understood to refer to acts of courtship that stopped short of the overtly sexual acts, come in the 1960s to refer to nothing but such acts? And how do such changes in definition reflect or even cause broader changes in social attitudes?

Definition can also be an important part of other sorts of essays, as Melissa Davis's writing illustrates. In establishing her position Melissa is careful to inquire into what constitutes *freedom of expression,* and to define it with reference both to legal rights as set out constitutionally, and to the reality of social practice. Notice that she does not rely here on a dictionary as her source; she is aware that dictionary definitions are usually inadequate to the needs of academic writing. (Indeed, if a term has a meaning particular to an academic discipline, dictionary definitions can be downright misleading.)

O GENERALIZATION AND ABSTRACTION

Generalization is the process of moving from an observation or conclusion about a single thing or a small number of things to a conclusion about all or most of that group. Abstraction, on the other hand, is at its most basic level the isolation of some particular quality of a thing from the rest of its properties—the consideration of the colour of a particular object, for example.

Many people are a bit hazy on the difference between abstraction and generalization—not surprisingly, since the two are related activities that we often perform simultaneously. Perhaps the best way of keeping them straight is to remember (as C.R. Hallpike puts it) that "while the opposite of *general* is *particular*, the opposite of *abstract* is *concrete*" (171). *Emotions* is a broad general category; love and hate are particular emotions. (*Neither* is a concrete thing.) The redness of the Canadian flag is an abstraction; the flag itself is a concrete thing. (We may also, of course, speak of one particular Canadian flag or of the Canadian flag in general, or of all flags in general; there can be numerous levels of both abstraction and generalization.)

Melissa Davis's essay is continually involved with the abstract (concepts such as *decency* and *freedom of expression*) and with the concrete (perhaps most memorably, the materials used in Ofili's piece). It is intensely involved, as well, with various generalizations—about the "Sensation" exhibit, for example, and about the appropriate role of government in a democratic society.

Most essays involve shifts not only from the general to the particular and back again, but also from one level of generalization to another:

- An art history essay on Chippendale chairs would probably refer to particular examples from the eighteenth-century studio of Thomas Chippendale himself, generalize about all chairs of that type, generalize further about the furniture of the period, and perhaps generalize at one higher level about how and why such designs suited the overall sensibilities of eighteenth-century England.

- An English literature essay might make a general claim about Jane Austen's use of irony. It might then descend one level of generality to discuss the differences in the degree to which the generalization applies in the various novels. It might then move to a lower level of generality, distinguishing between the scenes in *Northanger Abbey* that are suffused with the characteristic Austen sense of irony and those (apparently remaining from the first draft of the novel) that are almost pure melodrama with no irony to them whatsoever. Finally, the essay would doubtless give particular examples—quote sentences or paragraphs that exemplify an ironic tone and a melodramatic one.

Both abstraction and generalization are important mental processes for any writer; they help us, as Janet Giltrow puts it, to "name and manage otherwise unruly details" (141). But writers have to learn to use them with care. As a rule, generalizations must be supported by evidence. (Generalizations that are commonplace may be made without support; one does not need to provide evidence in support of the generalization that dogs have four legs or that war is a terrible thing, or cite sources to back up a claim that Jane Austen has been widely admired for her use of irony.) If an essay makes any claim that is not generally accepted (and if it is an interesting essay it usually will make several such claims), the claim must be supported. And if generalizations are made, the writer must be particularly careful to show that he is aware that his generalizations may not apply in all cases. He should make clear if he is writing about the way beaver build lodges that not all beaver do so; river beaver have quite different quarters, and behave differently in other ways as well.

And he should be precise. *Most Canadians voted against the Free Trade Agreement in the 1988 election* is an imprecise generalization. *In the 1988 election most Canadians voted for parties that opposed the Free Trade Agreement* is more accurate. Such concern for precision may seem like pedantry; is there any difference between the two statements? Yes, there is. In that election many Canadians who opposed Free Trade nevertheless voted for the Progressive Conservatives, just as many Canadians who supported Free Trade voted for the Liberals or New Democrats. Free Trade was the most contentious issue in the campaign, but not the only one; it was an election, not a referendum. Being careful about such distinctions is an important part of what is involved in a college or university education.

○ CAUSE AND EFFECT

A great deal of university and college writing involves discerning and analysing causes and effects. Whereas the natural connectives in narrative writing are *and* and *then*, the natural connectives in writing about causes and effects are words such as *because* and *therefore*. These connectives (and how they relate to causes and effects) are treated fully below (pages 295–300). Here we touch on a few general points.

Events often have more than one cause, and claims must often be justified by more than one reason. This sounds straightforward enough, but it is easy to forget, as the following examples show. Many of the arguments against military intervention in the Persian Gulf (both before the 1991 Gulf War and in 2003) took this form:

> Americans are willing to fight Saddam Hussein because they believe the oil reserves of the Gulf region are of strategic and economic importance to them. This is not a good moral justification for going to war. Therefore we should not fight.

To begin with, this sort of argument confuses explanation with justification. To ask what American motives were is to ask why the country went to war—a very different thing from asking if the country should have gone to war. Quite possibly America may have done "the right deed for the wrong reason."

Beyond this, however, the argument assumes that if one explanation can safely be advanced for an action, it is also safe to conclude that it is the only explanation. Surely it is entirely possible for the US and its allies to have been willing to go to war *both* out of a self-interested desire to protect oil reserves *and* out of unselfish desires to resist aggression or potential aggression, to prevent the development or deployment of chemical and biological weapons, and so on.

Reasoning used by many on the opposite side of such debates may be equally flawed. The gist of the argument of the American, British, and Canadian political leaders in 1991 was this:

> In an act of brutal aggression, Iraq invaded and annexed Kuwait, killing many of its citizens in the process. Aggression must be resisted. Therefore we should be willing to go to war.

And in 2003:

> In contravention of UN resolutions, Iraq has refused to allow
> monitoring of strategic sites on which it may have been devel-
> oping chemical and biological weapons. Contempt for interna-
> tional law must be resisted. Therefore we should be willing to
> go to war.

As with the anti-war arguments above, the pro-war arguments here suffer from incomplete reasoning—reasoning that fails
to allow for any multiplicity of causes, reasons, and effects. Did
Iraq in 1991 have a legitimate historical claim on the territory of
Kuwait (which, like Iraq, was carved out of what had been a part
of the Ottoman Empire by the British)? What are the casualties
likely to be in the event of war? Should aggression be resisted in
all circumstances, and at all costs? These are some of the questions
left unanswered.

And similarly in 2003: should defiance or partial defiance of
UN resolutions be punished at any cost? Who is likely to suffer,
and how much? Does military intervention in the Persian Gulf
carry with it the risk of sparking a larger conflict? Have other
means short of military action been exhausted? Depending on
the answers one gives to such questions, the appropriate course of
action may seem far less clear.

A useful distinction in sorting out the relative importance of
multiple causes, effects, and reasons is that between necessary and
sufficient conditions. The presence of oxygen is a necessary condition for there to be fire; there can be no fire without oxygen. But it
is not a sufficient condition; everything in the presence of oxygen
does not automatically catch fire.

Similarly (in the argument discussed above), the 1991 political
leaders were in effect arguing that the fact of Iraq having invaded
and annexed another sovereign country was in itself a sufficient
condition to justify going to war. Someone arguing against going
to war in the same circumstances might claim that the invasion of
one country by another was a necessary condition for going to war,

but not a sufficient one—that other, additional justification was required. And a third person might say that the invasion constituted neither a necessary nor a sufficient condition; that we should stay out of such affairs in any circumstances.

Another useful distinction—particularly in the sciences and social sciences—is between cause and correlation. Again, this may be made clear by example. A recent study has shown that the rate of breast cancer in women has increased markedly over the past twenty years. Over the same period, the average childbearing age has also increased dramatically. Now, it is possible that the connection between those two occurrences may be causal in nature—that, for example, waiting until later in life to have children increases one's risk of breast cancer. But researchers caution that we should not assume this to be the case; more research needs to be done. As it stands, the connection is merely a correlation: an interrelationship of variable qualities. In this case, over the same period and under the same conditions, both variables increased.

When a correlation between two things exists:

- there may be a common cause or common causes for both
- one may cause the other (or help to cause the other; again, more than one cause may be involved)
- the two may happen coincidentally as a result of quite separate causes

A detailed look at Melissa Davis's essay will show how different modes of thought combine to produce logical fluency. Her introduction (paragraph 1) moves quickly from a general topic—public galleries as forums for presenting new and controversial material—to the particular example of Ofili's work in the "Sensation" exhibit. She briefly describes the sequence of events involving the presentation of the "Sensation" exhibit and the flurry of discussion that ensued. This sets the stage for the statement of thesis at the end of the paragraph.

Both narrative and classification are important to paragraph 2, in which Melissa narrates the background of the "Sensation" exhibit and the controversy surrounding it. Notice here how she classifies different aspects of the controversy. She refers to the disagreements about Marcus Harvey's work—disagreements involving the issues of decency and freedom of expression that are her central concern—in the body of her essay. The controversy over the financing of the "Sensation" exhibit, on the other hand, she relegates to a note; it is not directly relevant to her topic.

Paragraph 3 is linked to paragraph 2 as an extension of the narrative of the controversy; it uses quotation judiciously to express the flavour of the debate. Paragraph 4 uses quotation much more extensively. Here Melissa is presenting the core argument of those opposed to the exhibit—and in analysing the thrust of their argument is beginning to elaborate her own.

Paragraph 5 extends the argument begun in paragraph 4. Here the writer moves beyond responding to Giuliani's argument, and begins to draw the distinctions between moral and legal obligations that will be central to her conclusion.

Paragraph 6 fills in the historical background regarding the tradition of government support for the arts, while paragraphs 7 and 8 present views on both sides of the contemporary debate. Paragraph 9 concedes that there are reasonable grounds on which the government may have no obligation to extend support, while paragraph 10 presents a case from first principles (fundamental assumptions) for encouraging *new ideas and new artistic expressions*. Notice that paragraph 10 includes an extended discussion on how freedom of expression needs to be defined both against a legal backdrop and in relationship to social practice.

The long paragraph 11 is an important digression in which the issue is discussed not in generalities or from first principles but in reference to a detailed consideration of the specific artwork at issue. Here Melissa relies on quotation of the artist himself, on quotation of a recognized authority in the field, and on her own arguments. She again touches on definition here—in this case not treating at length the question of "what is art?" but noting that

Introduction
- frame in historical context (galleries & freedom of expression)
- very brief summary of "Sensation" case
- touch on the issues — offence vs. decency / free expression / public funding

[THESIS] – opponents have some legitimate concerns BUT free expression a core principle

Body

① extended presentation of issues
- history of exhibit
- reactions — politicians / press

② analyse / examine Giuliani's argument
- the issue of prior commitment in this case

③ Ofili's work itself – aesthetic considerations (legitimate artistic activity?)

④ broader issues re, govt. support for arts & intellectual activity obligation? Probably not – but fabric of society would suffer if support withdrawn

Conclusion

① Since "Sensation" (change in climate?) — and looking forward

touch on thesis again → ② return to issue of principle — and not only a legal issue. Freedom of expression will always need to be defended.

Melissa Davis's planning and prewriting moves from mapping to an informal outline, which helps her to arrange the sequence of points in her argument. Notice the three-part skeleton (introduction/body/conclusion), with the essay's thesis as the focus of the introduction.

even a conservative definition of art would have to allow Ofili's work to qualify. Paragraph 13 turns again to narrative, recounting the resolution of the case in the courts and the repercussions since. Notice in this paragraph how cause-and-effect analysis is intertwined with the narrative.

The essay's conclusion is signalled at the outset of paragraph 14 by two statements of generalization. The topic of the essay is reiterated without being merely repeated. In other words, Melissa Davis makes the effort to find other words. She returns not only to the general topic of the essay but also to its all-important thesis, and she does so without simply cutting and pasting the introduction from paragraph 1. Melissa then punctuates her argument by recognizing the profound changes wrought by the 9/11 attacks—and by holding to her own position on freedom of expression. Her position is clearly elaborated. The essay is complete.

O Reasoning

Nothing sinks an essay more quickly than an illogical argument. Readers expect a writer's assertions to be supported by solid evidence. None of the modes of thought discussed in this book will succeed unless employed along a clear path of reasoning.

Consider once again Melissa Davis's essay. Her use of the various modes of thought—such as classification or narration—is complemented by a strong linkage between the essay's main points and the reasons supporting them. Chief among her main points is, of course, the essay's thesis at the end of paragraph 1: the thesis statement commits Melissa to the logical task of demonstrating (a) that the case against Ofili's work, as it was advanced in the context of the "Sensation" show, rests on an insufficiently strong foundation and (b) that, more generally, artistic and intellectual activity deserves government support in the interest of preserving and promoting freedom of expression.

In arguing (a) effectively, Melissa first demonstrates her understanding of the defects in Giuliani's arguments and then later defends the Ofili piece directly. Melissa advances two lines of argument for (b), first presenting the historical justifications for such support in paragraph 5, and then arguing the case from general principles in paragraph 8. Then, when she returns to the argument in paragraph 10, she gives further support to both lines of argument.

In structuring her essay, Melissa signals that she wishes to put more emphasis on (b) than on (a). She devotes far more space to arguing (b) than she does to arguing (a), and she returns in the essay's final paragraph to her general points regarding freedom of expression. Such decisions concerning an essay's structure, as well as the weight to be placed on its various points, are often as important as the essay's internal logic—which brings us to our next topic.

⊙Subordination and Paragraphing

For many pages now, *The Broadview Guide* has been discussing something that is impossible to fully describe in words—the transfer of human thought from mind to paper. Various natural functions of the mind (such as contrast, narration, deduction, argument, and classification) have been touched on. Certainly, the more a writer can be conscious of these functions while working on the draft of an essay, the better off she will be. But that sort of consciousness is liable to fade away. From time to time, writers' brains go on functioning—and writers keep on writing—in a less-than-fully-conscious-of-where-this-paper-is-going condition.

What saves the day at those moments is the paragraph. A competent writer will start new paragraphs on no surer a hunch than "something's gotta change here." Perhaps on reflection, or by looking back at the preliminary mapping of the essay, he will realize that example must give way to comparison, or that deduction must be followed by summation. Until such useful analysis kicks in, though, paragraphing is a compass for the reader; it gives visual form to the emerging sections of any essay. Of course, the movement from a first draft to a final draft may well require reordering of those sections. Paragraphs may have their original sequence shattered and reconstituted, a fact of writers' lives that makes one piece of advice particularly valuable: never underestimate the power of subordination to enhance logical fluency.

As a grammatical gesture, subordination turns what would have been a complete sentence (e.g., *Some find this art offensive*) into a sentence fragment (e.g., "*Even if some find this art offensive* ..."). This example comes from the end of Melissa Davis's twelfth paragraph. Because the first half of the sentence (before the comma) is subordinated, the second half (after the comma) is given prominence. Grammatically, the second half is stronger; it could stand alone as a complete sentence (*it is hard not to think that on its merits, Ofili's work deserves to be widely exhibited*). Its logical function is to sum up the argument of the paragraph. Meanwhile the first half—the grammatically weaker "subordinate clause"—looks back in the direction of the earlier paragraphs that have presented the views of those who find Ofili's work offensive.

Similarly, in the opening of paragraph 9, Melissa looks back with a subordinate phrase (*Despite the general support* ...) to the argument of the previous paragraph regarding the appropriateness of government support for artistic and intellectual endeavour. She then states, in the main clause of the sentence, the argument she wishes to advance in her new paragraph: *we should not assume an unlimited obligation on the part of government.*

On the Web

Exercises on paragraphing may be found at
www.broadviewpress.com/writing.
Click on **Exercises** and go to **C1**.

Thus, the grammar of subordination mirrors the logic of the ways in which an essay makes transitions from one sub-topic to the next. It allows the acknowledgement in one paragraph of a preceding paragraph's material, while still introducing (and grammatically asserting) its own. This sort of signalling can greatly enhance logical fluency, especially for the writer who tends to change the sequence of her paragraphs during the process of drafting and redrafting an essay.

O *Connectives*

If the paragraphs and the sentences in an essay are to convey a sense of logical fluency to the reader, connectives are of vital importance. *Even if ...* and *despite ...* in the above examples are connectives. So is the word *however*, used in the last sentence of Melissa's first paragraph: *... a greater concern, however, is ....* Like others of this kind (*moreover, consequently, therefore, furthermore, admittedly*), connectives such as *however* and *even if* are a writer's road signs, indicating to readers where the logical structure of the essay has come from, and where it is headed. (See pages 283–309 for a full treatment of the ways in which such words can be used.) Melissa's use of *however* conveys a clear message: the "greater concern" that is being introduced will be one that stands in contrast to the concerns just referred to. (If, on the other hand, she were to write *... a greater concern, moreover, is ...* the reader would be led to expect an extension of the ideas presented previously.)

On the Web

Exercises on connectives may be found at **www.broadviewpress.com/writing**. Click on **Exercises** and go to **C1–33**.

Sometimes connectives may be made up of more than one word; such is the case not only with *even if* but also with the phrases *by contrast, in addition, for example, to summarize,* and *all in all.* Whether through phrases such as these or through one-word connectives, an essay's fluency often depends on matching connectives with their appropriate logical contexts.

⊙Stylistic Fluency

Unfortunately, the achievement of logical fluency does not guarantee the achievement of its necessary other, stylistic fluency. Consider, for example, these meticulously thought-out instructions for patrons of the Bank of Nova Scotia:

> The annual rental fee for the lease of the box is subject to change from time to time by the Bank either giving notice in writing to the lessee by mailing the notice to the lessee at the address given hereunder (or such address as the lessee may from time to time in writing instruct the Bank to substitute thereof) and any such notice shall be deemed to have been duly given when mailed, or by posting a notice in a readily accessible place in the branch of the Bank.

Or this paragraph from a university student's critique of an assigned reading:

> Rembar simply uses refutation to make a greater distinction between impeachment and the judiciary system. Refutation, in this instance, clarifies the distinction. The natural confusion which exists initially is suppressed as Rembar offers explanation. The effect has tremendous influence and we progressively take stance with Rembar's viewpoint.

Neither writer is thoughtless or incompetent, but each has developed a case of what James Thurber once called "inflammation of the sentence structure." Fortunately, this stylistic disease is curable, provided the patient is willing to rehabilitate his diction (choice of words) and syntax (arrangement of words).

O *Diction*

As George Orwell warned repeatedly, the great danger of English is its insidious power over the human thought process. Words come in familiar, formulaic packages that often leap from a writer's pen or keyboard before she's had a chance to really think. Worse yet, the familiar and formulaic tends to be hypnotic; writers are often unaware that Language is leading Thought on its leash:

> Ready-made phrases come crowding in. They will construct your sentences for you—even think your thoughts for you, to a certain extent—and at need they will perform the important service of partially concealing your meaning even from yourself.... This invasion of one's mind by ready-made phrases ... can only be prevented if one is constantly on guard against them. (362)

Four eyes are better than two when it comes to sighting an invasion force. In dialogue with another person, any university essay-writer will resist more strongly the temptations of ready-made academic prose (what Northrop Frye calls "verbal cotton wool" [107]). Such temptations are very real. It is easy for any experienced consumer of university writing to summon a lifeless introductory sentence from her general memory-bank:

Certain	definite	elements	can be	identified
Several	key	components		illuminated
Three	crucial	factors		underlined
	aspects			isolated
	facets			
	areas			

... when discussing the topic of the "Sensation" show controversy.

Even the most attentive writers can inadvertently slip into this passive game of fill-in-the-blanks, dulling their topics (and their minds!) with phrases like *Certain crucial facets* or *Three key elements* or *Several definite components* or (even worse) *Certain crucial facets and several definite components*. Usually there is nothing at all "definite" or "certain" about such writing. Rather, its anesthetized perpetrator conjures up vague categories—factors, areas, components, etc.—without having any specific material to fill them in. "What is above all needed," as Orwell insists, "is to let the meaning choose the word, and not the other way about" (366).

Many people believe that their writing will be made more impressive by using long, unusual words and long, complicated sentences. About one per cent of us are capable of impressing in this way; the rest of us only end up making more mistakes than we would have otherwise, and looking rather foolish. Of course, academic writing depends upon the use of jargon—namely, the specialized language of any scholarly field. But the best writers always aim to express their ideas in the most straightforward manner possible. The goal is a varied and flexible style, one that utilizes simple words wherever possible without becoming simplistic.

Because they are involved in intellectual discourse, academic and professional writers must rigorously monitor their use of abstract and conceptual nouns. Too dense a concentration will sap an essay's clarity; the ideas will be—as the overused idiom has it—too difficult to grasp. But the metaphor is apt: readers can't put their hands on something that is too airy. They require, and deserve, a balance between abstraction and solidity. Competent writers choose from several techniques—including example, definition, reference to data, and quotation—in order to keep their abstract diction out of the rhetorical clouds.

Many who have written on style have advised against using too many adjectives or adverbs—though it is rare to find "too many" quantified. No doubt the widespread prejudice against adjectives and adverbs is in part a reaction against two unfortunate tendencies that many of us share. The first is to be repetitive in our use of adjectives; *tiny little* and *great big* are common conversational combinations that sometimes find their way onto the page as well. The second is to use adverbs as largely meaningless intensifiers; we don't usually need the *very* in *very important* or the *extremely* in *extremely tragic*. But in fact most good writers use adjectives and adverbs freely, and with great effect. Look, for example, at the following description by Charles Simic, a Pulitzer Prize–winning poet as well as a superb essayist:

> In Clarksdale, the former capital of the Cotton Kingdom which President Clinton visited during his 1999 tour focusing on the nation's poorest communities, I saw in a parking lot of a closed supermarket two ancient cars parked side by side with their four doors wide open. Over their hoods, roofs, and doors, spread out and draped, someone's once-pretty dresses and worn children's clothes were covering every available space. Two black women sat on low stools, one on each side, waiting for a customer. (45)

Notice in particular here that of the many adjectives used, none is at all rare, and none is used in a particularly striking or original fashion. *Ancient, once-pretty, worn, low*; these are everyday adjectives, carefully chosen. Writers can certainly create an effect with references to the *elaborate casualness* of a hostess or the *cerulean intensity* of an actor's blue eyes. But well-chosen adjectives and adverbs do not need to be unusual or showy; they simply need to fit the context, and help the writer convey to the reader the desired sense.

As mentioned earlier, word-choosing can also be perilous whenever a writer's topic involves jargon—that is, technical or specialized language. "In order to ensure that a truly regional renal care delivery structure will be optimally functional, there must be patient accessibility to a number of interdigitated modalities of care," writes the medical essayist, forgetting simplicity in his pursuit of kidney doctors' respect. Chances are he has misconstrued his audience, anyway; even professionals at ease with the jargon of their own specialty would prefer *work well* to *be optimally functional*; and *several interconnected clinics* to *a number of interdigitated modalities of care.* Who really wants to read *the plan is more philo-sophical than operational in terms of framework*, rather than *the plan is still an idea; it hasn't been tested yet?*

In addition to technical or specialized language, the word *jargon* also refers to unnecessarily vague and unfocused vocabulary. This second connotation—a very negative one—points more to a problem of psychology than to a problem of grammar and usage. It comes from people being more concerned with making themselves sound knowledgeable and intellectual than with acquiring knowledge or developing their intelligence; more concerned with making their ideas sound important than with thinking them through and expressing them clearly. Unfortunately, most students are sufficiently impressionable to be taken in by the pretence that some jargon puts forward. Even more sadly, many working adults who should know better are just as easily taken in. The best way to safeguard against jargon is to embrace simplicity of expression. Writers who are always willing to revise their choices, who realize that no word in any draft of an essay is inevitable, will best resist being hypnotized by jargon.

On the Web

Exercises on word choice may be found at **www.broadviewpress.com/writing**. Click on **Exercises** and go to **Style**.

O *Figures of Speech*

Yet another ingredient of stylistic fluency is figurative language, the persuasive use of images from beyond the realm of the essay's primary topic—most commonly in the form of metaphors or similes. By appealing to readers' senses, such images give life and clarity to abstract diction. An excellent example appears in George Orwell's famous essay on politics and language, where the writer complains about people who believe that "any struggle against the abuse of language is a sentimental archaism, like preferring candles to electric light or hansom cabs to aeroplanes" (353). His introduction of an abstract and difficult concept (*sentimental archaism*) is followed by two vivid figures of speech, which aid readers in understanding the point being made.

Orwell's use of the word *like* is enough to classify his figures of speech as similes, which are distinct from metaphors: *My love is a red, red rose* is a metaphor; *My love is like a red, red rose* is a simile. The difference is simply that similes make comparisons explicit through the use of words such as *like* or *as if*, whereas metaphors fuse the objects of comparison.

Of course, as Orwell himself warns, dull or overly familiar figures of speech can undermine not only stylistic but also logical fluency. Most writers drink from the well of stale imagery more often than they realize. When they do, what ends up on the page has little life to it: *that will be the acid test; the United States is a melting pot; he's barking up the wrong tree; I threw caution to the wind; we were told that we would have to bite the bullet; put that on the back burner; this university is a hotbed of unrest.*

For the most part these are what are known as dead metaphors—metaphors that have been used so frequently that they no longer conjure up any physical image in the minds of those who hear or read them. When we hear the phrase *miss the boat* we do not think of a boat, any more than we think of pavement when we hear the expression *paved the way for*. In similar fashion a phrase such as *the lifeblood of democratic society* has been used so often that the blood has been drained out of it. Melissa Davis realized exactly that on re-reading the second draft of her essay—and changed *that are the lifeblood of democratic society* to *that continually replenish the red blood cells of democratic society*. It is a moot point whether a dead metaphor is better than no metaphor at all, but certainly a fresh metaphor is far better than either. Instead of *paved the way*, for example, what about *blazed a path*? Instead of a *hotbed*, try a *cauldron*. Instead of *nipping something in the bud*, try *digging up the seedlings*. It may take a little longer, but the improvement in style will be worth it.

Of course, so many people have been using metaphors for so long that it is extremely difficult to find a fresh one for every situation. One useful compromise is to try to bring dead metaphors to life by using them in new ways. For example, no one thinks of a wave in this sentence:

- The Prime Minister of Britain has been riding a wave of popular support since his election.

Mention the wave again in a slightly different way, however, and it becomes water again to the reader:

- The Prime Minister of Britain has been riding a wave of popular support since the election. The question now is when that wave will crest.

Similarly, few people think of plants when they read of something having been *nipped in the bud*—unless the writer has made an effort to bring the dead metaphor back to life:

- The company wanted to nip the spreading unrest among its employees in the bud.

- The company wanted to nip the spreading unrest among its employees in the bud before it became a tangled, snake-infested jungle.

Writers who use dead metaphors are also more likely to mix their metaphors. A mixed metaphor occurs when we are not really thinking of the meaning of the words we use:

- If we bite the bullet we have to be careful not to throw the baby out with the bath-water.

As soon as one really thinks about such sentences one realizes that the bullet is really better off out of the baby's bath-water, and the best way to search for an avenue is not to turn stones over:

> *needs checking* Now the president is out on a limb and some of his colleagues are trying to pull the rug out from under him.
>
> *revised* Now the president is out on a limb and some of his colleagues are preparing to saw it off.

On the Web

Exercises on mixed metaphors may be found at **www.broadviewpress.com/writing**. Click on **Exercises** and go to **Style**.

O *Syntax*

The Broadview Guide begins by talking about "black marks on a page" moving "from left to right and from top to bottom" (13). It begins, in other words, by talking about word order, also known as syntax. As the following examples show, poor syntax can quite thoroughly disrupt stylistic fluency:

- Trapped in a 101-foot mine shaft abandoned for almost fifty years, two injured men were rescued over the weekend after they lit a fire to attract the attention of passers-by.
- The macadamia was named for Dr. John MacAdam, an enthusiastic scientist who promoted the nut in its native Australia, and was dubbed "the perfect nut" by Luther Burbank.

At times, words and phrases seem to have wills of their own, teaming up unexpectedly to completely undermine writers' intended meanings. Like some subversive magnet, the word *trapped* (in the first sentence) lures the prepositional phrase *for almost fifty years* to its side. And, in sentence 2, the verbal phrase *was dubbed* ignores the macadamia and aligns itself instead with poor Doctor MacAdam.

Writers must, however, shoulder the blame for such syntactical insurrections. They may not know the grammatical jargon—may not know that "a past participle preceding the object of a preposition will surrender control of a subsequent prepositional phrase to a second past participle that precedes either of the two prepositional phrases in question." But they must know that the phrase *for almost fifty years* in the first example is controlled by the word *abandoned*—not the word *trapped*. They may not know that "the second of two past-tense verbs in the passive voice, instead of aligning itself to the subject word of the sentence, will align itself to the relative pronoun that introduces an adjective subordinate clause, when that clause modifies a noun in apposition to the object of a prepositional phrase syntactically adjacent to the first past-tense verb in the passive voice." But they must know that in the second example the verb *was dubbed* refers to *the macadamia*—not the scientist.

Rare is the writer who always thinks in grammatical terms as she writes. Nevertheless, successful writers develop an eye for the syntax of English grammar by allowing time between successive drafts of an essay. A good night's sleep enhances objectivity, so that the person who wrote the sentences can respond more as their eventual readers will respond.

O *Rhythm*

A writer's pursuit of stylistic fluency is not complete without attention to the music created by words and sentences—to the rhythm of language. The most predictable syntax in the grammar of English is SUBJECT-VERB-PREDICATE, as in the sentence, *The response of the mayor was more vehement.* Upend that predictability, and a writer such as Melissa Davis is on her way (in paragraph 3 of the essay) to rhythmical distinctiveness: *Even more vehement was the response of ....*

An important element in rhythmical distinctiveness is balance. Sometimes a pleasing balance is achieved simply by deliberately repeating phrases or grammatical forms:

- We may not wish to deny academics the right to publish such research. But nor can we deny the harm that it causes.

Sometimes balance may be achieved by placing words or phrases in apposition:*

- Haldeman was Nixon's closest confidant, his most influential advisor.

- The generality of the images here has the effect of opening up the scene to the reader, of allowing her to graft her own archetypes of *river* and *hill* and *woods* onto the story.

Often paired connectives *(if … then, either … or, not only … but also)* can help in achieving balance. But here, as always, the writer must be careful that the words are in the right places; otherwise the fragile element of balance is lost:

needs checking	Hardy was not only a prolific novelist but wrote poetry too, and also several plays.
revised	Hardy was not only a prolific novelist but also a distinguished poet and a dramatist.

(Here the noun *novelist* is balanced by the later nouns *poet* and *dramatist*.)

needs checking	The experiment can either be performed with hydrogen or with oxygen.
revised	The experiment can be performed with either hydrogen or oxygen.

(Here the choice is between the two gases, not between performing and some other thing.)

---

* I.e., where successive words or phrases fulfill the same grammatical function in a sentence, with the second helping to elaborate on or explain the first.

needs checking   To subdue Iraq through sanctions, the United Nations felt, was better than using military force.

revised   To subdue Iraq through sanctions, the United Nations felt, was better than to use military force.

or   Subduing Iraq through sanctions, the United Nations felt, was better than using military force.

(Here infinitive balances infinitive; participle balances participle.)

needs checking   In 1984 there was a female Vice-Presidential candidate for a major American political party, and in 2008 too.

revised   In both 1984 and 2008 a major American political party chose a female Vice-Presidential candidate.

Repetition of some grammatical phrase allows readers to sense a pattern in the writing. To feel that pattern. To conclude that pattern. If parallel structure has been used to balance the parts of a sentence, even long sentences can be made easily digestible to the reader. Let's look again to Melissa Davis's essay for an example:

> The resulting uproar led both to a widely publicized court case and to an ongoing campaign to support "decency" in artistic expression. Should such art be banned? Should it be exhibited at public expense?

Notice here the balancing of *both to* ... with *and to* ..., as well as the common structure of the two sentences that follow.

But even careful balancing cannot make a steady diet of long sentences palatable; a rich source of rhythm in any well-written essay is the short sentence, a highly visible minority in the academic world of long, drawn-out sentences. No writer naturally thinks, as she is drafting an essay, "Now I must remember to vary the length of my sentences." But when she comes to revise her work—particularly if she has allowed a day or two to elapse after completing the rough draft—she is better able to notice if and when the writing becomes too dominated either by very long sentences or by very short ones. She is able too to notice such things as a preponderance of *it is ...*, *there is ...*, and *there are* sentences:

> *needs checking* It is important to remember that there are cultural as well as economic effects of Free Trade. There are many people who argue that over the long term these are just as significant.
>
> *revised* Free Trade has cultural as well as economic effects. Indeed, many argue that over the long term these are just as significant.

By making such changes as these, even when there are no actual errors in her rough draft, the careful writer is able—with very little effort expended—to make her prose clearer, crisper, and more concise. And by doing so she makes things considerably easier for her reader.

On the Web
Exercises on balance and parallelism may be found at **www.broadviewpress.com/writing**. Click on **Exercises** and go to **Style**.

O *Voice*

As many authorities have pointed out, in most cases writers can make their sentences less wordy and more effective by using the active voice rather than the passive:

> *needs checking* The election was lost by the premier. (Passive—7 words)
>
> *revised* The premier lost the election. (Active—5 words)

needs checking Union power was seen by them to have con-
       strained the possibilities for full investment, and
       for achieving full employment.

revised   The shareholders thought that union power had
       constrained the possibilities for full investment,
       and for achieving full employment.

It is too extreme, however, to suggest with George Orwell that you should "never use the passive when you can use the active" (367). Writers often want—for perfectly good reasons—to keep the focus of their writing on the recipient of an action rather than its agent. In such cases they are quite right to use the passive voice:

passive   Fifty millilitres of the solution were added to the
       serum.

active   I added fifty millilitres of the solution to the
       serum.

passive   John Paul Getty III was released in Italy after a
       2.8-million-dollar ransom had been paid.

active   His kidnappers released John Paul Getty III in
       Italy after they had been paid a 2.8-million-dollar
       ransom.

To the reader of a chemistry paper it is of no concern who added the fifty millilitres; that they were added is what matters, and there the focus of the sentence should be. Similarly in the second example, it is more appropriate to keep John Paul Getty III as the subject of the sentence than to shift the focus to his kidnappers.

The passive is also sometimes useful as a means of dealing with issues of gender and usage. Compare, for example, the following sentences:

- If a writer uses vivid adjectives, his or her descriptive writing will carry greater force.

- If vivid adjectives are used, descriptive writing will carry greater force.

The passive-voice version allows the wordy *his or her* to disappear. Altering syntax in this sort of way can help writers to write bias-free prose without resorting to awkward phrasing. (For a full discussion of this issue see below, page 433.)

The vice associated with the passive voice, then, is not the passive *per se*, but the wordiness it sometimes gives rise to.

On the Web
Exercises on active & passive voice may be found at
www.broadviewpress.com/writing.
Click on **Exercises** and go to **Style**.

O *Tone*

The voice of logical fluency is not supposed to gush or cajole or insult or amuse or exclaim. After all, most academic essays are formal pieces of writing, and should be approached as such. Your readers expect a calm and disinterested tone, free of extreme emotion or conversational touches (for advice on avoiding slang expressions and contractions, turn to page 339). Thinking rigorously about a topic does not, however, preclude feeling strongly about it. As Susan Cole demonstrates in her essay on Terry Fox, sentences that are both logically and stylistically fluent will convey emotion without the need for fanfare:

Terry's Marathon of Hope was a tremendous athletic accomplishment, and the physical punishment to which he subjected himself is almost beyond imagining. It is not a well-known fact that he was advised before his run that he had a heart condition.... As he approached Thunder Bay in late August, he experienced a persistent intense pain in his upper chest and he was unable to go any further. Terry's run was finished on the first of September, 114 days and 3,339 miles after it had begun. (255)

Cole's style is personal without being subjective. Like many a practiced writer, she maintains objectivity while relying on diction and syntax to express an earnestness of tone that complements her subject matter.

Notice in particular how Cole manages to personalize the tone of her writing without employing the first-person singular pronoun; indeed, most academic writers use *I* or *me* infrequently, if at all. The objective of most formal essays is to present a clear argument; writers succeed by letting the evidence speak for itself. Thus many instructors advise their students to avoid using first-person pronouns.

As with all stylistic guidelines, though, this one should not be regarded as written in stone. As the other introductory passage quoted earlier demonstrates, the acclaimed historian Garry Wills uses *I* and *me* frequently. So does George Orwell, often praised as the finest essayist of the past century.

O Revision

Perhaps the greatest failing among those learning to write well is a reluctance to spend sufficient time reworking and reorganizing their prose. Far too many students—not to mention people working in business and government—assume that completing a first draft means, essentially, finishing the job. Feeling the pressure of a deadline, they're inclined to ask the same rhetorical question that Louis Menand asks himself:

Why burn through limited time and brain cells trying to coax coherence out of a ramshackle string of half-baked ideas embedded in badly written sentences when you could be forging your verbal chain one exquisite and unbreakable link at a time? (94)

Menand himself is a truly extraordinary writer, who is indeed capable of forging marvellous essays one exquisite and unbreakable link at a time, but for most of us, exquisite first drafts are few and far between. As Ian Cameron puts it in *For All Practical Purposes*:

A few students feel that they are as likely to make more mistakes in checking and correcting their work as they are to correct the mistakes they have already made, but in fact almost every student is able to improve his or her work at least 15% by checking it slowly and carefully. Remember, you are not checking simply for details such as spelling; you should be trying to replace words, to re-arrange paragraphs, to cut entire sections, to alter almost every sentence. (276)

By its very nature revising is likely to lead to more cuts than additions. Might this not cause damage? "Aren't I more likely to do well," some students may ask themselves, "if I've written more than the prof asked for?" If the instructor has asked for 1,000 words, they feel they should write 1,500; if 2,500 words are requested, they are sure to top 3,000. Experienced writers have learnt that quantity matters much less than quality; unless an essay is well below the requested number of words the only thing that matters is what it says, and how well it says it.

O *Examinations and In-class Essays*

The discussion of essay-writing in these pages has presumed that the process is likely to extend over several days, or even several weeks. How does the situation change when the student is asked to write an essay in a much more limited time, as part of an in-class assignment or an examination? Many students have a natural—and understandable—tendency to assume that entirely different principles must apply to this second category of essay-writing.

There are differences, of course, but the basic similarities must also be kept in mind. Success in either situation depends upon clearly understanding the task at hand. By zeroing in on the command words (*explain, analyze, argue, compare, summarize,* etc.), an exam-writer will know precisely what kind of response (explanatory, argumentative, etc.) the professor wants. Reading the questions carefully and with an attitude of self-confidence; assessing the relative value of each question, so as to better apportion the time available; remembering (as the essay-writer must) that quantity matters much less than quality: these are the means to the mastery of examinations. Here too are a few additional pointers:

- Examination questions never ask the student to write down all he has in his head on the given topic. If the student is asked to write on Austen's use of irony in *Emma*, he will not do well by recounting the full story of the book, or discussing Emma's character at great length. If asked to comment on the claim that "the Treaty of Versailles caused World War II," he will not do well by simply reciting a list of the main historical developments between the two world wars.

- As in writing essays, the use of a map or plan is an asset. It won't, of course, be as well thought-out; indeed, it may well be just a frenzied clutter of words. But it's important to have some sense of structure, and some place to jot down ideas that come to mind unexpectedly. A rough sheet for notes and plans kept always at hand can help.

- Another similarity between essays and essay answers on exams is the importance of checking written work. Make sure nothing important has been left out; make sure the points are expressed concisely and clearly. And avoid writing madly right up to the end of the time allotted. Again, a well-written short answer will be better received than a sloppy and long-winded one.

Note: An excellent guide to the peculiarities of exam-writing is *Making Your Mark* by Catherine Taylor et al., published by the Academic Skills Centre at Trent University.

⊙ Collaboration and Research

Stop and think for a moment about the experiences of writers described in this book: putting together a voice; working out the argumentative structure for an essay; refining the stylistic fluency of phrases, sentences, and paragraphs. Some of those experiences are collaborative by nature, involving—for instance—the one-to-one dialogue of writing tutorials. There is simply no such thing as a hermetically sealed, totally isolated writer of utterly personal beliefs and insights. As long as he is acquiring new knowledge, a competent writer relies on collaboration, which is an honourable and occasionally miraculous activity to pursue.

O *Using the Library*

Among the most fertile territories for collaboration is the library, the traditional site of scholarly research. Regrettably, some university students approach research as an endeavour entailing nothing more than the finding and collating of old material on their assigned subject. The more imaginative and independent, however, will set out to discover new insights, seeking to arrange and examine what exists in order to present that which has never existed. Their essays' arguments are thereby strengthened through collaborative exposure to the work of others.

Consider the research presented by Melissa Davis—and, in particular, the authority she quotes in paragraph 9, Peter Levine. She quotes Levine only once (at a point where he makes a significant historical point succinctly and effectively), and she never paraphrases any of Levine's arguments; indeed, he reaches a substantially different conclusion than does Melissa Davis. Nevertheless, the Levine article was of considerable help to Davis: a strong, collaborative voice providing information and arguments that helped her to sort out a number of facts, and to clarify her own views—and pointing her in the direction of significant other voices.

How does an industrious student locate strong, collaborative voices of this sort—voices that she can be confident are responsible ones, regardless of whether or not she may in the end agree with their conclusions?

Research begins with a computer, whether in a library, in the student's residence, or wherever she may happen to be with her laptop. Sometimes an instructor will have provided the names of at least one or two books or articles in the area to look up; sometimes the researcher will be starting from scratch with only the subject, and will have to make up a list of books and articles on her own. More often than not, search engines will put her only a few clicks away from a vast array of material—more than could possibly be taken account of in a single essay, perhaps more than could be read in an entire academic year. How does she choose?

At this stage it is important not to simply take the path of least resistance. Articles that are not included in protected databases may be more readily accessible than those that are—but they are likely also to be less reliable. Search engines are enormously valuable, but they tend to put the most frequently consulted sources at the head of lists—a practice that may place pieces by popular astrologers or political cranks ahead of the less flamboyant but more reliable work of reputable scholars.* It is on the latter that the student researcher should focus—and she may do well to keep her initial list brief—no more than a handful of books or articles. Then, as the researcher is scanning those, she can notice which other books or articles are referred to most often by the authors; those are the

---

* Note that in this respect Google Scholar (scholar.google.com) is far preferable to the main Google search engine.

ones she knows she should be aware of in particular, both in order to keep the task of research manageable and to try to make sure that she does not ignore any of the most important authorities on the subject.

Where articles are concerned, the researcher should pay attention to the journal or newspaper in which the piece was originally published. Often she will be able to pick up on clues as to whether or not it is a publication with a good reputation. As Melissa Davis was following up a lead that Levine had mentioned, for example— an article by Arthur C. Danto in *The Nation*—she noticed on the masthead that *The Nation* had been published "since 1865," and that Danto had been for many years "Columbia University's Johnsonian Professor of Philosophy." At the other end of the spectrum, she found a vast amount of material on the Web the reliability of which seemed difficult to vouch for. An article on the Bush Watch website, for example, discussing George W. Bush's stance towards the "Sensation" exhibit, was by an unnamed author and referred to Bush as "Dubya." No doubt not by coincidence, the article in *The Nation* seemed both far better informed and far better written than the commentary on the Bush Watch site.

Where newspapers are concerned it is also helpful to acquire some sense of the reputation of the publication. *The New York Times*, *The Washington Post*, *Los Angeles Times*, and *The Wall Street Journal* are all American newspapers with strong reputations; in Canada the equivalents are *The Globe and Mail* and *National Post*; in the UK *The Times*, *The Telegraph*, *The Independent*, *The Guardian*, and *The Economist* (the latter now published weekly in a magazine format, but still resolutely styling itself as a "newspaper"). Though all these are reputable publications, it is also helpful to know that some (e.g., *The Wall Street Journal*, *National Post*, *The Telegraph*) tend to be ideologically very conservative, while others (e.g., *The Washington Post*, *The Guardian*) tend to be ideologically somewhat to the left.

If you are uncertain about how reputable a source may be, it is a good idea to consult your instructor. She will be able to tell you, for example, that *The American Historical Review* and *The Journal of American History* are both highly reputable, that *The Journal of*

Philosophy is a much more reputable publication than is *Animus: A Philosophical Journal for Our Time*, and so on. That should not lead you to agree with everything you find in *The Journal of Philosophy*, of course—but it should save you some time.

The experienced researcher will also notice the publishing companies of books published in the relevant area—but not put too much stock in their reputations. The university presses of Oxford, Cambridge, Harvard, and Princeton are far more reputable than is, for example, Three Rivers Press—but the most prestigious university presses have also published a few real clunkers in their time. And because librarians often have standing orders for all books from such prestigious presses as these, a clunker from them is more likely to find its way onto the shelves of the university library than a clunker from Wilfrid Laurier Press or from Hackett Publishing.

With its rich landscape only a fingertip away, the World Wide Web is a great temptation for any writer in search of information. When embarking on research in cyberspace, though, the importance of exercising caution cannot be emphasized too strongly. Whereas the material in the vast majority of the scholarly monographs and journals available through your university library (whether online or hard-copy-only) will have been vetted through a laborious process of peer review, no such vetting need occur with material posted on the Web outside of any academic framework. Some such work is good scholarship in electronic form; a good deal of it is trash. Complaining about a biography of the Russian composer Shostakovich, musicologist Alex Ross describes "a pedantic, fanatical mess of a book, a kind of hardbound website, in which fresh information is lost in reams of third-hand factoids" (126). Ross knows of what he speaks; anybody can slap anything onto a website, and it is not always easy for the student to distinguish reliable scholarly research from rubbish. Nowadays most reputable journals post their material online through one or more research databases, but the amount of unreliable material remains far larger than is the solid scholarship. You should always examine the quality and reliability of your sources with the utmost care; one step in learning how to do that is to rely initially on materials in the library (including materials in electronic databases) rather than materials available only on the Internet.

Finally, the experienced researcher is willing to trust her own judgement: to glance at the table of contents and skim quickly through two or three dozen works on a subject and in each case make a snap decision as to its likely usefulness. These decisions are not, of course, irreversible; she may well find that one of the books initially set aside with barely a moment's notice is generally regarded as among the two or three most important works in the field (in which case she will, of course, return to it with more care). But she must in the first instance have some way of making the mass of material manageable.

What of the opposite problem? What if there seems to be little or nothing published on the subject before? Perhaps it's an area on the border with one or more other territories; in that case, surveying those territories may be necessary. Perhaps it's a relatively new subject; in that case—as indeed for any research—it's always helpful to check the relevant indices of journal articles. Some of the most important of these for work in the arts and social sciences are as follows:

- *Humanities Index:* covers articles published from 1974 onwards in such disciplines as English, history, and philosophy.
- *MLA Bibliography:* offers articles on the English language and literature as well as on French, German, Italian, Spanish, and so on.
- *Philosopher's Index:* the most comprehensive listing of articles on philosophy.
- *Social Sciences Index:* covers articles published from 1974 onwards in such areas as anthropology, economics, political science, psychology, and sociology.

These days, virtually all indices appear in electronic form;* keyword searches are indispensable for researchers. The idea is to use

---

* For listings by academic discipline see pages 378–430.

a single word—or a combination of words—that you consider to be the "key" or main focus of your topic. The computer system will look through every author, title, and subject heading that includes the keywords (in any order). Queen's University provides its students with the following "Basic Search Tips":

Title or journal article
- Omit initial article (*a, the, le*)
- Type just the first few words
- Use journal title for magazines, journals, newspapers

Author
- Type last name first: *einstein, a*
- Add first initial if known
- For organizations use normal word order

Keyword
- Results can include any of your words
- Must use + to indicate essential terms
- Use ? to truncate; use quotes for phrases: "*meech lake*"

Call number
- Include punctuation and spaces

Regardless of whether a library exists electronically or in physical space, it can take time to become familiar with it. Finding the right research material—professional journal, book, or otherwise—often means asking energetic questions. Library staff are trained to know which standard reference books apply to which academic disciplines, and where they are located—and to know a good deal more than that. For instance, the student of literature who asked her librarian for advice about research in a paper on the imagery of Keats's poetry might learn, through polite and persistent interrogation, the value of a "concordance," a listing of words used by an author, with citations of the lines or passages in which each word appears. In that way, she could rapidly determine the frequency and location of "mortality" in the poems of John Keats, thereby saving time and enhancing evidence for, say, a thesis asserting the poet's preoccupation with death. Just one more instance of fruitful collaboration.

The old-fashioned (and sexist) image of the librarian as timid and bespectacled spinster is contradicted mightily by today's experts in "information retrieval and management." Since more and more research tools are being made available on CD-ROM, or on the Web, expertise with computers is an important professional service offered by modern reference librarians. Writers can at most institutions take advantage of in-library workshops on such topics as search strategy formulation, database access, online library catalogues, and file management.

Many writers nowadays conduct all their research for an academic paper without going near a physical library. There is still much to be said, though, for the experience of browsing the relevant shelves of hard-copy books and journals as a means of furthering research. Scanning those shelves and flipping through volumes of possible interest can be of enormous value in sparking unexpected connections, in bolstering arguments, and in adding both depth and breadth to one's base of knowledge. Moreover, it is generally possible to scan very large amounts of material in this way much more quickly and efficiently than may be done on a computer screen.

Whether one is reviewing bound volumes of printed material or articles in an electronic database, it is essential to strike an appropriate balance between one's own ideas and those of others; now is the time for establishing collaboration between one's own writing and the writing of others. The assertive attitude developed during the writer's voice work is crucial at this point, since quotations from experts can easily obscure or overwhelm an essay's thesis. Philip Levine or Arthur C. Danto are more qualified than is Melissa Davis. She is the writer, though, and must therefore remain in full control of the essay's argumentative force, while drawing on others' writing for much of her raw material.

O *Plagiarism*

Just as important as establishing one's own voice is being clear about what others have written—and being careful to attribute it properly. Collaborating with a secondary source means acknowledging that source in the final draft of the essay. Otherwise a writer commits plagiarism, defined by the *MLA Handbook for Writers of Research Papers* as "the act of using another person's ideas or expressions in your writing without acknowledging the source" (21). In her essay Melissa Davis quotes Lynn MacRitchie's description of Ofili's work as developing an "emotional range to match its decorative facility." Had she not included MacRitchie's name, and the quotation marks around MacRitchie's words, and the specifics regarding the reference to MacRitchie's article, Davis would have been guilty of plagiarism.

It is important to be aware that you may be guilty of plagiarism even if you do not use precisely the same words of another writer in precisely the same order. Following is an actual example of plagiarism, in which a newspaper columnist borrowed for his column from an article that had appeared a few days earlier in *The Economist*. The columnist does not always use exactly the same words, but no one reading the two passages can doubt that one writer is stealing from the other:

> From *The Economist*, 21 August 2004: During the run-up to independence in Rwanda, the Belgians changed their minds and started to favour the Hutus instead. The then-fashionable view was that the Hutus were oppressed, and therefore deserving. The Hutus took power, massacred Tutsis, and passed laws restricting the number of university places or civil-service jobs they could hold.

> From *The Lethbridge Herald*, 28 August 2004: But just before independence in Rwanda, the Belgians changed their minds and started to favour the Hutus, reasoning the oppressed major-

ity was deserving. The Hutus took power, massacred Tutsis, and restricted the number of university places and civil-service jobs they could hold.

The penalties for such theft are not trivial; the *Herald* columnist lost his job when a pattern of "borrowings" such as that above was discovered—and at most colleges and universities a student may be expelled for plagiarism.

How can you be sure to avoid plagiarism? First of all, be *extremely* careful in your note-taking, so as to make it impossible to imagine a few days later that words you have jotted down are your own if in fact they are a quotation. Second, use a variety of sources, and do not rely too heavily on any one source. If two or three sources are consulted in a situation such as that above, for example—and then all sources are set aside while the writer composes his own account—what emerges is something very different, in which information gleaned from different sources is incorporated into a summary paragraph:

> The Belgians had a change of heart in the late 1950s and early 1960s, and came round to the view that, as the majority group, the Hutus deserved more power. In 1959 a civil war engulfed the then-colony, with the Hutus defeating the Tutsis. In granting Rwanda independence in 1962, the Belgians accepted a structure that had little power to restrain abuses of power by the majority. Legalized discrimination by the Hutu majority—including the imposition of quotas for the number of university places and public-sector jobs that could be filled by Tutsis—followed, as did large-scale massacres of the minority group.

In the case of the facts provided in the paragraph above, the information being summarized may be classed as common knowledge, and the sources drawn on need only be listed in the bibliography for your essay; no specific source need be cited as evidence that a civil war erupted in 1959, or that the country was granted independence in 1962. If, on the other hand, you wished to present as part of your own essay the judgements of *The Economist*'s correspondent that "a showdown [between Congo government forces and Tutsi rebels] is expected around Goma," or that "few Congolese believe that [the scheduled election] will actually be held," you would be obliged to cite the source of the ideas, even if you were using none of the same words to express them. Far from being "common knowledge," such judgements are clearly the product of informed speculation.

Judgement of the writerly crime of plagiarism has no provision, by the way, for malice aforethought; whether or not a writer is willfully deceptive makes no difference. Therefore, competent writers are extremely careful on two counts. First, they keep thorough and well-organized notes while reading and researching, so as not to assume (weeks later) that some vivid turn of phrase (like *emotional range to match its decorative facility*) must have come to them (weeks earlier) in a burst of inspiration. Second, they continuously assess both the information they are using and the audience they are addressing. In paragraph 8 Davis summarizes the principles behind government support for the arts in Western democracies. She has consulted several sources to be sure the information she is providing here is correct, but in this case there is no need to cite any particular source; the material may safely be considered general knowledge.

O *Citation*

Notice that a parenthetical reference is included by Davis to cite MacRitchie's quoted phrase. She is following a system currently recommended by the *MLA Handbook* (an authoritative guide, published by the Modern Language Association of America). The parenthetical reference may be followed up by readers under "Works Cited" at the end of Davis's essay:

> MacRitchie, Lynn. "Ofili's Glittering Icons." *Art in America* Jan. 2000: n. pag. *Find Articles at BNET*. BNET, Web. 1 May 2009.

Under the MLA system, which dispenses with the traditional footnote, the parenthetical reference should include the author's last name unless that name is clearly linked to the cited material in the actual text of the essay. Thus, when Davis provides Arthur Danto's name in the body of her text, the parenthetical reference accompanying the quotation includes only the relevant page number:

> As Arthur C. Danto has pointed out, "since it is unlikely that as a black Anglo-African Ofili would have used dung to besmirch the slaves [in the picture "Afrobluff"], there is no reason to suppose he was bent on besmirching the Holy Virgin through its presence there either" (2).

Notice here that when Davis feels it appropriate to add a few words of explanation in the midst of the Danto quotation, she puts them in square brackets to indicate that these are not part of the quotation.

Melissa's list of "Works Cited" also demonstrates the format for arrangement of titles (alphabetical, according to the authors' last names), for indentation of successive lines, and for listing different sorts of sources. Notice in particular the sequence of information for a citation from a website. Following the date of the source's publication comes the date that the researcher visited the site.

The MLA system of citation is the most commonly employed system in many humanities disciplines; a full summary of how to use "MLA style" appears in a later section of this book—along with full summaries of other leading systems of citation.

All university professors, like all book publishers and all journal editors, are primarily concerned with two things when it comes to citing and documenting material: accuracy and consistency. Whatever system is recommended, a research writer must take the responsibility of following it closely—by consulting a manual or a style sheet (some professors compose their own) or, if accessible, exemplary essays. Just as audiences vary from discipline to discipline, so do systems of documentation; those provided by the MLA and the APA are certainly not the only ones. While their differences may at times seem trivial (professors have been known to penalize essays whose citations exhibit misplaced commas), accuracy and consistency should nevertheless be sought. This is the one facet of essay-writing that calls on a good writer to suspend his independent attitude in favour of slavish obedience and conformity.

Most systems currently in use have done away with citations at the bottoms of the pages (footnotes), but they have preserved a means for writers to offer marginal explanations to their readers. Called endnotes, or simply "notes," these explanations appear immediately after the text of an essay but before the list of "Works Cited." Endnotes have one of two purposes. The first is to direct readers towards additional sources of information on the topic, as does Melissa Davis's note 4. The second is to digress responsibly from a topic, as Davis does, for example, in her notes 1 and 3. The effect of such brief explanatory paragraphs is to enhance—from a peripheral position—the strength of the essay.

O *Proofreading*

The essay is done! The rough draft has been tidied up, and all the references are in place; it's ready to hand in. Or is it? Experienced writers will at this point always embark on one more step—proofreading. Checking once more (proofreading should never be confused with revising from first to subsequent drafts) for logical and stylistic fluency. Checking for mechanical errors that may—however unfairly—take away from the effect of the essay as a whole. Checking the spelling. Checking the accuracy and format of the references. A boring job, and yet one that brings satisfaction, for no writer is able to proofread an essay without finding things to fix, things to improve.

One final suggestion about proofing: try reading the essay aloud. Inevitably most writers feel silly at first reading aloud to themselves, but inevitably as well they catch things—a missing word, an extra letter—that even the most diligent silent proofing will have missed. For the few minutes it takes, it is always worth giving voice, in an entirely literal sense, to the written text.

O Computers

Word processing emphasizes the fluent and changeable nature of writing; texts are transferred, shared, and modified with unprecedented speed and frequency. In several ways the computer has revolutionized the process of writing over the past thirty years.

The advantages are obvious. No longer does the revision process require endless rewrites of the entire work; errors can be corrected, phrasing can be improved, paragraphs can be shifted around without re-writing or re-typing the whole. Moreover, even those whose spelling is (like that of Winnie the Pooh) "a little wobbly" can appear as perfect spellers through the wonders of spell-check. And yet....

Writers who have grown intimate with word-processing still often prefer to do their first draft in longhand. They know that writing directly onto the screen is more prone to wordiness, and they know as well that it can be difficult to keep the feel of the essay as a whole in mind if half a page is the most that can ever be before their eyes at one time. In short, they remain as aware of the limitations of word-processing as they are of its virtues. And they remain aware that a spell check is just that; it will not catch a substitution of *there* for *their*, or of *its* for *it's*, or of *poured over* for *pored over*. In short, it does not substitute for old-fashioned proofreading.

O Criticism

The ultimate, and often most volatile, collaboration occurs when a writer faces the criticism and responses of a reader. For journalists, such collaboration is fairly routine, since both editors and subscribers are only too eager to correct and modify articles. The university writer also expects regular doses of criticism and advice. Professorial zeal can, however, prove to be a shock, as one student explains:

> My problem is that my essays are perfect only up until the moment I hand them in to be marked. Suddenly, the paper undergoes a drastic transformation. Red marks appear scattered across the page. Words like *NO!* or *EXPLAIN!* appear, linked by arrows to the short forms *AWK* and *SP*. Then there's the ultimate in humiliation—a red line scribbling out my sentence, and a better one written in its place.

Warding off humiliation very often depends on active response to criticism. Collaboration is, after all, a two-sided affair; no red-penned advice or correction has the power to improve a writer's skills unless that writer evaluates it independently. Questions are bound to arise ("Sure, this passage is awkward, but how can I improve it?" "What's wrong with this?!"); finding satisfactory answers depends on continued dialogue and revision. When all is said and done, when all is written and submitted, competent assessors of essays—while experienced and qualified—are far from dictatorial. They look for logical coherence, not for reflections of their own beliefs; and for stylistic clarity, not for imitations of their own writing. Writers who take advantage of actually collaborating with their most demanding readers are the ones who progress most steadily.

O *Works Cited*

Cameron, Ian. *For All Practical Purposes*. Peterborough: Broadview, 1988. Print.

Cole, Susan. "The Legacy of Terry Fox." *Queen's Quarterly* 97.2 (1990): 253-76. Print.

Frye, Northrop. "Humanities in a New World." *Divisions on a Ground*. Ed. James Polk. Toronto: Anansi, 1982. 102-17. Print.

Giltrow, Janet. *Academic Writing*. 3rd ed. Peterborough: Broadview, 2002. Print.

Gould, Stephen Jay. "The Brain of Brawn." *New York Times* 25 June 2000: 17. Print.

Hallpike, C.R. *The Principles of Social Evolution*. Oxford: Clarendon, 1984. Print.

Lauer, Janice. "Writing as Enquiry: Some Questions for Teachers." *College Composition and Communication* 33.1 (1982): 89-93. Print.

Menand, Louis. "Comp Time." *New Yorker* 11 Sept. 2000: 92-94. Print.

Orwell, George. "Politics and the English Language." *Collected Essays*. London: Secker, 1961. 353-67. Print.

Ostry, Sylvia. "New Developments in Trade Policy." *Queen's Quarterly* 97.2 (1990): 215-25. Print.

Ross, Alex. "Shostakovich and Stalin." *New Yorker* 20 March 2000: 124-29. Print.

Taylor, Catherine, et al. *Making Your Mark*. Peterborough: Trent University Academic Skills Centre. 1988. Print.

Whitman, Walt. "Democratic Vistas." *Prose Works 1892: The Collected Writings of Walt Whitman*. Ed. Floyd Stovall. Vol. 2. New York: New York UP, 1964. 361-426. Print.

Wills, Garry. "The Negro President." *The New York Review of Books* 6 November 2003: 45-51. Print.

What Limits to Freedom? Freedom of Expression and
the Brooklyn Museum's "Sensation" Exhibit

*What Limits to Freedom? Freedom of Expression and
the Brooklyn Museum's "Sensation" Exhibit*

cover page (may not
be required by some
instructors)

What Limits to Freedom?

Freedom of Expression and the Brooklyn Museum's

"Sensation" Exhibit

by Melissa Davis

all text centred

Prof. K.D. Smith

Humanities 205

16 May 2009

Melissa Davis

Professor Smith

Humanities 205

16 May 2009

*name
and page
number in
top right
corner*

What Limits to Freedom?

Freedom of Expression and the Brooklyn Museum's

"Sensation" Exhibit

1   For over a century public galleries in Western democracies have

been forums not only for displaying works by "old Masters" but also

for presenting art that is new, as well as ideas that are sometimes

*first line
of all
paragraphs
indented*

radical and controversial. In the United States that tradition has

been under wide attack in the past generation. Various political and

religious leaders have criticized exhibits of works of art that they claim

offend against notions of public decency, and have crusaded against

providing public funding for the creation or display of such works.

The largest such controversy of the past generation was sparked by the

display of a painting entitled "The Holy Virgin Mary," by the British

*text left
justified
and
ragged
right*

artist Chris Ofili at the Brooklyn Museum in 1999. Though the

image appears inoffensive at a distance, the artist has affixed to the

painting cutouts of body parts from magazines, and has incorpo-

rated clumps of elephant dung into the piece, both below the main

body of the work as if supporting it and as part of the collage. The

text double-spaced throughout

Davis 2

resulting uproar led both to a widely publicized court case and to an

ongoing campaign to support "decency" in artistic expression. Should

such art be banned? Should it be exhibited at public expense? In the

course of the Ofili controversy cultural conservatives raised legitimate

concerns about the obligation of any society to provide funding for

activities of which it disapproves. This essay will argue, however, that

the greater concern is in the other direction; a free society must con-

tinue to provide opportunities for the free expression both of artistic

vision and of controversial thought.

first paragraph ends with a statement of the essay's thesis

The Ofili piece was part of a much-hyped exhibit entitled

"Sensation: Young British Artists from the Saatchi Collection." As

the title indicated, the show was made up entirely of works from one

collection, that of the wealthy British advertising executive Charles

Saatchi.[1] The exhibition had been shown first at the Royal Academy

of Arts in London and then at a major gallery in Berlin. (In London

what sparked controversy was not Ofili's work but rather a realistic

painting by Marcus Harvey of child-murderer Myra Hindley that

incorporated hundreds of children's handprints into the image.)

Bringing the show to Brooklyn cost one million dollars—a cost

covered in part by Christie's, a London auctioneer—and from the

outset it could be argued that the museum was courting controversy.

2

numbered note for additional information provided as an aside

paren-
thetical
reference;
Internet
source
has no
page
number

italics
used for
titles of
books,
news-
papers,
journals,
etc.

3

It claimed in its advertising that the exhibition "may cause shock, vomiting, confusion, panic, euphoria, and anxiety. If you suffer from high blood pressure, a nervous disorder, or palpitations, you should consult your doctor" (Barry and Vogel).

No doubt that warning was tongue-in-cheek, but there was nothing ironic about the angry reactions provoked by the show in general and directed toward the Ofili piece in particular. On one side art critics and civil libertarians were full of praise; in *The New York Times* the work was praised as "colorful and glowing" (Kimmelman). On the other side John Cardinal O'Connor called it "an attack on religion," and the president of the Catholic League for Religious and Civil Rights called on citizens to picket the exhibition (Vogel). The United States Senate and the House of Representatives both passed resolutions condemning the exhibit. Even more vehement was the response of New York Mayor Rudy Giuliani (later to become famous for his leadership in the wake of the September 11, 2001 terrorist attacks, and in 2008 to run for president); he declared himself "offended" and the work itself "sick" and "disgusting" (Barry and Vogel). He ordered that ongoing city funding of the museum be withheld until the offensive work was removed, and launched eviction proceedings against the museum. Other conservative politicians—then-Texas Governor George

Davis 4

W. Bush prominent among them—spoke out in support of Giuliani's stand ("Bush Backs Giuliani").

What was the substance of Mayor Giuliani's case? Here is how he explained his stance to the press:

> You don't have a right to a government subsidy to desecrate someone else's religion. And therefore we will do everything that we can to remove funding from the [museum] until the director comes to his senses and realizes that if you are a government subsidized enterprise then you can't do things that desecrate the most personal and deeply held views of people in society. (Brooklyn Institute of Arts and Sciences v. City of New York 7)
>
> "If somebody wants to do that privately and pay for that privately ... that's what the First Amendment is all about," he said. "You can be offended by it and upset by it, and you don't have to go see it, if somebody else is paying for it. But to have the government subsidize something like that is outrageous." (Vogel)

But is it outrageous? Let us examine the implications of Giuliani's argument. According to him, government should never provide funding for activities that some people may find deeply offensive. But governments have long funded much artistic and intellectual activity in advance on the grounds that such activity in general represents a

4

long quotations indented— no quotation marks used except for quotation within a quotation

parenthetical references at end of short quotations followed by punctuation

5

social good, without knowing precisely what sort of artistic work will be created or exhibited, what results academic research may come up with, and so on. If such funding were to be always contingent on no one ever being deeply offended by the results of the artistic or intellectual activity, the effect would be to severely damage freedom of speech and expression. (Here it is important to note that the actions Giuliani took were retroactive; the annual funding for the museum had not been provided with strings attached.)[2]

6   Social conservatives are often characterized as favouring censorship of any material they find offensive; to be fair, that is clearly not the position Giuliani takes here. Nor is the issue whether or not the material is offensive; Hilary Clinton, for example, agreed that works such as that by Ofili were "objectionable" and "offensive" (qtd. in Nagourney), while opposing any punitive actions against the museum. Rather, the issue at stake is under what conditions government has an obligation to fund controversial artistic or intellectual activity. To that question at least one short answer should be plain: an obligation exists where a prior commitment has been made. As Judge Nina Gershon put it in her eventual ruling on the case,

> the issue is ... whether the museum, having been allocated a
> general operating subsidy, can now be penalized with the loss

Davis 6

of that subsidy, and ejectment from a City-owned building,
because of the perceived viewpoint of the works in that exhibit.
The answer to that question is no. (Brooklyn Institute v. City of
New York 17)

Where such a commitment has been made it can only be fairly broken   7
if the activity has in some way contravened previously agreed-on
guidelines or if it has broken the law. If, for example, a work of art or
of literature is thought to violate laws against obscenity, laws concerning hate crimes, laws concerning libel and slander—or, indeed, laws
concerning cruelty to animals, as in the cases of certain "works of art"
in recent years[3]—then legal recourse is available. But not even the
most vociferous of the opponents of the "Sensation" exhibit suggested
that Ofili, the curators, or anyone else had broken the law. Moreover,
the ongoing funding for the Museum had never been made contingent on the institution's exhibits never offending anyone. There were
therefore no just grounds for taking punitive action as Giuliani did.

But how much further than this should the obligation of govern-   8
ment to fund controversial artistic or intellectual activity extend? Do
governments have a general or unrestricted obligation to support and
to fund such activity? The tradition of government support for artistic
and intellectual activity in Western democracies has for many genera-

no citation
needed
for
informa-
tion that is
common
knowledge

tions been one in which support was provided at "arm's length" from
the political process; if judgements based on the merit of individual
works need be made, they are typically made by bodies independent of government. That approach has stemmed from a number of
sensible general principles. One such principle has been a recognition
of the inherent value of intellectual and artistic activity. Another has
been a recognition that such activity will sometimes be challenging,
disturbing, even offensive or disgusting.[4] And a third has been that
if politicians are involved in judging individual artistic or intellectual
works, the judgements will tend to be made more on political and
religious grounds than on intellectual and esthetic ones. We value a
society in which a wide range of free expression is supported, and we
have come to expect that governments will provide a good deal of that
support.

9

Despite the general support for these principles that exists in our
society, we should not assume an unlimited obligation on the part of
government. In particular, liberals and civil libertarians are unwise if
they suggest that the obligation of the government to support artistic
or intellectual endeavour is always a strong and compelling one, or
that any failure of a government to provide financial support for such
endeavour somehow constitutes censorship.[5] There is no clear agree-

Davis 8

ment as to what constitutes art; it follows that there can be no legal
or moral obligation to fund everything that may be classified as art.
And to decide in advance not to subsidize an activity is not the same
as censoring that activity; civil libertarians do not advance their case
by equating the two. Indeed, as philosopher Peter Levine has pointed
out, attempts to remove all restrictions on government support can
easily backfire, since the law

> cannot compel governments to subsidize art in the first place.
> When the Supreme Court ruled in 1998 that individual artists
> may not be denied federal grants because of the content of their
> work, Congress simply cancelled all support for individual artists.
> (2)

If it is a great mistake for the artistic and intellectual com-
munities to press too hard for unrestricted government support, it is
perhaps an even greater mistake for cultural conservatives to seek to
restrict government support to work that conforms to their definition
of "decency." The moral obligation of government to support a broad
range of artistic and intellectual expression may be a relatively weak
one, but if we cast it aside we are choosing to narrow ourselves, to
discourage rather than encourage the sorts of challenge from new ideas
and new artistic expressions that continually replenish the red blood

(margin note) sentence structured so that it flows grammatically into quotation

(margin note) 10

cells of democratic society. In approaching such questions we should ask ourselves what really constitutes freedom of thought, speech, and expression. One defining pillar is legal: constitutional guarantees of freedom and the case law that has helped to define them.[6] But is that all there is to it? A moment's reflection should make it clear that a great deal else is involved. Regardless of what is allowed or prohibited, if there exists a scarcity of art galleries—or of book publishers, or of academic journals, or of newspapers, or of radio and television stations—that are willing to put forward original and controversial works of art, or works of scholarly research, or political treatises, then freedom of speech and expression is *in practice* severely limited.[7] And economic reality dictates that a number of valued activities, including academic research as well as many of the arts, would be severely curtailed without some degree of public funding. If we choose as a society not to fund such activities we will inevitably be erecting real barriers against freedom of speech and expression, even if we have passed no laws restricting such freedoms. That is the reality at the heart of the "Sensation" controversy.

11   It is interesting that in the midst of the controversy Ofili's work itself became oddly invisible, lost in the clamour of arguments from principle on both sides of the debate. Photographic representations

of "Holy Virgin Mary" are widely available on the Web,[8] and viewers coming to these after sampling the heat of the arguments surrounding the piece are likely to be surprised by how calm and pleasant an image is presented to them. Ofili himself was the recipient of the prestigious Turner Prize in 1998 and has been widely recognized as one of the most important of his generation of British artists. Fairly typical are the comments of a writer in *Art in America*, one of the most authoritative journals of contemporary art criticism: "his paintings are a joy to behold.... His technique, as it becomes ever richer and more complex, is developing an emotional range to match its decorative facility" (MacRitchie). The painter, who was born in Britain to parents of Nigerian background, was raised—and still remains—a church-going Catholic. (Clearly critics' claims that "The Holy Virgin Mary" is offensive to Catholics cannot be true of all Catholics!) Ofili has spoken interestingly of how he draws connections between the subjects of his work and the materials he uses, including shiny varnish to make it seem that the subject of a painting is "in some ways more imagined than real" (Vogel), and, of course, the notorious balls of elephant dung that adorn the work and on which it rests.[9] Significantly, Ofili has incorporated dung into many of his works, including those portraying slaves and other African subjects. As Arthur C. Danto has pointed

Davis 11

quotation with author named in signal phrase; page number in parentheses

out, "since it is unlikely that as a black Anglo-African Ofili would have used dung to besmirch the slaves [in the picture "Afrobluff"], there is no reason to suppose he was bent on besmirching the Holy Virgin through its presence there either" (2). From one angle, Ofili clearly sees the use of dung as a way of connecting his paintings to his African heritage and of giving the paintings "a feeling that they've come from the earth" (Vogel). But he also aims to create a tension between the superficially appealing nature of his images and the inherent unpleasantness of some of the materials he has used to create them:

title cited when work has no attributed author

> "The paintings themselves are very delicate abstractions, and I wanted to bring their beauty and decorativeness together with the ugliness of shit[10] and make them exist in a twilight zone—you know they're together, but you can't really ever feel comfortable about it" (qtd. in *Sensation*).

12

One does not need to endorse all of Ofili's theorizing about what he does, or agree fully with the favourable assessments of the critics in order to conclude that it would be unreasonable not to classify his work as art. Even the narrowest and most conservative definitions of art allow the term to be applied to work that many people find pleasing to the eye and that many agree demonstrates creative skill. Ofili's work unquestionably fulfills those criteria. More than that,

there is evidently a good deal of subtlety and nuance to both the
work and the ideas of this painter, far more than the polarized debate
swirling around the painting might suggest. Even if some find this art
offensive, it is hard not to think that on its merits Ofili's work deserves
to be widely exhibited.

    In a narrow sense the controversy of the Ofili work and the Sen-
sation exhibit ended with a clear victory for the Brooklyn Museum.
Federal Judge Nina Gershon ruled that in these circumstances the
City of New York's attempt to shut down the exhibit constituted a vio-
lation of the First Amendment—the Constitutional guarantee of freedom of expression—and in March of 2000 the City and the museum
reached an agreement under the terms of which all further lawsuits
were dropped and the City agreed to contribute 5.8 million dollars
towards a museum restoration project. (The museum re-opened in
2004 after the completion of restorations.) But in a wider sense the
outcome is far less certain. In 2001 Mayor Giuliani attempted to
develop "decency standards" intended to restrict these sorts of works
from being shown in future in publicly funded exhibitions, and such
initiatives received strong support from the administration of George
W. Bush. Among certain commentators the crusade against Ofili has
continued unabated long after the exhibit itself had ended. Phyllis

13

Schlafly is one such crusader (2004); Tammy Bruce is another. In
her best-selling book *The Death of Right and Wrong*, for example,
Bruce uses the case as an example in urging us to "make no mistake:
the degrading of symbols important to Christianity is ... propaganda
meant to change your view of Christianity as a whole" (52). Given the
persistence of attacks of this sort, major museums and galleries must
have real courage to mount exhibitions of work that they consider
likely to be controversial. Tellingly, the "Sensation" exhibit was never
seen after it closed in Brooklyn; the National Gallery of Australia
cancelled its plans to show the exhibit, and a Tokyo museum that had
expressed interest in exhibiting it thereafter did not in the end make
any commitment (Rosenbaum). More recently, the San Francisco Art
Institute closed Adel Abdessemed's controversial "Don't Trust Me"
show after only a few days "for safety reasons" (DeBare B1) in the face
of protests by animals' rights groups and some artists, though there
had been no suggestion that any law had been broken, and though
condemnation of the show had been far from universal.[11]

14   Legal victories in defense of freedom of expression, then, will
never in themselves suffice. The preservation of a truly open society
requires, on the part of those who wish to allow and to encourage
freedom of expression, a moral determination that is at least as strong

Davis 14

as the moral determination of those who wish to roll back its frontiers. Much as constitutional guarantees of freedom of expression are important, even more so is whether we wish as a society to narrow the range of what citizens may readily see or hear, or instead to encourage the wide dissemination of information, opinion, and artistic expression—even opinions and artistic expressions that some may find offensive. In the years since the September 11, 2001 attack, it is understandable that many both within the United States and around the world have been prepared to accept some new restrictions on freedom. But whatever justification there may be for such restrictions does not extend to the sphere of intellectual and artistic activity. If we wish to retain a robustly democratic society we should continue to choose the path of openness.

final paragraph restates and broadens the essay's main argument

Notes

notes
numbered
as in text

1. Saatchi contributed $100,000 to mounting the show, the economics of which became another subject for controversy when it was shown in Brooklyn. As well as complain about the content of the works in the exhibit, Mayor Rudy Giuliani and others suggested that the show had been intended in large part to raise the value of works in the Saatchi collection, and on those grounds, too, argued that the exhibit should not be receiving a subsidy from taxpayers.

each note
indented

2. Because its content was recognized as controversial, city officials had been provided in advance of the "Sensation" show with photographs and full descriptions of all pieces to be included in the exhibit, including the information that Ofili's works incorporated elephant dung into the images they portrayed. The mayor insisted that he personally had not been alerted to the content of the show beforehand, however.

3. Animal rights activists have protested against works by the renowned British artist Damien Hirst, which present, among other things, a sectioned cow and a bisected pig in formaldehyde cases. (Several such works by Hirst were included in the "Sensation" show.) In Toronto, art student Jesse Power and two friends pleaded guilty in

Davis 16

2001 to charges of animal cruelty and public mischief after making what they called an art video recording their torturing and killing a cat; the case again aroused controversy in 2004 following the release of a documentary film about the incident, *Casuistry: The Art of Killing a Cat*, directed by Noah Cowan and Piers Handling. See also the articles by Christie Blatchford and by Gayle MacDonald, and Note 11 below on the 2008 "Don't Trust Me" exhibition in San Francisco.

4. There are many defenses of the principle that an open society must make a place even for controversial or disgusting material. The case for the other side is put by John Kekes in *A Case for Conservatism*; he argues for what he terms "the moral importance of disgust" (100–109).

5. To be fair, although some individuals make assertions as extreme as this one, responsible civil liberties organizations such as the ACLU stop short of any such all-embracing claim.

6. The First Amendment to the American Constitution specifies that Congress "shall make no law ... abridging the freedom of speech, or of the press; or the right of the people to assemble...." In American legal practice it has long been established that "freedom of speech" should also cover other forms of expression—such as artistic works. Other, more recent constitutions tend to make such protections explicit; the Charter of Rights and Freedoms that forms a central

part of the Canadian Constitution, for example, protects "freedom of thought, belief, opinion, and expression, including freedom of the press and other media of communication."

7. A good example of how such freedoms may be constrained is the March 2003 case in which Natalie Maines of the Dixie Chicks criticized George W. Bush—and promptly found that two media conglomerates controlling over 1,300 radio stations refused to play Dixie Chicks music. That case is discussed by Robert B. Reich in *Reason: Why Liberals Will Win the Battle for America*.

8. Among the many Web addresses at which photographs of the work may be found are www.artsjournal.com/issues/Brooklyn.htm and www.postmedia.net/999/ofili.htm and www.geocities.com/southernhelle/sensation3.html.

9. Many who have attacked the piece have chosen to describe the dung as being "*smeared* on a Christian icon" (Bruce 39, my italics), which is substantially to misrepresent the nature of the work.

10. It is interesting to contemplate the impact diction may have on arguments such as this; it is difficult not to respond slightly differently depending on whether the material is referred to using the noun Ofili uses here or referred to less provocatively as "dung."

11. The show included video clips of the killing of animals in

rural Mexico. The artist had evidently not arranged for the killings; he was merely recording local practice. For more on this and other recent controversies, see the articles by Kenneth Baker and Phoebe Hoban.

Davis 19

works cited are
listed alphabetically

Works Cited

Baker, Kenneth. "Show's Cancellation a Rare Case of Artists Advocating Censorship." *San Francisco Chronicle* 1 Apr. 2008: E1. Print.

Barry, Dan, and Carol Vogel. "Giuliani Vows to Cut Subsidy over Art He Calls
Offensive." *New York Times* 23 Sept. 1999: n. pag. Web. 2 May 2009.

each
entry
begins
at left
margin;
subse-
quent
lines
are in-
dented

Blatchford, Christie. "Face to Face with Cruelty." *Globe and Mail* 4 Sept. 2004:
A13. Print.

Brooklyn Institute of Arts and Sciences v. City of New York 99CV 6071. *New
York Law Journal* 1 Nov. 1999: n. pag. Web. 1 May 2009.

Bruce, Tammy. *The Death of Right and Wrong.* New York: Three Rivers, 2003.
Print.

"Bush Backs Giuliani on Museum Flap." *Associated Press* 4 Oct. 1999: n. pag.
Washingtonpost.com. Web. 3 May 2009.

Danto, Arthur C. "'Sensation' in Brooklyn." *The Nation* 1 Nov. 1999: n. pag.
Web. 1 May 2009.

DeBare, Ilana. "Art Institute Halts Exhibition Showing Killing of Animals." *San
Francisco Chronicle* 30 Mar. 2008: B1. Print.

Hoban, Phoebe. "How Far Is Too Far?" *ArtNews* Summer 2008: 145-49. Print.

Kekes, John. *A Case for Conservatism.* Ithaca, New York: Cornell UP, 1988.
Print.

Davis 20

Kimmelman, Michael. "A Madonna's Many Meanings in the Art
World." *New York Times* 5 Oct. 1999: n. pag. Web. 2 May 2009.

Levine, Peter. "Lessons from the Brooklyn Museum Controversy."
Philosophy and Public Policy Quarterly 20.2/3 (2000): n. pag.
Web. 3 May 2009.

MacDonald, Gayle. "TIFF Contacts Police over Death Threat: Caller
Threatens Programmer over Cat-Killer Documentary." *Globe and
Mail* 1 Sept. 2004: R1. Print.

MacRitchie, Lynn. "Ofili's Glittering Icons." *Art in America* Jan. 2000:
n. pag. *Find Articles at BNET.* BNET. Web. 1 May 2009.

Nagourney, Adam. "First Lady Assails Mayor over Threat to
Museum." *New York Times* 28 Sept. 1999. n. pag. Web. 1 May
2009.

Reich, Robert B. *Reason: Why Liberals Will Win the Battle for America.*
New York: Knopf, 2004. Print.

Rosenbaum, Lee. "The Battle of Brooklyn Ends, the Controversy
Continues." *Art in America* June 2000: n. pag. *Find Articles at
BNET.* BNET, n.d.Web. 4 May 2009.

Schlafly, Phyllis. "Time to Abolish Federally Financed 'Hate Art.'"
Eagle Forum. Eagle Forum, 13 Oct. 1999. Web. 2 May 2009.

double
spacing
used
throughout

italics used
for titles
of books,
journals,
magazines,
etc.

Davis 21

Sensation: Young British Artists from the Saatchi Collection. Guide-
book. *Geocities.com*. Yahoo, n.d. Web. 2 May 2009.

"Turner Prize: Twenty Years." *Tate Gallery Online*. Tate Gallery,
2003. Web. 1 May 2009.

Vogel, Carol. "Chris Ofili: British Artist Holds Fast to His
Inspiration." *New York Times* 28 Sept. 1999: n. pag. Web.
2 May 2009.

◎ WRITING GRAMMATICALLY

⊙ Right and Wrong in Writing

In what sense are errors in grammar and usage wrong? *Are* they in fact wrong in any meaningful sense? Should "wrong" in this context be read as always having quotation marks around it?

Too often this sort of question becomes so infused with assumed political content that it is not taken seriously. On the one hand the conservative is likely to regard the question of whether *you* is a formation inherently superior to the vulgar *y'all* or *youse* as unworthy of debate. Of course the form established as correct is superior; of course the colloquialism is debased. On the other side are those who regard it as an article of faith that there are no universal or objectively verifiable truths, and that consequently there can be no rational justification for preferring *you* to *youse* or *y'all*.

Is *Would you like anything else?* correct and *Would youse like anything else?* incorrect in the same way that *12 x 3 = 36* is correct and *12 x 3 = 35* incorrect? Or in the same way that *The capital of Burkina Faso is Ouagadougou* is correct and *The capital of Burkina Faso is Harare* is false? No. It is not wrong in quite those sorts of ways; one pointer is that it would seem distinctly odd to describe *Would youse like anything else?* as false. In what sense, then, is it wrong? The problem is not that it fails to map onto a structure of reality. In fact, as the cognitive scientist Stephen Pinker points out, it makes such a connection with a greater degree of precision than does currently correct usage:

> The mavens lament the loss of conjugal distinction in *he don't* and *we was*. But this has been the trend in standard English for centuries. No one minds that we have abandoned the second-person singular form of verbs, as in *thou sayest*. And by this criterion it is the non-standard dialects that are superior, because they provide their speakers with second-person plural pronouns such as *y'all* and *youse*. (23)

Returning for a moment to Burkina Faso may help us to sense the way in which *youse* and *y'all* may fairly if in a limited sense be thought of as wrong. The sentence *The capital of Upper Volta is Ouagadougou* is wrong in something like the same sense that *Would youse like anything else?* is wrong. Both use the symbolic system of language to correspond to an understood reality. But in both cases the signs used are not those used under currently accepted conventions; though a few may still cling to the old usage, almost everyone has now adopted the late 1980s change of name (from Upper Volta to Burkina Faso) for the area surrounding the headwaters of the Volta River. Upper Volta certainly still corresponds to reality; it is not false. But nor is it right.

On the Web

A fascinating discussion of the ways in which issues of correctness are often confused with issues of style, tone, and voice in writing may be found in Louis Menand's review of *Eats, Shoots & Leaves: The Zero Tolerance Approach to Punctuation*. The review is entitled "Bad Comma: Lynne Truss's Strange Grammar"; it first appeared in the 28 June 2004 issue of *The New Yorker*, and may be found online at www.newyorker.com/critics/books/?critics/040628crbo_books1.

Similarly, if one were to transplant from Alberta to Massachusetts one of the Alberta highway signs that reads "Speed Limit 110," it would not be in any way false. Given that the convention in all Canadian provinces is to measure speed in kilometres and the convention in the United States is to measure it in miles, however, the sign would in an important sense be wrong (much more wrong, indeed, than would be the use of *youse*, even in the most formal of essays).

But why stick to the conventional where the essay or the business report is concerned? Is there any legitimate argument in favour of the conventions of standard English? One such argument may fairly be grounded in pedagogy; the acquiring of a knowledge of English grammar and syntax is an enormously helpful way of strengthening habits of abstract thought. But that speaks to the value of a byproduct, not of the thing itself. There may be only two *essential* justifications for standard English: ease of communication, and elegance of expression. The first of these is to a large extent obvious, but it is worth stressing that the ease of communication which standard forms or conventions of usage make possible extends not only from individual to individual but also from one culture to another, and over very long periods of time. It has been often noted that the ordinarily literate person in our own time is able to respond to the language of Shakespeare in a way that the ordinarily literate person in Shakespeare's day was quite unable to respond to *Beowulf,* simply because the conventional codification of grammar and usage that print made possible has drastically slowed down the rate of linguistic change. (Cullen Murphy has interestingly suggested that the development beginning in the late nineteenth century of electric and then of electronic methods of reproducing sound has given the sloppy and unruly nature of the spoken word a much greater influence on the shaping of the language and on the speed of change than it had in the sixteenth through nineteenth centuries.)

The second legitimate argument in favour of standard English is by far the weaker, and it should be readily conceded that elegance of expression is often achievable outside the confines of standard English. But complex syntactical and grammatical pathways will inevitably tend to have been worn smoother in a greater variety of ways in long-established conventions of formal expression. Colloquial or non-standard usages may have a freshness to them or in other syntactical ways may appeal strongly in ways that standard English cannot compete with. But they are unlikely to consistently lend themselves to long and elegantly balanced combinations of clauses and phrases in the way that the mainstream of our culture has been training standard English to do for centuries.

⊙ ⊙ ⊙

If this book is prescriptive, then, it should be understood that it is prescriptive only in a context that recognizes correct English as a matter of convention, not as one in which one form is understood to be necessarily or absolutely better than another. Sentences such as *use "aggravate" to mean "make worse," not to mean "annoy" or "irritate"* should always be taken as a convenient short form for "in formal written English, if you wish to conform to the most commonly accepted conventions of usage, use...." And, to return to the example with which this chapter began, *y'all* and *youse* are alternative, arguably superior forms, that we may legitimately reject only on the grounds of convention.

On other specific issues, though, the case for standard usage is sometimes considerably stronger. The confusion of *uninterested* and *disinterested*, for example, will if *disinterested* is driven from the field represent a measurable loss of the communicative capacity of the English language. If we lose *disinterested* it will be more difficult and more cumbersome to express a variety of meanings. Yet there can be no question that many who are unperturbed by *disinterested* having largely been swamped by *uninterested*—indeed, many who do not even recognize the distinction—cringe at the supposed abomination of *youse* or *y'all*. What such cases drive home to us is the degree to which the ways in which we use standard English (and the assumptions we make about standard English) may be linked to irrational sentiments such as social snobbery, or class or gender-based prejudice. (How many there still are who ludicrously claim *fisher* and *chair* to be "more awkward" than the longer and cumbersome forms *fisherman* and *chairman*.) There are good reasons for not abandoning standard English—but good reasons as well to keep questioning our own assumptions about it.

⊙ ⊙ ⊙

One of the ways in which this book differs from many other guides to grammar and usage is in its approach to change in language, and in the degree to which it attempts to resist the assumption that where the English language is concerned, change implies debasement. Thus in the chapter on part-of-speech conversions such previous entries as *liaise* and *mandate* have been dropped. The back formation of a verb from the noun *liaison* might not be a pretty thing. But a bias against it might not reflect anything more than habit; certainly it can be difficult in many cases to choose more economical replacements. The prejudice against such words might not be any better grounded than was the bias a generation or two ago against using *contact* as a verb. *Finalize* still grates slightly on some ears, too. But sometimes *finish* just does not capture the sense, and *finalize* is more concise than *make final* or *put into final form*. A comparison of the current state of attitudes today towards the word *finalize* with attitudes of the mid-twentieth century may be instructive as to whether or not there are any good grounds today for objecting to *finalize*:

> *Finalize* is not standard: it is special, and it is a peculiarly fuzzy and silly word. Does it mean *terminate*, or does it mean *put into final form*? One can't be sure, really, what it means, and one gets the impression that the person using it doesn't know, either, and doesn't want to know. (Strunk and White, *The Elements of Style*, [New York, Macmillan: 2/e, 1972] 75–76)

That may have been true in 1957, when the first edition of *The Elements of Style* appeared, or even in 1972, when the second edition was published. But no one today uses *finalize* to mean *terminate*; that denotation has dropped away, and the word's meaning has stabilized as *put into final form*.

If Strunk and White are out of date on the particulars, this remains a good example of the wisdom of their advice to writers that one danger of "adopting new coinages too quickly is that they will bedevil one by insinuating themselves where they do not belong" (75–76). What was a fuzzy coinage in the 1950s has found a clearly defined place in the language of today. And even conservative arbiters such as Strunk and White recognize that language must change, and that this is no bad thing. In the end guides such as this one should continually strive for a balance between the value of continuity in language and in usage, and the value of language as a living thing; without change there can be no life.

⊙   ⊙   ⊙

In one area in particular this guide is not only unresistant to change but embraces change: the move towards bias-free language. In this one area a different sort of *correctness* than the correctness spoken of elsewhere in these pages is involved. Call it political correctness if you will, but however it is referred to, it concerns things that are right and wrong in a sense that goes far beyond questions of what is conventional or convenient. The point involved here is that language can have an important part to play in helping us to do the right thing. To treat men and women on an equal footing, to avoid discrimination on the basis of religion, or race, or class—language can be used to help accomplish all of these goals.

David Foster Wallace is not alone in claiming that the "central fallacy" of the so-called politically correct is "that a society's mode of expression is productive of its attitudes rather than a product of those attitudes" (55). In fact, the fallacy is to assume that it need be either/or; research has suggested *both* that changes in attitudes produce changes in modes of expression *and* that modes of expression help shape attitudes. Of course it is not possible to eliminate elitism and unfairness simply by ceasing to use "vocabulary that is historically associated with elitism and unfairness" (55). But equally clear is that the perpetuation of such vocabulary can only help to perpetuate elitism and unfairness; precisely how much difference language makes may be open to dispute, but it *does* make a difference.

A strong emphasis on the ways in which language can help or hinder social change of this sort is thus an important part of this book; a discussion of bias-free language forms a substantial chapter in the book, and provides a much more thoroughgoing treatment of these issues than do most other guides to usage.

○ *Works Cited*

Murphy, Cullen. "The Lay of the Language: The Decline of Semantic Distinction, and What It Suggests about Linguistic Evolution." *The Atlantic Monthly* May 1995: 20–22. Print.

Pinker, Stephen. "Grammar Puss: The Fallacies of the Language Mavens." *New Republic* 31 Jan. 1994: 19–24. Print.

Strunk, William Jr., and E.B. White. *The Elements of Style*. 2nd ed. New York: Macmillan, 1972. Print.

Wallace, David Foster. "Tense Present: Democracy, English, and the Wars over Usage." *Harper's Magazine* Apr. 2001: 39–58. Print.

⊙ Verbs

● *Verbs and Verb Tense Difficulties*

○ THE INFINITIVE

Although not properly speaking a verb tense, the infinitive is the starting point for building a knowledge of verb tenses; the infinitive is the most basic form of the verb. Some examples of infinitives are *to go, to be, to do, to begin, to come, to investigate*. The infinitive form remains the same, of course, whether the action referred to happens in the past, the present, or the future.

> **ESL**
> For particular problems with verbs faced by those whose native language is not English, see the ESL section later in the book (pages 443–53).

A1. **split infinitives:** The most commonly made mistake involving infinitives is undoubtedly the slang substitution of *and* for *to*, especially in the expression *try and do it* for *try to do it* (see under "Usage" for a fuller treatment). The great issue in this area among grammarians, however, is the split infinitive—the infinitive which has another word or words inserted between *to* and the verb:

needs checking   The time has come to once again go to the polls. Economic conditions are likely to greatly influence the outcome, and the prime minister has promised to forcefully speak out in defense of the government's fiscal record.

With re-united infinitives, the same passage looks like this:

revised   The time has come to go once again to the polls. Economic conditions are likely to influence greatly the outcome, and the prime minister has promised to speak out forcefully in defense of the government's fiscal record.

On what grounds can the second passage be considered better? It comes down to a matter of sound and rhythm. To most ears *to go once again* and *to speak out forcefully* are preferable to the split alternatives, but *to influence greatly* seems more awkward than *to greatly influence*. Happily, most authorities are now agreed that it is not a grievous sin to split an infinitive; Philip Howard, former editor of *The Times* of London, calls the split infinitive "the great shibboleth of English syntax," and even the traditionalist H.W. Fowler allows that while "the split infinitive is an ugly thing, we must warn the novice against the curious superstition that splitting or not splitting makes the difference between a good and a bad writer."

This is not to say that the splitting of infinitives should be encouraged. In many cases a split infinitive is a sign of wordiness; in cases such as the following it is better to drop the adverb entirely:

poor   The chair said it was important to really investigate the matter thoroughly.

better	The chair said it was important to investigate the matter thoroughly.

Like all verb forms, most infinitives have both an *active* and a *passive* voice. The active, which is more common, is used when the subject of the verb is doing the action, whereas the passive is used when the subject of the verb is receiving the action, or being acted on. *To do, to hit, to write* are examples of infinitives in the active voice, while *to be done, to be hit, to be written* are examples of infinitives in the passive voice.

On the Web

Exercises on split infinitives may be found at **www.broadviewpress.com/writing**. Click on **Exercises** and go to **A1**.

○ THE SIMPLE PRESENT TENSE

	singular	*plural*
1st person	I say	we say
2nd person	you say	you say
3rd person	he, she, it says	they say

A2. **subject-verb agreement**: The simple present tense seems entirely straightforward, and usually it is. Most of us have no difficulty with the first person or the second person. But almost all of us occasionally have problems in writing the third person correctly. All too often the letter *s* at the end of the third person singular is left out. The simple rule to remember is that whenever you use a verb in the third person singular of the simple present tense, it must end in *s*:

needs checking	He go to Vancouver at least once a month.
revised	He goes to Vancouver at least once a month.
needs checking	The litmus paper change immediately when the solution is poured into the beaker.

revised	The litmus paper changes immediately when the solution is poured into the beaker.
	(*Paper*, which is the subject, is an *it* and therefore third person singular.)

It is not particularly difficult to ensure that the subject agrees with the verb in the above examples, but even professional writers often have trouble with more complex sentences. Here are two common causes of subject-verb agreement errors:

(a) The subject and verb are separated by a long phrase or clause.

needs checking	The state of Afghanistan's roads reflect the chaotic situation.
revised	The state of Afghanistan's roads reflects the chaotic situation.

Here the writer has made the mental error of thinking of *roads* as the subject of the verb *reflect*, whereas in fact the subject is the singular noun *state*. *The state reflect ...* would immediately strike most people as wrong, but the intervening words have in this case caused grammatical confusion.

needs checking	As the statement by Belgium's prime minister about his country's deficit and unemployment problems indicate, many nations are in the same shape, or worse.
revised	As the statement by Belgium's prime minister about his country's deficit and unemployment problems indicates, many nations are in the same shape, or worse.
	(The subject is the singular noun *statement*, so the verb must be *indicates* rather than *indicate*.)
needs checking	Courses offered range from the history of the Greek and Roman world to the twenty-first century, and covers Britain, Europe, North America,

| | Africa, and the Far East. (History Dept. Prospectus, Birkbeck College, University of London) |
| *revised* | Courses offered range from the history of the Greek and Roman world to the twenty-first century, and cover Britain, Europe, North America, Africa, and the Far East. |

Sometimes a long sentence can in itself throw off a writer's sense of subject-verb agreement, even if subject and verb are close together. In the following example the close proximity of the subject *simplifications* to the verb has not prevented error:

| *needs checking* | The decline in the quality of leadership is mirrored in the crude simplifications which characterizes the average person's view of the world. |
| *revised* | The decline in the quality of leadership is mirrored in the crude simplifications which characterize the average person's view of the world. |

(b) The error of using *there is* instead of *there are* when the subject is plural has become more and more frequent in writing as well as in speech. When these two expressions are used, remember that the subject comes after the verb; use *is* or *are* depending on whether the subject is singular or plural:

| *needs checking* | There's many more opportunities of that sort than there used to be. |
| *revised* | There are many more opportunities of that sort than there used to be. |

On the Web

Exercises on subject-verb agreement may be found at
www.broadviewpress.com/writing.
Click on **Exercises** and go to **A2**.

A3. habitual action: The simple present tense is often used to express what is called habitual action—the way an action ordinarily, or habitually, occurs. The simple present tense is used to name such action even if the main verb of the sentence is in the past or future tense:

needs checking	The professor told us that Jupiter was the largest planet.
revised	The professor told us that Jupiter is the largest planet.
	(Jupiter has not stopped being the largest since he spoke.)

○ THE PRESENT PROGRESSIVE (OR CONTINUOUS) TENSE

	singular	plural
1st person	I am saying	we are saying
2nd person	you are saying	you are saying
3rd person	he, she, it is saying	they are saying

A4. verbs not normally used in the continuous tenses: In English the continuous tenses are not normally used with many verbs which have to do with feelings, emotions, or senses. Some of these verbs are *to see, to hear, to understand, to believe, to hope, to know, to think* (meaning *believe*), *to trust, to comprehend, to mean, to doubt, to suppose, to wish, to want, to love, to desire, to prefer, to dislike, to hate.*

needs checking	He is not understanding what I meant.
revised	He does not understand what I meant.

○ THE SIMPLE PAST TENSE

	singular	plural
1st person	I finished	we finished
2nd person	you finished	you finished
3rd person	he, she, it finished	they finished

A5. **irregular verbs:** The occasional problems that crop up with the simple past tense usually involve irregular verbs—that is to say, verbs that do not follow a regular pattern in the formation of the simple past and other tenses. (See page 142 for a fuller discussion and list.) The use of *may, might* is a good example:

needs checking	Bands such as U2 and Simple Minds gained a foothold in North America through campus radio; without it they may not have broken through.
revised	Bands such as U2 and Simple Minds gained a foothold in North America through campus radio; without it they might not have broken through.

A6. **lie/lay:** Two other verbs that often cause problems with the simple past tense are *lie* and *lay*. The difficulty many people have in keeping these straight is often ascribed to other factors, but is in part also attributable simply to the forms of the tenses; the past tense of *lie* is the same as the present tense of *lay*. Also, the past participle of *lie* is *lain*, not *laid*:

needs checking	Many in our party have just laid down and rolled over; they cannot get over the fact that we have lost control of the House of Representatives.
revised	Many in our party have just lain down and rolled over; they cannot get over the fact that we have lost control of the House of Representatives.

Given the inherent confusion of the tense forms, the difficulty of getting one's tongue round *lain down* rather than *laid down*, and the fact that almost anyone will know what meaning is intended with these words, many authorities now feel that the distinctions are not worth troubling over except in formal written English.

○ THE PAST PROGRESSIVE (OR CONTINUOUS) TENSE

	singular	*plural*
1st person	I was leaving	we were leaving
2nd person	you were leaving	you were leaving
3rd person	he, she, it was leaving	they were leaving

The problems that sometimes occur with the past continuous tense are the same as those that occur with the present continuous (see above, number A4). Remember to avoid these tenses when using verbs having to do with feelings, emotions, or senses (e.g., *see, hear, understand, believe, hope, know, think, trust, comprehend*) and when using the verb *to have* to mean *own, possess,* or *suffer from*:

needs checking	At that time he was believing that everything on earth was created within one week.
revised	At that time he believed that everything on earth was created within one week.

○ THE SIMPLE FUTURE TENSE

	singular	*plural*
1st person	I will arrive	we will arrive
2nd person	you will arrive	you will arrive
3rd person	he, she, it will arrive	they will arrive

○ THE FUTURE PROGRESSIVE (OR CONTINUOUS) TENSE

	singular	*plural*
1st person	I will be finding	we will be finding
2nd person	you will be finding	you will be finding
3rd person	he, she, it will be finding	they will be finding

○ THE PERFECT TENSES

As used to refer to the perfect tenses, the word *perfect* means *completed*; as you might expect, then, the perfect tenses are often (though not always) used to express actions that have been completed. They are formed by combining some form of the verb *to have* with a past participle (e.g., *opened, finished, believed, done*).

○ THE PRESENT PERFECT TENSE

	singular	*plural*
1st person	I have worked	we have worked
2nd person	you have worked	you have worked
3rd person	he, she, it has worked	they have worked

A7. **continuing past actions**: One way in which this tense is used is to speak of past actions which may continue into the present, or be repeated in the present or future. In the sentence *Margaret Atwood has written a number of books*, for example, the form of the verb shows that she will probably write more; she has neither died nor given up writing.

Understanding this sort of thing is a simple enough practice in normal usage, but in the long sentences that often occur in academic writing, it is easy to become confused:

> *needs checking*   Since it called the First World Food Congress in 1963, the Food and Agriculture Organization has said clearly that the world, with the science and technology then known, had enough knowledge to ensure man's freedom from hunger. Successive world congresses and conferences have repeated this contention. (from a paper given by a distinguished professor at an academic conference)

Here the writer has evidently chosen the present perfect, thinking that he is referring to a situation which has continued on into the present. But when he refers to the science and technology then known and to successive world congresses and conferences, he has cut off the 1963 conference from any grammatical connection with the present. This is the sort of mistake that most writers can catch only during the revision process.

> *revised*   When it called the First World Food Congress in 1963, the Food and Agriculture Organization said clearly that the world, with the science and technology then known, had enough knowledge to ensure man's freedom from hunger. Successive world congresses and conferences have repeated this contention.

○ THE PAST PERFECT TENSE

	singular	*plural*
1st person	I had believed	we had believed
2nd person	you had believed	you had believed
3rd person	he, she, it had believed	they had believed

Since the verb remains unchanged in all these forms, the past perfect is one of the easiest tenses to remember. What is difficult is learning how and when to use it. In English, however, there are quite definite rules about when the past perfect tense should be used. Its chief use is to show that one action in the past was completed before another action in the past began. Here are some examples:

- I told my parents what had happened.
  (The happening occurred before the telling.)
- By the time the group of tourists left Mozambique, they had formed a very favourable impression of the country.
  (The forming occurred before the leaving.)
- When he had gone I thought very seriously about what he had said.
  (Both the going and the saying occurred before the thinking.)

The usefulness of the past perfect tense can be clearly seen in passages in which the writer wishes to flashback, or move backwards in time. If you compare the following passages, you will see that the use of the past perfect tense in the second passage removes any confusion about the order in which the events happened. In the example below, when only the simple past tense is used, it sounds as if the dead snake is able to crawl:

needs checking	The tail was still moving, but the snake itself was quite dead. It crawled out from under a rock and slowly moved towards me as I was lowering the canoe at the end of the portage.
revised	The tail was still moving, but the snake itself was quite dead. It had crawled out from under a rock and had moved slowly towards me as I had been lowering the canoe at the end of the portage.
	(In the second passage it is clear that the snake approached this person *before* it died, and not afterwards.)

Perhaps the most common occasions in which we use the past perfect tense are when we are using indirect speech:

- She said that she had knocked on my door in the morning, but that there had been no answer.
  (The knocking happened before the saying.)
- The chair of the committee repeatedly asked the witness when the president had known of the diversion of funds.
  (The knowing happened before the asking.)

In a few cases it is possible to speak correctly of two actions which happened one after the other in the past by using the simple past tense for both actions. The use of the word *after*, for example, often makes it clear that the first action was completed before the other began.

A8. **past actions at different times, or over a prolonged period**: Writers often neglect to use the past perfect to name the earlier action when they are speaking of two (or more) actions that happened at different times in the past:

needs checking	He asked me if I talked to his secretary before coming to him.
revised	He asked me if I had talked to his secretary before coming to him.
needs checking	By the time the Allies decided to resist Hitler, the Nazis built up a huge military machine.
revised	By the time the Allies decided to resist Hitler, the Nazis had built up a huge military machine.
needs checking	Johnson's girlfriend, Marsha Dianne Blaylock, said she knew Williams since October 2007, when she and Johnson began their relationship.
revised	Johnson's girlfriend, Marsha Dianne Blaylock, said she had known Williams since October 2007, when she and Johnson began their relationship.

(Note that like the present perfect, the past perfect is very frequently required with *since* or *for*.)

The past perfect is also used to indicate that a past action occurred over a prolonged period:

- In the early 1960s Sonny Bono was a dishevelled pop singer and songwriter with hippie tendencies; by the time of his death in 1998 he had become a conservative Republican member of the House of Representatives.

needs checking	In 1980, 10 per cent of Chile's families did not have sufficient income to satisfy the minimum food requirements recommended by international organizations; in 2000 the figure grew to 32 per cent.

revised	In 1980, 10 per cent of Chile's families did not have sufficient income to satisfy the minimum food requirements recommended by international organizations; by 2000 the figure had grown to 32 per cent.
revised	... in 2000 the figure was 32 per cent.
	(The original suggests that the figure had remained at 10 per cent in every year from 1980 to 2000, and then jumped in the course of one year to 32 per cent.)

○ THE FUTURE PERFECT TENSE

	singular	plural
1st person	I will have gone	we will have gone
2nd person	you will have gone	you will have gone
3rd person	he, she, it will have gone	they will have gone

○ OTHER TENSES

The present perfect continuous tense—*I have been running, you have been working*, etc.

The past perfect continuous tense—*I had been looking, you had been following*, etc.

The future perfect continuous tense—*I will have been sleeping, they will have been studying*, etc.

The conditional continuous tense—*I would be bringing, she would be starting*, etc.

The past conditional continuous tense—*I would have been working, he would have been driving*, etc.

○ *Mood: Indicative, Imperative, and Subjunctive*

The tenses discussed above are all in the **indicative mood**; that is the way we express ourselves most of the time as we name real or possible actions. The **imperative mood** is used for commands and instructions:

- Follow the path to the right.
- Come here immediately!

The mood that even many native English speakers find difficult to use correctly is the **subjunctive mood**. The subjunctive is used to denote actions that are wished for or imagined, or contrary to fact or expectation. In common English usage the indicative mood is now often employed where once the subjunctive was mandatory, but the subjunctive has by no means disappeared—and, particularly where conditional constructions are concerned, it is a frequent source of difficulty for writers. Here are a few examples of sentences that use the subjunctive:

- If I were you, I would do what she says.
  (not *if I was you*)
- The doctor advises that he stop smoking immediately.
  (not *that he stops*)
- If we can't even get this much done, God help us.
  (not *God helps us*)
- Suffice it to say that the subject is a controversial one.
- Be that as it may, the central assertion of Smith's book is irrefutable.
- If you went to Iceland, would you visit a volcano?
  (not *if you go*)

In the last of these examples one may use as a subjunctive form either *if you went* or *if you were to go*. Until the second half of the twentieth century it was far more common than it is today to form subjunctive constructions such as this only by using "were." Over the past fifty years it has become much more acceptable in formal writing as well as in conversation to use as a subjunctive a verb in the same form as that of the simple past tense in the indicative mood. Where people used to say *If I were to send her something...* (when they were not in fact planning to send anything), they would now typically say *If I sent her something....* Where they used to say *If the Cubs were to win...* when they believed a Cubs win to be extremely unlikely, they would now typically say *If the Cubs won....* In such sentences the simple past form (*sent, won*) has replaced the old subjunctive form (*were to send, were to win*).

Much as subjunctive forms are less widely used in these sorts of conditional constructions, there still are important rules as to the correct combinations in grammatical constructions dealing with conditions. Given the difficulties involved, it may be worth spending some time on these.

○ THE CONDITIONAL

	singular	*plural*
1st person	I would go	we would go
2nd person	you would go	you would go
3rd person	he, she, it would go	they would go

The above forms are used when we are speaking of actions which would or might happen if certain conditions were fulfilled. Here are some further examples:

- If I wanted to go to Australia, I would have to fly.
- If I drank a lot of gin, I would be very sick.
- I would lend Joe the money he wants if I trusted him.
- I might enjoy basketball more if I were taller.

Each of these sentences is made up of a main clause, in which a modal auxiliary verb (*would, might*) is used, and a subordinate clause beginning with *if*, with a verb in the same form as the simple past tense (*wanted, drank, trusted,* etc.). In all cases the action named in the *if* clause is considered by the speaker to be unlikely to happen, or quite impossible. The speaker does not really want to go to Australia; she is just speculating about what she would have to do if she did. Similarly the second speaker does not expect to drink a lot of gin; if he did, he would be sick, but he does not plan to. In the same way, the speaker of the third sentence does not trust Joe; he is speaking about what the situation would be if he did trust Joe. Situations like these which are not happening and which we do not expect to happen are called *hypothetical situations*: we speculate on what *would* or *might* happen *if* ... but we do not expect the *if* ... to come true.

If we think the *if* ... is likely to come true, then we use the future tense instead of the conditional in the main clause, and the present tense in the subordinate *if* clause, as in these examples:

- If I drink a lot of gin, I will be very sick.
  (Here the speaker thinks that it is very possible or likely that he will drink a lot of gin.)
- If I want to go to Australia, I will have to fly.
  (Here the speaker thinks that she may really want to go.)

Notice the difference between the following two sentences:

- If a socialist government is re-elected in Venezuela, the American administration will not be pleased.
  (Here the writer thinks that it is quite possible or likely that the socialists will be re-elected.)
- If a socialist government were elected in Venezuela, the American administration would not be pleased.
  (Here the writer is assuming that the socialists probably will not be re-elected.)

Following are listed the most commonly experienced difficulties in forming conditional constructions.

A9. **forming the subjunctive**: Although it is now acceptable with most verbs to form a verb in the subjunctive mood by using the same form as that of the simple past tense (see above), this is not the case with the verb *to be*. In formal writing *were* remains the only accepted subjunctive formation of the verb *to be*:

needs checking   If a bank was willing to lend new businesses very large amounts without proper guarantees, it would go bankrupt very quickly.

revised	If a bank were willing to lend new businesses very large amounts without proper guarantees, it would go bankrupt very quickly.
needs checking	If I was an NHL player, I would be happy to play for less than $500,000 per year.
revised	If I were an NHL player, I would be happy to play for less than $500,000 per year.

On the Web

Exercises on conditional sentences may be found at
www.broadviewpress.com/writing.
Click on **Exercises** and go to **A11**.

A10. **choosing the right verb when writing about conditions**: Some writers mistakenly use the auxiliary verb *would* in the *if...* clause when they are also using *would* in the main clause. Others use the present tense (instead of the past tense) in the *if...* clause when they are using *would* in the main clause. Both are incorrect.

needs checking	If television networks would produce fewer series about violent crime, parents would allow their children to watch even more television than they do now.
revised	If television networks produced fewer series about violent crime, parents would allow their children to watch even more television than they do now.
or	If television networks were to produce fewer series about violent crime, parents would allow their children to watch even more television than they do now.
needs checking	If I want to buy a car, I would look carefully at all the models available.
revised	If I wanted to buy a car, I would look carefully at all the models available.
	(The speaker does not want to buy a car.)

or If I want to buy a car, I will look carefully at all the models available.

(The speaker may really want to buy a car.)

Remember that the subjunctive (typically, identical in form to that of the simple past tense) is used in the conditional *if...* clause whenever one is referring in the main clause to present or future situations that are imagined, wished for, or in some other way contrary to fact.

O THE PAST CONDITIONAL

	singular	*plural*
1st person	I would have gone	we would have gone
2nd person	you would have gone	you would have gone
3rd person	he, she, it would have gone	they would have gone

This verb form is used in conditional sentences in which we are speaking of actions which never happened. It is used in the main clause, with the past tense in the subjunctive mood being used in the *if...* clause. Notice in the examples below that these past tense subjunctive forms are identical in form to the past perfect tense formations in the indicative mood.

- If I had studied harder, I would have passed.
  (meaning that in fact I did not study very hard, and did not pass)
- If Kitchener had arrived at Khartoum a day earlier, he would have saved Gordon and the rest of the British garrison force.
  (meaning that Kitchener did not come early enough, and was not able to prevent the 1885 massacre at Khartoum)

Here again the subjunctive used to be formed with a *were to...* construction much more commonly than is the norm today. Instead of saying *if I had studied harder ...* or *if Kitchener had arrived a day earlier ...* it was once common to say *if I were to have studied harder ...*, *if Kitchener were to have arrived a day earlier ...*, and so on. It is easy to understand why these more cumbersome formulations are now relatively rare.

A11. **choosing the right verbs when writing about past conditions:** Some people mistakenly use the past conditional in both clauses of sentences such as these; remember that the past conditional should be used only in the main clause:

needs checking	If the Titanic would have carried more lifeboats, hundreds of lives would have been saved.
revised	If the Titanic had carried more lifeboats, hundreds of lives would have been saved.
needs checking	If the Yes campaign in Quebec would have won 200,000 more votes, the course of Canadian politics in the mid-1990s would have been very different.
revised	If the Yes campaign in Quebec had won 200,000 more votes, the course of Canadian politics in the mid-1990s would have been very different.

Active and Passive Voice

Discussions of the active and passive in writing are often the site of considerable controversy—and considerable confusion. The most frequent reference point in such discussions is George Orwell's "Politics and the English Language," in which Orwell made "never use the passive where you can use the active" one of his six elementary rules of writing. In his essay Orwell persuasively suggests links between verbal subterfuge and political duplicity. Given this background, it is perhaps unsurprising that many have tended to conflate the use of a passive voice (in itself a matter purely of grammar and sentence construction) with the use in general of words to disguise agency—something that may be effected through a variety of verbal means. For example, the sentence *the police officer killed the protestor with a single baton blow to the head* is a simple sentence using the verb *to kill* in the active voice. One way to disguise agency here is to make *the protestor* the subject of the sentence and use the same verb in the passive voice. Such a construction readily allows for the omission of any mention of who wielded the baton: *the protestor was killed by a single baton blow to the head.* But one could also disguise agency with a sentence such as the following: *a blow to the head from a baton was the cause of the protestor's death.* In that case the change is not a matter of shifting from the active to the passive voice but of choosing a different verb.

As background here, it is essential to appreciate that the distinction between active and passive voice is not relevant to all verbs, but only to transitive verbs. You can hit someone or something, and someone or something can be hit by you; the active voice/passive voice distinction is certainly relevant to the verb *to hit.* But you cannot sleep someone or something, or be slept by someone or something; the active voice/passive voice distinction is not relevant to an intransitive verb such as *to sleep.* Nor is it relevant to that most common of verbs, the verb *to be.* In some cases agency may be disguised by using either the active voice or the passive voice of a verb. Such, for example, is the case with the verb *to violate,* which may be used with the agent as the subject but may also be used with the action itself as the grammatical subject:

The detention of the suspect without any charges violates her constitutional rights.

The suspect's constitutional rights are violated by her detention without any charges.

The prosecutor violated the defendant's constitutional rights by detaining her without laying any charges.

Agency is as much disguised in the first of these sentences as in the second, though the first is in the active voice, the second in the passive voice.

Let us look at another example of disguised agency. The sentence *I knocked that vase off the shelf* uses the past tense *knocked* in the active voice. Switching to the passive voice gives us *that vase was knocked off the shelf,* and of course allows for the option of omitting *by me*; this is one way of disguising agency. But if I wanted to disguise agency in such a situation I would be more likely to choose a different verb entirely, perhaps an intransitive verb such as *to fall* for which the active voice/passive voice distinction is not relevant: *that vase fell off the shelf.*

Many verbal stratagems that disguise agency use the pronoun *it* as the grammatical subject. If someone has just dumped a girlfriend or boyfriend, for example, the "dumper" is not always keen to say *I dumped her* or *I dumped him*. But nor is it likely that the speaker will shift to the passive voice and say *she was dumped by me/he was dumped by me*. Much more likely would be a shift to the use of *it* as the subject, together with intransitive verbs such as *to be* or *to work*: *it is over between us*, for example, or *it just didn't work out.*

It is important to recognize that there is nothing pernicious *in itself* in the passive voice. In many cases, indeed, one may wish to use the passive voice in making political points of the sort that Orwell himself would approve of. Orwell himself does precisely this when he wishes to place appropriate emphasis on the recipient of an action—as in the following example, where he is emphasizing the experience of victims as well as the duplicity of language used to describe their suffering: "People are imprisoned for years without trial, or are shot in the back of the neck, or are sent to die of scurvy in Arctic lumber camps: this is called *elimination of unreliable elements.*"

A12. **awkwardness or wordiness arising from inappropriate use of the passive voice:** The passive voice, then, is one means that *may* be used to disguise agency, and it is also a verbal construction that *may* involve awkwardness or unnecessary wordiness. If either is the case, it is often better to rephrase by using the active voice:

needs checking	The ceremonial first pitch was thrown by the president. (Passive—9 words)
revised	The president threw the ceremonial first pitch. (Active—7 words)

But again, the passive voice *per se* is not the problem. For more on this issue see the discussion of style in the first section of this text, and the section on writing in scientific disciplines such as biology (page 386).

O *Dangling Constructions*

The error that is made most frequently by writers at all levels of ability—including holders of graduate degrees in English—is that of allowing large chunks of their sentences to "dangle," unrelated grammatically to the core of the sentence. For that reason several pages are devoted here to that problem.

On the Web
Exercises on dangling constructions may be found at **www.broadviewpress.com/writing**. Click on **Exercises** and go to **A13–A16**.

● *Dangling Participles and Infinitives*

A present participle is an *-ing* word (*going, thinking,* etc.). When combined with a form of the verb *to be*, participles form part of a complete verb. They can also be used in a number of ways on their own, however:

- The president felt that visiting China would be unwise at that time.
  (Here *visiting China* acts as a noun phrase.)
- Having taken into account the various reports, the committee decided to delay the project for a year.
  (Here *having taken into account the various reports* acts as an adjectival phrase modifying the noun *committee*.)

A13. **dangling present participles or participial phrases:** The danger of dangling occurs with sentences such as the second example above. If the writer does not take care that the participial phrase refers to the subject of the main clause, some absurd sentences can result:

needs checking	Waiting for a bus, a brick fell on my head.
	(Bricks do not normally wait for buses.)
revised	While I was waiting for a bus, a brick fell on my head.
needs checking	Leaving the room, the lights must be turned off.
	(Lights do not normally leave the room.)
revised	When you leave the room you must turn off the lights.

In sentences such as these the amusing error is relatively easy to notice; it can be much more difficult with longer and more complex sentences. Experienced writers are especially alert to this pitfall if they begin a sentence with a participle or participial phrase that describes a mental operation; they are wary of beginning by *considering, believing, taking into account, remembering, turning for a moment,* or *regarding:*

needs checking	Believing that he had done no wrong, the fact of being accused of dishonesty infuriated the company's CEO.
revised	Believing that he had done no wrong, the company's CEO was infuriated at being accused of dishonesty.
or	The company's CEO was infuriated at being accused of dishonesty; he believed he had done no wrong.
needs checking	Considering all the above-mentioned studies, the evidence shows conclusively that smoking can cause cancer.
revised	Considering all the above-mentioned studies, we conclude that smoking causes cancer.
better	These studies show conclusively that smoking can cause cancer.

needs checking	Turning for a moment to the thorny question of Joyce's style, the stream of consciousness technique realistically depicts the workings of the human mind.
revised	Turning for a moment to the thorny question of Joyce's style, we may observe that his stream of consciousness technique realistically depicts the workings of the human mind.
better	Joyce's style does not make *Ulysses* easy to read, but his stream of consciousness technique realistically depicts the workings of the human mind.
needs checking	Taking into account the uncertainty as to the initial temperature of the beaker, the results are not conclusive.
revised	Taking into account the uncertainty as to the initial temperature of the beaker necessitates that the results be deemed inconclusive.
better	Since the initial temperature of the beaker was not recorded, the results are inconclusive.

Notice that in each case the best way to eliminate the problem is to dispense with the participial phrase entirely. More often than not one's writing is improved by using active verbs rather than participial phrases. Many people seem to feel that writing which is filled with participial phrases somehow sounds more important; in fact, such phrases tend to obscure the writer's meaning under unnecessary padding. This is true even when the participles are not dangling:

needs checking	Another characteristic having a significant impact on animal populations is the extreme diurnal temperature range on the desert surface.
	(Can a characteristic have an impact? A small point is here buried in a morass of meaningless abstraction.)

better	The extreme diurnal temperature range on the desert surface also affects animal populations.
needs checking	Referring generally to the social stratification systems of the city as a whole, we can see clearly that types of accommodation, varying throughout in accordance with income levels and other socio-economic factors, display an extraordinary diversity.
	(Is there anything either clear or extraordinary about this?)
better	In this city rich people and poor people live in different neighbourhoods, and rich people live in larger houses than poor people.

By cutting out the padding in this way the writer may occasionally find to his surprise that instead of saying something rather weighty and important as he had thought he was doing, he is in fact saying little or nothing. But he should not be discouraged if this happens; the same is true for all writers. The best response is simply to chuckle and scratch out the sentence!

A14. **dangling past participles** (e.g., *considered, developed, regarded*): The same sorts of problems that occur with present participles occur frequently with past participles as well:

needs checking	Considered from a cost point of view, Combarp Capital Corporation could not really afford to purchase Skinflint Securities.
	(Combarp is not being considered; the purchase is.)
poor	Considered from the point of view of cost, the purchase of Skinflint Securities was not a wise move by Combarp Capital Corporation.
better	Combarp Capital Corporation could not really afford to buy Skinflint Securities.

needs checking   Once regarded as daringly modern in its portrayal of fashionable *fin de siècle* decadence, Wilde draws on traditional patterns to create a powerful new Gothic tale. (*The Cambridge Guide to Literature in English*)

(The novel is an *it*; Oscar Wilde was a *he*.)

revised   *The Picture of Dorian Gray* was once regarded as daringly modern in its portrayal of fashionable *fin de siècle* decadence. In the novel Wilde draws on traditional patterns to create a powerful new Gothic tale.

needs checking   Used with frequency, a man will feel refreshed and rejuvenated. (aftershave advertisement)

revised   Used with frequency, this product will help a man feel refreshed and rejuvenated.

A15. dangling infinitive phrases:

needs checking   To conclude this essay, the French Revolution was a product of many interacting causes.

(The French Revolution concluded no essays.)

poor   To conclude this essay, I would like to say that the French Revolution was a product of many causes.

better   The explanations given for the French Revolution, then, are not mutually exclusive; it was a product of many interacting causes.

(A good writer does not normally need to tell her readers that she is concluding an essay; they can see the space at the bottom of the page. A little word such as *then*, set off by commas, is more than enough to signal that this is a summing-up.)

needs checking   To receive a complimentary copy, the business reply card should be returned before June 30.

(The card will not receive anything.)

revised	To receive a complimentary copy, you should return the business reply card before June 30.
needs checking	To appreciate the full significance of the Camp David Accords, a range of factors needs to be considered.
	(A factor cannot appreciate.)
poor	To appreciate the full significance of the Camp David Accords, we need to consider many things.
better	The Camp David Accords were important in many ways.

A16. dangling gerund or prepositional phrases:

needs checking	In reviewing the evidence, one point stands out plainly.
	(A point cannot review evidence.)
poor	In reviewing the evidence, we can see one point standing out plainly.
better	One point stands out plainly from this evidence.
needs checking	When analysing the figures, ways to achieve substantial savings can be discerned.
	(The ways cannot analyse.)
poor	When we analyse the figures we can see ways to achieve substantial savings.
better	The figures suggest that we can greatly reduce our expenses.

Other sorts of phrases can be caught dangling too. But almost all writers are capable of attaching them properly if they re-read and revise their work carefully.

needs checking	On behalf of city council and the people of Windsor, it gives me great pleasure to welcome you to our city. (from an announcement by the mayor)
	(The mayor, not a faceless *it*, is acting on behalf of the others.)

revised	On behalf of city council and the people of Windsor, I am pleased to welcome you to our city.
needs checking	By adding more component parts to the prototype, this would cause an increase in the price of the product.
revised	By adding more component parts to the prototype, we force an increase in the price of the product.
or	Adding more component parts to the prototype makes it necessary to increase the price of the product.

⭕ Sequence of Tenses

If the main verb of a sentence is in the past tense, other verbs must also express a past viewpoint (except when a general truth is being expressed). Some writers have trouble keeping the verb tenses they use in agreement, particularly when indirect speech is involved, or when a quotation is incorporated into a sentence.

A17. agreement of tenses in indirect speech—past plus subjunctive:

needs checking	He said that he will fix the engine before the end of the year.
revised	He said that he would fix the engine before the end of the year. (*He said that he will fix the engine* implies that the fixing has not yet occurred but may still occur.)

A18. agreement of tenses in indirect speech—past plus past perfect:

needs checking	He claimed that he smoked drugs many years earlier, but that he never inhaled.
revised	He claimed that he had smoked drugs many years earlier, but that he had never inhaled.

A19. agreement of tenses—quoted material:

needs checking	Prime Minister Rudd admitted that "such a policy is not without its drawbacks."
	(The past tense *admitted* and the present tense *is* do not agree.)

There are two ways of dealing with a difficulty such as this:

(a) Change the sentence so as to set off the quotation without using the connecting word *that*. Usually this can be done with a colon. In this case the tense you use does not have to agree with the tense used in the quotation. The words before the colon, though, must be able to act as a complete sentence in themselves.

(b) Use only that part of the quotation that can be used in agreement with the tense of the main verb:

revised	Prime Minister Rudd did not claim perfection: "such a policy is not without its drawbacks," he admitted.
or	Prime Minister Rudd admitted that such a policy was "not without its drawbacks."

Here are some other examples:

needs checking	Churchill promised that "we shall fight on the beaches, ... we shall fight in the fields and in the streets, we shall fight in the hills; we shall never surrender."
	(This suggests that you, the writer, will be among those fighting.)
revised	Churchill made the following promise: "We shall fight on the beaches, ... we shall fight in the fields and in the streets, we shall fight in the hills; we shall never surrender."
	(Notice that the word *that* is now removed.)

or	Churchill promised that the British people would "fight on the beaches, ... in the fields and in the streets, ... in the hills," and that they would "never surrender."
needs checking	In the 1974 election campaign the Liberals claimed that "the Land is strong."
revised	In the 1974 election campaign the Liberals' slogan was "The Land is Strong."
or	In the 1974 election campaign the Liberals asserted that the Land was strong.

On the Web

Exercises on sequence of tenses may be found at **www.broadviewpress.com/writing**. Click on **Exercises** and go to **A17–A19**.

O *Irregular or Difficult Verbs*

The majority of verbs in English follow a regular pattern—*I open* in the simple present tense, *I opened* in the simple past tense, *I have opened* in the present perfect tense, and so forth. However, most of the more frequently used verbs are in some way or another irregular. To pick an obvious example, we say *I went* instead of *I goed*, and *I have gone* instead of *I have goed*. What follows is a list of the main irregular or difficult verbs in English. The past participle (column 3) is used in tenses such as the present perfect (e.g., *I have grown, he has found*) and the past perfect (*I had grown, I had found*).

The verbs that most frequently cause problems are given special treatment in the following list:

(Note: In both regular and irregular verbs, the present tense is formed by using the infinitive without the preposition *to*.)

Present & Infinitive	Simple Past	Past Participle
arise	arose	arisen

A20.

check	A problem had arose even before the discussion began.
revised	A problem had arisen even before the discussion began.

Present & Infinitive	Simple Past	Past Participle
awake	awoke	awoken/woken
	(passive: *was awakened*)	
be	was/were	been

A21.

bear	bore	borne

check	It was heartbreaking for her to lose the child after having bore it for so long.
revised	It was heartbreaking for her to lose the child after having borne it for so long.

A22.

beat	beat	beaten

check	The Yankees were badly beat by the Blue Jays.
revised	The Yankees were badly beaten by the Blue Jays.

become	became	become

A23.

begin	began	begun

check	He had already began treatment when I met him.
revised	He had already begun treatment when I met him.

bend	bent	bent
bite	bit	bitten
bleed	bled	bled
blow	blew	blown
break	broke	broken

Present & Infinitive	Simple Past	Past Participle
bring	brought	brought
build	built	built
burn	burned/burnt	burned/burnt

A24.

burst	burst	burst

check The pipes bursted while we were on holiday.
revised The pipes burst while we were on holiday.

buy	bought	bought
can	could	been able
catch	caught	caught

A25.

choose	chose	chosen

check In 1948 Newfoundlanders choose to join Canada.
revised In 1948 Newfoundlanders chose to join Canada.

cling	clung	clung
come	came	come
cost	cost	cost
dig	dug	dug
do	did	done

A26.

dive	dived/dove	dived

less accepted He dove into the shallow water.
more formal He dived into the shallow water.

A27.

drag	dragged	dragged

check The newspapers drug up a lot of scandal about her.
revised The newspapers dragged up a lot of scandal about her.

draw	drew	drawn
dream	dreamed/dreamt	dreamed/dreamt

	Present & Infinitive	Simple Past	Past Participle
A28.	drink	drank	drunk

check He has drank more than is good for him.
revised He has drunk more than is good for him.

	Present & Infinitive	Simple Past	Past Participle
	drive	drove	driven
	eat	ate	eaten
	fall	fell	fallen
	feel	felt	felt
	fight	fought	fought
	find	found	found
	fit	fit (US) fitted (UK)	fitted
	flee	fled	fled
A29.	fling	flung	flung

check George flinged his plate across the room.
revised George flung his plate across the room.

	Present & Infinitive	Simple Past	Past Participle
	fly	flew	flown

On the Web

Exercises on irregular or difficult verbs may be found at
www.broadviewpress.com/writing.
Click on **Exercises** and go to **A20–A44**.

	Present & Infinitive	Simple Past	Past Participle
A30.	forbid	forbade	forbidden

check Yesterday he forbid us to climb the fence.
revised Yesterday he forbade us to climb the fence.

	Present & Infinitive	Simple Past	Past Participle
A31.	forecast	forecast	forecast

| *check* | The weather office has forecasted more rain. |
| *revised* | The weather office has forecast more rain. |

	Present & Infinitive	Simple Past	Past Participle
	forget	forgot	forgotten
	forgive	forgave	forgiven
	freeze	froze	frozen
	get	got	got
	give	gave	given
	go	went	gone
	grind	ground	ground

(e.g., *I have ground the coffee.*)

	Present & Infinitive	Simple Past	Past Participle
	grow	grew	grown
A32.	hang	hanged/hung	hanged/hung

Note: *Hanged* is used only when referring to a person being killed by hanging. Say *The criminal has been hanged*, but *We have hung the picture on the wall*:

| *check* | No one has been hung in Canada since 1962. |
| *revised* | No one has been hanged in Canada since 1962. |

	Present & Infinitive	Simple Past	Past Participle
	have	had	had
	hear	heard	heard
	hide	hid	hidden
	hit	hit	hit
	hold	held	held
	hurt	hurt	hurt
	keep	kept	kept
	kneel	knelt	knelt
	know	knew	known

Present & Infinitive	Simple Past	Past Participle

A33.   lay   laid   laid

(Note: Although many authorities feel that the distinction is not worth troubling over in informal English, formal English still distinguishes between *lay* and *lie*; you *lay* something on a table, and a hen *lays* eggs, but you *lie* down to sleep. In other words, *lie* is an intransitive verb; it should not be followed by a direct object. *Lay*, by contrast, is transitive.)

check   That old thing has been laying around for years.
revised   That old thing has been lying around for years.

lead	led	led
lean	leaned/leant	leaned/leant
leap	leaped/leapt	leaped/leapt
learn	learned/learnt	learned/learnt
leave	left	left
lend	lent	lent
let	let	let

A34.   lie   lay   lain

check   He asked if I would like to lay down and rest.
revised   He asked if I would like to lie down and rest.

See also above, number A33.

light	lighted/lit	lighted/lit
lose	lost	lost
make	made	made
may	might	
mean	meant	meant
meet	met	met
must	had to	had to
pay	paid	paid

| | *Present &* | *Simple* | *Past* |
| | *Infinitive* | *Past* | *Participle* |

A35. plead · pleaded/pled pleaded/pled

(Note: The growing use of *pled* rather than *pleaded* irks some traditionalists, but is difficult to see why *pleaded* should not follow *leaded* to the grave where the latter was long ago led. If you are trying to please a traditionalist professor, it is probably still best to avoid *pled*. Otherwise, use consistently whichever of the two you prefer.)

accepted He had pled guilty to the same offence previously.
accepted He had pleaded guilty to the same offence previously.

A36. prove proved proven

check We have proved the hypothesis to be correct.
revised We have proven the hypothesis to be correct.

| put | put | put |
| read | read· | read |

A37. ride rode ridden

check The actor had never rode a horse before.
revised The actor had never ridden a horse before.

A38. ring rang rung

check I rung the bell three times, but no one answered.
revised I rang the bell three times, but no one answered.

rise·	rose	risen
run	ran	run
saw	sawed	sawed/sawn
say	said	said
see	saw	seen
seek	sought	sought

Present & Infinitive	Simple Past	Past Participle
sell	sold	sold
sew	sewed	sewed/sewn
shake	shook	shaken
shall	should	

A39.

shine	shone	shone

check The moon shined almost as brightly as the sun.

revised The moon shone almost as brightly as the sun.

(Note: *Shined* is the accepted formation of the simple past tense where the verb is transitive. Thus we say *she shined her shoes*.)

shoot	shot	shot
show	showed	showed/shown

A40.

shrink	shrank	shrunk

check The government's majority shrunk in the election.

revised The government's majority shrank in the election.

shut	shut	shut
sing	sang	sung

A41.

sink	sank	sunk

check The Edmund Fitzgerald sunk on Lake Superior.

revised The Edmund Fitzgerald sank on Lake Superior.

sit	sat	sat
sleep	slept	slept
slide	slid	slid
smell	smelled/smelt	smelled/smelt
sow	sowed	sowed/sown
speak	spoke	spoken
speed	speeded/sped	speeded/sped

	Present & *Infinitive*	*Simple* *Past*	*Past* *Participle*
	spell	spelled/spelt	spelled/spelt
	spend	spent	spent
	spill	spilled/spilt	spilled/spilt
	spin	spun	spun
	spit	spat	spat
	split	split	split
	spread	spread	spread

A42.   spring   sprang   sprung

check   The soldiers hurriedly sprung to their feet.
revised The soldiers hurriedly sprang to their feet.

	stand	stood	stood
	steal	stole	stolen
	stick	stuck	stuck
	sting	stung	stung
	strike	struck	struck
	swear	swore	sworn
	sweep	swept	swept

A43.   stick   stuck   stuck

A44.   swim   swam   swum

check   Pictures were taken while the royal couple swum in
           what they thought was a private cove.
revised Pictures were taken while the royal couple swam in
           what they had thought was a private cove.

	swing	swung	swung
	take	took	taken
	teach	taught	taught
	tear	tore	torn
	tell	told	told

Present & *Infinitive*	Simple *Past*	Past *Participle*
think	thought	thought
throw	threw	thrown
tread	trod	trodden/trod
understand	understood	understood
wake	woke	woken
wear	wore	worn
weep	wept	wept
win	won	won
wind	wound	wound
wring	wrung	wrung

(e.g., *She wrings out her clothes if they are wet.*)

write	wrote	written

O *Infinitives, Gerunds, Objects: "To Be or Not To Be?"*

gerunds and prepositions: Gerunds have the form of verbs but act as nouns, and as such they do not necessarily require any preposition to introduce them. In particular, when a gerund does not relate to a preceding verb, it should not be accompanied by a preposition. Nor does it require a pronoun to stand in for it as the subject of a verb:

needs checking	With using coal-fired generators, it is bad for the environment.
revised	Using coal-fired generators is bad for the environment.

When a gerund follows a verb, however, it often must be introduced by a preposition—and unfortunately, there are no rules governing when this happens, or which preposition should be used. More broadly, there are no rules in English to explain why some words must be followed by an infinitive (*to go*, *to do*, *to be*, etc.), while others must be followed by a preposition plus a gerund (*of going*, *in doing*, etc.), and still others by a direct object. Following are some of the words with which difficulties of this sort most often arise:

A45. **accept something** (not *accept to do something*): It needs a direct object.

needs checking	The committee accepted to try to improve the quality of the postal service.
revised	The committee accepted the task of trying to improve the postal service.
or	The committee agreed to try to improve the postal service.

A46. **accuse someone of doing something** (not *to do*)

needs checking	Klaus Barbie was accused to have killed thousands of innocent civilians in WW II.
revised	Klaus Barbie was accused of having killed thousands of innocent civilians in WW II.

A47. **appreciate something**: When used to mean *be grateful*, this verb requires a direct object.

needs checking	I would appreciate if you could respond quickly.
revised	I would appreciate it if you could respond quickly.
or	I would appreciate a quick response.
	(The verb *appreciate* without an object means *increase in value*.)

A48. **assist in doing something** (not *to do*)

needs checking	He assisted me to solve the problem.
revised	He assisted me in solving the problem.
or	He helped me to solve the problem.

A49. capable of doing something (not *to do*)

needs checking	He is capable to run 1500 meters in under four minutes.
revised	He is capable of running 1500 meters in under four minutes.
or	He is able to run 1500 meters in under four minutes.

A50. confident of doing something (not *to do*)

needs checking	She is confident to be able to finish the job before dusk.
revised	She is confident of being able to finish the job before dusk.
or	She is confident that she will finish the job before dusk.

A51. consider something or someone to be something or consider it something (not *as something*)

needs checking	According to a recent policy paper, the party now considers a guaranteed annual income as a good idea.
revised	According to a recent policy paper, the party now considers a guaranteed annual income to be a good idea.
or	According to a recent policy paper, the party now regards a guaranteed annual income as a good idea.

A52. discourage someone from doing something (not *to do*)

needs checking	The new Immigration Act is intended to discourage anyone who wants to come to Canada to enter the country illegally.
revised	The new Immigration Act is intended to discourage anyone who wants to come to Canada from entering the country illegally.

A53. forbid someone to do something (not *from doing*)

needs checking The witnesses were forbidden from leaving the scene of the crime until the police had completed their preliminary investigation.

revised The witnesses were forbidden to leave the scene of the crime until the police had completed their preliminary investigation.

ESL

For particular problems with infinitives, gerunds, and objects faced by those whose native language is not English, see the ESL section later in this book.

A54. insist on doing something or insist that something be done (but not *insist to do*)

needs checking The customer has insisted to wait in the front office until she receives a refund.

revised The customer has insisted on waiting in the front office until she receives a refund.

A55. intention: *Have an intention of doing something* but *someone's intention is/was to do something*

needs checking Hitler had no intention to keep his word.

revised Hitler had no intention of keeping his word.

or Hitler did not intend to keep his word.

or Hitler's intention was to break the treaty.

A56. justified in doing something (not *to do something*)

needs checking He is not justified to make these allegations.

revised He is not justified in making these allegations.

A57. **look forward to doing something** (not *to do something*)

needs checking	I am looking forward to receive your reply.
revised	I am looking forward to receiving your reply.

A58. **opposed to doing something** (not *to do something*)

needs checking	He was opposed to set up a dictatorship.
revised	He was opposed to setting up a dictatorship.
or	He was opposed to the idea of setting up a dictatorship.

A59. **organize something** (not *to do something*)

needs checking	We organized to meet at ten the next morning.
revised	We organized a meeting for ten the next morning.
or	We arranged to meet at ten the next morning.

A60. **persist in doing something** (not *to do something*)

needs checking	Despite international disapproval, the Reagan administration persisted to help the rebels in Nicaragua.
revised	Despite international disapproval, the Reagan administration persisted in helping the rebels in Nicaragua.

A61. **plan to do** (not *on doing*)

needs checking	They planned on closing the factory in Windsor.
revised	They planned to close the factory in Windsor.

A62. **prohibit someone from doing something** (not *to do*)

needs checking	Members of the public were prohibited to feed the animals.
revised	Members of the public were prohibited from feeding the animals.

A63. regarded as (not *regarded to be*)

needs checking	He is commonly regarded to be one of Canada's best musicians.
revised	He is commonly regarded as one of Canada's best musicians.
or	He is commonly thought to be one of Canada's best musicians.

A64. responsible for doing (not *to do*)

needs checking	Mr. Dumphy is responsible to market the full line of the company's pharmaceutical products.
revised	Mr. Dumphy is responsible for marketing the full line of the company's pharmaceutical products.

A65. sacrifice something (not *to do*): The use of *sacrifice* without a direct object may have crept into the language through the use of the verb as a baseball term (*Delgado sacrificed in the ninth to bring home Chavez*):

needs checking	He sacrificed to work in an isolated community with no electricity or running water.
revised	He sacrificed himself to work in an isolated community with no electricity or running water.
or	He sacrificed a good deal; the isolated community he now works in has no electricity or running water.

A66. seem to be (not *as if*)

needs checking	The patient seemed as if he was in shock.
revised	The patient seemed to be in shock.
	Exception: When the subject is *it*, *seem* can be followed by *as*. (e.g., *It seemed as if he was sick, so we called the doctor.*)

A67. suspect someone of doing something (not *to do*)

needs checking	She suspected him to have committed adultery.
revised	She suspected him of committing adultery.
or	She suspected that he had committed adultery.

A68. tendency to do something (not *of doing*)

needs checking	Some Buick engines have a tendency of over-revving.
revised	Some Buick engines have a tendency to over-rev.
or	Some Buick engines have a habit of over-revving.

⊙ Preposition Problems: *"Up With Which I Will Not Put"*

The prepositions used in English often make little or no sense. What good reason is there for saying *inferior to* but *worse than*? None whatsoever, but over the centuries certain prepositions have come to be accepted as going together with certain verbs, nouns, etc. There are no rules to help one learn the combinations; here are some of the ones that most commonly cause difficulty:

A69. agree with someone, with what someone says; agree to do something, to something; agree on a plan, proposal, etc.

needs checking	The union representatives did not agree with the proposed wage increase.
revised	The union representatives did not agree to the proposed wage increase.
or	The union representatives did not agree with management about the proposed wage increase.

A70. angry with someone; angry at or about something

needs checking	He was angry at me for failing to keep our appointment.
revised	He was angry with me for failing to keep our appointment.

A71. annoyed with someone; annoyed by something

needs checking	The professor is often annoyed with the attitude of the class.
revised	The professor is often annoyed by the attitude of the class.
or	The professor is often annoyed with the class.

A72. appeal to someone for something

needs checking	The premier appealed for the residents to help.
revised	The premier appealed to the residents for help.

A73. argue with someone about something

needs checking	They argued against each other for half an hour.
revised	They argued with each other about the merit of exams.

A74. arrive in a place, at a place (not *arrive a place*, except *arrive home*). Airlines have led the way in using both *arrive* and *depart* without prepositions. In formal writing one should still say *arrive in* or *arrive at*, and *depart from*.

needs checking	He won't join the Yankees until tomorrow night when they arrive Milwaukee.
revised	He won't join the Yankees until tomorrow night when they arrive in Milwaukee.

A75. attach two or more things (not *attach together*)

needs checking	The Siamese twins were attached together at the hip.
revised	The Siamese twins were attached at the hip.

A76. borrow something from someone

needs checking	I borrowed him a pair of trousers.
revised	I borrowed a pair of trousers from him.

A77. cancel something (not *cancel out*, except when the verb is used to mean *counterbalance* or *neutralize*)

needs checking	She cancelled out all her appointments.
revised	She cancelled all her appointments.
or	After playing hockey, he ate a huge snack that cancelled out the calorie loss of the exercise.

A78. care about something (meaning *to think it worthwhile or important to you*)

needs checking	George does not care for what happens to his sister.
revised	George does not care what happens to his sister.
or	George does not care about what happens to his sister.

A79. centre: centred on something (not *around something*; for one thing to be centred around another is physically impossible)

needs checking	The novel is centred around the conflict between British imperialism and Native aspirations.
revised	The novel centres on the conflict between British imperialism and Native aspirations.

On the Web
Exercises on preposition problems may be found at
www.broadviewpress.com/writing.
Click on **Exercises** and go to **A69–148**.

A80. chase someone or something away for doing something:
Despite the way the word is used in baseball slang, in formal writing the verb *chase* with no preposition means *run after*, not *send away*.

informal   Starting pitcher Pedro Martinez was chased in the
                fifth inning.

more formal   Starting pitcher Pedro Martinez was pulled from
                the game in the fifth inning.

A81. collide with something (not *against something*)

needs checking   The bus left the road and collided against a tree.
revised   The bus left the road and collided with a tree.

A82. compare to, compare with: To compare something *to* something else is to liken it, especially when speaking metaphorically (e.g., *Shall I compare thee to a summer's day?*). To compare something *with* something else is to judge how the two are similar or different (*If you compare one brand with another you will notice little difference*). Use *compare with* when noting differences:

needs checking   The First World War was a small conflict com-
                   pared to the Second World War, but it changed
                   humanity even more profoundly.
revised   The First World War was a small conflict com-
                   pared with the Second World War, but it changed
                   humanity even more profoundly.

A83. concerned with something (meaning *having some connection with it, having something to do with it*) and concerned about something (meaning *being interested in it or worried about it*)

needs checking   The ministry is very concerned with the level of
                   pollution in this river.
revised   The ministry is very concerned about the level of
                   pollution in this river.

A84. conform to (not *with*)

needs checking   The building does not conform with current
                   standards.
revised   The building does not conform to current
                   standards.
or   The contractors did not comply with current
                   standards.

A85. congratulate someone on something (not *for*)

needs checking	The Opposition leaders congratulated the prime minister for his success.
revised	The Opposition leaders congratulated the prime minister on his success.

A86. connect two things, connect one thing with another (not *connect up with*)

needs checking	As soon as he connects up these wires, the system should work.
revised	As soon as he connects these wires, the system should work.

A87. conscious of something (not *that*)

needs checking	He was not conscious that he had done anything wrong.
revised	He was not conscious of having done anything wrong.
	(Note: Unlike *conscious*, *aware* can be used with *of* or with a *that* clause.)

A88. consist in/consist of: *Consist in means to exist in, to have as the essential feature; consist of means to be made up of.*

needs checking	Success consists of hard work.
	(i.e., *The essence of success is hard work.*)
revised	Success consists in hard work.
needs checking	The U.S. Congress consists in two houses—the House of Representatives and the Senate.
revised	The U.S. Congress consists of two houses—the House of Representatives and the Senate.

A89. consult someone (not *consult with someone*)

needs checking	She will have to consult with the board of directors before giving us an answer.
revised	She will have to consult the board of directors before giving us an answer.

or   She will have to talk to the board of directors before giving us an answer.

A90. continue something, with something, to a place (not *continue on*)

needs checking   We were told to continue on with our work.

revised   We were told to continue with our work.

A91. convenient for someone, for a purpose; convenient to a place

needs checking   This house is very convenient to me; it is only a short walk to work.

revised   This house is very convenient for me; it is only a short walk to work.

A92. cooperate with someone (not *cooperate together*)

needs checking   The provinces should cooperate together to break down interprovincial trade barriers.

revised   The provinces should cooperate with one another to break down interprovincial trade barriers.

A93. correspond to (*be in agreement with*); correspond with (*exchange letters with*)

needs checking   The fingerprints at the scene of the crime corresponded with those of the suspect.

revised   The fingerprints at the scene of the crime corresponded to those of the suspect.

A94. couple of things, times, people, etc.

needs checking   The body had been partially hidden under a pier on Lake Union, a couple hundred feet from the Aurora Avenue Bridge.

revised   The body had been partially hidden under a pier on Lake Union, a couple of hundred feet from the Aurora Avenue Bridge.

or	The body had been partially hidden under a pier on Lake Union, approximately two hundred feet from the Aurora Avenue Bridge.
	(In formal writing it is better to use *two* than *a couple of.*)

A95. criticism of something or somebody (not *against*)

needs checking	His criticisms against her were completely unfounded.
revised	His criticisms of her were completely unfounded.

A96. depart from a place: See also arrive (A74).

needs checking	One woman was heard saying to a friend as they departed Wrigley Field....
revised	One woman was heard saying to a friend as they departed from Wrigley Field....
or	One woman was heard saying to a friend as they left Wrigley Field....

A97. die of a disease, of old age; die from injuries, wounds

needs checking	My grandfather died from cancer when he was only forty-two years old.
revised	My grandfather died of cancer when he was only forty-two years old.

A98. different from, to, than: *Different to* and *different from* are both accepted British usage; *different from* is the preferred form in Canada and the US. (*Different than* is a common alternative in the United States, but in formal writing *different from* is the more widely accepted of the two.)

UK	These results are different to those we obtained when we did the same experiment yesterday.
North America	These results are different from those we obtained when we did the same experiment yesterday.
US informal	These results are different than those we obtained when we did the same experiment yesterday.

A99. **discuss something** (not *discuss about something*; no preposition is needed)

> *needs checking*   They discussed about what to do to ease tensions in the Middle East.
>
> *revised*   They discussed what to do to ease tensions in the Middle East.

A100. **divide something** (no preposition necessary)

> *needs checking*   Lear wants to divide up his kingdom among his three daughters.
>
> *revised*   Lear wants to divide his kingdom among his three daughters.

A101. **do something for someone** (meaning *something that will help*); **do something to someone** (meaning *something that will hurt*)

> *needs checking*   Norman Bethune did a lot to the people of China.
>
> *revised*   Norman Bethune did a lot for the people of China.

A102. **end: at the end of something; in the end:** *In the end* is used when the writer does not say which end he means, but leaves this to be understood by the reader. *At the end of* is used when the writer mentions the end he is referring to.

> *needs checking*   In the end of *Things Fall Apart*, we both admire and pity Okonkwo.
>
> *revised*   At the end of *Things Fall Apart*, we both admire and pity Okonkwo.
>
> *or*   In the end, we both admire and pity Okonkwo.

A103. **end at a place** (not *end up at*)

> *needs checking*   We do not want to end up at the same place we started from.
>
> *revised*   We do not want to end at the same place we started from.

A104. **fight someone or with someone** (not *against*; *fight* means *struggle against*, so to add *against* is redundant)

needs checking	They fought against each other for almost an hour.
revised	They fought with each other for almost an hour.
or	They fought each other for almost an hour.

A105. **frightened by something** (when it has just frightened you); **frightened of something** (when talking about a constant condition)

needs checking	He was suddenly frightened of the sound of a door slamming.
revised	He was suddenly frightened by the sound of a door slamming.

A106. **graduate from a school**

needs checking	He graduated McGill in 2004.
revised	He graduated from McGill in 2004.

A107. **help doing**, as in *be unable to refrain from doing* (not *help from doing*)

needs checking	She could not help from agreeing to his suggestion.
revised	She could not help agreeing to his suggestion.

A108. **hurry** (not *hurry up*)

needs checking	She told me to hurry up if I didn't want to miss the train.
revised	She told me to hurry if I didn't want to miss the train.

A109. **identical to** (not *with*)

needs checking	This hotel is identical with the Holiday Inn we stayed in last week.
revised	This hotel is identical to the Holiday Inn we stayed in last week.

A110. **in/into/throughout:** Whereas *in* typically indicates a particular location, *into* implies motion, and *throughout* implies omnipresence. Particularly when using such words as *whole* or *entire*, be careful to use *throughout*.

> *needs checking*   Political repression is common in the whole world.
>
> *revised*   Political repression is common throughout the whole world.

(Note as well that *in to* should not always be converted to *into*; often the word *in* goes together with a previous verb rather than with *to*.)

> *needs checking*   The authorities keep giving into her demands.
>
> *revised*   The authorities keep giving in to her demands.

A111. **independent of something or someone** (not *from*)

> *needs checking*   I would like to live entirely independent from my parents.
>
> *revised*   I would like to live entirely independent of my parents.

A112. **inferior to someone or something** (not *than*)

> *needs checking*   Most people think that margarine is inferior than butter.
>
> *revised*   Most people think that margarine is inferior to butter.
>
>   (*Inferior* and *superior* are the only two comparative adjectives which are not followed by *than*.)

A113. **inside or outside something** (not *of something*)

> *needs checking*   Within thirty minutes a green scum had formed inside of the beaker.
>
> *revised*   Within thirty minutes a green scum had formed inside the beaker.

A114. **interested in something, in doing something** (not *to*)

needs checking   She is very interested to find out more about plant genetics.

revised   She is very interested in finding out more about plant genetics.

A115. **investigate something** (not *investigate about or into something*)

needs checking   The police are investigating into the murder in Brandon last week.

revised   The police are investigating the murder in Brandon last week.

A116. **join someone** (not *join up with*)

needs checking   Conrad Black joined up with his brother Montagu in making the proposal to buy the company.

revised   Conrad Black joined his brother Montagu in making the proposal to buy the company.

A117. **jump** (not *jump up*)

needs checking   Unemployment has jumped up to record levels recently.

revised   Unemployment has jumped to record levels recently.

A118. **lift something** (not *lift up*)

needs checking   I twisted my back as I was lifting up the box.

revised   I twisted my back as I was lifting the box.

A119. **lower something** (not *lower down something*)

needs checking   They lowered the coffin down into the grave.

revised   They lowered the coffin into the grave.

A120. mercy: have mercy on someone; show mercy to or towards someone

needs checking	We should all have mercy for anyone who is suffering.
revised	We should all have mercy on anyone who is suffering.

A121. meet/meet with: *Meet with* in the sense of *attend a meeting with* is a recent addition to the language. If one is referring to a less formal or less prolonged encounter, however, there is no need for the preposition.

needs checking	Stanley finally met with Livingstone near the shores of Lake Victoria.
revised	Stanley finally met Livingstone near the shores of Lake Victoria. (The meaning here is *came face to face with for the first time.*)

A122. near something (not *near to something*)

needs checking	The village of Battle is very near to the place where the Battle of Hastings was fought in 1066.
revised	The village of Battle is very near the place where the Battle of Hastings was fought in 1066.

A123. object to something (not *against*)

needs checking	Some people have objected against being required to wear a seat belt.
revised	Some people have objected to being required to wear a seat belt.

A124. off something (not *off of*)

needs checking	The man stepped off of the platform into the path of the moving train.
revised	The man stepped off the platform into the path of the moving train.

A125. opposite: When used as a noun, *opposite* is followed by *of*; when used as an adjective, it is followed by *to* or *from*, or by no preposition.

needs checking	His conclusion was the opposite to mine.
	(Here, *opposite* is a noun.)
revised	His conclusion was the opposite of mine.
or	His conclusion was opposite to mine.
	(Here, *opposite* is an adjective.)

A126. partake of something; participate in something

needs checking	They have refused to partake in a new round of talks on the subject of free trade.
revised	They have refused to participate in a new round of talks on the subject of free trade.
or	They have refused to partake of a new round of talks on the subject of free trade.

A127. prefer one thing or person to another (not *more than another*)

needs checking	They both prefer tennis more than squash.
revised	They both prefer tennis to squash.

A128. protest something (not *protest against*). *To protest* means *to argue against*; the preposition is redundant.

needs checking	The demonstrators were protesting against the government's decision to allow missile testing.
revised	The demonstrators were protesting the government's decision to allow missile testing.

A129. refer to something (not *refer back to something*)

needs checking	If you are confused, refer back to the diagram on page 24.
revised	If you are confused, refer to the diagram on page 24.

A130. regard/regards: With regard to something; as regards something

needs checking   I am writing in regards to the balance owing on your account.

fair   I am writing with regard to the balance owing on your account.

better   I am writing about the balance owing on your account.

(Note that *in regard to*, *with regard to*, and *as regards* may often be used interchangeably [*in regard to the issue you have raised*, *with regard to the issue you have raised*, *as regards the issue you have raised*]. All tend towards wordiness, however; usually there is a better way.)

A131. rejoice at something (not *for something*)

needs checking   He rejoiced for his good fortune when he won the lottery.

revised   He rejoiced at his good fortune when he won the lottery.

A132. repeat something (not *repeat again*)

needs checking   If you miss an answer you must repeat the whole exercise again.

revised   If you miss an answer you must repeat the whole exercise.

A133. request something or request that something be done (but not *request for something* unless one is using the noun—*a request for something*)

needs checking   He has requested for two more men to help him.

revised   He has requested two more men to help him.

or   He has put in a request for two more men to help him.

A134. **retroactive to a date** (not *from*)

needs checking The tax changes are retroactive from July 1.
revised The tax changes are retroactive to July 1.

A135. **return to a place** (not *return back*)

needs checking He wanted to return back to Edmonton as soon as possible.
revised He wanted to return to Edmonton as soon as possible.

A136. **seek something or someone** (not *seek for something*)

needs checking She suggested that we seek for help from the police.
revised She suggested that we seek help from the police.

A137. **sight: in sight** (*near enough to be seen*); **out of sight** (*too far away to be seen*); **on sight** (*immediately after being seen*)

needs checking The general ordered that deserters be shot in sight.
revised The general ordered that deserters be shot on sight.

A138. **speak to someone** (when one speaker is giving information to a listener); **speak with someone** (when the two are having a discussion)

needs checking She spoke harshly with the secretary about his spelling mistakes.
revised She spoke harshly to the secretary about his spelling mistakes.

A139. **suffer from something** (not *with*)

needs checking He told me that he was suffering with the flu.
revised He told me that he was suffering from the flu.

A140. **superior to someone or something** (not *than someone or something*)

needs checking The advertisements claim that this detergent is superior than the others.
revised The advertisements claim that this detergent is superior to the others.

A141. **surprised at or by something**: *At* is used to suggest that the person is disappointed or scandalized; unless one wishes to suggest this, *by* is the appropriate preposition.

needs checking	I was surprised at the arrival of my sister.
revised	I was surprised by the arrival of my sister.

A142. **type of person or thing**

needs checking	This type carburetor is no longer produced.
revised	This type of carburetor is no longer produced.

A143. **underneath something** (not *underneath of*)

needs checking	When we looked underneath of the table, we found what we had been looking for.
revised	When we looked underneath the table, we found what we had been looking for.

A144. **until a time or an event** (not *up until*)

needs checking	Up until 1967 the National Hockey League was made up of only six teams.
revised	Until 1967 the National Hockey League was made up of only six teams.

A145. **warn someone of a danger, against doing something** (*not about something or to do something*)

needs checking	She warned me about the danger involved in the expedition.
revised	She warned me of the danger involved in the expedition.

A146. **worry about something** (not *at something or for something*)

needs checking	He is always worried at what will happen if he loses his job.
revised	He is always worried about what will happen if he loses his job.

A147. **prepositions in pairs or lists:** If a sentence includes two or more nouns or verbs that take different prepositions, make sure to include all the necessary words:

needs checking	The fire was widely reported in the newspapers and television.
revised	The fire was widely reported in the newspapers and on television.

A148. **ending a sentence with a preposition:** Some authorities have argued that it is poor English to end a sentence with a preposition. The best answer to them is Winston Churchill's famous remark upon being accused of ending with a preposition: "This is the sort of pedantic nonsense up with which I will not put." Obviously such awkwardness as this can be avoided only by ending with a preposition. It is surely true that in many other cases ending sentences with prepositions is awkward. In practice, however, these are situations that we are already likely to avoid. The following dialogue (a version of which was passed on to me by Prof. A. Levey of the University of Calgary) provides in dramatic form another demonstration of the absurdity of strictures against ending with prepositions:

"Where do you come from?"
"From a place where we don't end sentences with prepositions."
"Let me rephrase. Where do you come from, you stupid pedant?"

⊙ Nouns and Pronouns: *Singular Difficulties*

A149. **unusual nouns:** A number of nouns are unusual in the way that either the singular or the plural is formed. Here is a list of some that frequently cause mistakes. The most troublesome—as well as a few pronouns that cause similar difficulties—are also given individual entries below:

appendix	appendices
attorney general	attorneys general
bacterium	bacteria
basis	bases
court martial	courts martial
crisis	crises
criterion	criteria
curriculum	curricula
datum	data
daylight-saving time	[no plural]
ellipsis	ellipses
emphasis	emphases
erratum	errata
father-in-law	fathers-in-law
focus	foci
governor general	governors general
index	indexes or indices
matrix	matrixes or matrices
medium	media
millennium	millennia
nucleus	nuclei
parenthesis	parentheses
referendum	referenda or referendums
runner-up	runners-up
stratum	strata
symposium	symposia
synthesis	syntheses
thesis	theses

A150. **accommodation**: The plural form is not normally used:

needs checking	My family and my friend's family were both unable to find accommodations downtown.
revised	My family and my friend's family were both unable to find accommodation downtown.

A151. **anyone/anybody/each/every/no one/nobody**: All are singular. It is often necessary to spend a few moments puzzling over how to phrase one's ideas before one finds a way to get all the verbs and subjects to agree, and at the same time avoid awkwardness. Ironically, however, the correct solution may in this case not be the best one. (See the "Bias-free Language" section, page 431.)

not in agreement	Anyone may visit when they like.
in agreement	Anyone may visit when he or she likes.
in agreement	Anyone may visit at any time.
not in agreement	No one likes to leave a place that they have grown fond of.
in agreement	No one likes to leave a place that he or she has grown fond of.
in agreement	No one likes to leave a place that has fond memories attached to it.
not in agreement	Each person applying for the job must fill out this form before they will be granted an interview.
in agreement	Each person applying for the job must fill out this form before he or she will be granted an interview.
in agreement	Each person applying for the job must fill out this form before being granted an interview.

Following is a list of common indefinite pronouns:

always plural: *both, many*

always singular: *another, anybody, anyone, anything, each, either, every, everybody, everyone, everything, neither, nobody, no one, nothing, one, somebody, someone, something* singular or plural, depending on the context: *all, any, more, most, none, some*

A152. bacteria: A plural word; the singular is *bacterium*.

needs checking	There were many bacterias in the moldy bread.
revised	There were a lot of bacteria in the moldy bread.

A153. behaviour: Although social scientists speak of *a behaviour* or of *behaviours* in technical writing, in other disciplines and in conversational English the word is uncountable (i.e., it cannot form a plural or be used with the indefinite article). Say *types of behaviour*, not *behaviours*:

needs checking	He has a good behaviour.
revised	His behaviour is good.
or	He behaves well.

A154. between/among: It is often supposed that *between* should always be used for two, *among* for more than two. As the *Oxford English Dictionary* points out, however, "in all senses *between* has been, from its earliest appearance, extended to more than two." Perhaps the most important difference is that *between* suggests a relationship of things or people to each other as individuals, whereas *among* suggests a relationship that is collective and vague. Thus we say *the ball fell among the hollyhocks* where we are expressing the relationship of the ball to many flowers collectively, and where the precise location of the ball is unspecified. But we should not say, as we watch a baseball game, *the ball fell among the three fielders*; here we know the precise location of the ball and are expressing the relationship between it and the three individuals.

A155. both/all: Use *both* to refer to two, and *all* to refer to more than two.

needs checking	Harris and Waluchow were the chief speakers in the debate yesterday. They all spoke very well.
revised	Harris and Waluchow were the chief speakers in the debate yesterday. They both spoke very well.

A156. **brain**: One person can have only one brain. The use of the plural to refer to the brain of one person (e.g., *He blew his brains out*) is slang, and should not be used in formal written work.

> *needs checking*   He used his brains to solve the problem.
> *revised*   He used his brain to solve the problem.

A157. **children**: Be careful when forming the possessive; the apostrophe should come before the *s*.

> *needs checking*   All the childrens' toys had been put away.
> *revised*   All the children's toys had been put away.

A158. **confusion**: Uncountable—we do not normally speak of *a confusion* or of *confusions*:

> *needs checking*   The misunderstanding about his time of arrival caused a confusion.
> *revised*   The misunderstanding about his time of arrival caused confusion.

A159. **criteria**: Plural; the singular is *criterion*.

> *needs checking*   The chief criteria on which an essay should be judged is whether or not it communicates clearly.
> *revised*   The chief criterion on which an essay should be judged is whether or not it communicates clearly.

ESL

For particular problems with nouns faced by those whose native language is not English, see the ESL section later in this book.

A160. **damage**: In its usual meaning, this noun has no plural, since it is uncountable. We speak of *damage*, not *a damage*, and of *a lot of damage*, not *many damages*. The word *damages* means *money paid to cover the cost of any damage one has caused*:

needs checking	The crash caused many damages to his car, but he was unhurt.
revised	The crash caused a lot of damage to his car, but he was unhurt.

A161. **data**: Like *bacteria, media,* and *phenomena,* the noun *data* is plural. The singular form, which is rarely used, is *datum*:

needs checking	This data proves that the lake is badly polluted.
revised	These data prove that the lake is badly polluted.

A162. **each other/one another**: Use *each other* for two, *one another* for more than two:

needs checking	The three brothers always tell stories to each other before going to sleep.
revised	The three brothers always tell stories to one another before going to sleep.
needs checking	The two men had long since begun to get on one another's nerves. (Alan Moorehead, *The White Nile*)
revised	The two men had long since begun to get on each other's nerves.

A163. **either/neither**: *Either* and *neither* are both singular. This can create considerable awkwardness in structuring sentences. (See also "Bias-free Language" on this point.)

needs checking	Somehow, neither Sally nor Great Uncle Magnus were as tidy as they had been when they set out. (Margaret Mahy, *Ultra-Violet Catastrophe*)

Trying to correct the error here by simply changing *were* to *was* creates a new problem with the word *they* in the second half of the sentence; a further change is also necessary:

revised	Somehow, neither Sally nor Great Uncle Magnus was as tidy as both had been when they set out.
needs checking	So far neither the party rank and file nor the electorate seem satisfied with the leader's performance.
revised	So far neither the party rank and file nor the electorate seems satisfied with the leader's performance.

A164. **either/any; neither/none:** Use *either* and *neither* for two, *any* and *none* for more than two:

needs checking	Shirley has six sisters, but she hasn't seen either of them since Christmas.
revised	Shirley has six sisters, but she hasn't seen any of them since Christmas.

A165. **government:** A singular noun:

needs checking	The government are intending to build a new terminal at this airport before 2015.
revised	The government is intending to build a new terminal at this airport before 2015.

A166. **graffiti:** A plural noun; the singular form is *graffito*:

needs checking	Graffiti covers most of the subway cars in the city.
revised	Graffiti cover most of the subway cars in the city.

A167. **media:** Plural; the singular is *medium*:

needs checking	The media usually assumes that the audience has a very short attention span.
revised	The media usually assume that the audience has a very short attention span.

A168. money: Some people seem to think that *monies* has a more official ring to it than *money* when they are talking of business affairs, but there is no sound reason for using this plural form in good English:

> *needs checking*   The council has promised to provide some monies for this project.
>
> *revised*   The council has promised to provide some money for this project.

A169. news: Despite the *s*, this is a singular collective noun. Make sure to use a singular verb with it:

> *needs checking*   Today's news of troubles in the Middle East are very disturbing.
>
> *revised*   Today's news of troubles in the Middle East is very disturbing.

A170. none: Although *no one* and *not one* are always singular, common usage allows *none* to be either singular or plural depending on the context. In a sentence such as *Of all European cities, none is more beautiful than Prague* the pronoun *none* is clearly singular—just as *not one* would be if used in its place. In the sentence *None of the field is dry* the pronoun *none* refers to the singular noun *field*—though here, we notice, it would not be possible to substitute *not one*. In the sentence *None of the girls want to leave* the word *none* refers to the plural noun *girls*, and may thus take a plural verb. In the same way the pronouns *all, any, more, most,* and *some* may be either singular or plural depending on whether they refer to a singular or a plural referent. *Most of the sugar is gone*, but *most of the people are happy*. Some argue, however, that *none* should be treated grammatically as *no one* and *not one* are treated, and should always take a singular verb (i.e., that we should say *none of the girls* **wants** *to leave, none of the things she wants* **is** *available*, and so on). If in doubt (or in fear of a grammatical traditionalist) treat *none* as always singular; otherwise, make it agree with its referent.

widely accepted	None of the issues concerning indefinite pronouns are of earth-shattering importance.
universally accepted	None of the issues concerning indefinite pronouns is of earth-shattering importance.

A171. phenomena: Plural; the singular is *phenomenon*:

needs checking	The great popularity of disco music was a short-lived phenomena.
revised	The great popularity of disco music was a short-lived phenomenon.

A172. police: a plural noun. Be sure to use a plural verb with it:

needs checking	The police is investigating the case, and hope to make an arrest soon.
revised	The police are investigating the case, and hope to make an arrest soon.

A173. someone/somebody: Both are singular. Be careful with sentences involving one of these pronouns and the pronoun *they*; getting the phrasing right is not always easy:

needs checking	Someone has forgotten to turn off the stove; they should be more careful.
revised	Someone has forgotten to turn off the stove; he or she should be more careful.
or	Some careless person has forgotten to turn off the stove.

On the Web

Exercises on singular and plural nouns and pronouns may be found at **www.broadviewpress.com/writing**. Click on **Exercises** and go to **A149–173**.

⊙ Pronouns: *Who Cares About Whom?*

Those unfamiliar with the territory may wish to refer to the section on pronouns in the "Reference Guide to Basic Grammar" at the back of the book. Readers may also wish to refer to the discussion of *y'all* and *youse* on pages 107–08 above.

A174. **extra pronoun:** It is easy to add an extra pronoun, particularly if the subject of the sentence is separated from the verb by a long adjectival clause:

needs checking	The countries which Hitler wanted to conquer in the late 1930s they were too weak to resist him.
revised	The countries which Hitler wanted to conquer in the late 1930s were too weak to resist him.
needs checking	The line that is longest in a right-angled triangle it is called the hypotenuse.
revised	The line that is longest in a right-angled triangle is called the hypotenuse.

A175. **first person:** In formal writing it is customary to use *I* and *me* infrequently or not at all. The object of a formal piece of writing is normally to present an argument, and writers realize that they can best argue their case by presenting evidence rather than by stating that such and such is what they think. Thus many teachers advise their students always to avoid using the first person singular (*I* and *me*) in their writing.

This guideline should not be regarded as a firm and fast rule. George Orwell, often praised as the finest essayist of the last century, uses *I* and *me* frequently. As the following example illustrates, however, he employs the first person to guide the reader through his argument, not to make the points in the argument:

If one gets rid of these habits one can think more clearly, and to think more clearly is a necessary first step towards political regeneration: so that the fight against bad English is not frivolous and is not the exclusive concern of professional writers. I will come back to this presently, and I hope that by that time the meaning of what I have said will become clearer. (*Politics and the English Language*)

Phrases such as *I think* and *I feel*, on the other hand, will not help you convince the reader of the strength of your main points.

needs checking   Many authorities assume inflation to be a cause of high interest rates, but I think that high interest rates are a cause of inflation. This essay will prove my argument through numerous examples.

revised   Many authorities assume inflation to be a cause of high interest rates; in fact, high interest rates are often a cause of inflation. Let us take the years 1978 to 1983 in the US as an example.

A176. **I/me/myself:** Perhaps as a result of slang use of *me* as a subject pronoun (*Me and him got together for a few beer last night*), the impression seems to have lodged in many minds that the distinction between *I* and *me* is one of degree of politeness or formality. It's not; the distinction is simply between subject pronoun (*I*) and object pronoun (*me*).

needs checking   There is no disagreement between you and I.
revised   There is no disagreement between you and me.
         (Both *you* and *I* are here objects of a preposition—*between*. *Between you and I* is no more correct than is *I threw the ball at he*.)

Many are also sometimes uncertain as to how *myself* should be used. One way is as a reflexive pronoun used as a direct or indirect object (*I hurt myself*; *I talk to myself*). Another is as an intensifier, to point up a contrast or add emphasis (*Someone from our company will attend, but I won't be there myself*). Note that *myself* is used in conjunction with another first person pronoun, however, not in place of *I* or *me*.

> *needs checking*   There was no need to consult Carol and myself about this.
>
> *revised*   There was no need to consult Carol and me about this.

On the Web
Exercises on pronoun problems may be found at
www.broadviewpress.com/writing.
Click on **Exercises** and go to **A174–179**.

A177. **than**: Does *than* take a subject or an object pronoun? Purists argue that we should say *She's brighter than I* [*am*], and *He's louder than she* [*is*]—that the verb is always understood in such sentences, even when we do not say it or write it, and that the unspoken verb requires a subject. It's hard to argue, however, that the increasingly widespread use of object pronouns after *than* is either ugly or confusing.

> *less formal*   She always sleeps later than him.
>
> *more formal*   She always sleeps later than he [does].

A178. **unreferenced or wrongly referenced pronoun**: Normally a pronoun must refer to a noun in the previous sentence or clause. In the following sentence, for example, the pronoun *she* clearly refers to the noun *Charity*, which is the subject of the first clause in the sentence:

- Charity told Alfred that she would start work at nine.

Notice how confusing the sentence becomes, however, if there are two possible *shes* in the first part of the sentence:

- Charity told Mavis that she would start work at nine.

Does this mean that Charity will start work at nine, or that Mavis will? From the sentence it is impossible to tell. In cases like this, where it is not absolutely clear whom or what a pronoun refers to, use the noun again instead:

clear	Charity told Mavis that she (Charity) would start work at nine.

In the following case the writer has gone astray by mentioning two things—one singular, one plural—and then matching only one of the two with a pronoun. In this instance the best remedy is to substitute a noun for the pronoun:

needs checking	Shields's characters are so exquisitely crafted and her plot so artfully conceived that it keeps the reader riveted until the final page.
revised	Shields's characters are so exquisitely crafted and her plot so artfully conceived that the book keeps the reader riveted until the final page.

Similar mistakes are often made in writing about a general class of people, such as police officers, or doctors, or football players. When writing in this way one can use either the third person singular (e.g., *A doctor helps patients. She* ....) or the third person plural (*Doctors help patients. They* ....). Mixing the two in such situations often leads people to write unreferenced pronouns:

needs checking	A herbalist knows a lot about plants. They can often cure you by giving you medicine.
	(Here the pronoun *they* is presumably meant to refer to the plural noun *herbalists*, but the writer has referred only to *a herbalist*.)
revised	A herbalist knows a lot about plants. He can often cure you by giving you medicine.
or	Herbalists know a lot about plants. They can often cure you by giving you medicine.

It may also not be clear what or whom a pronoun refers to if it is placed too far away from the noun:

needs checking   The finance minister increased corporate taxes by an average of 43 per cent. Other measures in the budget included $100 million in student assistance and new funding for the ombudsman. He also introduced a variety of measures to help small businesses.

revised   The finance minister increased corporate taxes by an average of 43 per cent. Other measures in the budget included $100 million in student assistance and new funding for the ombudsman. The minister also introduced a variety of measures to help small businesses.

Be particularly careful when using *this* as a pronoun; if the preceding sentence is a long one, it may not be at all clear what *this* refers to:

needs checking   The deficit was forecast to be $800 million, but turned out to be over $6 billion. This reflected the government's failure to predict the increase in interest rates and the onset of a recession.
    (*This what?*)

revised   The deficit was forecast to be $800 million, but turned out to be over $6 billion. This vast discrepancy reflected the government's failure to predict the increase in interest rates and the onset of a recession.

Sometimes the meaning may be clear, but the omission of a pronoun may create unintended and humorous ambiguity:

needs checking   She visited a doctor with a bad case of the flu.
    (Did the doctor have the flu?)

revised	She visited a doctor when she had a bad case of the flu.
needs checking	The Cougar was a sporty car aimed at the youthful-feeling who wanted luxury in their automobiles. Its buyers were similar to Mustangs, but more affluent.
revised	The Cougar was a sporty car aimed at the youthful-feeling who wanted luxury in their automobiles. Its buyers were similar to those who bought Mustangs, but more affluent.

A179. **who/whom:** The subject pronoun and the object pronoun, but it's not as simple as that. Nor is the distinction merely a matter of stuffiness or pedantry on the part of grammar purists. Sound has a great deal to do with it. Even purists must sometimes find themselves saying, *I didn't know who I was talking to*, even though the rules say it should be *whom* (subject—*I*; object—*whom*). In similar fashion the enemies of *whom* must surely be tempted to sacrifice principle rather than attempt such an owlish mouthful as *To who was he talking?* They would do so not on the grammatical grounds of *whom*, the object pronoun, being correct since it is acting as the object of the preposition *to*, but on the grounds of *whom*, the word with an *m* on the end, being in that sentence a lot easier to say. In such circumstances convenience of pronunciation occasionally overrides arguments either for or against formality.

less formal	Scott Fitzgerald never cared who he irritated.
more formal	Scott Fitzgerald never cared whom he irritated.

⊙ Part-of-speech Conversions: *A Question of Principle?*

A well-known Calvin and Hobbes cartoon strip nicely conveys the amusement that part-of-speech conversions may engender:

Calvin:	"I like to verb words."
Hobbes:	"What?"
Calvin:	"I take nouns and adjectives and use them as verbs. Remember when *access* was a thing? Now it's something you do. It got verbed....Verbing weirds language."
Hobbes:	"Maybe we can eventually make language a complete impediment to understanding."

In fact, however, there is no good reason why a word that has become established as one part of speech should not be used as another; the language has always been changing and growing in this way. As Tom Shippey asks:

What can be the matter with using nouns as adjectives? Everyone does it; how about *stonewall*? It has been built into the language since before English settlers found Ireland, let alone America.... As for converting nouns to verbs, what about *water*? *Watering the horses* is recorded from before the Conquest. (*Times Literary Supplement*, 19–25 October 1990)

For that matter, what about *chair, table, paper, shelf, bottle, cup, knife, fork, eye, mouth, finger*? The list of nouns that have also become verbs or other parts of speech is a very long one, and it includes many of the most basic words in the language. (Ironically enough, the adjective *weird*, used humorously in the cartoon as a verb, began life as a noun; in Old English a weird was the personification of a powerful but unpredictable natural force.) The point in being aware of the conversion of one part of speech to another, then, is not that the practice is always a bad one. Rather it is to keep oneself aware of whether or not one is saying something in the best possible way. If the new creation fills a need, saying something more clearly and concisely than it is possible to do otherwise, then it deserves to survive. But if it fulfils no useful purpose—if clearer and more concise ways of saying the same thing already exist—then it's better to avoid it.

A180. **access:** For many years authorities felt, except in the vocabulary of computers, *access* should be used as a noun, not a verb. The use of *access* as a verb is now much more widely accepted, but some purists still argue that alternatives such as *enter* and *reach* are usually more precise:

less widely accepted	The cafeteria may be accessed from the warehouse or the accounts department.
more widely accepted	The cafeteria may be reached through the warehouse or the accounts department.

A181. **adjective for adverb:** If a word is modifying a verb, it should as a general rule be an adverb rather than an adjective. This is normally the case when the descriptive word comes directly after the verb. We say *The boy laughed quietly*, for example (rather than *The boy laughed quiet*), because the descriptive word *quietly* refers to the verb *laughed*, not the noun *boy*. Similarly, in the sentence *The quiet boy laughed* we use the adjective *quiet* to refer to the noun *boy*.

In most cases a descriptive word following a verb will apply to that verb, and should take the form of an adverb:

needs checking	She asked us not to talk so loud.
revised	She asked us not to talk so loudly.
needs checking	According to Mr. Adams, "most books will go heavier into evolution, which is a good thing."
revised	According to Mr. Adams, "most books will go more heavily into evolution, which is a good thing."
needs checking	He performs bad whenever he is under pressure.
revised	He performs badly whenever he is under pressure.

In some cases, however, a descriptive word following a verb may refer not to the verb, but to the subject. This happens most frequently with the verb *to be*, which of course does not name an action in the way that other verbs do. Thus we say *The boy is quiet*, not *The boy is quietly*; we use the adjective rather than the adverb because we are describing the boy, not the action of being. Verbs such as *taste*, *smell*, and *feel* resemble *be* in this respect; it is correct to say *I feel good* rather than *I feel well*, since the descriptive word is clearly intended to describe your condition, and not the act of feeling. Similarly, we say *it tastes good*, not *it tastes well*, and *it smells sweet*, not *it smells sweetly*. In some other cases, too, an adjective rather than an adverb will be appropriate after a verb. It makes perfect sense, for example, to write that *someone sliced the bread thin* (rather than *sliced the bread thinly*), since the descriptive word is intended to refer to the resulting slices, and not to the action of slicing.

The principles outlined above also apply to the comparative and superlative forms of adjectives and adverbs:

needs checking	They both ran quicker in the final than they had in the semi-final.
revised	They both ran more quickly in the final than they had in the semi-final.
needs checking	He performs worse under pressure than he does when he is relaxed.
revised	He performs less well under pressure than he does when he is relaxed.
needs checking	Of all the contestants, Hawkins ran the quickest.
revised	Of all the contestants, Hawkins ran the most quickly.

Given that comparative and superlative adverbs are often more long-winded compound formations, it is not surprising that in everyday speech the shorter adjectival equivalents are often used in their stead. And such usages are becoming more and more common as well in written English. Should the *Financial Post* editor have corrected the headline that read "Northern Miners Breathe Easier"? Certainly it's easier to use the adjective here in place of the two-part adverb *more easily*. Whether or not it's better is less clear; certainly many purists are not pleased by the practice.

less widely accepted	The purpose of desktop publishing is to do the same old thing cheaper, easier, and quicker.
more widely accepted	The purpose of desktop publishing is to do the same old thing more cheaply, more easily, and more quickly.

A182. **advice/advise**: *Advice* is the noun; *advise* is the verb.

needs checking	They refused to take our advise.
revised	They refused to take our advice.

A183. **affect/effect**: *Effect* is normally used as a noun meaning *result*. (It can also be used as a verb meaning *put into effect*, as in *The changes were effected by the committee*.) *Affect* is a verb meaning *cause a result*.

needs checking	When the acid is added to the solution, there is no visible affect.
revised	When the acid is added to the solution, there is no visible effect.
needs checking	"The issues that effect us here on the reserve are the same issues that effect the whole constituency," Mr. Littlechild said. (*The Globe and Mail*)
revised	"The issues that affect us here on the reserve are the same issues that affect the whole constituency," Mr. Littlechild said.

A184. **author**: A noun, not a verb. If you wish to suggest that someone's name appears on the cover as the author but that in fact the book has been ghost-written, "authored" may be a good choice. Otherwise, there is no need to find a substitute for *write*.

needs checking	Smith is a member of the Appeals Court, and has authored two books on the judicial system.
revised	Smith is a member of the Appeals Court, and has written two books on the judicial system.

A185. **bear/birth/give birth to**: Twenty years ago a woman would *bear children* or *give birth to children*, but there was no single word to describe the process of giving birth. The word *birthing* was coined to fill the linguistic gap, and from there the use of *birth* as a transitive verb quickly became common. The new coinage *birth a child* is certainly more concise than *give birth to a child*, and is widely felt to better reflect the active nature of the process.

A186. **breath/breathe**: *Breath* is the noun, *breathe* the verb.

needs checking	When you breath, your lungs take in oxygen.
revised	When you breathe, your lungs take in oxygen.

A187. **dependent/dependant**: *Dependent* is the adjective, *dependant* the noun. You are dependent on someone or something, and your young children are your dependants; they are dependent on you.

needs checking	Emily is still dependant on her parents for financial support.
revised	Emily is still dependent on her parents for financial support.

A188. **dialogue**: As a verb, *talk* serves perfectly well, even after all these years.

awkward	The two department heads should dialogue with each other more frequently.
better	The two department heads should talk to each other more frequently.

A189. **enthuse/enthusiastic:** The verb *enthuse* is a relatively recent back formation from the adjective *enthusiastic*; *enthused* is its simple past tense form. Confusion between the two forms is now common.

needs checking	In 2008 millions were enthused about China's Olympic performance.
revised	In 2008 millions were enthusiastic about China's Olympic performance.
or	In 2008 millions enthused over China's Olympic performance.

A190. **first/firstly:** *Firstly* is now generally thought of as archaic, though it is not incorrect. Be sure to be consistent, though, in the use of *first, second,* etc., in lists.

needs checking	There were several reasons for France's reluctance to commit more resources to the New World. First, she was consumed with the battle for supremacy in Europe. Secondly, the returns on previous investments had been minimal.
revised	There were several reasons for France's reluctance to commit more resources to the New World. First, she was consumed with the battle for supremacy in Europe. Second, the returns on previous investments had been minimal.

A191. **give/gift:** Until relatively recently it was universally understood that *give* is a verb and *gift* is a noun. The use of *gift* as a verb seems to have arisen in the context of institutional fundraising; it is difficult to see any reason to say "thank you" for this *gift*.

needs checking	Mr. Dench has generously gifted the university with funding for a new library.
revised	Mr. Dench has generously given the university funding for a new library.

A192. **good/well**: The most common of the adjective-for-adverb mistakes.

needs checking	As the manager put it, "He pitched good, but not real good."
fair	He pitched well, but not really well.
better	He did not pitch very well.

A193. **impact**: The use of *impact* as a verb has become widespread even in formal English, but *affect* remains an attractive option.

awkward	The government's decision will impact upon wholesalers in all areas of the country.
better	The government's decision will affect wholesalers in all areas of the country.

A194. **like/as**: *Like* is a preposition, not a conjunction; it introduces a noun or pronoun in a phrase. If introducing a clause, which always includes a verb, use *as* in formal writing.

- He looks like his father.
  (*Like* introduces the noun *father*.)
- He looks as his father did at his age.
  (*As* introduces the clause *as his father did at his age*.)
- He is acting like a drunkard.
  (*Like* introduces the noun *drunkard*.)
- He is acting as if he were drunk.
  (*As* introduces the clause *as if he were drunk*.)

needs checking	Like I said before, smoking is forbidden.
revised	As I said before, smoking is forbidden.
needs checking	He runs like I do—with short, choppy strides.
revised	He runs as I do—with short, choppy strides.
or	He runs like me. We both take short, choppy strides.
needs checking	Duvalier ran Haiti like his father had done.
revised	Duvalier ran Haiti the way his father had.

The attempt is also sometimes made to use *like what* in place of *as*.

needs checking	Bush Sr. wanted to appear tough, like what Reagan had when he ordered the invasion of Grenada.
revised	Bush Sr. wanted to appear tough, as Reagan had when he ordered the invasion of Grenada.

A195. **its/it's**: *Its* is an adjective meaning *belonging to it*. *It's* is a contraction of *it is*—a pronoun plus a verb. (Similarly, *whose* is an adjective meaning *belonging to whom*, whereas *who's* is a contraction of *who is*. See A211.)

needs checking	Its important to remember that the population of North America in this period was less than 10 million.
revised (less formal)	It's important to remember that the population of North America in this period was less than 10 million.
revised (more formal)	It is important to remember that the population of North America in this period was less than 10 million.
needs checking	A coniferous tree continually sheds it's leaves.
revised	A coniferous tree continually sheds its leaves.

A196. **lend/loan**: In formal English *loan* should be used only as a noun; *lend* is the verb.

needs checking	He was unwilling to loan his sister any money.
revised	He was unwilling to lend his sister any money.

On the Web
Exercises on part-of-speech conversions may be found at **www.broadviewpress.com/writing**.
Click on **Exercises** and go to **A180–211**.

A197. **loath/loathe:** *Loath* is the adjective; *loathe* is the verb.

needs checking	He told me he is beginning to loath his job.
revised	He told me he is beginning to loathe his job.
or	He is loath to return to his old job.

A198. **loose/lose:** *Loose* is normally used as an adjective meaning *not tight*; as a verb it means to *make loose* (e.g., *He loosed the reins*). *Lose* is, of course, always a verb.

needs checking	As soon as it became dark she began to loose control of herself.
revised	As soon as it became dark she began to lose control of herself.
needs checking	If this movie doesn't bring the song back to the hit parade, then you know it's flopped—and that Spielberg is loosing his touch.
revised	If this movie doesn't bring the song back to the hit parade, then you know it's flopped—and that Spielberg is losing his touch.

A199. **maybe/may be:** *Maybe* is an adverb that should be replaced by *perhaps* in formal writing. *May be* is a compound verb.

needs checking	May be he will come, but I doubt it.
revised	Maybe he will come, but I doubt it.
or	Perhaps he will come, but I doubt it.
needs checking	The prototype maybe ready by 2013.
revised	The prototype may be ready by 2013.

A200. **meantime/meanwhile:** *Meantime* is a noun, used most frequently in the phrase *in the meantime*. *Meanwhile* is an adverb.

needs checking	The Germans were preparing for an attack near Calais. Meantime, the Allies were readying themselves for the invasion of Normandy.

revised	The Germans were preparing for an attack near Calais. Meanwhile, the Allies were readying themselves for the invasion of Normandy.

A201. **medal/win a medal**: Until quite recently English lacked a one-word verb meaning *win a medal*. The verb *to medal* now fills that function, but many feel the new coinage has the feel of a counterfeit. In formal writing it is probably still best to use the more widely accepted currency.

less widely accepted	She medalled twice at the 2008 Olympics.
more widely accepted	She twice won medals at the 2008 Olympics.
or	She won two medals at the 2008 Olympics.

A202. **orgasm/have an orgasm**: Until recently the only one-word synonyms for *have an orgasm* or *achieve orgasm* were vulgar terms that clearly had no place in formal writing. In recent years *orgasm* itself has begun to be used as a verb as well as a noun. The new usage has as yet not excited much attention, and it is too early to say if it will come to be accepted in formal English; for the moment it is probably best to use more established constructions.

less widely accepted	Twenty per cent of the respondents reported that on average they had orgasmed fewer than three times per month.
more widely accepted	Twenty per cent of the respondents reported that on average they had experienced orgasm fewer than three times per month.
or	Twenty per cent of the respondents reported that on average they had had fewer than three orgasms per month.

A203. **practice/practise**: In the US *practice* serves as both noun and verb. In Canada and Britain *practise* (verb) and *practice* (noun) should be distinguished.

US	The team will practice on Thursday.
UK/CDA	The team will practise on Thursday.

A204. **predominate/predominant**: *Predominate* is the verb, *predominant* the adjective. (Either *predominately* or *predominantly* may be used as adverbs.)

needs checking	The Social Credit movement was predominate only in Alberta and British Columbia.
revised	The Social Credit movement was predominant only in Alberta and British Columbia.
or	The Social Credit movement predominated only in Alberta and British Columbia.

A205. **principal/principle**: *Principal* can be either a noun or an adjective. As a noun it means *the person in the highest position of authority in an organization* (e.g., *a school principal*) or *an amount of money*, as distinguished from the interest on it. As an adjective it means *first in rank or importance* (*The principal city of northern Nigeria is Kano*). *Principle* is always a noun, and is never used to describe a person; *a principle* is *a basic truth or doctrine, a code of conduct*, or *a law describing how something works.*

needs checking	We feel this is a matter of principal.
revised	We feel this is a matter of principle.
needs checking	Up went the shares of the two principle companies in this emerging field.
revised	Up went the shares of the two principal companies in this emerging field.

A206. **prophecy/prophesy**: *Prophecy* is the noun, *prophesy* the verb.

needs checking	His comment should be regarded as a prediction, not a prophesy.
revised	His comment should be regarded as a prediction, not a prophecy.

A207. **quality**: Although in colloquial English *quality* is frequently used as a replacement for *good* or *worthwhile*, in formal writing it should be used as a noun, not an adjective. It is useful to remember that something may as easily be of poor quality as of good quality.

needs checking	The salesperson claims that this is a quality product.
revised	The salesperson claims that this is a product of high quality.
or	The salesperson claims that this is a good product.
needs checking	"It was Mother's Day. I was trying to spend some quality time with my wife." (An NHL vice-president explaining why he had not attended an important playoff game, as quoted in *The Toronto Star*)
revised	"It was Mother's Day. I was trying to spend some time with my wife."

A208. **quote/quotation:** In formal English *quote* is the verb, *quotation* the noun.

needs checking	The following quote shows just how determined she is to change the Constitution.
revised	The following quotation shows just how determined she is to change the Constitution.

A209. **real/really:** One of the most commonly made adjective-for-adverb mistakes.

needs checking	Some of the fish we caught were real big.
fair	Some of the fish we caught were really big.
better	Some of the fish we caught were very big.

A210. **verb-noun confusion:** Where verbs and nouns have similar forms, be careful not to confuse them. Some of the most common examples are: *advice* (noun) and *advise* (verb); *extent* (noun) and *extend* (verb); *device* (noun) and *devise* (verb); *revenge* (noun) and *avenge* (verb); *loan* (noun) and *lend* (verb).

needs checking   Gerald Ford, president from 1974 to 1976, has now to a large extend been forgotten.

revised   Gerald Ford, president from 1974 to 1976, has now to a large extent been forgotten.

needs checking   She wanted to revenge the harm he had caused her.

revised   She wanted to avenge the harm he had caused her.

A211. whose/who's: *Whose* means *belonging to whom*; *who's* is a contraction of *who is.*

needs checking   Kennedy is not normally remembered as the president who's policies embroiled the US in the Vietnam conflict, but several scholars have suggested that he was as much responsible as was Johnson.

revised   Kennedy is not normally remembered as the president whose policies embroiled the US in the Vietnam conflict, but several scholars have suggested that he was as much responsible as was Johnson.

◉ WORDS

◉ Word Order Problems

Word order problems are of many sorts. See also, for example, the discussions elsewhere in this book of syntax; of ambiguity; of split infinitives; of indefinite pronouns such as *each*, *every*, and *anyone*; and of *not only ... but also*.

B1. **ambiguity/confusion**: Inappropriate word order is one of the most common sources of ambiguity and confusion. Often a change in punctuation may also be required to correct the problem.

needs checking	The liner tilted dramatically after fire broke out in the engine room, 50 miles south of Cyprus.
revised	The liner tilted dramatically after fire broke out in the engine room. At the time the ship was 50 miles south of Cyprus.
needs checking	He has not come under any pressure to make way for a new leader, despite the failure of any tangible benefits from his government's economic policies.
revised	He has not come under any pressure to make way for a new leader, despite the failure of his government's economic policies to bring any tangible benefits.
needs checking	Proportion of overweight people between 18 and 64 years trying to lose weight by sex in Alberta, 1990. (Heading on chart, Alberta Heart Health Survey, reprinted in *The Calgary Herald*)
revised	Proportion in Alberta of overweight people between 18 and 64 years, by sex, who were trying to lose weight, 1990.

B2. **amounts**: For no good reason, adjectives having to do with amounts or quantities (e.g., *much*, *few*, *many*) normally precede the noun or pronoun to which they refer, even when the verb *to be* is used. In this way such adjectives differ from other adjectives. For example, we can talk about a happy man, putting the adjective *happy* before the noun *man*, or we can use the present tense of the verb *to be* and say, *The man is happy*, in which case the adjective *happy* comes after the noun *man*. In contrast, it is considered awkward to say, *We were many at the meeting*, or *The people here are few*. Instead the sentence should be changed around, and the adjectives put before the nouns. The easiest way to do this is by using *there* and the verb *to be*. The revised versions of the above sentences are as follows:

revised	There were many of us at the meeting.
revised	There are few people here.

A further example:

needs checking	The students at the football game were many.
revised	There were many students at the football game.

ESL

For particular problems with word order faced by those whose native language is not English, see the ESL section later in this book.

B3. **balance**: As discussed earlier (61), paired connectives (*if ... then*, *either ... or* [given a separate entry below], *not only ... but also*, *both ... and*) can help in achieving balance. But difficulties in getting all the words in the right order can easily arise.

needs checking	As a critic she is both fully aware of the tricks used by popular novelists to score easy successes with readers through stylized depictions of sex and violence, as well as realizing that "serious" novelists are sometimes not above resorting to the very same tricks.

revised	As a critic she is fully aware both of the tricks used by popular novelists to score easy successes with readers through stylized depictions of sex and violence, and of the fact that "serious" novelists are sometimes not above resorting to the very same tricks.

B4. direct object position: The normal position for direct objects is after the verb. When the direct object is put at the beginning of a sentence it sounds awkward, and the word order may lead writers to include an extra, unwanted pronoun later in the sentence. It is therefore always best to keep the direct object after the verb.

needs checking	Some of the money I put it in the bank. (Notice the extra pronoun *it*.)
revised	I put some of the money in the bank. (*I* is the subject; *some of the money* is the direct object of *put*.)

B5. either ... or: These words should directly precede the pair of things to which they refer. The same applies to *neither ... nor*.

needs checking	I will either pick an apple or a banana.
revised	I will pick either an apple or a banana. (*Either* and *or* refer to *apple* and *banana*. Therefore they must come immediately before those words.)
needs checking	He will go either to New York for the holiday or remain here.
revised	He will either go to New York for the holiday or remain here. (The choice is between *going* and *remaining*.)
needs checking	We will either buy a poodle or a spaniel.
revised	We will buy either a poodle or a spaniel. (The choice is between breeds of dogs, not between *buying* and a dog breed.)

B6. except: A phrase beginning with *except* should appear directly after the noun or pronoun to which *except* refers.

needs checking	We all had to wait except for those who had bought tickets in advance.
revised	All except those who had bought tickets in advance had to wait.

B7. first person last: When speaking about both yourself and another person (or other people), always mention the other person first. The first person pronoun (*I, me*) should come last.

needs checking	I and my brother decided to go shopping.
revised	My brother and I decided to go shopping.

On the Web

Exercises on word order may be found at
www.broadviewpress.com/writing.
Click on **Exercises** and go to **B1–10**.

B8. only: The adverb *only* should come directly before the word or words it refers to. *She could only see him* implies that she could not hear, smell, or touch him; *She could see only him* implies that she had eyes for no one else.

needs checking	She only asked six people to the party.
revised	She asked only six people to the party.

B9. questions in indirect speech: In a question we normally reverse the order of the subject and the verb. For example, to change the statement *She was sad* to a question, we reverse the order of *she* and *was* and ask, *Was she sad?* The same rule does not apply, however, to questions in indirect speech. These are considered to be part of a statement and, as in any other statement, the entire verb should come after the subject. For example, to turn the above sentence into indirect speech we would say, *I asked her if she was sad* (not *I asked her was she sad*).

needs checking	I asked him how was he.
revised	I asked him how he was.
needs checking	She asked her brother where was he going.
revised	She asked her brother where he was going.

Notice as well that these sentences are statements, not questions. They therefore do not end with a question mark.

B10. **relative pronouns**: Relative pronouns (*who, which, whom, whose*, etc.) normally refer to the word that has come immediately before them. This may sometimes turn out to be difficult, in which case the word order may have to be changed.

needs checking	He purchased his friend's shop, whom he had known for many years.
	(The relative pronoun *whom* refers to *friend*, not *shop*. Change the word order to put *whom* directly after *friend*.)
revised	He purchased the shop from his friend, whom he had known for many years.
needs checking	On Saturday I went to my brother's wedding, whose new wife is a senior government official.
revised	On Saturday I went to the wedding of my brother, whose new wife is a senior government official.

⊙ One Word or Two?

A number of very commonly used English words have over many years become accepted as one word because they are combined so often. Other similar combinations, however, should still be written as two words. In a few cases one can see English usage changing on this point right now. A generation ago, for example, *alright* as one word could not have been found in any dictionary. Now numerous authorities regard *alright* as acceptable, and perhaps in another generation or two it will have completely replaced *all right*. For the moment, though, it is best to stick with *all right* rather than the more colloquial *alright*.

B11. **one word preferred**: What has been written as two words should be one. Here are some common examples:

already:	one word when used as an adverb (*He has finished already.*)
altogether:	one word when used as an adverb to mean *completely* or *entirely* (*He is not altogether happy with the result.*)
another	
anybody	
anyone:	one word unless it is followed by *of*
awhile:	one word when used as an adverb
bathroom	
bloodshed	
businessman	(but see "Bias-free Language" on page 440)
cannot:	*can not* is less common, but still acceptable
everybody	
everyday:	one word when used as an adjective (e.g., *Brushing your teeth should be part of your everyday routine*—here *everyday* is an adjective modifying the noun *routine*.)

needs checking	Doctors perform procedures of this sort everyday.
revised	Doctors perform procedures of this sort every day.

needs checking	Doctors perform procedures of this sort as part of their every day routine.
revised	Doctors perform procedures of this sort as part of their everyday routine.

everyone:	one word unless it is followed by *of*
everything	
forever	
furthermore	
indeed	
intact	
into:	one word except in the relatively few cases where the senses of *in* and *to* are clearly separate (e.g., *She brought the craft in to land.*)
maybe:	when used as an adverb meaning *perhaps* (e.g., *Maybe I will join you later*—here the verb is *will join* and *maybe* is an adverb.)
nearby	
nobody	
onto:	see *into*
ourselves	
somebody	
someone	
straightforward	
themselves	
wartime	
whatever	
whenever	

B12. **two words preferred**: What has been written as one word should be two words. Here are some common examples:

a lot	
all ready:	two words when not used as an adverb (*We are all ready to go.*)
all right	

all together: two words when not used as an adverb (e.g., *They were all together when I left them.*)

every day: two words when not used as an adjective (e.g., *We see each other every day.*)

every time

in fact

in front

in order

in spite of

may be: two words when used as a verb (e.g., *He may be here later tonight—may be* is the verb in the sentence.)

no one

On the Web

Exercises on one-word/two-word problems may be found at
www.broadviewpress.com/writing.
Click on **Exercises** and go to **B11–12**.

⊙ Word Meanings: *Are Cars Ever Stationery?*

B13. **accept/except**: These two words are often confused because of their similar sounds. *Accept* is a verb meaning *to receive something favourably* (or at least without complaining). Examples:

- We accepted the invitation to his party.
- We will have to accept the decision of the judge.

Except, on the other hand, is a conjunction (or sometimes a preposition) which means *not including* or *but*.

needs checking	All the permanent members of the Security Council accept China voted to authorize the use of force.
revised	All the permanent members of the Security Council except China voted to authorize the use of force.

B14. **adapt/adopt/adept**: *To adapt something* is *to alter or modify it*; *to adopt something* is *to approve it* or *accept responsibility for it*; *adept* is an adjective meaning *skilful*.

needs checking	The board adapted the resolution unanimously.
revised	The board adopted the resolution unanimously.

B15. **adverse/averse**: *Adverse* means *unfavourable*; *averse* means *reluctant* or *unwilling*.

needs checking	The plane was forced to land because of averse weather conditions.
revised	The plane was forced to land because of adverse weather conditions.
or	The pilot was averse to the idea of landing in the fog.

B16. **afflict/inflict:** A person *inflicts* pain or hardship on someone else, who is *afflicted* by the pain and hardship.

needs checking	The Mugabe government began as early as 1983 to afflict terrible suffering on large numbers of Zimbabweans living in Matabeleland.
revised	The Mugabe government began as early as 1983 to inflict terrible suffering on large numbers of Zimbabweans living in Matabeleland.

B17. **aggravate/annoy/irritate:** *Aggravate* means *make worse*. Here is an example:

- The injury was aggravated by the bumpy ride in the ambulance.

In formal English *aggravate* should not be used to mean *annoy* or *irritate*.

needs checking	She found his constant complaints very aggravating.
revised	She found his constant complaints very irritating.

B18. **alliterate/illiterate:** *Alliterate* is a verb meaning *to use consecutively two or more words that begin with the same sound*.

- The big, burly brute was frighteningly fat.

Illiterate is an adjective meaning either *unable to read* or *unable to read and write well*. Those who confuse the two are sometimes, if unfairly, accused of being illiterate.

needs checking	Over forty per cent of the population of Zambia is functionally alliterate.
revised	Over forty per cent of the population of Zambia is functionally illiterate.

B19. **alternately/alternatively:** *Alternately* means *happening in turn, first one and then the other*; alternatively means *instead of*. Be careful as well with the adjectives *alternate* and *alternative*.

needs checking	An alternate method of arriving at this theoretical value would be to divide the difference between the two prices by the number of warrants.
revised	An alternative method of arriving at this theoretical value would be to divide the difference between the two prices by the number of warrants. (or *Another method of ...*)
needs checking	Professor Beit-Haliahmi seems to have trouble alternatively in reading his own book accurately and in reading my review of it correctly.
revised	Professor Beit-Haliahmi seems to have trouble alternately in reading his own book accurately and in reading my review of it correctly.

B20. ambiguity: There are many types of ambiguity; for other references see the chapters on "Pronouns" and "Word Order Problems," and the entries below for such words as *flammable*. Also see the box overleaf.

B21. amiable/amicable: *Amiable* is used to describe someone's personality; *amicable* describes the state of relations between people.

needs checking	Navratilova said that the split with her former tennis partner had been an amiable one.
revised	Navratilova said that the split with her former tennis partner had been an amicable one.

B22. amoral/immoral: An *amoral* act is one to which moral standards do not apply; an *immoral* act, on the other hand, is one that goes against a moral standard.

needs checking	The reader is unlikely to share Austen's views as to what constitutes amoral behaviour.
revised	The reader is unlikely to share Austen's views as to what constitutes immoral behaviour.

B23. **anti/ante:** If you remember that *anti* means *against* and *ante* means *before* you are less likely to misspell the many words that have one or the other as a prefix.

needs checking	The UN had many anticedents—most notably the League of Nations formed after World War I.
revised	The UN had many antecedents—most notably the League of Nations formed after World War I.

B24. **antonym/homonym/synonym:** Antonyms are opposites–two words with opposite meanings (e.g., *hot* and *cold*, *good* and *bad*). Homonyms have different meanings but the same spelling or sound. There are thus two types of homonyms; homophones (e.g., *sight* and *site*) have the same sound but different spellings, while homographs (e.g., *slough* meaning *swampy area*, pronounced *sloo*, and *slough* meaning *shed tissue*, pronounced *sluff*) have the same spelling, though they may be pronounced differently. *Pole* meaning *long stick* and *pole* meaning *extremity of a planet* are homonyms that are both homophones and homographs. Synonyms (e.g., the verbs *shut* and *close*) are words with the same meaning.

B25. **anxious/eager:** The adjective *anxious* means *uneasy, nervous, worried*; it should not be used in formal writing to mean *eager*.

needs checking	He was anxious to help in any way he could.
revised	He was eager to help in any way he could.

B26. **appraise/apprise:** *To appraise something* is *to estimate its value; to apprise someone of something* is *to inform him or her of it.*

needs checking	The house has been apprised at $160,000.
revised	The house has been appraised at $160,000.
or	He apprised her of the house's jump in value.

B27. **assure/ensure/insure:** *To assure someone of something* is *to tell her with confidence or certainty; to insure* (or *ensure*, in common Canadian, UK, and Australian usage) *that something will happen* is *to make sure that it does; to insure something* is *to purchase insurance on it so as to protect yourself in case of loss.*

Red Tape Holds Up New Bridge

The following are all examples of ambiguity in newspaper headlines. In some cases it may take several moments to decipher the intended meaning.

> Two pedestrians struck by bridge
> Man held over giant L.A. brush fire
> Illegal aliens cut in half by new law
> Passerby injured by post office
> Red tape holds up new bridge
> Village water holds up well
> Jerk injures neck, wins award
> Bishop thanks god for calling

(The above examples come courtesy of columnist Bob Swift of Knight-Ridder Newspapers, and Prof. A. Levey of the University of Calgary.)

Here are two gems provided by editor Beth Humphries:

> The fossils were found by scientists
> embedded in red sandstone.
> She walked into the bathroom tiled in
> sea-green marble.

And, from a Global News weather telecast, the following prediction:

> "Out west tomorrow, they're going to see the sun,
> as well as Atlantic Canada."

needs checking	Our inventory is ensured for $10,000,000.
revised	Our inventory is insured for $10,000,000.
needs checking	I will insure you that this will not happen again.
revised	I assure you that it will not happen again.
or (US)	I will insure that it does not happen again.
or (CDA, UK, AUS)	I will ensure that it does not happen again.

B28. **be/become:** The difference between the two is that *to be* simply indicates existence, while *to become* indicates a process of change. Whenever you are talking about a change, use *become* instead of *be*.

needs checking	I had been quite contented, but as time went by I was unhappy.
revised	I had been quite contented, but as time went by I became unhappy.
needs checking	After years of struggle, East Timor finally was independent in 2002.
revised	After years of struggle, East Timor finally became independent in 2002.

B29. **beg the question:** The original meaning of *beg the question* is *take for granted the very thing to be argued about*—not *invite the question*. In the words of philosopher Thomas Hurka, "'begging the question' is not what Alex Trebek does on Jeopardy." The extension of the phrase to mean *invite the question* has become so widespread in recent years that it may be vain to think of the tide being reversed, but the original concept of question begging is a useful one, and we should be reluctant to allow it to disappear.

needs checking	This sort of sexual abuse case begs the question as to how such behaviour could be hidden for so many years.
revised	This sort of sexual abuse case makes us wonder how such behaviour could be hidden for so many years.

Note: For more on *begging the question* see C8 below.

B30. **beside/besides:** *Besides* can mean *in addition to, moreover* (as in the sentence *Besides, he deserved to lose*), *other than*, or *except* (as in *no one was there besides me*). *Beside* may mean *at the side of* (as in *no one was there beside me*) or *irrelevant to* (as in the common phrase *beside the point*); in this latter meaning confusion with *besides* sometimes arises.

needs checking	Much of Dawkins's argument is besides the point.
revised	Much of Dawkins's argument is beside the point.

B31. **bored/boring:** *Bored* is the opposite of *interested* and *boring* is the opposite of *interesting*. In other words, one is quite likely to be bored when someone reads out what one has already read in the newspaper, or when one is watching a football game when the score is 38–0, or when one is doing an uninteresting job. To be bored, however, is not the same as to be sad, or depressed, or irritated, or angry.

needs checking	She was so bored with her husband that she tried to kill him.
revised	She was so angry with her husband that she tried to kill him.

B32. **breach/breech:** *To breach a wall or a contract* is *to break or break through it*, and *the breach* is *the breaking*. *Breech* refers to a part of a cannon or rifle—or to *the buttocks* (hence a *breech birth*, in which the buttocks or feet emerge before the head).

needs checking	The lawyers claimed that her actions constituted a breech of contract.
revised	The lawyers claimed that her actions constituted a breach of contract.

B33. **brusque/brisk:** *To be brusque* is *to be abrupt or slightly rude in speech or manner*; *brisk* means *quick* or *lively*.

needs checking	He didn't say anything rude to me, but his manner was rather brisk.
revised	He didn't say anything rude to me, but his manner was rather brusque.

B34. **can/may**: In formal writing *can* should be used to refer to *ability*, *may* to refer to *permission*.

needs checking	Can I leave the room? (This makes literal sense only if you are an injured person conversing with your doctor.)
revised	May I leave the room?

B35. **capital/capitol**: As a noun, *capital* can refer to *wealth*, to *the city from which the government operates*, to *an upper case letter*, or to *the top of a pillar*. It can also be used as an adjective to mean *most important* or *principal*. *Capitol* is much more restricted in its meaning—*a specific American legislative building or Roman temple*.

needs checking	The prosecution alleged that he had committed a capitol offence.
revised	The prosecution alleged that he had committed a capital offence.

B36. **career/careen**: As a verb, *career* means *to swerve wildly*. *Careen* originally meant *tilt or lean*, but now in North America especially is often treated as a synonym for *career*. Since *careen* has other specifically nautical meanings, some authorities resist the conflation of the two verbs—but the fact that *career* carries unintended echoes of the noun meaning *profession* leads many, not unreasonably, to prefer *careen*.

B37. **careless/uncaring**: *Careless* means *negligent* or *thoughtless*; you can be careless about your work, for example, or careless about your appearance. Do not use *careless*, however, when you want to talk about *not caring enough about other people*.

| *needs checking* | He acted in a very careless way towards his mother when she was sick. |
| *revised* | He acted in an uncaring way towards his mother when she was sick. |

B38. **censor/censure**: *To censor something* is *to prevent it, or those parts of it that are considered objectionable, from being available to the public. To censure someone* is *to express strong criticism or condemnation.*

| *needs checking* | The Senate censored the attorney general for his part in the scandal. |
| *revised* | The Senate censured the attorney general for his part in the scandal. |

B39. **childish/childlike**: The first is a term of abuse, the second a term of praise.

| *needs checking* | Her writing expresses a childish innocence. |
| *revised* | Her writing expresses a childlike innocence. |

B40. **classic/classical**: As an adjective *classic* means *of such a high quality that it has lasted or is likely to last for a very long time. Classical* is used to refer to *ancient Greece and Rome*, or, particularly when speaking of music, to refer to *a traditional style.*

| *needs checking* | Sophocles was one of the greatest classic authors; his plays are classical. |
| *revised* | Sophocles was one of the greatest classical authors; his plays are acknowledged classics. |

B41. **climatic/climactic**: Weather is not necessarily the high point of life.

| *needs checking* | Difficulties in predicting long-term trends are inherent in any climactic projections. |
| *revised* | Difficulties in predicting long-term trends are inherent in any climatic projections. |

B42. **collaborate/corroborate:** *To collaborate* is *to work together,* whereas *to corroborate* is *to give supporting evidence.*

needs checking   He collaborated her claim that the Americans had corroborated with the Nazi colonel Klaus Barbie.

revised   He corroborated her claim that the Americans had collaborated with the Nazi colonel Klaus Barbie.

B43. **compliment/complement:** *To compliment someone* is *to praise him,* and a *compliment* is the *praise; to complement something* is *to add to it to make it better or complete,* and a *complement* is *the number or amount needed to make it complete.*

needs checking   None of the divisions had its full compliment of troops.

revised   None of the divisions had its full complement of troops.

needs checking   Gretzky's mission in New York was to compliment Mark Messier, the team's captain.

         (Literally, this would mean that the hockey player's job was to keep saying, "Nice work, Mark," and so on.)

revised   Gretzky's mission in New York was to complement Mark Messier, the team's captain.

On the Web

Exercises on word meanings may be found at **www.broadviewpress.com/writing**. Click on **Exercises** and go to **B13–153**.

B44. **comprise/compose/constitute:** The whole *comprises* or includes the various parts; the parts *compose* the whole. The verb *constitute*, similar in meaning to *compose*, is commonly used to refer to abstract concepts (e.g., *The point you make does not constitute an argument*, *The case you refer to constitutes a legal precedent*).

needs checking	The British government is comprised of far fewer ministries than is the Canadian government.
revised	The British government comprises far fewer ministries than does the Canadian government.
or	The British government is composed of far fewer ministries than is the Canadian government.

B45. **conscience/conscious/consciousness**: *To be conscious* is *to be awake and aware of what is happening*, whereas *conscience* is *the part of our mind that tells us it is right to do some things and wrong to do other things (such as steal or murder)*. *Conscience* and *consciousness* are both nouns; the adjectives are *conscientious (aware of what is right and wrong)* and *conscious (aware)*.

needs checking	She was tempted to steal the chocolate bar, but her conscious told her not to.
revised	She was tempted to steal the chocolate bar, but her conscience told her not to.

B46. **contemptuous/contemptible**: We are *contemptuous* of anyone or anything we find *contemptible*.

needs checking	The judge called the delinquent's behaviour utterly contemptuous.
revised	The judge called the delinquent's behaviour utterly contemptible.

B47. **continual/continuous**: If something is *continuous* it *never stops*; something *continual* is *frequently repeated but not unceasing*. The same distinction holds for the adverbs *continually* and *continuously*.

needs checking	He has been phoning me continuously for the past two weeks.
	(Surely he stopped for a bite to eat or a short nap.)

B48. decimate: Most etymologists agree that originally this word meant *kill one of every ten*. It has come to be used more loosely to mean *destroy a considerable number of,* and sometimes *kill nine of every ten,* but it is best not to use it in a way that some authorities feel, as H.W. Fowler puts it, "expressly contradicts the proper sense."

needs checking	The regiment was decimated; fewer than 40 per cent of the troops survived.
revised	The regiment suffered extreme losses; fewer than 40 per cent of the troops survived.

B49. deduce/deduct: *Deduction* is the noun stemming from both these verbs, which is perhaps why they are sometimes confused. *To deduce* is *to draw a conclusion,* whereas *to deduct* is *to subtract.*

needs checking	Sherlock Holmes deducted that Moriarty had committed the crime.
revised	Sherlock Holmes deduced that Moriarty had committed the crime.

B50. definite/definitive: If something is *definite* then there is *no uncertainty about it*; a *definitive* version of something *fixes it in its final or permanent form*—just as a dictionary definition attempts to fix the meaning of a word. Often a sentence is better with neither of these words.

needs checking	Glenn Gould's recording of Bach's *Goldberg Variations* is often thought of as the definite modern version.
revised	Glenn Gould's recording of Bach's *Goldberg Variations* is often thought of as the definitive modern version.
needs checking	Once we have completed our caucus discussion I will be making a very definitive statement.
revised	Once we have completed our caucus discussion I will be making a statement.

or	Once we have completed our caucus discussion I will have something definite to say.

B51. degradation/decline: *Degradation* carries the connotation of *shame and disgrace.* *To degrade something* is not *to reduce it,* or *downgrade it,* or *destroy it.*

needs checking	Among those units in which women played a combat role there was no degradation in operational effectiveness.
revised	Among those units in which women played a combat role there was no decline in operational effectiveness.
or	... there was no reduction in operational effectiveness.
needs checking	According to some authorities, the Iraqi threat has now been significantly degraded.
revised	According to some authorities, the Iraqi threat has now been significantly reduced.

B52. deny/rebut/refute: *To deny something* is *to assert that it is not true*; *to rebut an argument* is *to oppose it*; *to refute it* is *to prove conclusively that it is not true.*

needs checking	During yesterday's press conference the president angrily refuted the allegations: "There has been no improper relationship," he said.
revised	During yesterday's press conference, the president angrily denied the allegations: "There has been no improper relationship," he said.

B53. deprecate/depreciate: *To deprecate something* is *to suggest that it is not valuable or worthy of praise*; something that *depreciates* loses its value.

needs checking	Leonard Cohen was very self-depreciating throughout the interview.
revised	Leonard Cohen was very self-deprecating throughout the interview.

B54. **discrete/discreet**: *Discrete* means *separate* or *distinct*, whereas *discreet* means *prudent* and *tactful; unwilling to give away secrets.*

needs checking	Madonna is not renowned for being discrete.
revised	Madonna is not renowned for being discreet.

B55. **disinterested/uninterested**: A *disinterested* person is *unbiased; uninfluenced by self-interest, especially of a monetary sort.* It is thus quite possible for a person who is entirely disinterested in a particular matter to be completely fascinated by it. If one is *uninterested in* something, on the other hand, one is *bored by* it.

needs checking	He was so disinterested in the game that he left after the fifth inning with the score at 2–2.
revised	He was so uninterested in the game that he left after the fifth inning with the score at 2–2.
needs checking	The controlling shareholders had grown tired of the CEO's futuristic strategies and disinterest in day-to-day operations.
revised	The controlling shareholders had grown tired of the CEO's futuristic strategies and lack of interest in day-to-day operations.

B56. **disorient/disorientate**: Both are considered correct by many authorities, but the extra syllable of the second grates on the ear.

needs checking	I was entirely disorientated in the darkness.
revised	I was entirely disoriented in the darkness.

B57. **dissemble/disassemble**: *To dissemble* is *to disguise your feelings*—a mild form of lying (e.g., *Some still claim that Bill Clinton was guilty of little more than dissembling*). *To disassemble* is *to take apart.*

needs checking	For the test we are required to first assemble and then dissemble a six-cylinder engine.
revised	For the test we are required to first assemble and then disassemble a six-cylinder engine.

B58. dissociate/disassociate: There is no need for the extra syllable.

needs checking	T.S. Eliot speaks of a disassociation of sensibility that began in the seventeenth century.
revised	T.S. Eliot speaks of a dissociation of sensibility that began in the seventeenth century.

B59. distinct/distinctive: *Distinct* means *able to be seen or perceived clearly; easily distinguishable from those around it. Distinctive* means *unusual; not commonly found.* There is a similar contrast between the adverbs *distinctly* and *distinctively*, and the nouns *distinction* and *distinctiveness.*

needs checking	I distinctively heard the sound of a car engine.
revised	I distinctly heard the sound of a car engine.

B60. economic/economical: *Economic* means *pertaining to economics*, or *sufficient to allow a reasonable return for the amount of money or effort put in. Economical* is a word applied to people, which means *thrifty.* The difference applies as well to *uneconomic* and *uneconomical.*

needs checking	Controversy over whether it would be economical to develop the vast Hibernia oilfield continued for many years.
revised	Controversy over whether it would be economic to develop the vast Hibernia oilfield continued for many years.

B61. effective/efficacious/effectual/efficient: *Effective, efficacious,* and *effectual* all mean *sufficient to produce the desired effect. Efficacious,* however, applies only to *strategies* or *things* (though it strikes many as a rather pompous word in any application). A person, then, cannot be efficacious. *Effectual* was once applied only to actions, but is now sometimes applied to people as well. *Effective* can apply to actions or people. *Efficient* has an added connotation:

producing results with little waste of money or effort. Thus a promotional campaign to persuade people to buy a product by giving away free samples to every man, woman, and child in the country might be effective, but it would certainly not be efficient; a good deal of waste would be involved. The same difference applies to the nouns *effectiveness* and *efficiency*. (*Efficacy* is a rather pretentious noun that is usually best avoided.)

needs checking	The board wants to increase the efficacy of the machinery we use.
revised	The board wants to increase the efficiency of the machinery we use.
needs checking	He is the most efficacious worker in the office.
revised	He is the most effective worker in the office.

B62. **e.g./i.e.**: The abbreviation *e.g.* is short for *exemplum gratia* ("example given"; or, in the plural *exempli gratia*, "examples given"). It is sometimes confused with the abbreviation *i.e.*, which is short for *id est* ("that is to say").

needs checking	Those citizens of India who speak Hindi (e.g., over 400 million people) are being encouraged to learn a second language.
revised	Those citizens of India who speak Hindi (i.e., over 400 million people) are being encouraged to learn a second language.

B63. **elemental/elementary**: A thing is *elemental* if it forms *an important or essential element of the whole*; it is *elementary* if it is *easy to understand*, or *at a relatively simple level*.

needs checking	He lacked even the most elemental understanding of the problem.
revised	He lacked even the most elementary understanding of the problem.

B64. elicit/illicit: *Elicit* is a verb; one elicits information about something. *Illicit* is an adjective meaning *illegal* or *not approved*.

needs checking	She has been dealing in elicit drugs for some time.
revised	She has been dealing in illicit drugs for some time.
or	The police elicited details about her drug use.

B65. eligible/illegible: One is *eligible* for a job or for membership in an organization if one *meets the standard* set for applicants. One of the requirements might be that one's handwriting not be *illegible*.

needs checking	He regretted that I was not illegible to join his club.
revised	He regretted that I was not eligible to join his club.

B66. emigrant/immigrant: *To migrate* is *to move from one place to another*. The prefix *ex*, shortened to *e*, means *out of*, so an *emigrant* from a country is *someone who is moving out of it*. The prefix *in* or *im* means *in* or *into*, so an *immigrant* to a country is *someone moving into it*. Similarly, *emigration* is *the movement of people out of a country*, while *immigration* is *the movement of people into a country*. Notice the spelling in both cases: *e-migrant* (one *m*), *im-migrant* (two *ms*).

needs checking	More than 100,000 emigrants entered America last year.
revised	More than 100,000 immigrants entered America last year.

B67. eminent/imminent/immanent: A person is *eminent* if she is *well-known and well-respected*; an event is *imminent* if it is *about to happen*; a quality (or a god) is *immanent* if it *pervades* everything.

needs checking	Even those working for the party in the campaign did not believe that a majority victory was immanent.

revised	Even those working for the party in the campaign did not believe that a majority victory was imminent.

B68. enervate/invigorate: Because of the similarity in sound between *enervate* and *energy*, *enervate* is often thought to mean *make more energetic*. In fact *enervate* means just the opposite—*to lessen the strength of.* If something makes you more *energetic* it *invigorates* you.

needs checking	She found the fresh air quite enervating; I haven't seen her so lively in months.
revised	She found the fresh air quite invigorating; I haven't seen her so lively in months.

B69. enormity/enormousness: Originally the adjective *enormous* simply meant *deviating from the norm*, but by the early nineteenth century it had also come to mean *abnormal, monstrous,* or *extraordinarily wicked.* Today the only meaning is of course *vast in size or quantity*, but the connotation of wickedness is preserved in the noun *enormity*. We may speak of the enormity of a person's crime, but if we want a noun to express vast size we should use *enormousness* or *vastness*.

needs checking	What most impresses visitors to the Grand Canyon is its sheer enormity.
revised	What most impresses visitors to the Grand Canyon is its sheer enormousness.
better	What most impresses visitors to the Grand Canyon is its vastness.

B70. epithet/epigraph/epitaph/epigram: four words often confused. Here are their meanings:

- Epithet—an adjective or short phrase describing someone (*The Golden Brett, the epithet often used to describe Brett Hull, involves an allusion to the nickname of his famous father*).

- Epigraph—an inscription, especially one placed upon a building, tomb, or statue to indicate its name or purpose; or a motto or quotation appearing at the beginning of a book (or the beginning of a chapter in a book).
- Epitaph—words describing a dead person, often the words inscribed on the tomb.
- Epigram—a short, witty, or pointed saying.

needs checking	His epigram will read, "A good man lies here."
revised	His epitaph will read, "A good man lies here."

B71. **equal/equitable/equable**: Things that are *equal* have the *same value*. Arrangements that are *equitable* are *fair and just*. An *equable* person is one who is *moderate and even-tempered*.

needs checking	The distribution of Commons and Senate seats is an equable one; in almost every case the percentage of combined seats allocated to a province closely approximates the percentage of the Canadian population made up by its inhabitants.
revised	The distribution of Commons and Senate seats is an equitable one; in almost every case the percentage of combined seats allocated to a province closely approximates the percentage of the Canadian population made up by its inhabitants.

B72. **explicit/implicit**: If something is *explicit* it is *unfolded—stated in precise terms, not merely suggested or implied*. Something that is *implicit* is *folded in—not stated overtly*. By extension *implicit* has also come to mean *complete or absolute* in expressions such as *implicit trust* (i.e., trust so complete that it does not have to be put into words).

needs checking	I told you implicitly to have the report on my desk first thing this morning.
revised	I told you explicitly to have the report on my desk first thing this morning.

B73. **financial/fiscal/monetary/economic**: The terms used in personal, business, and government finance are not always the same. Here are four that are often not clearly understood:

- Financial—having to do with finance or the handling of money.
- Fiscal—having to do with public revenue.
- Monetary—having to do with the currency of a country. (Only in very limited circumstances, such as the expression *monetary value*, can *monetary* have the more general meaning of *having to do with money*.)
- Economic—having to do with the economy. Thus a government's economic program embraces both fiscal and monetary policies.

needs checking	My brother is a nice person, but he has no monetary ability.
revised	My brother is a nice person, but he has no financial ability.

B74. **finish/be finished/have finished**: In slang usage *to be finished* means *to be at the end of one's life or career* (*If that player's knee is seriously injured again, he will be finished*). This special use should not be extended to the verb *finish* in its normal meaning.

needs checking	Are you finished your work?
revised	Have you finished your work?

B75. **flammable/inflammable**: The two words share the same meaning; *flammable* may have originated because of the possibility for confusion with the word *inflammable*, which looks like a negative but isn't. *Non-flammable* should be used to mean *difficult or impossible to burn*.

needs checking	Asbestos is an inflammable material.
revised	Asbestos is a non-flammable material.

B76. flout/flaunt: *To flout* is *to disobey or show disrespect for*; *to flaunt* is *to display very openly.*

needs checking	Aggressive policing seems to have increased the number of people flaunting the law.
revised	Aggressive policing seems to have increased the number of people flouting the law.

B77. formerly/formally: The similarity of sound often leads to confusion.

needs checking	In August Mr. Laurel formerly broke with Mrs. Aquino.
revised	In August Mr. Laurel formally broke with Mrs. Aquino.

B78. fortunate/fortuitous: *Fortunate* means *lucky* and can refer to people as well as occurrences; *fortuitous* means *happening by chance*, and can refer only to occurrences or situations, not people.

needs checking	This combination of circumstances is not a fortuitous one for our company; we shall have to expect reduced sales in the coming year.
revised	This combination of circumstances is not a fortunate one for our company; we shall have to expect reduced sales in the coming year.

B79. forward/foreword: You find a *foreword* before the other words in a book.

needs checking	The author admits in the forward to her book that the research was not comprehensive.
revised	The author admits in the foreword to her book that the research was not comprehensive.

B80. **founder/flounder**: As a verb, *founder* means *to get into difficulty, to stumble or fall, to sink* (when speaking of a ship), or *to fail* (when speaking of a plan). *To flounder* is *to move clumsily or with difficulty,* or *to become confused in an effort to do something.*

needs checking	He foundered about in a hopeless attempt to solve the problem.
revised	He floundered about in a hopeless attempt to solve the problem.

B81. **fulsome/effusive**: *Fulsome* means *insincere* or *excessively flattering*; fulsome praise is not the sort one wants to receive. But we all like to receive *effusive* (or *enthusiastic*) praise.

needs checking	He was pleased to be showered with fulsome compliments.
revised	He was pleased to be showered with effusive compliments.

B82. **further/farther**: *Farther* refers only to *physical distance.*

needs checking	Eisenhower argued that the plan should receive farther study.
revised	Eisenhower argued that the plan should receive further study.

B83. **historic/historical**: *Historic* means *of sufficient importance that it is likely to become famous in history*; *historical* means *having to do with history* (*historical research, historical scholarship,* etc.).

needs checking	We are gathered here for a historical occasion— the opening of the city's first sewage treatment plant.
revised	We are gathered here for a historic occasion— the opening of the city's first sewage treatment plant.

B84. **hopefully**: one of the greatest causes of disagreement among grammarians. Traditionalists argue that the correct meaning of the adverb *hopefully* is *filled with hope*, and that the use of the word to mean *it is to be hoped that* is therefore incorrect. On the other side it is plausibly argued that many adverbs can function as independent comments at the beginning of a sentence. (*Finally, let me point out that* ... ; *Clearly, we have much to do if we are to* ... ; *Obviously, it will not be possible to* ...). Why should *hopefully* be treated differently? Why indeed? Using *hopefully* for this purpose might not make for beautiful English, but it should not be regarded as a grievous error.

needs checking	Hopefully, it will be possible to finish before tomorrow.
	(As usually happens, *hopefully* is here used with the passive, making for a wordy sentence.)
revised	We hope we can finish before tomorrow.
needs checking	Hopefully, we will arrive before dusk.
	(This sentence should be rewritten in order to ensure that the sentence does not suggest the meaning, *we will arrive filled with hope before dusk.*)
revised	I hope we will arrive before dusk.

B85. **human/humane**: Until the eighteenth century there was no distinction made between the two in either meaning or pronunciation; they were simply alternative ways of spelling the same word. In recent centuries *humane* has come to be used to refer exclusively to the more attractive human qualities—kindness, compassion, and so forth.

needs checking	Their group is campaigning for the human treatment of animals.
revised	Their group is campaigning for the humane treatment of animals.

B86. idioms: Similarity in sound and meaning between words often leads to the mixing-up of idioms.

needs checking	Authorities termed it a democratic transition, but for all intensive purposes it was a *coup d'état*.
revised	Authorities termed it a democratic transition, but for all intents and purposes it was a *coup d'état*.
needs checking	The new recruits were reminded that they would have to tow the line.
revised	The new recruits were reminded that they would have to toe the line.

B87. illusion/allusion: An *allusion* is *an indirect reference to something*; an *illusion* is *something falsely supposed to exist.*

needs checking	Joyce is making an illusion in this passage to a Shakespearean sonnet.
revised	Joyce is making an allusion in this passage to a Shakespearean sonnet.

B88. imply/infer: *To imply something* is *to suggest it without stating it directly*; the other person will have to *infer* your meaning. It may be a comfort to the many who have confused the two to know that the mistake goes back at least as far as Milton:

needs checking	Great or Bright infers not Excellence. (*Paradise Lost* viii, 91)
revised	Great or Bright implies not Excellence. (The fact that a thing is great or bright does not imply that it is also excellent.)
needs checking	I implied from his tone that he disliked our plan.
revised	I inferred from his tone that he disliked our plan.

B89. in to/into: The difference is that *into* is used to indicate movement from outside to inside.

needs checking	Writers in Britain generally expressed sympathy for Rushdie's decision, although some said he was caving into pressure.
revised	Writers in Britain generally expressed sympathy for Rushdie's decision, although some said he was caving in to pressure.

Note: See also pages 166, 207.

B90. **incidents/incidence**: *Incidents* is the plural of *incident* (*happening*), whereas *incidence* is a singular noun meaning *the rate at which something occurs*.

needs checking	The incidents of lung cancer is much lower in Zambia than it is in North America.
revised	The incidence of lung cancer is much lower in Zambia than it is in North America.

B91. **ingenious/ingenuous**: *Ingenious* means *clever*; *ingenuous* means *pleasantly open and unsophisticated*.

needs checking	Her manner was completely ingenious; I cannot imagine she was trying to deceive us.
revised	Her manner was completely ingenuous; I cannot imagine she was trying to deceive us.

B92. **innumerable**: *so numerous that it is impossible to count*; do not use this word as a synonym for *many*.

needs checking	Scholars have advanced innumerable explanations for the dinosaurs' disappearance.
revised	Scholars have advanced many explanations for the dinosaurs' disappearance.

B93. **insist/persist**: To *insist* (that something be done, or on doing something) is to *express yourself very forcefully*. To *persist in doing something* is to *keep on doing it, usually despite some difficulty or opposition*.

needs checking	Even after he had been convicted of the crime, he persisted that he was innocent.
revised	Even after he had been convicted of the crime, he insisted that he was innocent.

B94. **instinctive/instinctual**: There is no difference in meaning; it is thus better to stay with the older (and more pleasant sounding) *instinctive*.

needs checking	Biologists disagree as to what constitutes instinctual behaviour.
revised	Biologists disagree as to what constitutes instinctive behaviour.

B95. **judicial/judicious**: *Judicial* means *having to do with law courts and the administration of justice*. *Judicious* means *having good judgement*.

needs checking	He made one or two judicial comments about the quality of the production.
revised	He made one or two judicious comments about the quality of the production.

B96. **know**: When one *knows* something, that piece of knowledge has been in one's mind for some time. The process of gathering or acquiring knowledge is called *discovering*.

needs checking	Although I noticed the new employee on Monday, I did not know her name until today.
revised	Although I noticed the new employee on Monday, I did not discover her name until today.

B97. **later/latter**: *Later* means *afterwards in time*, whereas the *latter* is the *last mentioned (of two things)*.

needs checking	I looked up the battle of Stalingrad in both the *Encyclopedia Britannica* and Wikipedia. The later provided much more information.
revised	I looked up the battle of Stalingrad in both the *Encyclopedia Britannica* and Wikipedia. The latter provided much more information.

B98. **laudable/laudatory**: *Laudable* means *worthy of praise*; *laudatory* means *expressing praise*.

needs checking	His efforts to combat poverty are very laudatory.
revised	His efforts to combat poverty are very laudable.

B99. **liable/likely**: *Liable* means *obliged by law* or *responsible under the law* (*You will be liable for any damage caused when you are driving the vehicle*); or *in danger of doing or suffering from something undesirable* (*That chimney is liable to fall*). Since in the latter meaning *likely* can often be used in place of *liable*, it is often assumed that there is really no distinction between the two. Careful writers, however, do not use *liable* unless they are referring to possible consequences of an undesirable nature.

needs checking	Last Sunday Singh won the Colonial Open. He's liable to win again before the end of the year.
revised	Last Sunday Singh won the Colonial Open. He's likely to win again before the end of the year.

B100. **libel/slander**: *Libel* is written (and published); *slander* is oral.

needs checking	He was careful in his speech to avoid making any libellous remarks.
revised	He was careful in his speech to avoid making any slanderous remarks.

B101. **lightning/lightening**: One is not likely to see the sky *lightening* until after the thunder and *lightning* are over.

needs checking	Three of the men were severely injured by the lightening.
revised	Three of the men were severely injured by the lightning.

B102. literally: *Literal* means *by the letter—in exact agreement with what is said or written*. A literal meaning is thus the opposite of a figurative or metaphorical meaning. Do not use the adverb *literally* simply to emphasize something.

needs checking	As silviculturalists, we are—literally—babes in the woods. (Ken Drushka, *Stumped: The Forest Industry in Transition*)
	(Silviculturalists may be literally in the woods, but they are not literally babes.)
revised	As silviculturalists, we are babes in the woods.

B103. make/allow/make possible: *To make someone do something is to force them to do it (often against their wishes); to allow someone to do something is to permit them or make it possible for them to do something that they want to do.*

needs checking	A new hospital wing is being built; this will make many more people come for treatment.
revised	A new hospital wing is being built; this will allow many more people to come for treatment.
or	A new hospital wing is being built; this will make it possible for many more people to come for treatment.

B104. masterful/masterly: *Masterful* means *domineering*; *masterly* means *exhibiting mastery or great skill*.

needs checking	Once again last night, Liona Boyd gave the audience a masterful performance.
revised	Once again last night, Liona Boyd gave the audience a masterly performance.

B105. **meretricious/meritorious**: *Meretricious* derives from the Latin word *meretrix*, meaning *prostitute*; if you are looking for a word meaning *very worthy* rather than one meaning *cheap and showy*, *meritorious* is a worthy choice.

<table>
<tr><td>needs checking</td><td>The award is given for meretricious service to the department over an extended period.</td></tr>
<tr><td>revised</td><td>The award is given for meritorious service to the department over an extended period.</td></tr>
</table>

B106. **mitigate/militate**: To *mitigate something* is to *make it less harsh or severe*; thus, mitigating circumstances are those that make a criminal offence less serious. *To militate against something* is *to act as a strong influence against it*.

<table>
<tr><td>needs checking</td><td>The natural history orientation of early anthropology also mitigated against studies of change. (Bruce G. Trigger in Natives and Newcomers)</td></tr>
<tr><td>revised</td><td>The natural history orientation of early anthropology also militated against studies of change.</td></tr>
</table>

B107. **momentarily**: *Momentarily* means *lasting only a moment (He was momentarily confused)*. Common usage also allows the word to mean *in a moment* or *soon*; in formal writing it is best to avoid this use.

<table>
<tr><td>needs checking</td><td>Ms. Billings has informed me that she will join us momentarily.</td></tr>
<tr><td>revised</td><td>Ms. Billings told me that she will join us soon.</td></tr>
</table>

B108. **moot/mute**: A *moot court* discusses a hypothetical case; a *moot point* is one that may be argued from either side but typically has no great significance. *Mute* means *silent* or *incapable of speech*.

<table>
<tr><td>needs checking</td><td>In her recent article Nussbaum suggests that Williams's point is mute.</td></tr>
<tr><td>revised</td><td>In her recent article Nussbaum suggests that Williams's point is moot.</td></tr>
</table>

B109. **need/want:** The verb *need* conveys the idea that it would be difficult or impossible for you to do without the needed thing. If you are talking about acquiring something that is not necessary or essential, use *want* instead; everyone *needs* water and food, but no one really *needs* a flat-screen television. Be careful too not to commit to paper the slang use of *need to* for *should*.

needs checking	I need to marry someone who is very beautiful, very intelligent, very kind, and very rich.
revised	I want to marry someone who is very beautiful, very intelligent, very kind, and very rich.
needs checking	The government needs to improve the roads in this area.
revised	The government should improve the roads in this area.

B110. **non sequitur:** A *non sequitur* is a *statement that has no clear relationship with what has preceded it.* There may be some connection within the mind of the speaker or writer, but it has not been expressed in words.

needs checking	It's time our government did something to help southern Africa. Besides, consumers appreciate inexpensive clothes.
revised	It's time our government did something to help southern Africa. Lowering the current barriers against importing cheap food and textiles would be an important step in that direction. Such a move would benefit our own citizens too; consumers appreciate inexpensive food and clothing.

B111. **obligate/oblige:** These two words share the same Latin root but have different shades of meaning and are used rather differently. One feels a *sense of obligation*, but feels *obliged to do something*.

needs checking	She felt obligated to finish the book her friend had lent her.

revised   She felt obliged to finish the book her friend had lent her.

On the Web

Exercises on word meanings may be found at
www.broadviewpress.com/writing.
Click on **Exercises** and go to **B13–153**.

B112. **of/have**: The difference in meaning is obvious, but the similarity in sound consistently leads people to write sentences involving such meaningless expressions as *should of, would of, could of, may of, might of*, and *must of*.

needs checking	The experiment would of succeeded if the solution had been prepared correctly.
revised	The experiment would have succeeded if the solution had been prepared correctly.
needs checking	Hitler believed that Rommel should of been able to defeat Montgomery at El Alamein.
revised	Hitler believed that Rommel should have been able to defeat Montgomery at El Alamein.

B113. **other**: if one uses the words *the other* it suggests that the thing or person one is about to mention is the only other one is going to write about. If there are several others to be mentioned, *another* is the word to choose.

needs checking   One reason Germany lost the Second World War was that Hitler underestimated the importance of keeping the United States out of the conflict. The other reason was that the German intelligence network was inferior to that of the Allies. Moreover, Hitler's decision to invade Russia was a disastrous mistake.

(Here the use of *the other* in the second sentence leads the reader to believe this is the only other reason. When a third reason is mentioned in the next sentence, the reader is taken by surprise.)

revised　　One reason Germany lost the Second World War was that Hitler underestimated the importance of keeping the United States out of the conflict. Another reason was that the German intelligence network was inferior to that of the Allies. Moreover, Hitler's decision to invade Russia was a disastrous mistake.

B114. our/are: Like the substitution of *of* for *have*, the confusion of *our* and *are* should never survive the rough draft stage.

needs checking　　Almost all are time is spent together.
revised　　Almost all our time is spent together.

B115. palate/palette/pallet: Your *palate* is in your mouth. An artist uses a *palette* to mix paint on. (By extension people often refer to the range of colours typically used by a painter as her *palette*.) Finally, a *pallet* (or skid) is a *wooden frame designed for transporting goods*.

needs checking　　In his later work Matisse's pallet was more limited; much of his work was in unmodulated, primary colours.
revised　　In his later work Matisse's palette was more limited; much of his work was in unmodulated, primary colours.

B116. partake/participate: *Partake* refers to *things* (especially food and drink), *participate* to *activities*.

needs checking　　The governor general made a brief appearance, but did not partake in the festivities.

revised	The governor general made a brief appearance, but did not participate in the festivities.

B117. **persecute/prosecute:** *To persecute someone is to treat them in a harsh and unfair manner, especially because of their political or religious beliefs. To prosecute someone is to take legal action against them in the belief that they have committed a crime.*

needs checking	Catholics began to be prosecuted in England in the sixteenth century.
revised	Catholics began to be persecuted in England in the sixteenth century.

B118. **persuade:** *To persuade someone of something is to make that person believe that it is true. To persuade someone to do something is to lead that person, through what one says, to do the desired thing.* If one does not succeed in making people believe or do what one wants, then one has not persuaded or convinced them, but only tried to persuade them. (The confusion of *refute* with *deny* [page 221] is a parallel mistake.)

needs checking	After all Portia's persuasion Shylock still refuses to change his mind.
revised	After all Portia's attempts to persuade him, Shylock still refuses to change his mind.

B119. **pore/pour:** As *The Globe and Mail Style Book* puts it, one should "not write of someone pouring over a book unless the tome in question is getting wet."

needs checking	After pouring over the evidence, the committee could find no evidence of wrongdoing.
revised	After poring over the evidence, the committee could find no evidence of wrongdoing.

B120. practical/practicable: *Practical* means *suitable for use*, or *involving activity rather than theory*. *Practicable* means *able to be done*. Changing the railway system back to steam locomotives would be practicable but extremely impractical. In most cases *practical* is the word the writer wants; excessive use of *practicable* will make writing sound pretentious rather than important.

needs checking	We do not feel that the construction of a new facility would be practicable at this time.
revised	It would not be practical to construct a new facility now.

B121. prescribe/proscribe: *To prescribe something* is *to recommend or order its use*; *to proscribe something* is *to forbid its use*.

needs checking	One local physician has already proscribed this new drug for a dozen of her patients, and in every case their condition has improved after they take it.
revised	One local physician has already prescribed this new drug for a dozen of her patients, and in every case their condition has improved after they take it.

B122. presently: The subject of much disagreement among grammarians; should *presently* be restricted to its original meaning of *soon*, or should common usage of the word to mean *now* be allowed to spread unopposed? Traditionalists argue that the acceptance of both meanings encourages ambiguity, but in fact the verb tense usually makes clear whether the speaker means *soon* or *now* (*I will be there presently, I am presently working on a large project*, etc.). Perhaps the best solution is to avoid the rather pompous *presently* altogether, and stick to those fine Anglo-Saxon words *soon* and *now*.

needs checking	I am seeing Mr. Jones presently.
revised	I am seeing Mr. Jones now.
or	I will be seeing Mr. Jones soon.

B123. **proposition/proposal**: The only formally correct meaning of *proposition* is *a statement that expresses an idea*, as in *This country is dedicated to the proposition that all humans are created equal*. It is better not to use it to mean *proposal*.

needs checking	The department has put forward a proposition for increasing sales.
revised	The department has put forward a proposal for increasing sales.

B124. **prove**: *To prove something* is *to eliminate any doubt whatsoever as to its truth*. Outside of mathematic or philosophical logic, proof is rarely possible; what one is doing when writing about history or political science or literature is presenting an argument, not a proof. Be cautious in the claims you make in formal writing.

needs checking	The following passage proves that T.S. Eliot was anti-Semitic.
revised	The following passage strongly suggests that T.S. Eliot was anti-Semitic.
or	Anti-Semitic feeling is clearly present in the following passage.

B125. **raise/rise**: As a verb, *raise* means *to lift*; *rise* means *to come up*.

needs checking	They rose the curtain at 8 o'clock.
revised	They raised the curtain at 8 o'clock.
or	The curtain rose at 8 o'clock.
	(Note: Both words are also used as nouns; in North America a *raise* is an *increase in salary*; the UK equivalent is a *rise* in salary.)

B126. **rational/rationale**: *Rational* is an adjective meaning *logical* or *sensible*. A *rationale* is *an explanation for something*.

needs checking	The underlying rational for the proliferation of soaps and detergents is not to make our skin or clothes any cleaner, but to increase the profits of the manufacturers.
revised	The underlying rationale for the proliferation of soaps and detergents is not to make our skin or clothes any cleaner, but to increase the profits of the manufacturers.

B127. **ravish/ravage**: *Ravish* has two quite unrelated meanings—*to rape*, or *to fill with delight*. *To ravage* is *to damage or destroy*.

needs checking	The tree had been ravished by insects.
revised	The tree had been ravaged by insects.

B128. **real/genuine**: The basic meaning of *real* is *existing*; the opposite of *fake* or *forged* is *genuine*.

needs checking	The buyer had thought the painting was a Cezanne, but he soon discovered it was not real.
revised	The buyer had thought the painting was a Cezanne, but he soon discovered it was not genuine.

B129. **regime/regimen/regiment**: A *regime* is either a *system of government* or a *period in which a particular government is in power* (e.g., *military regime, democratic regime*). A *regimen* is a *precisely fixed course of activity* (e.g., a *program of daily exercise and dieting*, a *schedule according to which medication must be taken*). A *regiment* is an *army unit*. Sometimes medical authorities use *regime* and *regimen* interchangeably; there is some benefit to keeping all three clearly separate.

needs checking	A regiment of exercise and heavy medication kept Kennedy performing into his third year as president. (*The National Post*, 7 June 2003)
revised	A regimen of exercise and heavy medication kept Kennedy performing into his third year as president.

B130. **reign/rein:** A monarch *reigns* over a territory; to control a horse you *rein* it in (using the reins).

needs checking	The new leader has so far shown no signs of reigning in the armed forces.
revised	The new leader has so far shown no signs of reining in the armed forces.

B131. **respectively/respectfully:** *Respectively* means *in the order mentioned; respectfully* means *done with respect,*

needs checking	Philadelphia, Denver, and New England were, respectfully, the three best teams in the NFL last season.
revised	Philadelphia, Denver, and New England were, respectively, the three best teams in the NFL last season.

B132. **reticent/reluctant:** *Reticent* means *reluctant to speak; reserved about speaking.* A country may be *reluctant* to go to war; it cannot be *reticent* to go to war. And to say *reticent to speak* is to repeat oneself.

needs checking	She was reticent to speak up, even when her family's reputation had been attacked.
revised	She was reluctant to speak up, even when her family's reputation had been attacked.
or	She remained reticent, even when her family's reputation had been attacked.

B133. **rite/right:** A *rite* is a *ceremonial or ritualistic act;* the word is most frequently used to denote formal acts, such as those of religious ceremonies (e.g., *marriage rites*). Many cultures have formal ceremonies to mark a new stage in a person's life—ceremonies referred to by social scientists as *rites of passage.* That phrase has come to be used informally to refer to any event marking a significant life change. Perhaps because rights and privileges are sometimes conferred during a ceremonial *rite*, the two words are sometimes confused and two *right*s end up making a wrong.

| needs checking | For many students, deconstruction was a right of passage into the world of rebellious intellect. (*New York Times*, 10 October 2004) |
| revised | For many students, deconstruction was a rite of passage into the world of rebellious intellect. |

B134. **sensory/sensuous/sensual**: Advertising and pornography have dulled the distinction among these three adjectives. The meanings of *sensory* and *sensuous* are similar—*sensual* is the sexy one:

- Sensory—having to do with the senses.
- Sensuous—having to do with the senses, or appealing to the senses.
- Sensual—offering physical pleasure, especially of a sexual sort.

| needs checking | Boswell suggested they go to a house of ill repute, but Johnson had no desire for sensuous pleasures. |
| revised | Boswell suggested they go to a house of ill repute, but Johnson had no desire for sensual pleasures. |

B135. **set/sit**: *To set* means *to place something somewhere.*

needs checking	I could remember everything, but I had difficulty sitting it down on paper.
revised	I could remember everything, but I had difficulty setting it down on paper.
needs checking	He asked me to set down on the couch.
revised	He asked me to sit down on the couch.

B136. **shall/will**: Historically *shall* was used primarily for simple statements or questions in the first person—both singular (*I*) and plural (*we*)—and *will* primarily for simple statements or questions in the second person and third person. When *shall* was used in the second or third person it implied control or authority, expressing promises, commands, or a sense of determination. The old "distinctions" are still maintained in questions (*shall I eat a peach?*, *will you have some tea?*) but in other respects the distinctions long ago weakened. A sense of control is expressed with just as much force in the second person using *will* (*you'll do as I say*) and expressions of determination in the first person often use *shall* (*we shall overcome*). At most, then, a slight difference in tone lingers. In legal documents, for example, *shall* is often used rather than *will*, but either wording carries with it the same meaning—and confers the same legal obligation.

correct	The undersigned shall fulfill the said requirements on or before December 31, 2012.
also correct	The undersigned will fulfill the said requirements on or before December 31, 2012.

B137. **simple/simplistic**: *Simplistic* is a derogatory word meaning *too simple* or *excessively simplified*.

needs checking	The questions were so simplistic that I was able to answer all but one correctly.
revised	The questions were so simple that I was able to answer all but one correctly.

B138. **somehow**: *Somehow* means *by some method* (*Somehow I must repair my car so that I can arrive in time for my appointment*). It does not mean *in some ways*, *to some extent*, or *somewhat*.

needs checking	His brother is somehow mentally disturbed.
revised	His brother is mentally disturbed in some way.
or	His brother is somewhat disturbed mentally.

B139. **specially/especially**: *Specially* means *for a particular purpose* (*These utensils are specially designed for left-handed people*). *Especially* means *particularly* or *more than in other cases*.

| *needs checking* | The entire system pleased her, but she was specially happy to see that the computer program had been especially created for small business users. |
| *revised* | The entire system pleased her, but she was especially happy to see that the computer program had been specially created for small business users. |

B140. **stationary/stationery**: *Stationary* means *not moving*; *stationery* is *what you write on*.

| *needs checking* | As Mr. Blakeney remembered it, Lord Taylor "would always park his car in the no-parking zone outside the Bessborough Hotel, leaving House of Lords stationary on the windshield." |
| *revised* | As Mr. Blakeney remembered it, Lord Taylor "would always park his car in the no-parking zone outside the Bessborough Hotel, leaving House of Lords stationery on the windshield." |

B141. **stimulant/stimulus**: *Stimulus* (plural *stimuli*) is the more general word for *anything that produces a reaction*; *stimulant* normally refers to *a drink or drug that has a stimulating effect*.

| *needs checking* | The shocks were intended to act as stimulants to the rats that we used as subjects for the experiment. |
| *revised* | The shocks were intended to act as stimuli to the rats that we used as subjects for the experiment. |

B142. **tack/tact**: *Tack* is a sailing term; *a different tack* means *a different direction relative to the wind*. *Tact* is *skill in saying or doing the right or polite thing*.

| *needs checking* | We will have to exercise all our tack in the coming negotiations. |
| *revised* | We will have to exercise all our tact in the coming negotiations. |

B143. **then/than/that**: The difference in meaning is obvious, but slips of the pen or keyboard too often allow the error to make it to the final draft. Spell-check won't help, of course.

needs checking	It turns out that the company needs more money that we had expected.
revised	It turns out that the company needs more money than we had expected.
needs checking	There were fewer people in attendance then had been predicted.
revised	There were fewer people in attendance than had been predicted.

B144. **they/their/there/they're**: Four words that are confused perhaps more frequently than any others. *They* is a pronoun used to replace any plural noun (e.g., books, people, numbers). *There* can be used to mean *in* (or *at*) *that place*, or can be used as an introductory word before various forms of the verb *to be* (*there is, there had been*, etc.). *Their* is a possessive adjective meaning *belonging to them*. Beware in particular of substituting *they* for *there*:

needs checking	They were many people in the crowd.
revised	There were many people in the crowd.

The easiest way to check whether one is making this mistake is to ask if it would make sense to replace *they* with a noun. In the above sentence, for example, it would obviously be absurd to say, *The people were many people in the crowd*.

The confusion of *they*, *there*, and *their* is the sort of mistake that all writers are able to catch if they proofread carefully—particularly if they do so out loud.

needs checking	Soviet defenceman Mikhail Tatarinov is considered to be there enforcer. (*Peterborough Examiner*)
revised	Soviet defenceman Mikhail Tatarinov is considered to be their enforcer.

needs checking	There all going to the dance this Saturday.
revised	They're all going to the dance this Saturday.
or	They are all going to the dance this Saturday.

B145. tiring/tiresome: Something that is *tiring makes you feel tired,* though you may have enjoyed it very much. Something that is *tiresome* is *tedious and unpleasant.*

needs checking	Although it is tiresome for him, my father likes to play tennis at least twice a week.
revised	Although it is tiring for him, my father likes to play tennis at least twice a week.

B146. to/too/two: Too can mean *also* or be used to indicate *excess* (*too many, too heavy*); *two* is of course the number.

needs checking	She seemed to feel that there was to much to do.
revised	She seemed to feel that there was too much to do.

B147. to/towards: *To* indicates *direction*; *towards* indicates *motion.*

(Note that *toward* and *towards* may be used interchangeably.)

needs checking	The deer moved slowly to me through the tall grass.
revised	The deer moved slowly towards me through the tall grass.

B148. unexceptional/unexceptionable: *Unexceptional* means *ordinary, not an exception*; *unexceptionable* is used when you do not object (or take exception) to the thing or person in question.

needs checking	One way the president pays for this is in the confusion and controversy that surround the unexceptional White House plan to reflag 11 Kuwaiti

tankers with the Stars and Stripes. It is a modest proposal that in itself should not cause the hand-wringing now being observed on Capitol Hill.

(The plan to reflag the tankers clearly was an exception; the U.S. had not done anything similar for years. What the writer means to say is that the plan is unexceptionable—that no one should have any objection to it.)

revised   One way the president pays for this is in the confusion and controversy that surround the unexceptionable White House plan to reflag 11 Kuwaiti tankers with the Stars and Stripes. It is a modest proposal that in itself should not cause the hand-wringing now being observed on Capitol Hill.

B149. **unique/universal/perfect/complete/correct**: None of these can be a matter of degree. Something is either *unique* or *not unique*, *perfect* or *imperfect*, and so on.

needs checking   Frida Kahlo made a rather unique contribution to twentieth-century art.

revised   Frida Kahlo made a unique contribution to twentieth-century art.

or   It is arguable that Frida Kahlo made a unique contribution to twentieth-century art.

B150. **valid/true/accurate**: An *accurate* statement is one that is *factually correct*. A combination of accurate facts may not always give a true picture, however. For example, the statement *former Canadian Prime Minister Mackenzie King often visited prostitutes* is entirely accurate, but gives a false impression; in fact King visited prostitutes not to use their services but rather to try to convince them to give up their profession. *Valid* is often used carelessly and as a consequence might seem fuzzy in its meaning. Properly used it can mean *legally acceptable*, or *sound in reasoning*; do not use it to mean *accurate, reasonable, true*, or *well-founded*.

needs checking	Churchill's fear that the Nazis would become a threat to all of Europe turned out to be valid.
revised	Churchill's fear that the Nazis would become a threat to all of Europe turned out to be well-founded.

B151. **vein/vain**: *Veins* run through your body; *to be vain* is *to be conceited*; an effort that fails to brings any of the desired results has been *in vain*.

needs checking	Shakespeare portrays Sir John Oldcastle—or Falstaff, as he is usually known—as vein and irresponsible but immensely amusing and likeable.
revised	Shakespeare portrays Sir John Oldcastle—or Falstaff, as he is usually known—as vain and irresponsible but immensely amusing and likeable.

B152. **verbal/oral**: *Oral* means *spoken* rather than written, whereas *verbal* means *having to do with words*. A person who is unable to speak may have a high level of verbal skill.

needs checking	I can write well enough, but I have difficulty in expressing ideas verbally.
revised	I can write well enough, but I have difficulty in expressing ideas orally.

B153. **were/where**: *Were* is of course a past tense form of the verb *to be*, while *where* refers to a place. Spell-check will not tell you if you have used the correct word.

needs checking	This is the place were Dante met Beatrice.
revised	This is the place where Dante met Beatrice.

Some other words over which issues of meaning often cause confusion:

amused/bemused: If you are *bemused*, you are a bit puzzled about something—though not in any troubled fashion, and perhaps even in a somewhat amused one. From that slight point of connection (as well as the similarity in sound) has arisen the erroneous belief that the two words are synonymous.

demur/demure: To *demur* is to raise an objection; to be *demure* is to be modest and shy in an appealing way.

ecology/environment: *Ecology* is the study of some aspects of the environment; you cannot "harm the ecology."

empathy/sympathy: To *sympathize* with another person is to feel for that person; to *empathize* is to do so in a way that identifies oneself with that person.

England/Britain/Great Britain/United Kingdom: England + Scotland + Wales = Great Britain (less formally, "Britain"); Great Britain + Northern Ireland = United Kingdom (full title, "United Kingdom of Great Britain and Northern Ireland").

envious/jealous: One is envious of someone else's good fortune, jealous of one's own possessions. In common parlance *jealous* is often used as a synonym for *envious*, but arguably the distinction between the two words is worth preserving.

fleshing/flushing: The expression *flesh out* means add to—just as flesh is added to a growing animal. The similarity in sounds often leads people to write *flush* instead of *flesh*, but if you suggest someone *flush out* their argument, you are surely not suggesting they expand it.

gender/sex: The word *gender* is used to refer to characteristics that are associated with one's sex but that have been formed through social influences. When we refer to the *female sex* or the *male sex*, on the other hand, we are speaking of biological difference.

herbs/spices: The difference lies in the origin; *herbs* come from the stems, leaves, or flowers of plants, while *spices* come from the roots, the bark, the seeds, or the buds.

moral/morale: The *morale* of a group is their level of confidence, optimism, shared positive feeling—not to be confused with the *moral* of a story, or with *moral* issues.

nauseous/nauseated: Something that is *nauseous* makes you feel *nauseated*. Informally many people speak of feeling *nauseous*; in the context of formal writing they should feel *nauseated* instead.

obsolescent/obsolete: Something *obsolescent* is becoming out of date; something *obsolete* is completely outmoded.

obtuse/abstruse: *Obtuse* means *rounded* or *blunt* (as opposed to sharp)—and by extension, when used about humans, *dull* or *dim-witted* (sometimes with the implication that the person is willfully refusing to see the truth). *Abstruse* refers to ideas, not people, and means *obscure, difficult to understand* (sometimes with the implication that the material is of considerable weight or importance).

penultimate/ultimate: The *penultimate* one comes just before the last one; the *ultimate* one is the last one. A widespread misconception is that *penultimate* carries the implication of being higher than or better than or beyond the *ultimate*; not so.

tortuous/torturous: *Tortuous* means *full of twists and turns*; *torturous* means *having to do with torture*.

⊙ Usage: *Word Conventions*

B154. **according to**: This expression normally is used only when one is referring to a person or to a group of people (e.g., *According to his lawyer, the accused was nowhere near the scene when the crime was committed*; *According to Shakespeare, Richard III was an evil king*).

needs checking	According to geography, Congo is larger than all of Western Europe.
revised	As we learn in geography, Congo is larger than all of Western Europe.
needs checking	According to the story of *Cry the Beloved Country*, Stephen Kumalo has a quick temper.
revised	The events of the story show that Stephen Kumalo has a quick temper.

B155. **age/aged**: Do not use the noun *age* as a participle.

needs checking	A woman age 35 was struck and killed by the car.
revised	A woman aged 35 was struck and killed by the car.

B156. **all of**: Many authorities advise that the expression *all of* should be avoided in the interests of economy. Perhaps so, but there is certainly no error involved, and in many cases the addition of the word *of* improves the rhythm of the sentence; Lincoln's famous maxim "You can not fool all the people all of the time" would not be improved by dropping the *of*.

B157. **amount**: This word should be used only with things that are uncountable (sugar, goodwill, etc.).

needs checking	A large amount of books were stolen from the library last night.
revised	A large number of books were stolen from the library last night.

B158. **and**: In most cases *or* rather than *and* should be used as a connective if the statement is negative.

> *needs checking*   Moose are not found in South America, Africa, and Australia.
>
> *revised*   Moose are not found in South America, Africa, or Australia.

B159. **anyways/anywheres**: There is never a need for the *s*.

> *needs checking*   We were unable to find him anywheres.
>
> *revised*   We were unable to find him anywhere.

B160. **as**: When this word is used to relate the times at which two actions happened, the actions must have happened at the same time (e.g., *As I got out of bed, I heard the sound of gunfire*, where the hearing happens during the action of getting out; *As he was walking to work, he remembered that he had left the stove on*, where the remembering happens during the walking). *As* should not be used in this way if the two actions happened at different times. If one action is completed before the other begins, always use *when*.

> *needs checking*   As I had finished my geography assignment, I started my history essay.
>
> *revised*   When I had finished my geography assignment, I started my history essay.
>   (The finishing happens before the starting.)
>
> *needs checking*   As she discovered that the engine was overheating, she stopped the car immediately.
>
> *revised*   When she discovered that the engine was overheating, she stopped the car immediately.
>   (The discovering happens before the stopping.)

Note: Since *when* can be used both when actions happen simultaneously and when they happen at different times, anyone who is at all uncertain about this point is wise to avoid using *as* to refer to time, and always stick to *when*. This has the added advantage of avoiding the possible ambiguity as to whether *as* is being used to mean *because* or to mean *when*.

B161. **as/that/whether**: Do not use *as* to mean *that* or *whether*.

needs checking	I don't know as how I can do the job in time.
revised	I don't know whether I can do the job in time.

B162. **back formations**: A back formation is the formation of a word from what one would expect to be its derivative. The verb *laze*, for example, is a back formation from the adjective *lazy*; a more recent (and similar-sounding) back formation is the verb *liaise* from the noun *liaison*. Many back formations may be created from negatives that lack a positive form (*kempt, gruntled, ruthful, solent*, etc.). These may constitute amusing colloquialisms, but should be avoided in formal written English except where the writer is striving for a humorous effect.

informal	Toronto is a pretty ruly place to watch a game. (Baseball manager Lou Piniella, as quoted by Robertson Cochrane in *The Globe and Mail*, 29 Oct. 1994)
more formal	Toronto is a pretty civilized place to watch a game.

B163. **because of the following reasons/some reasons/many reasons**: The word *because* makes it clear that a cause or reason is being introduced. The addition of a phrase such as *of the following reasons* is redundant. Either use *because* on its own, or use *for the following reasons/many reasons*, etc.

needs checking	During her first few years in Canada, Susanna Moodie was unhappy because of several reasons.
revised	During her first few years in Canada, Susanna Moodie was unhappy for several reasons.

B164. **both:** The expressions *both alike*, *both equal*, and *both together* all tend to involve repetition.

needs checking	Macdonald and Cartier both arrived together at about eight o'clock.
revised	Macdonald and Cartier arrived together at about eight o'clock.

B165. **can be able:** *I can do it* and *I am able to do it* mean the same thing. Using the verbs together is redundant.

needs checking	He thinks Minnesota can be able to win the Cup.
revised	He thinks Minnesota can win the Cup.
or	He thinks Minnesota will be able to win the Cup.

B166. **cannot help but:** One too many negatives; use *can but* or *cannot help*.

needs checking	He couldn't help but think he had made a mistake.
revised	He couldn't help thinking he had made a mistake.
or	He could but think he had made a mistake.

B167. **change:** You *make a change* (not *do a change*).

needs checking	The manager did several changes to the roster before the match with Russia.
revised	The manager made several changes to the roster before the match with Russia.

On the Web

Exercises on conventions of English usage may be found at
www.broadviewpress.com/writing.
Click on **Exercises** and go to **B154–207**.

B168. **comment:** We *make comments* (not *say* or *do them*).

needs checking	Anyone who wishes to say any comments will have a chance to speak after the lecture.
revised	Anyone who wishes to make any comments will have a chance to speak after the lecture.

B169. **compared to/than:** The use of *compared to* as a participial phrase often leads to ambiguity and error. Unless one is speaking of one person comparing something to something else, it is usually better to use *than*.

needs checking	There were far fewer frogs in the area in 2008 compared to previous years.
revised	There were far fewer frogs in the area in 2008 than there had been in previous years.

B170. **convince:** You *convince* people that they should do something, or *persuade* them to do it.

needs checking	Reagan's advisers convinced him to approve the arms-for-hostages deal with Iran.
revised	Reagan's advisers persuaded him to approve the arms-for-hostages deal with Iran.

B171. **elder/older:** *Elder* can act as an adjective (*my elder son*) or a noun (*the elder of the two*). *Older* can act only as an adjective. If using *than*, use *older*.

needs checking	She is four years elder than her sister.
revised	She is four years older than her sister.

B172. **for:** One use of this preposition is to show purpose. Normally, however, *for* can be used in this way only when the purpose can be expressed in one word (e.g., *for safety*, *for security*). It is not usually correct to try to express purpose by combining *for* with a pronoun and an infinitive: expressions such as *for him to be happy, for us to arrive safely* are awkward and should be avoided. Instead, one can express purpose either by beginning with *in order to* (e.g., *in order to make life easier, in order to increase yield per hectare*), or by using *so that* (e.g., *so that life will be made easier, so that yield per hectare will be increased*).

needs checking	Please speak slowly for me to understand what you say.
revised	Please speak slowly so that I can understand what you say.
needs checking	The team must work hard for it to have a chance at the Grey Cup.
revised	The team must work hard if it is to have a chance at the Grey Cup.

B173. **forget:** *To forget something* is *to fail to remember it*, not *to leave it somewhere.*

needs checking	I forgot my textbook at home.
revised	I left my textbook at home.
or	I forgot to bring my textbook from home.

B174. **had ought/hadn't ought:** Use *ought* or *ought not* instead.

needs checking	He hadn't ought to have risked everything at once.
revised	He ought not to have risked everything at once.
or	He should not have risked everything at once.

B175. **hardly:** *Hardly* acts as a negative; there is thus no need to add a second negative.

needs checking	The advertisers claim that you can't hardly tell the difference.
revised	The advertisers claim that you can hardly tell the difference.

B176. **how/what:** One may talk about *how something* (*or someone*) is, or *what something* (*or someone*) is like, but not *how they are like.*

needs checking	Tell me how it looks like from where you are.
revised	Tell me how it looks from where you are.
or	Tell me what it looks like from where you are.
needs checking	I do not know how the roads are like between St. John's and Corner Brook.
revised	I do not know what the roads are like between St. John's and Corner Brook.
or	I do not know how the roads are between St. John's and Corner Brook.

B177. **increase:** Numbers can be *increased* or *decreased*, as can such things as production and population (nouns which refer to certain types of numbers or quantities). Things such as houses, however, or books (nouns which do not refer to numbers or quantities) cannot be increased; only the number of houses, books, etc. can be increased or decreased, raised or lowered.

needs checking	The government has greatly increased low-rent houses in the suburbs of Seattle.
revised	The government has greatly increased the number of low-rent houses in the suburbs of Seattle.

B178. **information:** One *gives information* (not *tells it*).

needs checking	He told me all the information I wanted about how to apply.
revised	He gave me all the information I wanted about how to apply.

B179. **investigation:** We *make, carry out,* or *hold an investigation* (not *do one*).

needs checking	The manager did a thorough investigation into the disappearance of funds from his department.

revised	The manager made a thorough investigation into the disappearance of funds from his department.

B180. irregardless: The result of confusion between *regardless* and *irrespective*. Use *regardless*.

needs checking	She told us to come for a picnic, irregardless of whether it is rainy or sunny.
revised	She told us to come for a picnic, regardless of whether it is rainy or sunny.

B181. is when/is where: Many people use these phrases when attempting to define something. There is always a better way.

needs checking	Osmosis is when a fluid moves through a porous partition into another fluid.
revised	Osmosis occurs when a fluid moves through a porous partition into another fluid.
or	Osmosis is the movement of a fluid through a porous partition into another fluid.

B182. journey: You *make a journey* (not *do one*).

needs checking	If we do not stop along the way, we can do the journey in an hour.
revised	If we do not stop along the way, we can make the journey in an hour.

B183. law: A law is *passed, made,* or *put into effect* by the government, and *enforced* by the police. Laws are not *put* or *done*.

needs checking	I think the government should put a law increasing the penalty for drunk driving.
revised	I think the government should pass a law increasing the penalty for drunk driving.

B184. **less/fewer**: When something can be counted (e.g., people, books, trees), use *fewer*. Use *less* only with uncountable nouns (e.g., *sugar, meat, equipment*).

needs checking	As the modern economy spreads through the countryside, less people will die of tropical diseases or infected wounds. (*The New York Times*, 12 May 1997)
revised	As the modern economy spreads through the countryside, fewer people will die of tropical diseases or infected wounds.
needs checking	There are less steps, and that means there is more room for error.
revised	There are fewer steps, and that means there is more room for error.

B185. **lie** (meaning *speak falsely*): You *lie about something*, not *that something*.

needs checking	He lied that he was eighteen years old.
revised	He lied about his age, stating that he was eighteen.
or	He lied when he said he was eighteen years old.

B186. **mistake**: Mistakes are *made* (not *done*).

needs checking	He did seven mistakes in that short spelling exercise.
revised	He made seven mistakes in that short spelling exercise.

B187. **more/most**: Most adjectives and adverbs have comparative and superlative forms; the comparative is used when comparing two things, the superlative when comparing three or more.

needs checking	Smith was the most accomplished of the two.
revised	Smith was the more accomplished of the two.

To use *more* with a comparative adjective, or *most* with a superlative adjective is to repeat oneself.

needs checking	The bride looked like the most happiest person in the world.
revised	The bride looked like the happiest person in the world.
or	The bride looked like the most happy person in the world.
needs checking	Gandalf is much more wiser than Frodo.
revised	Gandalf is much wiser than Frodo.

B188. **nor**: This word is usually used with *neither*. Do not use it with *not*; when using *not*, use *or* instead of *nor*.

needs checking	She does not drink nor smoke.
revised	She does not drink or smoke.
or	She neither drinks nor smokes.
needs checking	Graham does not have the money nor the organization to work with that Atkins enjoys.
revised	Graham does not have the money or the organization to work with that Atkins enjoys.
or	Graham has neither the money nor the organization to work with that Atkins enjoys.

B189. **nothing/nobody/nowhere**: These words should not be used with another negative word such as *not*. If one uses *not*, then one should use *anything* instead of *nothing*, *anybody* instead of *nobody*, *anywhere* instead of *nowhere*.

needs checking	He could not do nothing while he was in prison.
revised	He could not do anything while he was in prison.

B190. **old-fashioned**: Be sure not to leave off the *-ed* in this adjectival expression.

needs checking	Let's do it the old-fashion way.
revised	Let's do it the old-fashioned way.

B191. opposed: You are opposed *to* something or someone (not *with* or *against*)

needs checking	Charles Darwin was opposed against the literal interpretation of the story of Creation, as found in Genesis.
revised	Charles Darwin was opposed to the literal interpretation of the story of Creation, as found in Genesis.

B192. per cent/percentage: If you use *per cent*, you must give the number. Otherwise, use *percentage*.

needs checking	The per cent of people surveyed who reported any change of opinion was very small.
revised	The percentage of people surveyed who reported any change of opinion was very small.
or	Only six per cent of the people surveyed reported any change of opinion.

Note: *Percentage* is always one word; authorities differ as to whether *per cent* should always be written as two words, or whether it also may be written as one word (*percent*).

B193. preclude: *To preclude something* is *to exclude any possibility of it happening*; people cannot be precluded.

needs checking	Our cash flow problems preclude us from entering into any new commitments before 2008.
revised	Our cash flow problems preclude any new commitments before 2008.
or	We do not have enough money to make a commitment to you now.

B194. position/theory: Positions and theories *are held* or *are argued*; they do not hold or argue themselves.

needs checking	Devlin's position holds that a shared public morality is essential to the existence of society.
revised	Devlin's position is that a shared public morality is essential to the existence of society.
or	Devlin holds that a shared public morality is essential to the existence of society.

B195. **reason**: The phrase *the reason is because* involves repetition; use *that* instead of *because*, or eliminate the phrase completely.

needs checking	The reason ice floats is because it is lighter than water.
revised	The reason ice floats is that it is lighter than water.
or	Ice floats because it is lighter than water.
needs checking	The reason I have come is because I want to apply for a job.
revised	I have come to apply for a job.

B196. **short/scarce**: If a person is *short of something*, that thing is *scarce*.

needs checking	Food is now desperately short throughout the country.
revised	Food is now extremely scarce throughout the country.
or	The country is now desperately short of food.

B197. **since/for**: Both these words can be used to indicate length (or duration) of time, but they are used in slightly different ways. *Since* is used to mention the point at which a period of time began (*since 6 o'clock, since the beginning of 2004, since last Christmas,* etc.). *For* is used to mention the amount of time that has passed (*for two years, for six months, for centuries,* etc.).

needs checking	She has been staying with us since three weeks.
revised	She has been staying with us for three weeks.
or	She has been staying with us since three weeks ago.

B198. so: When used to show degree or extent, *so* is normally used with *that*: *so big that* ... , *so hungry that* ... , etc. *So* should not be used as an intensifier in the way that *very* is used.

needs checking	When George stepped out of the church he looked so handsome.
revised	When George stepped out of the church he looked very handsome.
or	When George stepped out of the church he looked so handsome that it was hard to believe he had once been thought of as unattractive.

B199. some/any/someone/anyone: With negatives (*not, never,* etc.) *any* is used in place of *some.*

needs checking	He never gives me some help with my work.
revised	He never gives me any help with my work.

B200. speech: You *make a speech* or *give a speech* (not *do a speech*).

needs checking	The dean was asked to do a speech at the convocation.
revised	The dean was asked to give a speech at the convocation.

B201. start: If both the time at which an event begins and the time that it finishes are mentioned, it is not enough to use only the verb *start.*

needs checking	The dance started from 9 p.m. till midnight.
revised	The dance started at 9 p.m. and finished at midnight.
or	The dance continued from 9 p.m. until midnight.
or	The dance lasted from 9 p.m. until midnight.

B202. **suppose/supposed**: Be sure to add the *d* in the expression *supposed to*.

needs checking	We are suppose to be there by eight.
revised	We are supposed to be there by eight.

B203. **supposed to/should**: These two are very similar in meaning, and may often be used interchangeably; if a person is *supposed to* do something, then that is what she *should* do. In the past tense, however, the question of when and when not to use *supposed to* is quite tricky. You may use it when you are clearly talking about a fixed plan that has not been carried out (e.g., *He was supposed to arrive before two o'clock, but he is still not here*). You should not use it to apply to any action that you think was wrong, or you feel should not have been carried out. The safe solution to this problem is always to use *should* instead of *supposed to*.

needs checking	What she said was impolite, but he was not supposed to hit her for saying it.
revised	What she said was impolite, but he should not have hit her for saying it.
needs checking	The National Party government was not supposed to keep Nelson Mandela in jail for so many years.
revised	The National Party government should not have kept Nelson Mandela in jail for so many years.

B204. **thankful/grateful**: We are *thankful* that something has happened, and *grateful* for something we have received.

needs checking	I am very thankful for the kind thoughts expressed in your letter.
revised	I am very grateful for the kind thoughts expressed in your letter.

B205. **too**: The word *too* suggests that something is *more than necessary*, or *more than desired*. Do not use it indiscriminately to lend emphasis.

needs checking	He looked too handsome in his new suit.
revised	He looked very handsome in his new suit.

B206. **try/sure:** Perhaps the most common error of all, in published books and articles as well as in less formal writing, is the use of *and* rather than *to* after *try* and *sure*.

needs checking	No Montrealers stepped in to try and save the franchise.
revised	No Montrealers stepped in to try to save the franchise.
needs checking	Burton had agreed with the Sultan not to try and convert the Africans to Christianity. (Alan Moorehead, *The White Nile*)
revised	Burton had agreed with the Sultan not to try to convert the Africans to Christianity.
needs checking	Be sure and take out the garbage before you go to bed.
revised	Be sure to take out the garbage before you go to bed.

B207. **use/used:** Be sure to add the *d* in the expression *used to*.

needs checking	He use to be much more reckless than he is now.
revised	He used to be much more reckless than he is now.

B208. **where:** Do not use *where* for *that*.

needs checking	I read in the paper where the parties are now tied in popularity.
revised	I read in the paper that the parties are now tied in popularity.

◎ PUTTING IDEAS TOGETHER

⊙ Paragraphing

C1. There is a degree of flexibility when it comes to the matter of where and how often to start new paragraphs. Sometimes a subtle point in an argument will require a paragraph of almost an entire page to elaborate; occasionally a single sentence can form an effective paragraph. Yet separating ideas into paragraphs remains an important aid to the processes of both reading and writing. Here are some guidelines as to when it is appropriate to begin a new paragraph:

O *In Narration:*

- whenever the story changes direction.
  (*This was the moment Paul Martin had been waiting for ...,
  When Napoleon left Elba he....*)
- when there is a gap in time in the story.
  (*Two weeks later the issue was raised again in cabinet....*)

O *In Description:*

- whenever you switch from describing one place, person, or thing to describing another.
  (*Even such a brief description as this is enough to give some sense of the city and its pretensions. Much more interesting in many ways are some of British Columbia's smaller cities and towns....*)

O *In Persuasion or Argument:*

- when a new topic is introduced.
  (*There can be little doubt that Austen's asides on the literary conventions of her time provide an amusing counterpoint to her story. But does this running commentary detract from the primary imaginative experience of* Northanger Abbey?)

- when there is a change in direction of the argument.
  (*To this point we have been looking only at the advantages of a guaranteed annual income. We should also ask, however, whether or not it would be practical to implement.*)

Description, narration, and argument are commonly blended together in writing, and it is usually also advisable to start a new paragraph when changing from one mode to another. If, for example, a text moves from describing an experiment to analysing its significance, it's a good time to start a new paragraph. If it moves from telling where Napoleon went and what he did to discussing why events unravelled in this way, the same holds true.

There are many ways of putting ideas together. Much of this chapter is concerned with the particulars of joining words and how to use them. It may be useful, however, to begin with a look at some of the mental processes involved in putting ideas together into strong and coherent arguments.

⊙ Argument

It is widely accepted that problems with writing are often closely intertwined with a lack of training in thinking critically; for that reason coverage of some basic concepts in critical thinking is included here. Of course thousands of books have been written on critical thinking and logical argument—and on the subtleties of logical argument in English. In a book of this sort it is not possible to do more than touch on a few key distinctions.

deductive/inductive: The conclusion of a deductive argument is based on its premises, and the conclusion must follow logically from the premises if the argument is sound. The classic examples of deductive arguments are syllogisms—logical structures in which a conclusion is drawn from two premises. Here is an example:

- A successful baseball team must have good starting pitchers to succeed. This year's White Sox team does not have good starting pitching. Therefore, this year's White Sox team will not be successful.

Note that the reasoning of a deductive argument may be sound even if one of its premises is false. For example, the above syllogism makes a valid argument in terms of its reasoning regardless of whether or not it is in fact true that to be successful a team must have good starting pitching.

Inductive arguments, on the other hand, rest on factual evidence; typically they generalize from a particular number or percentage to a general conclusion. Here is an example:

- Since the creation of the National League, every World Series winner has had at least three outstanding starting pitchers on its roster. It seems reasonable to conclude from this that a team with fewer than three outstanding starting pitchers has an extremely slight chance of winning the World Series.

From this observation it seems safe to generalize that a team needs outstanding starting pitchers if it is to succeed. Notice that inductive arguments are based on numbers, percentages, and estimates of probabilities.

In practice, arguments very frequently combine inductive and deductive elements. Here is another example:

- Almost no one ever dies from this sort of operation. If Frank dies during the operation, then it must be as a result of malpractice on the part of the surgeons. We should sue!

The initial claim here involves an inductive claim. It can only be settled by reference to the facts:

- What percentage of people have in fact died during this sort of operation?

The follow-up claim represents a deductive argument, and can be addressed by reasoning, without reference to the facts of the case:

- If it is indeed true that others have not died during this sort of operation, then what are the possible explanations? Is it in fact true that the *only* possible explanation is medical malpractice?

C2. **some/all**: It is particularly important in sorting out both inductive and deductive arguments to be sensitive to the difference between *some* and *all*. This may seem an obvious point, but it is one that it is easy to lose in the twists and turns of an argument—or indeed in making off-hand observations about things that seem self-evident:

- "I don't know about that job candidate. We've hired people from that school before and, to be honest, they really haven't worked out. Let's look again at the other candidates."

The implicit assumption here is of course that since *some* graduates of a particular school have not worked out, it follows that *all* graduates of the same school will not work out at this particular sort of job.

The distinction between *some* and *all* should also be kept in mind when it comes to arguments with several interconnected strands. Does what one is saying apply to all the facts of the argument, or only to some of them? Here is an example:

- What on earth is wrong with *spinster*, *chairman*, *mankind*, or, for that matter, adjectives such as *blind* and *deaf*, to name just a few? These are perfectly legitimate and serviceable terms, yet an arbitrary, malevolent connotation has been assigned them. In their place we are asked to draw from a silly artificial glossary of convoluted euphemisms to describe people and events, a glossary replete with all manner of adverbs with the word *challenged* suffixed leech-like to them.

The writer here is arguing against bias-free language. The core of the argument is that the new terms we are asked to use are silly, artificial, and convoluted. That may well be true of a term such as *mentally challenged*. But notice how difficult it is to make such claims stick with all or even most of the examples here. The non-sexist alternatives for *chairman* and *mankind*—*chair, humanity*, and the like—are hardly silly, artificial, or convoluted. And are we in fact asked to replace the word *deaf* with *aurally-challenged*? Not at all. Those working in the field do indeed use *aurally-challenged* as a blanket term to refer to all those who have any hearing impairment, ranging from mild loss of hearing to complete deafness, but they do not shy away from using terms such as *deaf* and *partially deaf.* In short, the objection raised by this writer to "politically correct" language in general turns out to apply only to a very few instances.

C3. **if/then**: The *if ... then* syntactical structure is a basic form of both deductive and inductive arguments. It may be helpful here to look out for *necessary* and *sufficient* conditions; these are discussed above under the section on "Cause and Effect" (p. 42).

C4. **trends**: In matters of any complexity involving numbers and trends, it is easy to lose sight of the big picture—and many verbal arguments are constructed in a way that encourages those listening to the arguments to lose sight of the big picture. Here is an example:

- Even many of those who support the proposed global warming treaty say that it will cost jobs in industries ranging from oil and gas to mining to automobile manufacturing—perhaps hundreds of thousands of jobs. We cannot afford to let our economy shrink; it is essential that we oppose ratification of this treaty.

An unstated premise in this argument is that if jobs are lost in the stated sectors, the economy shrinks. But no estimate is given of the number of jobs that would in this sort of situation be created (in industries such as solar and wind power) or jobs that would be saved (for example at ski resorts) if strong action were taken against global warming. Some have suggested that the economy in general would grow just as fast if such action were taken. Others have estimated it would grow more slowly, but few have suggested it would actually shrink. Here, as in many other cases, it is important to be aware of distinctions between a decline, a decline in the rate of increase, and so on.

C5. **relevance**: It is often much more difficult than one would think to judge what is relevant or irrelevant to a given argument. Here is an example:

- I don't agree with the arguments of the animal rights activists. Before we worry about any troubles the animals might have, we should take care of the problems that people have.

The argument here may seem at first glance quite powerful, but in fact the claims being made are entirely irrelevant to all but one of the arguments put forward by animal rights activists. The argument here says nothing as to the inductive claims made by these activists about the prevalence of cruelty to animals in factory farming, for example, and nor does it address the argument from first principles that it is wrong to cause unnecessary pain to other creatures. The only argument that it does address is the claim that we should pay *some* attention to the plight of animals even while we are also attempting to address human problems. There are no doubt legitimate arguments of a variety of sorts to be made concerning the priority we should give to the plight of animals in relation to that of humans who are suffering. But that is not the question this argument purports to be addressing.

O *Fallacies*

A fallacious argument is one that suffers from faulty reasoning. Many forms of faulty reasoning have been identified; following is a list of some of the most common forms of fallacy.

C6. **ad hominem**: The Latin *ad hominem* means *directed at the person*; an attempt to persuade through ad hominem comments entails attacking the person making the claim rather than attacking the claim itself. In both the following examples the pieces of information supplied may be of interest, but do not constitute arguments:

- What George W. Bush says about energy policy makes no sense at all. Remember, he made a fortune in the oil industry.

- Any arguments John McCain makes about the beer industry cannot be taken seriously; he is married to a beer distributor heir.

C7. **straw man argument**: A common practice in argument is to ascribe to one's opponent an extreme view that in fact one's opponent has never put forward, and then suggest that in knocking down the extreme "straw man" argument you have won. Here are two examples:

- I fully support capital punishment. How can anyone claim that the life of a convicted murderer is as valuable as the life of the innocent person he has killed?

- I oppose capital punishment. How can anyone claim that there is no chance of a criminal reforming, and no intrinsic value in human life itself?

Of course, neither the opponents nor the supporters of capital punishment make the suggested claims—but often people are able to get away with this sort of sleight of hand in the midst of an argument.

C8. **begging the question**: *To beg the question* is *to avoid the question by taking for granted the very thing to be argued about.* Here is an example:

- The situation in Afghanistan remains turbulent, and in this context it is vital that we support good government. Clearly we have an obligation to support the present Afghan government; the only question is how this should best be done.

By moving straight to a conclusion that we are obliged to support the present government, the arguer here avoids (or *begs*) the question of whether or not the current government of Afghanistan is indeed providing good government. (For the common misunderstanding of *beg the question* to mean *raise the question*, see above, page 214.)

C9. **formally invalid arguments**: If the formal structure of one's argument is not sound, then the argument is fallacious.

Two common forms of formally invalid arguments are those which *deny the antecedent*, and those which *affirm the consequent*. Here is an example of the former:

- If water starts dripping from this ceiling during a rainstorm, then you can be sure there is a problem with your roof. No water has dripped from the ceiling during a rainstorm. Therefore, there is no problem with the roof.

In this case it is certainly true that water dripping from the ceiling is a reliable sign of there being some problem with the roof. But of course there can be a problem with the roof even without there being such a visible sign; very frequently, roof leaks result in water saturating rafters and seeping down inside walls without there being any drips from the ceiling. (Like so many elements of reasoning, the ability to recognize this fallacy connects to the ability to be sensitive to the distinction between *some* and *all*; some roof leaks result in dripping ceilings, but others don't.) The *if ...* part of an argument such as this is known as the *antecedent*. And, as the example shows, denying the antecedent has no argumentative force.

- If a lake is very seriously affected by acid rain, no fish can survive in it. This lake has no fish living in it whatsoever. This lake must be seriously affected by acid rain.

It is entirely true that lakes seriously affected by acid rain cannot support any aquatic life. But that is not the only possible cause for the disappearance of aquatic life from a lake. If, for example, a company had been using the lake as a toxic waste dump, that would also have the effect of killing all the fish. (Again, the distinction between *some* and *all* is crucial; some lifeless lakes got that way because of acid rain, but not all). The *then ...* part of an argument is called the *consequent*. As the example shows, affirming the consequent does nothing to prove the argument.

C10. **slippery slope arguments:** The fallacy of the slippery slope argument is the suggestion that one development in a certain direction will inevitably lead to further developments in the same direction or *down the same slope*. Here is an example:

> The idea of people being required to carry identity cards may seem innocuous enough, but in fact it should be resolutely opposed. If we allow the government to force us to carry identity cards, pretty soon they'll be keeping track of all our movements with video cameras, and placing all sorts of restrictions on our privacy. We have to stop these government intrusions into our lives!

This argument says nothing about the issue of identity cards per se. It is entirely based on the premise of one move by the government being followed by other, more drastic moves. Sometimes, of course, developments are part of long-term trends, but sometimes they are not part of any trend—or may represent the furthest extent of a particular trend. Certainly there is no inevitability about any particular move in one direction being followed by subsequent moves in the same direction.

C11. **false dichotomy**: A *dichotomy* occurs when *things or ideas are split into two distinct alternatives.* An argument that tries to insist on two and only two alternatives when in fact three or more possibilities exist (or gradations among possibilities exist) is one that poses a false dichotomy. Here is an example:

A.   There should be laws prohibiting people from inciting hate against those of other races or religions.

B.   So you're against freedom of speech? Without freedom of speech we wouldn't have a democracy!

A.   No, I support freedom of speech—but with certain limits to prevent the most harmful extreme views from being promulgated. It sounds to me as if you are not willing to do anything to combat bigotry and racism.

B.   Not at all. But I believe that people speaking out freely against freely expressed bigoted or racist opinions will combat them more effectively than government attempts to prohibit them.

In this case both arguers pose false dichotomies in their characterizations of the other's viewpoint—whereas in fact both hold nuanced views.

C12. **missing or unacknowledged premises**: Many real-life arguments take shortcuts and do not spell out all the underlying premises. In many cases this does not in fact damage the argument, but sometimes a missing or unacknowledged premise is the key to a fatal weakness in an argument. Here is an example:

- Many have suggested that the presence of extreme poverty and oppression in the world makes it more likely that terrorism will take root. But that just doesn't square with the facts; the vast majority of the September 11th terrorists and the Al

Qaeda leadership did not come from backgrounds of extreme hardship. Some, including Osama bin Laden, were among the most privileged members of Saudi Arabian society.

The missing or unacknowledged premise in this argument is that people will always struggle only on behalf of those from their own nationality or social class. In fact, however, history is filled with examples of individuals from one nation or social class who became so involved with the plight of another that they devoted all their energies to fighting for change.

An example like this illustrates just how readily our perceptions of argument are influenced by emotion and ideology. In this case, an entirely appropriate sense of anger and revulsion at the terrorist acts makes it difficult for us to imagine that the terrorists might consider themselves as acting altruistically on behalf of the poor and the oppressed. And maybe most of them do not in fact think of themselves in this way. The only point here is that the fact of someone coming from a privileged background does not in itself preclude the possibility that such a person will act in a way he or she perceives as benefiting the less privileged.

C13. **post hoc, propter hoc:** The fallacy here is to imagine that if one thing happens after the other, then it will have happened because of the other. (The Latin *post hoc, propter hoc* translates as *after this, because of this*). Here is an example:

- The decline of frog populations throughout the world started to happen just after the thinning of the ozone layer; there has to be a connection!

But there doesn't have to be a connection—as becomes plain if we substitute a different event in the same logical structure:

- The decline of frog populations throughout the world started to happen just after the Montreal Canadiens stopped winning the Stanley Cup with any degree of frequency; there has to be a connection!

In the first case damage from ultraviolet radiation is indeed one possible cause for the decline of frog populations—but scientists are still weighing the evidence, and are far from certain if it is one of several contributing causes, the primary cause, or simply an unrelated event. (For more on this sort of problem in reasoning, see page 42 above).

⊙ Joining Words

The art of combining correct clauses and sentences logically and coherently is as much dependent on taking the time to think through what we are writing—and how the reader will respond to what we write—as it is on knowledge of correct usage. It is all too easy for most of us to assume that the flow of our thoughts will be as clear to the reader as it is to us. In practical terms this leads to the omission of links in the argument or of joining words that help the reader to see those links. Almost as common is the tendency to give too many or contradictory cues to the reader—a tendency that is often an indication that ideas have not yet been thoroughly thought out. That in itself is nothing to be ashamed of; the key is to be willing to take the time to re-read and revise the work. Every good writer makes at least two and sometimes as many as five or six drafts of any piece of writing before considering it finished. Here are two examples, both taken from early drafts of books published by Broadview Press:

- At the end of World War II there was substantial optimism that the application of Keynesian analysis would lead to economic stability and security. Over the post-war period optimistic rationalism weakened in the face of reality.

- A short report in which you request an increase in your department's budget should be written in the persuasive mode. Most reports, however, do not have persuasion as their main objective. Persuasion, though, will often be one of their secondary objectives.

C14. **too few cues** (see also "Non Sequitur"): The first of these passages gives the reader too few cues. What is the connection between the idea of the first sentence and that of the second? One can figure it out without too much difficulty, but the flow of the argument is briefly interrupted while one does so. The problem is easily solved by the addition of one word to the second sentence:

> *revised*   At the end of World War II there was substantial optimism that the application of Keynesian analysis would lead to economic stability and security. Over the postwar period, however, optimistic rationalism weakened in the face of reality.

C15. **too many or contradictory cues**: The second passage suffers from the opposite problem; the use of *however* and *though* in consecutive sentences gives the reader the sense of twisting back on himself without any clear sense of direction. This sort of difficulty can be removed by rewording or rearranging the ideas:

> *revised*   A short report in which you request an increase in your department's budget should be written in the persuasive mode. Most reports, however, do not have persuasion as their main objective. Persuasion will thus be at most a secondary objective.

The following pages list the chief words and expressions used in English to join ideas together, and discuss problems that are often experienced with them.

O *Words to Connect Ideas Opposed to Each Other*

All these words are used to indicate that the writer is saying two things which seem to go against each other, or are different from each other. For example, in the sentence, *He is very rich, but he is not very happy,* the fact that he is not happy is the reverse of what we might expect of a rich man. The word *but* indicates this opposition of ideas to the reader.

although	nevertheless
but	though
despite	whereas
even if	while
however	yet
in spite of	

● *Although*

This word indicates that in the same sentence two things that seem to go against each other are being said. *Although* is usually used to introduce subordinate clauses, not phrases.

- Although he has short legs, he can run very quickly.
- Hume and Dr. Johnson, indeed, have a good deal in common, although Hume's attitude towards religion earned him Johnson's scorn.

C16. **although/but**: Be careful not to use both *although* and *but* in the same sentence; one is enough:

needs checking	Although in many African countries the government is not elected by the people, but in Botswana the government is democratically elected.
revised	Although in many African countries the government is not elected by the people, in Botswana the government is democratically elected.
or	In most African countries the government is not elected by the people, but in Botswana the government is democratically elected.

● *But*

This word is usually used in the middle of a sentence to show that the two ideas in the sentence oppose or seem to oppose each other. It is also quite correct, however, to use *but* at the beginning of a sentence, if what one is saying in the sentence forms a complete clause and if the idea of the sentence seems to oppose the idea of the previous sentence. Examples:

- The civilization of ancient Greece produced some of the world's greatest works of art and gave birth to the idea of democracy, but the Greeks also believed in slavery.

- The civilization of Greece produced some of the world's greatest works of art and gave birth to the idea of democracy. But the Greeks also believed in slavery.

C17. **opposing or supporting ideas**: When one is dealing with complex combinations of ideas it is sometimes easy to forget which ideas are in fact in opposition and which in support.

needs checking   Brandy and bourbon, with the most "congenors," have the highest hangover ratings. Red wine is a close second, followed by dark rum, sherry, scotch, rye, beer, white wine, gin, and vodka. Vintage red wines have 15 times as much histamine (it triggers allergic reactions) as white wine, but vintage whites have fewer congenors.

    (The use of *but* is inappropriate here; that whites have both less histamine and fewer congenors is as one would expect; the two facts are both instances of white wines having fewer side effects than reds.)

revised   Brandy and bourbon, with the most "congenors," have the highest hangover ratings. Red wine is a close second, followed by dark rum, sherry, scotch, rye, beer, white wine, gin, and vodka. Vintage red wines also have 15 times as much histamine (it triggers allergic reactions) as white wine does.

C18. **but**: Experienced writers are careful not to use *but* more than once in a single sentence, or in consecutive sentences; they realize that doing so tends to confuse the reader. (It is also unwise to use any combination of *but* and *however* in this way.)

needs checking	Chief Constable Smith said that Ryan had been legally in possession of three handguns and two rifles, but he thought it "incredible" that some-one should be allowed to keep ammunition at his home. But he said any change in the firearms law was something which would not be discussed by him.
revised ·	Chief Constable Smith said that Ryan had been legally in possession of three handguns and two rifles. Smith said he thought it "incredible" that someone should be allowed to keep ammunition at his home, but he would not comment directly on whether there should be a change in the fire-arms law.

● *Despite*

This word means the same as *although*, but it is used to introduce phrases, not clauses.

- Despite his old age, his mind is active and alert.
  (*Despite his old age* is a phrase; it has no verb.)
- Although he is very old, his mind is active and alert.
  (*Although he is very old* is a clause, with *he* as a subject and *is* as a verb.)
- Despite the rain, she wanted to go out to the park.
- Although it was raining, she wanted to go to the park.

C19. **despite:** Remember not to introduce clauses with *despite*.

needs checking	Despite that the drink tasted very strong, there was very little alcohol in it.
revised	Despite its strong taste, there was very little alcohol in the drink.

or   Although the drink tasted very strong, there was
                        very little alcohol in it.

● *Even if*

This expression is used when one is introducing a clause giving a
condition. The word *even* emphasizes that the condition is surprising or unusual. Examples:

- Even if I have to stay up all night, I am determined to finish
  the job.
  (Staying up all night would be very unusual.)
- Even if Bangladesh doubled its food production, some of its
  people would still be hungry.
  (Doubling its food production would be very surprising.)

● *However*

When used as a joining word, *however* shows that what one is saying seems to go against what one has said in the previous sentence.
It should normally be set off by commas when used in this way:

- The country suffered greatly during the three-year drought.
  This year, however, the rains have been heavy.

C20. **however:** *However* should not be used to combine ideas
within one sentence, unless a semicolon is used.

needs checking   Hitler attempted to conquer the Soviet Union
                      however he was defeated.

revised   Hitler attempted to conquer the Soviet Union;
                      however, he was defeated.

or   Hitler attempted to conquer the Soviet Union.
                      However, he was defeated.

or   Hitler attempted to conquer the Soviet Union
                      but he was defeated.

needs checking	There will not be regular mail pick-up from boxes this Friday, however regular mail pick-up will resume Saturday.
revised	There will not be regular mail pick-up from boxes this Friday, but regular mail pick-up will resume Saturday.
or	There will not be regular mail pick-up from boxes this Friday. However, regular mail pick-up will resume Saturday.

(Note that *however* in the sense of *to whatever extent* is an adverb, and does not need to be set off by commas. *However tired we are, we must finish the job tonight.*)

● *Nevertheless*

C21. Like *however*, *nevertheless* is normally used to show that the idea of one sentence seems to go against the idea of the previous sentence. It should not be used to join two clauses into one sentence. Example:

- According to the known laws of physics it is not possible to walk on water. Nevertheless, this is what the Bible claims Jesus did.

On the Web
Exercises on joining words may be found at
www.broadviewpress.com/writing.
Click on **Exercises** and go to **C14–46**.

● *Whereas*

This word is commonly used when one is comparing two things and showing how they differ. Like *although*, it must begin a subordinate clause, and may be used either at the beginning or in the middle of a sentence. Examples:

- Whereas Americans are usually thought of as being loud and confident, Canadians tend to be more quiet and less sure of themselves.

- Americans are usually thought of as being loud and confident, whereas Canadians tend to be more quiet and less sure of themselves.

C22. **whereas**: Any sentence that uses *whereas* must have at least two clauses—a subordinate clause beginning with *whereas* and a main clause.

needs checking	In "The Rain Horse" a young person feels unhappy when he returns to his old home. Whereas in "The Ice Palace" a young person feels unhappy when she leaves home for the first time.
revised	In "The Rain Horse" a young person feels unhappy when he returns to his old home, whereas in "The Ice Palace" a young person feels unhappy when she leaves home for the first time.

● *While*

C23. **while**: *While* can be used in the same way as *although*. If there is any chance of confusion with the other meanings of *while*, however, it is better to use *although* in such circumstances.

needs checking	While I support free trade in principle, I think it hurts this industry.
revised	Although I support free trade in principle, I think it hurts this industry.

● *Yet*

This word can be used either to refer to time (e.g., *He is not yet here*), or to connect ideas in opposition to each other. When used in this second way, it may introduce another word or a phrase, or a completely new sentence.

- His spear was firm, yet flexible.

- Barthes decries the language of "realism"—the pretense that one can represent on the page life as it really is. Yet it is difficult to see how following his prescriptions for an art of signs that "draw attention to their own arbitrariness" can entirely escape a tendency towards art that calls too much attention to its own surface, even art that is self-indulgent.

C24. **yet:** *Yet*, like the other words in this group, should not be paired with another conjunction in such a way as to create too many twists and turns in the argument.

needs checking	Varying the pace, altering the tone, director Joseph Rubens keeps us off balance. Ultimately, though, the pedestrian script catches up with him, yet not before *Sleeping with the Enemy* has made its point.
	(The combination of *yet* and *though* is confusing for the reader.)
revised	Varying the pace, altering the tone, director Joseph Rubens keeps us off balance. Ultimately, the pedestrian script catches up with him, yet not before *Sleeping with the Enemy* has made its point.

O *Words to Join Linked or Supporting Ideas*

also	indeed
and	in fact
as well	moreover
further	similarly
furthermore	: [colon]
in addition	; [semicolon]
not only ... but also	

● *Also, as well*

These two are very similar both in meaning and in the way that they are used. It is best not to use *also* to start sentences or paragraphs. Examples:

- He put forward his simplistic credo with enormous conviction. "To do well at school," he assured us, "you must be willing to study. It is also important to eat the right foods, exercise regularly, and get plenty of sleep." All the while, the one thing we all wanted, and none of us had managed to get, was plenty of sex.

- He put forward his simplistic credo with enormous conviction. "To do well at school," he assured us, "you must be willing to study. It is important as well to eat the right foods, exercise regularly, and get plenty of sleep." All the while, the one thing we all wanted, and none of us had managed to get, was plenty of sex.

C25. **also:** *Also* should not be used in the way that we often use *and*—to join two clauses together into one sentence.

needs checking	We performed the experiment with the beaker half full also we repeated it with the beaker empty.
revised	We performed the experiment with the beaker half full, and we repeated it with the beaker empty.
or	We performed the experiment with the beaker half full. We also repeated it with the beaker empty.

● *And*

C26. **and:** If this word appears more than once in the same sentence, it's worth stopping to ask if it would not be better to start a new sentence. Usually the answer will be yes.

needs checking	All my family attended the celebration and most of my friends were there and we enjoyed ourselves thoroughly.
revised	All my family attended the celebration, and most of my friends were there, too. We enjoyed ourselves thoroughly.

C27. **as ... as**: When making comparisons one may use the *as ... as* combination or use a comparative adjective with *than*. But the two should not be combined.

needs checking	Recent studies indicate that the average smoker is three times as likely to develop cancer than his non-smoking counterpart.
revised	Recent studies indicate that the average smoker is three times more likely to develop cancer than is his non-smoking counterpart.

C28. **as well**: To avoid repetition, do not use *as well* in combination with *both*.

needs checking	This method should be rejected, both because it is very expensive as well as because it is inefficient.
revised	This method should be rejected, both because it is very expensive and because it is inefficient.

● *In addition*, *further*, *furthermore*, *moreover*

All of these are commonly used to show that what the writer is saying gives additional support to an earlier statement she has made. An example:

- It was easy to see why many countries, despite their intense dislike of apartheid, still traded with South Africa. For one thing, it was the richest country in Africa. Many of its resources, moreover, were of strategic importance.

Notice that all four expressions are often used after sentences that begin with words such as *for one thing* or *first*.

● *Indeed, in fact*

Both of these are used to indicate that what the writer is saying is a restatement or elaboration of the idea he has expressed in the previous sentence. Notice that a colon or semicolon may also be used to show this. Examples:

- Asia is the world's most populous continent. In fact, more people live there than in all the other continents combined.
- Asia is the world's most populous continent: more people live there than in all the other continents combined.

● *Not only ... but also*

C29. **not only ... but also**: This combination is used to join two pieces of supporting evidence in an argument. The combination can help to create balanced, rhythmic writing, but if it is to do so it must be used carefully. Notice that it is not necessary to use *but also* in all cases, but that if the phrase is omitted a semicolon is normally required in order to avoid a run-on sentence.

needs checking	Not only was Nirvana a commercial success, it was also among the first grunge bands to achieve musical respectability.
revised	Not only was Nirvana a commercial success; it was also among the first grunge bands to achieve musical respectability.
or	Nirvana was not only a commercial success, but also a critical one; it was among the first grunge bands to achieve musical respectability.

● *Plus*

C30. **plus**: Do not use this word in the same way as *and* or *as well*.

needs checking	For one thing, the council did not much like the design for the proposed new City Hall. Plus, there was not enough money available to build it that year.
revised	For one thing, the council did not much like the design for the proposed new City Hall. As well, there was not enough money available to build it that year.

O *Words Used to Introduce Causes or Reasons*

Relationships of cause and effect are at the heart of many arguments. It is common to experience some difficulty at first in understanding such relationships clearly. The discussion below of the word *because* may be helpful in this respect. To begin with, though, here is a list of words that are used to introduce causes or reasons:

> as
> for
> as a result of
> on account of
> because
> since
> due to

● *As*

This word can be used either to show the relationship between two events in time, or to indicate that one event is the cause of another. This sometimes leaves room for confusion about meaning (ambiguity). The following sentence is a good example:

- As he was riding on the wrong side of the road, he was hit by a car.

This can mean either *When he was riding on the wrong side of the road ...* or *Because he was riding on the wrong side of the road ....*

Unless the writer is absolutely certain that the meaning is clear, it may be better to use *while* or *when* instead of *as* to indicate relationships in time, and *because* instead of *as* to indicate relationships of cause and effect.

● *Because*

This word creates many problems for writers. The first thing to remember is that any group of words introduced with *because* must state a cause or reason. It must not state a result or an example.

C31. **because**: In the following sentences, *because* has been wrongly used:

needs checking	The wind was blowing because the leaves were moving to and fro.
needs checking	He had been struck by a car because he lay bleeding in the road.

A moment's reflection leads to the realization that both of these sentences are the wrong way round. The movement of the leaves is the result of the blowing of the wind, and the man's bleeding is the result of his having been hit. When the sentences are turned around, they become correct:

revised	The leaves were moving to and fro because the wind was blowing.
revised	He lay bleeding on the road because he had been struck by a car.

What leads many people to make mistakes like these is the sort of question that begins, *How do you know that...* or *Prove that...* or *Show that....* The person who is asked, "How do you know that the wind is blowing?" is likely to answer wrongly, "The wind is blowing because the leaves are moving to and fro." What he really means is, "I know the wind is blowing because I see the leaves moving to and fro." That answer is quite correct, since here the seeing is the cause of the knowing. Similarly, someone who is asked to show that the man in a newspaper story had been hit by a car might answer wrongly, "He had been struck by a car because he lay bleeding in the road." What he really means is, "I know that he had been struck by a car because I read that he lay bleeding in the road." It is of course awkward to use a lot of phrases such as *I know that* and *I see that*. Here are some easier and better ways of answering such questions:

- The movement of the trees shows that the wind is blowing.
- The fact that the leaves are moving proves that the wind is blowing.
- Since the man lay bleeding in the road, it seems likely that he had been hit by a car.

C32. **because**: *Because* is also often used incorrectly to introduce examples.

Look carefully at the following sentences:

needs checking   The Suharto regime detained people in jail for long periods without ever bringing them to trial because it had little respect for the law.

needs checking   In the story "The Hero," Dora feels sorry for Julius because she sheds tears when he is expelled from school.

In these sentences the source of confusion might not be immediately clear. If we ask ourselves whether the regime's actions caused it to have little respect for the law, however, we realize that the answer is no. Are Dora's tears a cause of her feeling sorry for Julius? Again, no. It might be a result of her feeling sorry, or an example chosen to show that she feels sorry, but it is certainly not a cause. Again, it is possible to correct these sentences as we did the ones above—by reversing the order of the ideas. But this might not always be an appropriate solution to the problem, particularly if what the writer is trying to show is an example or an illustration rather than a relationship of cause and effect. If, for example, one had been asked, "How do you know that Dora feels sorry for Julius?" or told to "Show that the Suharto regime had little respect for the law," one would not normally want to answer using *because*. Here are various ways of dealing with such difficulties:

- Dora feels sorry for Julius when he is expelled; that is made clear when she sheds tears for him.
- It is clear that Dora feels sorry for Julius, since she sheds tears for him.
- We can see from the fact that Dora sheds tears for Julius that she feels sorry for him.
- The fact that the Suharto regime in Indonesia detained people for long periods without ever bringing them to trial shows that it had little respect for the law.
- The Suharto regime in Indonesia showed little respect for the law. It detained people for long periods, for example, without ever bringing them to trial.
- The Suharto regime in Indonesia had little respect for the law; it detained people for long periods without ever bringing them to trial.

Of all these examples the last is perhaps the best, since it is the most succinct.

C33. **because**: It is best not to use *because* when listing several reasons for something; otherwise the writer gives the reader the impression that the first reason given is to be the only reason. The reader will then be surprised when others are mentioned.

needs checking   He was happy because it was Friday. He was also happy because his team had won the game that morning and he had scored the winning goal. Finally, he was happy because he had done well on his exams.

revised	He was happy for several reasons: it was Friday, he had scored the winning goal for his team that morning, and he had done well on his exams.
needs checking	Frederick was able to enjoy such success because he was adroit at waiting for the right opportunity, and seizing it when it was handed him. He was also successful because he created a military machine that had no equal.
revised	One reason Frederick was able to enjoy such success was that he was adroit at waiting for the right opportunity, and seizing it when it was handed him. But none of this would have been possible had he not also created a military machine that had no equal.

C34. **because**: Some people like to answer *How ...?* questions by using *because*. Instead, the word *by* should be used.

needs checking	How did she help him? She helped him because she lent him some money.
revised	How did she help him? She helped him by lending him some money.

● *Due to*

C35. **due to**: *Due* is an adjective and therefore should always modify a noun (as in the common phrase *with all due respect*). When followed by *to* it can suggest a causal relationship, but the word *due* must in that case refer to the previous noun:

- The team's success is due to hard work.
  (*Due* refers to the noun *success*.)

It is not a good idea to begin a sentence with a phrase such as *Due to unexpected circumstances* ... or *Due to the fact that*.... To avoid such difficulties it is best to use *because*.

needs checking   Due to the sudden resignation of our sales manager, the marketing director will take on additional responsibility for a short time.

revised   Because our sales manager has resigned suddenly, the marketing director will take on additional responsibility for a short time.

● *Since*

When used to introduce causes or reasons (rather than as a time word) *since* is used in essentially the same way as *because*.

○ *Words Used to Introduce Results or Conclusions*

as a result	therefore
consequently	thus
hence	to sum up
in conclusion	in consequence
it follows that ...	so

● *As a result, hence*

Both of these are used to show that the idea being talked about in one sentence follows from, or is the result of, what was spoken of in the previous sentence.

- His car ran out of gas. As a result, he was late for his appointment.
- His car ran out of gas. Hence, he was late for his appointment.

Notice the difference between these two and words such as *because* and *since*; we would say *Because* (or *since*) *his car ran out of gas, he was late for the appointment.*

C36. **hence**: Hence should not be used to join two clauses into one sentence, or to join words or phrases.

needs checking	Her phone is out of order hence it will be impossible to contact her.
revised	Her phone is out of order. Hence, it will be impossible to contact her.
needs checking	It is not the film but the advertising that is exploitative, hence pornographic.
revised	It is not the film but the advertising that is exploitative, and hence pornographic.

● *So*

This word may be used to introduce results when one wants to mention both cause and result in the same sentence (e.g., *Her phone is out of order, so it will be impossible to contact her*). It is usually best not to use *so* to begin a sentence, in order to avoid writing sentence fragments.

C37. **so**: If *so* is used, *because* is not needed, and vice versa. One of the two is enough.

needs checking	Because he was tired, so he went to bed early.
revised	Because he was tired, he went to bed early.
or	He was tired, so he went to bed early.

● *Therefore*

C38. **therefore**: *Therefore* should not be used to join two clauses into one sentence.

needs checking	Training is perceived as good, therefore the payment of a $30 million subsidy to McDonalds can be made to look like a benign act.
revised	Training is perceived as good; therefore the payment of a $30 million subsidy to McDonalds can be made to look like a benign act.

○ *Words Used to Express Purpose*

in order to	so that
in such a way as to	so as to

● *So that*

C39. **so that**: When used beside each other (see also *so ... that* below) these two words show purpose; they indicate that we will be told why an action was taken. Examples:

- He sent the parcel early so that it would arrive before Christmas.
- She wants to see you so that she can ask you a question.

The words *such that* should never be used in this way to indicate purpose.

needs checking	The doctor will give you some medicine such that you will be cured.
revised	The doctor will give you some medicine so that you will be cured.
needs checking	Fold the paper such that it forms a triangle.
revised	Fold the paper so that it forms a triangle.
or	Fold the paper in such a way that it forms a triangle.

○ *Words Used to Introduce Examples*

for example	such as
for instance	: [colon]
in that	

● *For example, for instance, such as*

The three expressions are used differently, even though they all introduce examples. *Such as* is used to introduce a single word or short phrase. It always relates to a plural noun that has appeared just before it.

- Crops such as tea and rice require a great deal of water.
  (Here *such as* relates to the noun *crops*.)
- Several African peoples, such as the Yoruba of Nigeria and the Makonde of Tanzania, attach a special ceremonial importance to masks.
  (*Such as* relates to *peoples*.)

For example and *for instance*, on the other hand, are complete phrases in themselves, and are normally set off by commas. Each is used to show that the entire sentence in which it appears gives an example of a statement made in the previous sentence. Examples:

- Some crops require a great deal of water. Tea, for example, requires an annual rainfall of at least 1500 mm.
- Several African peoples attach a special ceremonial importance to masks. The Yoruba and the Makonde, for example, both believe that spirits enter the bodies of those who wear certain masks.
- Tornadoes are not only a Deep South phenomenon. In 1987, for instance, more than 20 people were killed by a tornado in Edmonton, Alberta.

C40. **for example, for instance:** *For example* and *for instance* should not be used to introduce phrases that give examples. In such situations use *such as* instead.

needs checking	In certain months of the year, for example July and August, Penticton receives very little rainfall.
revised	In certain months of the year, such as July and August, Penticton receives very little rainfall.
or	In certain months of the year Penticton receives very little rainfall. July and August, for example, are almost always extremely dry.

● *In that*

C41. **in that:** Do not confuse with *in the way that*.

needs checking	He is cruel in the way that he treats his wife harshly.

revised	He is cruel in that he treats his wife harshly.
or	He is cruel in the way that he treats his wife.

● *Such as*

C42. **such as:** The addition of *and others* at the end of a phrase beginning with *such as* is redundant.

needs checking	In contrast to this perspective, sociological studies of ethnicity written from the "class" perspective (such as Bollaria and Li's 2008 paper, Chan's 1999 monograph, and others) have argued that ethnic inequality is only a special class of inequality in general.
revised	In contrast to this perspective, sociological studies of ethnicity written from the "class" perspective (such as Bollaria and Li's 2008 paper, and Chan's 1999 monograph) have argued that ethnic inequality is only a special class of inequality in general.

○ *Words Used to Indicate Alternatives*

either ... or	otherwise
if only	rather than
instead, instead of	unless
in that case	whether ... or
neither ... nor	

● *If only*

This expression is normally used when we wish that something would happen, or were true, but it clearly will not happen, or is not true.

- If only he were here, he would know what to do.
  (This indicates that he is not here.)
- "If only there were thirty hours in a day ...," she kept saying.

● *In that case*

This expression is used when we wish to explain what will happen if the thing spoken of in the previous sentence happens, or turns out to be true. Examples:

- He may arrive before six o'clock. In that case we can all go out to dinner.
- It is quite possible that many people will dislike the new law. In that case the government may decide to change it.

Do not confuse *in that case* with *otherwise*, which is used in the reverse situation (i.e., when one wishes to explain what will happen if the thing spoken of in the previous sentence does not happen, or turns out to be false).

● *Otherwise*

This word has two meanings. The first is *in other ways* (e.g., *I have a slight toothache. Otherwise I am healthy*). The second meaning can sometimes cause confusion: *otherwise* used to mean *if not*. Here the word is used when we want to talk about what will or might happen if the thing spoken of in the previous sentence does not happen. Examples:

- I will have to start immediately. Otherwise, I will not finish in time.
  (This is the same as saying, *If I do not start now, I will not finish in time.*)
- The general decided to retreat. Otherwise, he believed, all his troops would be killed.
  (This is the same as saying, *The general believed that if he decided not to retreat, all his troops would be killed.*)
- You must pay me for the car before Friday. Otherwise, I will offer it to someone else.
  (i.e., *If you do not pay me for the car before Friday, I will offer it to someone else.*)

C43. otherwise: When used to mean *if not*, *otherwise* should normally be used to start a new sentence. It should not be used in the middle of a sentence to join two clauses.

needs checking	I may meet you at the party tonight, otherwise I will see you tomorrow.
revised	I may meet you at the party tonight. Otherwise, I will see you tomorrow.

O *Words Used to Show Degree or Extent*

for the most part	to some extent
so ... that	too ... for ... to
such ... that	to some degree
to a certain extent	

● *So ... that*

C44. so ... that: When separated from each other by an adjective or adverb, these two words express degree or extent, answering questions such as *How far ...?*, *How big ...?*, *How much ...?* Examples:

- How fat is he? He is so fat that he cannot see his feet.
- How large is Canada? It is so large that you need about six days to drive across it.

So ... that is the only combination of words that can be used in this way; it is wrong to say *very fat that* ... or *too large that*, just as it is wrong to leave out the word *so* and simply use *that* in such sentences.

needs checking	She was very late for dinner that there was no food left for her.
revised	She was so late for dinner that there was no food left for her.
needs checking	Dominic speaks quickly that it is often difficult to understand him.

306 | PUTTING IDEAS TOGETHER

<table>
<tr><td>revised</td><td>Dominic speaks so quickly that it is often difficult to understand him.</td></tr>
</table>

● *Such ... that*

C45. **such ... that**: Like *so ... that*, the expression *such ... that* is used to express degree or extent, answering questions such as, *How big ...?*, *How long ...?*, *How fast ...?* Notice the difference in the way the two are used.

- How far is it? It is such a long way that you would never be able to get there walking.
- It is so far that you would never be able to reach there walking.
- How fat is he? He is such a fat man that his trousers need to be made specially for him.
- He is so fat that his trousers need to be made specially for him.

The difference between the two is of course that only one word is normally used between *so* and *that*, whereas two or three words (usually an article, an adjective, and a noun) are used between *such* and *that*. Be careful not to confuse the two, or to leave out *such*.

<table>
<tr><td>needs checking</td><td>It was a hot day that nobody could stay outside for long.</td></tr>
<tr><td>revised</td><td>It was such a hot day that nobody could stay outside for long.</td></tr>
</table>

O *That and Which*

To understand when to use *that* and when to use *which* (according to traditional grammatical principles), one must first understand the difference between a restrictive clause and a non-restrictive clause. A restrictive clause restricts the application of the noun it modifies. Here is an example:

- The horse that was injured yesterday should recover.

Here the clause *that was injured yesterday* restricts the meaning of the subject of the sentence—*horse*—to a particular horse. The clause helps to define the subject more narrowly. A non-restrictive clause does not restrict the application of the noun it modifies; instead it tells us more about the subject. Again, here is an example:

- The injured horse, which was the favourite to win today's race, should recover in time for the Derby.

Here the clause *which was the favourite to win today's race* tells us more about the horse but is not necessary to its definition. Notice that the non-restrictive clause is set off by commas, while the restrictive clause follows on directly after the noun it describes, with no intervening comma. As these examples illustrate, *that* is typically used with restrictive clauses, *which* with non-restrictive clauses.

C46. **that/which**: Students have long been taught that it is correct to use *that* in restrictive clauses and *which* in non-restrictive clauses.

needs checking	The only store which sells this brand is now closed.
revised	The only store that sells this brand is now closed.
needs checking	The position which Marx adopted owed much to the philosophy of Hegel.
revised	The position that Marx adopted owed much to the philosophy of Hegel.

Although the use of the word *which* in any restrictive clause provokes a violent reaction among some English instructors, there are clearly instances in which one is quite justified in using *which* in this way. Such is the case when the writer is already using at least one *that* in the sentence:

needs checking	He told me that the radio that he had bought was defective.

revised   He told me that the radio which he had bought was defective.

Better yet, in many cases, is to avoid the use of a second relative pronoun by rephrasing:

revised   He told me that the radio he had bought was defective.

Indeed, instructors who object to *which* point out that rephrasing can often make the sentence shorter and crisper:

needs checking   The ending, which comes as a surprise to most readers, is profoundly unsettling.
revised   The ending is both surprising and unsettling.
needs checking   The 2008 campaign, which had been carefully planned, was an enormous success.
revised   The carefully planned 2008 campaign was an enormous success.

But *which* is not a special case in this regard. *That*, *who*, and *whose* can often be fruitfully removed in the same way:

needs checking   The surplus that we now project for 2010 will probably be exceeded in 2011.
revised   The projected 2010 surplus will probably be exceeded in 2011.
needs checking   Eisenhower hired as his personal driver a woman who turned into a long-term friend.
revised   Eisenhower and his driver became close friends.

The vice, then, is not *which* per se, but wordiness in general. Those who focus their attention on the one word and rail that "witches ride on broomsticks" might do better to treat the excessive use of *which* as a symptom of a much broader disease.

Interestingly, the rule about *that* and *which* seems to be a relatively recent invention, dreamt up by Henry and Francis Fowler and first propounded in their book *The King's English* in 1906. In the words of Joseph M. Williams, they felt

> the random variation between *that* and *which* in restrictive clauses [to be] messy, so they simply asserted that henceforth writers should (with some exceptions) limit *which* to non-restrictive clauses. (*Style: Ten Lessons in Clarity and Grace*, New York, Longman, 2000, 24–25)

Many instructors today are as anxious as were the Fowlers to limit the messiness in English. But, as Robert M. Martin fairly observes, it is "hard to imagine real contexts in which observation of the *that/which* distinction would result in better communication" (*Dalhousie Review*, Spring 2003, 19). Again, the better reason for observing the distinction is that doing so may help to reduce wordiness—not that the distinction itself rests on a particularly strong foundation.

O *Words Used to Make Comparisons*

by comparison	on the one hand ...
in contrast	... on the other hand

O *Other Joining Words and Expressions*

as illustrated above/below	in other words
as mentioned above/below	in the event of
as we can see/we can see that	in light of
assuming that	in this respect/in some respects
as shown in the diagram	above/below
in that	firstly/in the first place
these findings indicate that	secondly/in the second place
to begin with	for one thing
whereby	

⊙ Sentence Combining

As they become more and more skilled, writers become more adept at manipulating and varying the structures of their sentences. Such flexibility is a goal all serious writers should aspire to reach, and one of the best ways to achieve it is to engage in a process called sentence combining. As a means of helping students develop facility with more mature sentence structures, this technique goes back to the writing classrooms of the nineteenth century. But it wasn't until the 1960s that sentence combining gained a substantial following among writing teachers, largely because Noam Chomsky's new, highly influential linguistic theory, transformational-generative grammar, appeared to provide a theoretical rationale for this writing exercise. Subsequent research into the effectiveness of sentence combining in improving the fluency and maturity of developing writers' sentence structures gave the technique firm support (Connors 103–07). Since then, newer alternatives to and further development of Chomsky's grammar may also give some insight into the basis for the efficacy of sentence combining (Myers 611–12). But since it works, many are content to leave theoretical discussion to the specialists and simply take advantage of this useful practice.

In its most elementary practice, writers join two or more simple sentences, called "kernels," into a longer sentence or group of sentences. Kernels can be kept as they are and joined with conjunctions or conjunctive adverbs, or they can be embedded into other kernels, a process that often involves shortening the inserted structures. The corollary to combining short sentences is taking apart long sentences in order to examine how they were put together in the first place. Writers can analyze their own sentences in this way as well as those of other, admired authors, becoming conversant with the many options present whenever a writer considers how to express and even create a thought with words. Together, these combining and analyzing procedures are simple but effective. Mastering them confers an important component of the stylistic fluency described in the "Writing Process" chapter of this guide;

writers gain greater conscious control over and facility with their sentence structures and sentence variety, become better able to avoid problems like wordiness and repetition, and find elegance and strategic emphasis easier to achieve. Research into writing practices has shown that when unskilled writers revise a draft, they tend to focus exclusively on deleting and changing single words and phrases (Sommers 381–82). What these basic writers often fail to do is reorder and add to their initial material (386); experienced writers, on the other hand, use all of these revision techniques, especially the latter two. Rewriting for them is an entire reworking and rethinking of their arguments (see pages 66–67 of this book for more advice in this regard). At the level of sentence style, then, inexperienced writers would do well to include in their studies practice in the reordering of sentences. The work of sentence combining, "de-combining," and recombining affords just such practice.

For many students, another plus of sentence combining and its offshoots is that they don't require an extensive knowledge of grammatical terminology. The exercises work on writers' intuitive understanding of language structures and help practitioners build an increased "feel" for them, which translates into yet another benefit: the ability to avoid certain kinds of grammatical sentence errors. For example, because some sentence combining exercises require kernels to be shortened and embedded as modifiers into other sentences, practice makes it easier to spot dangling constructions and other modifier errors (see as well the discussion on dangling constructions starting on page 134). Working with kernels, which are always short but full sentences, helps students internalize what constitutes a full sentence or main clause and so avoid sentence fragments, run-ons, and comma splices (see also 455–61 of *The Guide*). Developing writers are also better able to recognize and write balanced, parallel structures (see pages 60–63 and 202–03 in *The Guide*) after gaining greater awareness of sentence constituents.

A key ability of more experienced writers is reading well. Writers who are also good readers are able to see their own work as a reader would see it and allow that crucial insight to guide their revisions. Combining kernels and reconfiguring the results a few times gives writers more practice in reading at the level of the sentence, and because the process generates a variety of arrangements of the same words, students have an opportunity to compare them and decide which of the structures are most effective and why. It's important to note, though, that sentence combining alone cannot confer the ability to judge such matters well. Enthusiastic combining sessions can produce all manner of unfortunate sentences; an important complementary exercise is analysis both of sentences that work well and of ones that work less well. Those that work well may of course be used as models. Practice in analyzing the work of others also yields another benefit: greater ease in reading more sophisticated and difficult texts. Along the way, students can also examine the elements that make up an individual author's style. All told, diligent sentence "de-combining" and recombining leads to better reading skills, and better reading leads to better writing.

These exercises in sentence manipulation and analysis have been shown to be particularly useful for students who are learning to write in English as an additional language. The kernels and guidelines for combining them in various ways contain both explicit and implicit instructions on how English sentences are structured and on which words can combine with others in which ways (Myers 615-17). All of this information provides ESL students with useful models for their own writing.

For a closer look at sentence combining in action, see the books by William Strong and the articles by Sharon A. Myers, and Glenn J. Broadhead and James A. Berlin, and Charles R. Cooper listed in Works Cited at the end of this chapter; these works inform what follows.

O *Combining*

● *Joining Kernels*

One of the simplest ways to combine kernel sentences is to join them with a connecting word or phrase. Deciding on the best connector, of course, depends on the relationship among the kernels' ideas; see the section on joining words (282-309) for advice on appropriate choices.

Consider the following kernels:

1) My ruse was sloppy.
2) My ruse deceived everyone.

Two noticeable features of a list of kernels are their choppiness of style and their tendency towards unnecessary repetition of words and phrases. Two of the tasks of sentence combining, consequently, are to create more fluent structures out of the kernel lists and to avoid wordiness. An obvious strategy in the case of the kernels above is to use a pronoun to replace one of the "my ruse" phrases. Joining the kernels will take care of the choppiness. Because the second kernel reverses the expectations raised by the first, a helpful joining word may be used to signal the contrast between the two. Here are some options for joining them.

A coordinating conjunction:

My ruse was sloppy, but it deceived everyone.

A subordinating conjunction (note that this conjunction does join the kernels despite its position before one of the kernels rather than between the two):

Even though my ruse was sloppy, it deceived everyone.

A conjunctive adverb:

> My ruse was sloppy; nevertheless, it deceived everyone.

In some cases, word order can be rearranged somewhat, as in the following example that joins the kernels with the subordinating conjunction "though":

> Sloppy though my ruse was, it deceived everyone.

If a pair of kernels consists of linked or supporting ideas, several connecting words would be suitable (see, for examples, those listed on pages 290-94), but it might also be stylistically effective to join the kernels with only a mark of punctuation. This option makes for a punchier sentence that emphasizes the closeness of relationship between the joined ideas. Consider the following kernels:

1) My ruse was brilliant.
2) My ruse deceived everyone.

Joined with a conjunction, the kernels make a sentence that is satisfactory:

> My ruse was brilliant, and it deceived everyone.

Using only a semicolon as a connector, however, makes a more dramatic alternative:

> My ruse was brilliant; it deceived everyone.

Using a dash instead heightens the drama even further:

> My ruse was brilliant—it deceived everyone.

If one kernel illustrates, specifies, or provides an explanation for the other, a colon is an appropriate connector:

On the Web
Exercises on sentence combining may be found at
www.broadviewpress.com/writing
Click on **Exercises** and go to **C47**.

1) She had only one thing to say.
2) Don't touch the chocolate.

   She had only one thing to say: don't touch the chocolate.

● *Embedding Kernels*

Structurally more complex sentences can be built by embedding one kernel within another. The embedded kernel can stay whole or substantially so, or parts of it can be deleted to create phrases and even single words for insertion into what then becomes the sentence's main kernel.

O WHOLE CLAUSES EMBEDDED WITH PUNCTUATION

Certain marks of punctuation—paired dashes and parentheses, for example—allow for an entire kernel to be embedded in another unchanged.

1) The secret to Edith's success is her stubbornness.
2) The secret cannot be denied.

   The secret to Edith's success—it cannot be denied—is her stubbornness.

1) She hung on to the bitter end.
2) She is so very stubborn.

   She hung on (she is so very stubborn) to the bitter end.

O RELATIVE CLAUSES

An embedded kernel left whole can also take the form of a relative clause, that is, an adjective clause introduced by a relative pronoun (see pages 583-84). Like other pronouns, relative pronouns eliminate some repetition of words or phrases by substituting for them. Below are examples of embedded relative clauses using the relative pronouns *that, who, which, where,* and *when.*

1) The music is the best music of all.
2) The music plays only in Chester's head.

> The music that plays only in Chester's head is the best music of all.

Note that in the next two examples, which involve the relative pronoun *who*, the kernel that will become the relative clause in the combined sentence indicates which form, *who* or *whom*, the pronoun should take. In the first example, the pronoun takes the place of the kernel's subject and so takes the subject form, *who*. In the second, the pronoun takes the place of the kernel's object and so takes the object form *whom*. Here is one instance of the ways in which sentence combining practice can help writers master some grammatical rules.

1) Lewis writes the best books.
2) Lewis is despicable.

> Lewis, who is despicable, writes the best books.

1) Lewis writes the best books.
2) I despise Lewis.

> Lewis, whom I despise, writes the best books.

1) Lewis is despised by all.
2) Lewis's books are the best.

> Lewis, whose books are the best, is despised by all.

1) That book is everyone's favourite.
2) No one can understand that book.

That book, which no one can understand, is everyone's favourite.

1) Frieda's thoughts turned to evil at a precise moment.
2) No one knows the precise moment.

No one knows the precise moment when Frieda's thoughts turned to evil.

1) She left him in the attic.
2) No one ever goes to the attic.

She left him in the attic, where no one ever goes.

● *Abbreviated Kernels Joined as Absolute Phrases*

Absolute phrases are shortened kernels that contain nouns and modifiers but no main verb (see pages 584-85 for a definition of verbs). Absolutes often modify entire sentences and attach to them with commas.

1) Willard is an impatient man.
2) The experiment went badly.

Willard being an impatient man, the experiment went badly.

1) No one waited for the banana flambé.
2) The party was already wrecked by Shirley's antics.

The party already wrecked by Shirley's antics, no one waited for the banana flambé.

● *Abbreviated Kernels Embedded as Verb and Noun Phrases*

Kernels can be abbreviated to phrases or even single words before being inserted into other kernels. When the ideas of paired kernels have an equal, independent status, they can be shortened to phrases and joined with coordinating conjunctions.

○ NOUN PHRASE

1) Dolores always cries at *Casablanca*.
2) Stan always cries at *Casablanca*.

Dolores and Stan always cry at *Casablanca*.

○ VERB PHRASE

1) Morton sang "Danny Boy."
2) Morton expected our applause.

Morton sang "Danny Boy" and expected our applause.

● *Abbreviated Kernels Embedded as Modifiers*

Shortened kernels can also serve as various kinds of modifiers, including adjectives, adverbs, prepositional phrases, past and present participles, infinitive phrases, and appositives.

○ KERNELS EMBEDDED AS SINGLE-WORD ADJECTIVES

1) Herman's handshake was floppy.
2) Herman's handshake irritated his in-laws.

Herman's floppy handshake irritated his in-laws.

○ KERNELS EMBEDDED AS SINGLE-WORD ADVERBS

1) Estelle was doubtful.
2) Estelle frowned at the chocolate mousse bombe.

Estelle frowned doubtfully at the chocolate mousse bombe.

○ KERNELS EMBEDDED AS PREPOSITIONAL PHRASES

   1) The glove looked suspiciously familiar.
   2) The glove was in the hallway.

   The glove in the hallway looked suspiciously familiar.

   1) Terrence threw Mabel's letter.
   2) Mabel's letter landed on the fire.

   Terrence threw Mabel's letter on the fire.

○ KERNELS EMBEDDED AS PRESENT PARTICIPLES

   1) Walter paddled doggedly.
   2) Walter finished another lap of the pool.

   Paddling doggedly, Walter finished another lap of the pool.

○ KERNELS EMBEDDED AS PAST PARTICIPLES

   1) Rita's insight was wrapped in obscurity.
   2) Rita's insight went unnoticed.

   Rita's insight, wrapped in obscurity, went unnoticed.

○ KERNELS EMBEDDED AS INFINITIVE PHRASES

   1) They went home.
   2) They reflected on their bad behaviour.

   They went home to reflect on their bad behaviour.

○ KERNELS EMBEDDED AS APPOSITIVES

   1) Carl is a wily tactician.
   2) Carl always wins at checkers.

   A wily tactician, Carl always wins at checkers.

O *Combining and Recombining*

For building effective revision practices, exercises in recombining kernels work very well. The idea is to combine the same list of kernels into several combinations and compare the results. An important decision in any combination is which kernel will form the main clause or clauses of the sentence. The rule of thumb is that the main idea should rest in the main clause. Varying the way the kernels are combined can change the emphasis or even the fundamental idea of a sentence. Consider the following kernels:

    1) I love ice cream.
    2) I don't eat ice cream often.

The two could be given equivalent status and joined by a coordinating conjunction or conjunctive adverb into a sentence with two main clauses:

    I love ice cream, but I don't eat it often.

    I love ice cream; however, I don't eat it often.

In combinations such as this, notice that *but* must stay where it is, while *however* is able to move to a variety of spots in the sentence:

    I love ice cream; I don't, however, eat it often.

    I love ice cream; I don't eat it often, however.

Each option is subtly different from the others. Placed at the beginning of its clause, *however* signals an upcoming contrast right away, so readers anticipate some sort of reversal of the first idea. Placed after *I don't*, the transition word interrupts its clause and so emphasizes the idea of not doing something; the shift from the first clause's affirmative statement to the second's negative one is thus immediately more specific than the first sentence's broader signal of contrast. The third sentence delays the transition word until the very end, confronting the readers with a starker contrast between the affirmative and negative statements as their expectations after reading the first clause are suddenly reversed without notice.

Coordinating main clauses is not the only option for these kernels; one clause can be subordinated to the other for still different effects.

> Although I love ice cream, I don't eat it often.

> Although I don't eat it often, I love ice cream.

Each kernel becomes the sole main clause in each of the variations above. In the first, the emphasis is on not eating ice cream, while in the second, the focus is on loving it.

Embedding each kernel as a relative clause achieves a similar effect, but again, there are subtle differences:

> I love ice cream, which I don't eat often.

> I don't often eat ice cream, which I love.

There, the relative clauses feel more like wistful afterthoughts and less like blunt statements of fact (as in the sentences using *although*).

Here are still more variations with still different effects:

> I love but don't often eat ice cream.

> I don't often eat my beloved ice cream.

> Despite loving ice cream, I don't often eat it.

> Despite not often eating it, I love ice cream.

Depending on a writer's rhetorical purposes, any of these sentences would work well in a larger context. Sentence recombining helps writers see what options are available to them so that they can consider which would be preferable.

● *Combining Several Kernels into a Single Sentence*

The next step after the simple combining of pairs of kernels is to work on joining three, four, and even more kernels. Consider the following list of kernels:

1) Clutter is far from causing certain things.
2) Clutter does not make the mind disorganized.
3) Clutter does not make the mind distracted.
4) Clutter does not make the mind distressed.
5) Clutter can foster thinking.
6) The thinking is creative.
7) Clutter can contain order.
8) The order is of a high degree.
9) The order is not visible to observation.
10) The observation is initial.
11) The observation is casual.

The more kernels in a list, the more options there are for combining them, and the more choices a writer must make. Not all possibilities are equally felicitous, however. It is very possible for an excited sentence combiner to produce questionable sentences. Here is one example:

> You might say that clutter makes the mind disorganized, that it makes the mind distracted, and that it makes the mind distressed, but clutter is far from having these effects; instead, it can foster thinking in a creative manner, and it can also contain a kind of order that is of a high degree but that is not visible to the first glance of the casual observer.

The sentence above is grammatically correct and makes some interesting substitutions and additions to the original list of kernels, but it is unnecessarily wordy and needn't be so long. The goal of sentence combining is never to write the longest, most complex sentence possible. Good writers vary their sentence lengths and recognize the rhetorical value of short, simple sentences for emphasis. For combining exercises involving more than two kernels, leaving one or more kernels uncombined is always an option. Other stylistic choices that such exercises call for are whether kernels should be joined or embedded, where embedded kernels should be placed within the finished sentence, whether transitions or conjunctions would be effective and which ones would work best, and, importantly, which kernel should become the main clause of a combined sentence. The section on stylistic fluency in this book, starting on page 52, gives some guidance on how to make such choices well. Some writers also find reading sentences out loud helpful, and many solicit the opinions of other readers. But particularly beneficial is taking the time to configure and then reconfigure a list of kernels, and then compare the results. Here are two more arrangements of the kernel list above:

> Clutter, far from making the mind disorganized, distracted, and distressed, can foster creative thinking and, moreover, contain a high degree of order not at first visible to casual observation.

> Clutter seems sure to make the mind disorganized, distracted, and distressed. Not so, however—it can actually foster creative thinking. Even more surprising, it can contain a high degree of order, which casual observation may not at first reveal.

Both of the recombinations above are less wordy than the first try and seem better for that reason. Which of the last two you prefer, however, will likely depend on what context you imagine the passages belonging to. The final combination includes more transitional words and so directs readers more strongly toward conclusions to be drawn from the claims it makes. It is also more casual in tone, largely because of phrases like *seems sure to*, and *not so*, and the use of a dash rather than, say, a semicolon. The middle combination is leaner and gives the impression of a less familiar, perhaps more professional voice behind the words.

● *"De-Combining" and Recombining*

While combining kernels improves a writer's understanding of sentence structure, analyzing a complete sentence into its possible constituent kernels yields even more insights. The practice can clarify certain grammar problems (as in the relative clause examples above that use *who* and *whom*), helping writers to avoid them, and in the process, become better readers of their own work, an important skill that sets experienced writers apart from the less skilled. "De-combining" sentences can also help students become better able to read even difficult texts and more adept at grasping the components that make up the styles of a variety of writers and types of writing.

○ *Help with Some Grammatical Errors: Two More Examples*

● *Dangling Modifiers*

Inexperienced writers sometimes dangle modifiers (see the section beginning on page 134 for more information on dangling constructions). Sentence combining can help writers recognize and so better avoid this common problem. Consider the following sentence:

> While watching an abominable film, even the popcorn tasted vile.

Dividing the sentence into kernels gives the following result:

1) The popcorn tasted vile.
2) _____ watched a film.
3) The film was abominable.

There is an obvious problem with kernel 2; it has no subject. That's what causes it to dangle when combined with the others. Embedded as a modifier, it attaches to the closest noun, *popcorn*, and creates the unintentionally amusing image of popcorn watching a film. Once the problem is clearly laid out in a kernel list, it's easy to see and to fix:

1) The popcorn tasted vile.
2) We watched a film.
3) The film was abominable.

> Because we were watching an abominable film, even the popcorn tasted vile.
> We were watching an abominable film; even the popcorn tasted vile.

● *Syntactic Ambiguity*

Sometimes, unwanted ambiguity in a sentence comes from its syntax, or the arrangement of its words. The following is the title of an anthology of key philosophical texts:

Enduring Issues in Philosophy

The title is not an entire sentence, but there are nonetheless abbreviated kernels underlying it. Analyzing the title shows that it has two possible underlying groups of kernels:

1) Philosophy has issues.
2) The issues have endured.

1) Philosophy has issues.
2) People can endure the issues.

It's doubtful that the publisher of that book intends us to read the second possible meaning of the title, but that reading is nonetheless available. An unambiguous title would combine one of the pairs of kernels above, presumably the first. Here are two possible reconfigurations:

> *Some Enduring Issues in Philosophy*
> *Philosophy's Enduring Issues.*

O *Help with Reading Challenging Texts*

Often, students have difficulty reading the work of authors from earlier eras simply because the language has changed considerably in the interval. Some of the challenge comes from changes in vocabulary, of course, for which the best remedy is to consult a good dictionary or glossary of words from the period. But some confusion can result from unfamiliar sentence structure, too; careful analysis of some sample sentences into their constituent kernels will, with practice, help students raise their literacy skills to the point where such texts no longer pose a problem. Look, for example, at the following passage from Thomas Hobbes's *Leviathan* (16):

> A LAW OF NATURE (*lex naturalis*) is a precept or general rule, found out by reason, by which a man is forbidden to do that which is destructive of his life, or taketh away the means of preserving the same, and to omit that by which he thinketh it may be best preserved. (98)

Here is a possible division of this sentence into kernels:

1) The Latin for "law of nature" is *lex naturalis*.
2) A law of nature is a precept.
3) A law of a nature is a general rule.
4) A law of nature is found out by reason.

5) A law of nature forbids a man to do certain things.
6) Some things are destructive of the man's life.
7) Some things take away means.
8) The means are for preserving his life.
9) A law of nature forbids the man to omit certain things.
10) Some things preserve the man's life.
11) The man thinks this.

Recombining these kernels into more contemporary language and, for better understanding, expanding them somewhat can help elucidate Hobbes's meaning.

> A law of nature, which in Latin is called a *lex naturalis*, is a precept or general rule. This kind of law can be discovered by reasoning; that is, the law does not need to be revealed to us by any other agent. A law of nature forbids a person[*] to do anything that would destroy his life or that would take away the means by which he preserves his life. A law of nature also obliges a person to follow any course of action that he thinks will help preserve his life.

The result is perhaps a little more cumbersome than it need be, but it is clear, and the point of this exercise in any case is to understand a challenging passage rather than offer a rewrite of it to a reader.

Here is another example, this time a passage from Sonnet 116 by William Shakespeare.

> Let me not to the marriage of true minds
> Admit impediments. Love is not love
> Which alters when it alteration finds,

---

[*] In working through the meaning of a passage such as this, we may also need to ask whether the writer intended words such as man to apply only to males, or to all humans. In this case context makes clear that Hobbes intended the latter.

Or bends with the remover to remove.
O, no, it is an ever-fixèd mark
That looks on tempests and is never shaken;
It is the star to every wandering bark,
Whose worth's unknown, although his height be taken.

Part of our potential puzzlement on reading this passage comes again from unfamiliar vocabulary (for example, *remove* means *leave*, not *take away*, and *bark* is a noun meaning *ship*), but the glosses that are now almost always published with Shakespeare's work can help with that. Beyond gaining experience with his words and terms, readers of Shakespeare must gain skill interpreting the structures of his lines of verse. An important first step is to realize that a line does not necessarily constitute a sentence; the periods in the passage above show that it consists of three sentences divided over eight lines. Here is a list of kernels generated from the passage above, with more modern expressions substituted as needed. For ease of analysis, the kernels are grouped according to the sentences they make up, and the kernel that underlies each sentence's main clause or clauses are underlined:

Sentence One

1) <u>Do not let me allow certain things</u>.
2) The things are impediments.
3) The impediments interfere with a marriage.
4) The marriage is between minds.
5) The minds are true.

Sentence Two

1) Certain things can seem like love.
2) <u>These things are not love</u>.
3) One thing changes under a certain circumstance.
4) This thing finds a change (in the one loved).
5) Another thing changes (*bends*) under a certain circumstance.

6) The loved one (*the remover*) goes away.
7) This thing departs (*removes*).

Sentence Three

1) Love is not this thing.
2) <u>Love is a landmark that never moves or changes</u>.
3) The landmark looks at tempests.
4) The landmark is not shaken.
5) <u>Love is a star</u>.
6) The star guides ships.
7) The ships are off course.
8) The star has a worth.
9) The worth is unknown.
10) The star has a height (above the horizon).
11) The height has been measured.

Note that some of the kernels include understood elements that don't appear in the original but that must nonetheless be included in the kernels in order to make them complete. Consider the clause *when it alteration finds*; in order to understand the point of this clause, we need to answer the question *alteration in what*? The line does not directly say what it is that alters, but the context of the rest of the poem, with its focus on the properties of true love, strongly suggests that this hypothetical alteration is in the object of such love.

Once the kernels are carefully written, recombining them yields a paraphrase of the passage. The meaning of much poetic language lies condensed in the structures of its words; the rendering below of the ideas of this sonnet includes an interpretive expansion of the metaphors used in the poem.

Do not let me allow impediments to the marriage of minds that are true to one another. Some things can seem like love, but they are not love. For example, if a supposed lover changes his or her attitude when there is a change in the loved one, it is not love. Similarly, when a supposed lover stops loving if the beloved is gone, it is not love. Love is like an unchanging landmark at sea. Such a landmark is witness to tempests, but storms cannot move or change it. Likewise, love does not change or fall if there is any upheaval in its circumstances. Love is like a guiding star that helps every ship that's gone off course find its way. Such a star has a worth so great that it cannot be known, even if its physical height above the horizon has been measured. Likewise, the worth of love is too great to know, even if love's more mundane details can be described.

The process of analysis again helps to clarify the original meaning and points to the places where material must be added to or expanded on in order to facilitate this illumination. The subsequent recombination of the kernels is thus an exercise in careful interpretation of what rests within the poetic language. The paraphrase is again ungraceful, and because it provides a single reading with little possibility of variation in its own interpretation, it paints a unidimensional picture of a deeply textured original. But all that just serves to highlight the beauty and mastery of the sonnet, in which multiple meanings are folded into musical lines.

O Gaining Awareness of Writing Style

A particular benefit of sentence "de-combining" comes from analyzing the work of admired writers. A close look at their sentences reveals sentence strategies that less experienced writers can use as models for their own writing. It may also serve to illuminate the characteristics of a given writer's style or the characteristics of a particular genre of writing.

Below is a passage by Lewis Thomas, a non-fiction writer justly praised for his prose style:

I am a member of a fragile species, still new to the earth, the youngest creatures of any scale, here only a few moments as

evolutionary time is measured, a juvenile species, a child of a
species. We are only tentatively set in place, error-prone, at risk
of fumbling, in real danger at the moment of leaving behind
only a thin layer of our fossils, radioactive at that. (25)

Here is a list of kernels generated from the passage by Thomas.
Again, the kernels are grouped according to the sentences they are
part of, with the main clause kernels underlined:

Sentence One

1) <u>I am a member of a species.</u>
2) The species is fragile.
3) The species is new to the earth.
4) The species consists of creatures.
5) The creatures are the youngest.
6) All creatures are ranked on many scales.
7) The creatures are here over moments.
8) The moments are few.
9) The moments are measured.
10) The measurement is of evolutionary time.
11) The species is juvenile.
12) The species is a child.

Sentence Two

1) <u>We are set in place.</u>
2) The setting is temporary.
3) We are error-prone.
4) We are at risk.
5) The risk is of fumbling.
6) We are in danger.
7) The danger is real.
8) The danger is now.
9) The danger is of leaving a residue.
10) The residue is the only one.

11) The residue is a layer.
12) The layer is of fossils.
13) The layer is thin.
14) The fossils are radioactive.

The list of kernels makes some aspects of Thomas's style jump out. Both of the two sentences that make up the passage start with a main clause made up of a whole kernel without any kind of transition leading in to it. Each of the sentence-opening kernels has another kernel embedded in it as a single-word modifier: *fragile* and *tentatively*. A series of abbreviated kernels acting as modifiers then follows each main clause. In the first sentence, if we consider the first three phrases following the main clause, *still new to the earth*, *the youngest creatures of any scale*, and *here only a few moments as evolutionary time is measured*, we can see that they are progressively more complex—each contains more embedded kernels than the last. The final two phrases of sentence one, *a juvenile species* and *a child of a species*, are then again made up of simple abbreviated kernels.

The pattern of the second sentence is similar, though not exactly the same. Set off by commas after the main clause are three phrases that are again progressively more complex: *error-prone*, *at risk of fumbling*, and *in real danger at the moment of leaving behind only a thin layer of our fossils*. The sentence then ends with one simple abbreviated kernel: *radioactive*. The two sentences together, then, create a pleasing symmetry that is varied just enough to keep it from being rigid. Another graceful touch is the pairing of a whole kernel with a list of abbreviated kernels in each sentence. Within the lists themselves, the movement in the modifying phrases toward greater complexity gives each sentence a momentum that is softly slowed with the simple closing kernels. In all, these structural elements contribute to the elegance of the passage.

Here, from Ursula K. Le Guin's novel *Lavinia*, is a passage of fictional prose that reveals the author's skill in crafting language. The speaker is Lavinia, a young woman. Her future husband, Aeneas, is looking with his people for a new homeland and has just arrived in her country.

And in the twilight of morning of the next day, alone, kneeling in the mud by Tiber, I saw the great ships turn from the sea and come into the river. I saw my husband stand on the high stern of the first ship, though he did not see me. He gazed up the dark river, praying, dreaming. He did not see the deaths that lay before him, all along the river, all the way to Rome. (95)

This passage can be "de-combined" into kernels as follows (the italicized kernel of sentence two is a full but subordinate clause):

Sentence One

1) It was twilight.
2) It was morning.
3) It was the next day.
4) I was alone.
5) I was kneeling in the mud.
6) The mud was by the Tiber.
7) <u>I saw ships</u>.
8) The ships were great.
9) The ships turned from the sea.
10) The ships came into the river.

Sentence Two

1) <u>I saw my husband</u>.
2) My husband stood on the stern.
3) The stern was of the first ship.
4) The stern was high.
5) *My husband did not see me.*

Sentence Three

1) <u>My husband gazed up the river</u>.
2) The river was dark.
3) My husband was praying.
4) My husband was dreaming.

Sentence Four

1) <u>My husband did not see the deaths</u>.
2) The deaths lay before him.
3) The deaths lay all along the river.
4) The deaths lay all the way to Rome.

Kernel analysis shows that Le Guin's passage also has an overall symmetry, though again it is not strict. The passage pulls the reader along from sentence to sentence with a pattern in which structures are mirrored by what follows next across sentence boundaries. After opening with six abbreviated kernels, the first sentence consists of one main clause, *I saw the great ships*, with three kernels embedded in it. The very next clause at the start of sentence two, *I saw my husband stand*, also contains three shortened kernels serving as modifiers. In structure (as well as wording), it closely repeats the pattern of the first sentence's main clause: *I saw the great ships turn* and *I saw my husband stand* echo one another substantially, and both are similarly followed by a short series of abbreviated kernels.

The next full clause is the second, subordinate clause of the second sentence, *he did not see me*. This clause, again a whole kernel, is itself echoed, though again not rigidly, by the next clause, which opens sentence three: *He gazed up the dark river*. This clause also consists of an unshortened kernel, though it has one embedded modifier. Attached to the end of this clause are two kernels abbreviated into a pair of present participles, *praying* and *dreaming*. That structure is loosely repeated in the next sentence, which features a whole kernel, *He did not see the deaths*, with one embedment (the relative clause *that lay before him*), to which are attached a pair of kernels shortened into two prepositional phrases, *all along the river* and *all the way to Rome*.

All of these echoed structures are contained within a whole that has its own mirror symmetry: the passage begins with six abbreviated kernels leading into a main clause, and ends with a main clause leading to three abbreviated kernels. These strings of shortened kernels slow the reader's progress, creating a heightened anticipation at the start of the passage and a sense of ending and inevitability at the close. In addition, the four kernels that are left whole are similar in wording and thematically linked; *I saw, I saw, He gazed*, and *He did not see* are all about seeing and not seeing, key themes in the novel as a whole. That these clauses have little or nothing embedded directly within them makes them stand out, startling and grave; the important themes they embody are thus highlighted and reinforced.

As the structure of such samples suggests, an almost but not quite exact symmetry is a common feature of powerful prose—both fictional and non-fictional.

Finally, consider the opening to the play *Glengarry Glen Ross* by David Mamet. The speaker is Shelly Levene, a real estate salesman in imminent danger of losing his job; he is addressing John Williamson, his supervisor:

> **Levene:** John ... John ... John. Okay. John. John. Look: *(Pause.)* The Glengarry Highland's leads, you're sending Roma out. Fine. He's a good man. We know what he is. He's fine. All I'm saying, you look at the *board*, he's throwing ... wait, wait, wait, he's throwing them *away*, he's throwing the leads away. All that I'm saying, that you're wasting leads. I don't want to tell you your *job*. All that I'm saying, things get *set*, I know they do, you get a certain *mindset*.... A guy gets a reputation. We know how this ... all I'm saying, put a *closer* on the job. There's more than one man for the ... Put a ... wait a second, put a *proven man out* ... (15)

A possible breakdown of the passage into kernels is as follows:

1) John, listen. (uttered four times)
2) John, look.
3) You are sending Roma out.
4) Roma (is to do something).
5) Roma (will close) the Glengarry Highland leads.
6) That is fine.

7) Roma is a good man.

8) We know Roma.

9) Roma is (a certain kind of salesman).

10) Roma is fine.

11) I am saying only one thing.

12) Look at the board.

13) Roma is throwing the leads away. (uttered three times)

14) John, wait. (uttered three times)

15) I am saying only one thing.

16) You are wasting leads.

17) I don't want to tell you something.

18) Your job (is a certain thing).

19) I am saying only one thing.

20) Things get set.

21) I know they do.

22) You get a mindset.

23) The mindset is a certain kind.

24) A guy gets a reputation.

25) We know something.

26) This happens (in a certain way).

27) I am only saying one thing.

28) Put a closer on the job.

29) More than one man is suitable.

30) The suitability is for the (job).

31) Put a (closer on the job).

32) John, wait a second.

33) Put a man out.

34) The man is proven.

The kernel list makes several remarkable features of the passage immediately apparent. Four kernels (1, 11, 13, and 14) are repeated several times, with three of the repetitions (all but kernel 11) occurring in sequence. Other kernels are close but not exact repetitions: *Roma is a good man* and *Roma is fine*, and *put a closer on the job* and *put a proven man out*, for example. Very few kernels are embedded into others; in fact, almost all of the passage's sentences either consist of single, unembellished kernels or are a string of simple kernels. Some of the kernels as represented in the passage are incomplete: for example, *John* for *John, listen to me*; *all I'm saying* for *I'm only saying one thing*; and *The Glengarry Highland's leads, you're sending Roma out*, with the connection between the two elements left unspoken. Several of the kernels are also conceptually incomplete: how do things get set, and what are those things? What sort of mindset does one get about what? What kind of reputation does a guy get, and how?

These arresting features create some important effects. With its many broken and repeated kernels, the passage closely mimics spontaneous speech and implies non-verbal responses by Williamson to which Levene subsequently reacts. Both stylistic effects are common to drama, particularly modern drama. The choppy strings of simple and incomplete kernels also help establish Levene's emotional agitation. But the structure of the passage has thematic significance, as well. Throughout the play, salesmen use words to manipulate one another and their clients ruthlessly; what is implied by and left out of the utterances creates a subtext that has a crucial importance to the circumstances of each man. Unspoken completions to fragmented kernels imply a shared understanding and friendly intimacy, neither of which may actually exist. But their apparent existence is all that matters. Levene is clearly trying hard to play this game well, to manoeuvre Williamson into giving him a break. The gradual deterioration of the speech graphically illustrates Levene's growing desperation as he feels his skill at closing a "sale" slip away.

With great skill, Mamet has built word structures that fulfill a writing purpose quite different from Le Guin's.

○ Works Cited

Broadhead, Glenn J., and James A. Berlin. "Twelve Steps to Using Generative Sentences and Sentence Combining in the Composition Classroom." *College Composition and Communication* 32.3 (1981): 295-307. *JSTOR*. Web. 15 Aug. 2008.

Connors, Robert J. "The Erasure of the Sentence." *College Composition and Communication* 52.1 (2000): 96-128. *JSTOR*. Web. 27 June 2008.

Cooper, Charles R. "An Outline for Writing Sentence-Combining Problems." *The English Journal* 62.1 (1973): 96-108. *JSTOR*. Web. 27 June 2008.

Eichhoefer, Gerald W., ed. *Enduring Issues in Philosophy*. San Diego: Greenhaven, 1995. Print.

Hobbes, Thomas. *Leviathan*. 1651. Ed. A.P. Martinich. Peterborough, ON: Broadview, 2002. Print.

Le Guin, Ursula K. *Lavinia*. Orlando: Harcourt, 2008. Print.

Mamet, David. *Glengarry Glen Ross*. New York: Grove, 1982. Print.

Myers, Sharon A. "ReMembering the Sentence." *College Composition and Communication* 54.4 (2003): 610-28. *JSTOR*. Web. 27 June 2008.

Shakespeare, William. Sonnet 116. *The Longman Anthology of British Literature*. Ed. David Damrosch. Vol. 1. Ed. David Damrosch. New York: Longman-Addison, 1999. 1176. Print.

Sommers, Nancy. "Revision Strategies of Student Writers and Experienced Adult Writers." *College Composition and Communication* 31.4 (1980): 378-88. *JSTOR*. Web. 15 Aug. 2008.

Strong, William. *Sentence Combining: A Composing Book*. 3rd ed. New York: McGraw Hill, 1994. Print.

———. *Writer's Toolbox: A Sentence-Combining Workshop*. New York: McGraw Hill, 1996. Print.

Thomas, Lewis. "The Art and Craft of Memoir." *The Fragile Species*. New York: Touchstone, 1992. 16-27. Print.

◎ STYLE

⊙ Slang and Informal English

D1. **slang/informal English**: The column to the left below lists words and expressions often used in conversation, but not in formal English. The corresponding formal words are listed to the right. The most frequently troublesome entries are given a separate number.

anyways	anyway
anywheres, anyplace	anywhere
awful	poor, miserable, sick
awfully	very, extremely

Some authorities continue to hold that *awful* should retain its original meaning of *filled with or inspiring awe*. In any case, a better replacement can always be found. The same is even more true of the use of the adverb *awfully* as an intensifier to mean *very* (*awfully good, awfully small*, etc.).

boss	manager, supervisor
bunch	group
(except for grapes, bananas, etc.)	
buy	bargain
(as a noun—*a good buy*, etc.)	
kid	child, girl, boy
kind of, sort of	rather, in some respects
let's us	let us
lots of	a great deal of
mad	angry
(unless the meaning is *insane*)	

All contractions (*it's, he's, there's, we're*, etc.) should be avoided in formal writing, as should conversational markers such as *Well*, ...

D2. **attitude**: In colloquial English in recent years *attitude* has undergone a considerable transformation, becoming first a synonym for *bad attitude* and then a word that (depending on context) may denote an air of superiority or suggest the audacity and forceful irreverence of an "in-your-face" personality. In formal written English such colloquial usages as *she's got attitude* should be avoided.

D3. **could care less/couldn't care less**: In the early 1990s people started to say sarcastically *I could care less* to mean the opposite—that they couldn't care less. For some time *I could care less* seemed to be taking over, regardless of the tone of voice used, and the meaning of the words themselves seemed in danger of being lost. In recent years *couldn't care less* has made something of a comeback.

needs checking	Most of the time most people could care less about what their elected representatives are doing.
revised	Most of the time most people couldn't care less about what their elected representatives are doing.

D4. **get**: should not be used to mean *come*, *go*, *be*, or *become*. Such expressions as *get a hold of* are also inappropriate in formal writing.

needs checking	Henry and Jane Seymour got married in 1536, only ten days after the death of Anne Boleyn.
revised	Henry and Jane Seymour were married in 1536, only ten days after the death of Anne Boleyn.

D5. **go** (to mean *say*)

needs checking	He goes, "What do you mean?"
revised	He said, "What do you mean?"

D6. **have got** (to mean *have*)

needs checking	He has got two houses and three cars.
revised	He has two houses and three cars.

In conversational English *got* has become widely used as an auxiliary verb, probably because of the awkwardness of pronouncing certain combinations involving common contractions. Thus we would never shorten *I have you covered* to *I've you covered*; instead we would say, *I've got you covered*. *Have got* is also an informal synonym for *have* in the sense of *possess*. Both these uses of *got* are usually to be avoided in formal writing.

D7. **let's say:** This expression should be omitted entirely from writing.

needs checking	Let's say for example a relative dies, a poor family will have to deal with financial worries as well as with grief.
revised	If a relative dies a poor family will have to deal with financial worries as well as with grief.

D8. **like** (to mean *say* or *indicate through gesture*): An expressive idiom, but one to be avoided in writing.

conversational	She's like, "Why do we have to be here?" and I'm like, "Duh!"
formal	She wondered why we had to be there; to me it was obvious.

D9. **look to:** In formal writing one may speak of *looking to the future*, but the informal use of *look to* to mean *attempt* or *intend* should be avoided.

needs checking	From the moment he took power in France, Napoleon was looking to conquer Europe.
revised	From the moment he took power in France, Napoleon intended to conquer Europe.

D10. **off** (to mean *from*)

needs checking	I got it off him for two dollars.
revised	I bought it from him for two dollars.

D11. **put across, get across** (one's point): *Express, convince.*

needs checking	He could not get his point across.
revised	He could not persuade us he was right.

D12. **till/until**: In conversation or in literature *till* is a perfectly acceptable informal substitute for *until*. In formal written English, however, *until* should be used.

needs checking	They waited till dawn to launch the attack.
revised	They waited until dawn to launch the attack.

D13. **well**: In conversation *well* is often added to sentences while you are thinking of what to say. Do not do this in writing.

needs checking	Well, at the end of the war there was some doubt within the cabinet as to which course to take.
revised	At the end of the war there was some doubt within the cabinet as to which course to take.

D14. **when you get right down to it**: usually best omitted; use *otherwise, indeed,* or *in fact.*

⊙ Wordiness

Wordiness is perhaps the most persistent disease afflicting modern writing; references to it permeate this book. Its opposite—the mistake of including too few words in a sentence—is also discussed in this section.

D15. **actual/actually**: Usually redundant.

needs checking	Many people assume that Switzerland is made up entirely of bankers and watchmakers. In actual fact, the Swiss economy is very diversified.

revised   Many people assume that Switzerland is made up entirely of bankers and watchmakers. In fact, the Swiss economy is very diversified.

D16. **as regards**: Use *about*, or rephrase.

needs checking   As regards your request for additional funding, we have taken the matter under advisement.

revised   We are considering your request for more money.

D17. **as stated earlier**: If so, why state it again?

needs checking   The Venus flytrap, which as stated earlier is an insectivorous plant, grows only in a restricted area of New Jersey.

revised   The Venus flytrap grows only in a restricted area of New Jersey.

D18. **as you know, as we all know**: Usually better omitted.

needs checking   As we all know, George W. Bush was elected president in 2000, even though more votes were cast for Al Gore.

revised   George W. Bush was elected president in 2000, even though more votes were cast for Al Gore.

On the Web
Exercises on wordiness may be found at
www.broadviewpress.com/writing
Click on **Exercises** and go to **D15–48**.

D19. **aspect:** Often a pointer to an entire phrase or clause that can be cut.

needs checking	The logging industry is a troubled one at the present time. One of the aspects of this industry that is a cause for concern is the increased production of cheaper timber in South America.
revised	The logging industry is now a troubled one. Increased production of cheaper timber in South America has reduced the market for North American wood.

D20. **at a later date:** *Later.*

needs checking	We can decide this at a later date.
revised	We can decide this later.

D21. **at the present time:** *Now,* or nothing.

needs checking	At the present time the company has ten employees.
revised	The company has ten employees.

D22. **attention:** *It has come to my attention* that this expression is almost always unnecessarily wordy.

needs checking	It has come to my attention that shipments last month were 15 per cent below targeted levels.
revised	Shipments last month were 15 per cent below targeted levels.

D23. **basis/basically:** Both are often pointers to wordiness.

needs checking	On the basis of the information we now possess it is possible to see that William Bligh was not the ogre he was once thought to be. Basically, he was no harsher than most captains of the time.

revised	Recent research suggests that William Bligh was not the ogre he was once thought to be. He was no harsher than most captains of the time.

D24. cause: Sentences using *cause* as a verb can often be rephrased more concisely; try to think of other verbs.

needs checking	The increased sales tax caused the people to react with fury.
revised	The increase in sales tax infuriated the people.
needs checking	The change in temperature caused the liquid to freeze within seventeen minutes.
revised	The liquid froze within seventeen minutes of the temperature change.

D25. close proximity to: *Near.*

needs checking	The office is situated in close proximity to shops and transportation facilities.
revised	The office is near a shopping centre and a bus stop.

D26. e.g. ... etc.: If you begin by saying *for example*, it is redundant to add *and others* at the end of your list. See *also* and *such as* in "Joining Words."

needs checking	In several African nations (e.g., Rwanda, Malawi, Zaire, etc.) tyrannical or murderous regimes were overthrown in the 1990s.
revised	In several African nations (e.g., Rwanda, Malawi, Zaire) tyrannical or murderous regimes were overthrown in the 1990s.

D27. etc.: The Latin *et cetera*, or *etc.* for short, means *and the rest* or *and others*. To say *and etc.* is really to say *and and others*. Beware as well of combining *etc.* with expressions such as *such as.*

needs checking	During recent years several countries (Haiti, Argentina, and etc.) have amassed huge debts, which they are now unable to pay.
revised	During recent years several countries (Haiti, Argentina, etc.) have amassed huge debts, which they are now unable to pay.
needs checking	Plants such as Venus flytraps, pitcher plants, etc. feed on insects.
revised	Plants such as Venus flytraps and pitcher plants feed on insects.
or	Some plants (Venus flytraps, pitcher plants, etc.) feed on insects.

D28. **exists:** Often a pointer to wordiness.

needs checking	A situation now exists in which voters suspect the government's motives, regardless of whether or not they approve of its actions.
revised	Voters now suspect the government's motives even if they approve of its actions.

D29. **fact:** Be wary of *the fact that* (as well as *in point of fact* and *actual fact*).

needs checking	Due to the fact that we have discontinued this product, we are unable to provide spare parts.
revised	Because we have discontinued this product, we are unable to provide spare parts.
needs checking	The fact that every member nation has one vote in the General Assembly does not give each one equal influence.
revised	Each member nation has one vote in the General Assembly, but some have more influence than others.
needs checking	Despite the fact that virtually no one in those days could foresee the end of American surpluses, Jones could.

revised	Jones was one of the few to foresee the end of American surpluses.

D30. **factor**: Heavily overused, and a frequent cause of wordiness.

needs checking	An important factor contributing to the French Revolution was the poverty of the peasantry.
revised	The poverty of the peasantry was a major cause of the French Revolution.

D31. **from my point of view, according to my point of view, in my opinion**: All three expressions are usually redundant.

needs checking	From my point of view, basic health care is more important than esoteric and expensive machines or procedures that benefit few.
fair	I think that basic health care is more important than esoteric and expensive machines or procedures that benefit few.
better	Basic health care is more important than esoteric and expensive machines or procedures that benefit few.

D32. **I myself**: In almost all cases the addition of *myself* is needlessly repetitive.

needs checking	I myself believe in freedom of speech.
revised	I believe in freedom of speech.

(Note: For more on *myself* see pages 183–84.)

D33. **in all probability**: *Probably.*

needs checking	In all probability we will be finished tomorrow.
revised	We will probably be finished tomorrow.

D34. **include**: Often a needed word or two is omitted after this verb. The best solution may be to rephrase or find another verb.

needs checking	The report includes both secondary and post-secondary education.
revised	The report includes material on both secondary and post-secondary education.
or	The report deals with both secondary and post-secondary education.
needs checking	The Thirty Years War included most countries in Europe.
revised	The list of countries that fought in the Thirty Years War includes almost every European nation.
revised	Almost every European country fought in the Thirty Years War.

D35. **interesting**: In most cases the writer should not have to tell the reader that what he is saying is interesting.

needs checking	It is interesting to observe that illiteracy affects almost as high a proportion of native-born Americans as it does immigrants.
revised	Illiteracy affects almost as high a proportion of native-born Americans as it does immigrants.

D36. **mean for**: The preposition is unnecessary.

needs checking	I did not mean for him to do it all himself.
revised	I did not want him to do it all himself.

D37. **nature**: Often contributes to wordiness.

needs checking	The nature of the brain is to process information incredibly swiftly.
revised	The brain processes information extremely swiftly.

D38. **personally**: As a way of distinguishing views expressed by the same person acting in different capacities, *personally* serves a very useful function (e.g., *As a member of the cabinet he is obliged to support the measure, but personally he has doubts as to its appropriateness*). If you are not making this sort of distinction, though, it is safe to let your reader take it for granted that you are speaking for yourself rather than on behalf of others.

needs checking	Personally, I feel that the Supreme Court has usually exercised its constitutional authority wisely in recent years.
revised	I feel the Supreme Court has usually exercised its constitutional authority wisely in recent years.

D39. **point in time:** *Now* or *then.*

needs checking	At that point in time central Africa was very sparsely populated.
revised	Central Africa was then very sparsely populated.

D40. **really:** The adverb *really* has a place in formal writing when used to mean *in reality, truly* (*Vervoerd said he would change the regulations, but really he had no intention of doing so*). If you want to use an intensifier, however, *very* is preferable.

needs checking	It is really important that this be done today.
revised	It is very important that this be done today.
or	This must be done today.

Often in such cases your point may be made more effectively without using intensifiers—and even without using adjectives:

needs checking	Like any other animal raised in a modern factory farm, a factory-farmed pig leads a very appalling life. It spends its entire life in really hideous pens that do not permit it to turn around, let alone to walk or run. Such incredibly barbaric cruelty is justified on the grounds that without it, humans would be forced to pay somewhat more for bacon and ham.

revised	Like any other animal raised in a modern factory farm, a factory-farmed pig leads an appalling life. It spends its entire life in pens that do not permit it to turn around, let alone to walk or run. Such cruelty is justified on the grounds that without it, humans would be forced to pay somewhat more for bacon and ham.

D41. regard, with regard to, as regards: Try *about* or *over*, or rephrase.

needs checking	I am writing with regard to your proposal to centralize production.
revised	I am writing about your proposal to centralize production.
needs checking	As regards the trend in interest rates, it is likely to continue to be upward.
revised	Interest rates are likely to continue to increase.
needs checking	This Act gave the government powers with regard to the readjustment of industry.
revised	This Act gave the government powers over the readjustment of industry.

D42. redundancy: *Redundancies* are words or expressions that repeat in different words a meaning already expressed. Commonly used expressions that involve redundancy include *ATM machine, NDP party, end result, plans for the future, general public, nod your head, optimistic about the future, a personal friend of mine*, and *mutual cooperation*. Sometimes a case may be made for using a phrase of this sort in order to emphasize a point. What is to be avoided is thoughtless and purposeless wordiness.

needs checking	This property will appreciate greatly in value.
revised	This property will appreciate greatly.
needs checking	The house is very large in size.
revised	The house is very large.

needs checking	It was decided it would be mutually beneficial to both of us if he left.
revised	It was decided it would be mutually beneficial if he left.
revised	We agreed it would be better for both of us if he left.

D43. **situation**: By avoiding this word you will usually make your sentence shorter and better.

needs checking	This treaty created a situation in which European countries gave up a degree of autonomy in return for greater security.
revised	Through this treaty European countries gave up a degree of autonomy in return for greater security.

D44. **there is/are/was/were**: These constructions often produce sentences that are needlessly long.

needs checking	There were many factors which undermined the government's popularity in this period.
revised	Many things undermined the government's popularity in this period.
needs checking	There are many historians who accept this thesis.
revised	Many historians accept this thesis.

On the Web
Exercises on wordiness may be found at
www.broadviewpress.com/writing.
Click on **Exercises** and go to **D15–48**.

D45. **too few words**: This mistake can happen anywhere in a sentence. One of the best tests of whether or not a writer has checked her work is whether or not there are missing words. In almost all cases, such omissions will be noticed through careful proofreading.

needs checking	She rushed home to tell my family and about the accident.
revised	She rushed home to tell my family and me about the accident.
needs checking	Gandhi reminded the Conference that just one intercontinental ballistic missile could plant 200 million trees, irrigate one million hectares of land, or build 6,500 health care centres.
revised	Gandhi reminded the Conference that the money spent on just one intercontinental ballistic missile could be used to plant 200 million trees, irrigate one million hectares of land, or build 6,500 health care centres.

D46. too many words: Many of the causes of this problem have been given separate entries.

needs checking	So far as the purpose of this essay is concerned, it will concentrate on the expansion of Chinese influence.
revised	This essay will concentrate on the expansion of Chinese influence.
needs checking	Although the author does not claim to be writing a social study, the question arises whether the social implications of his analysis can be ignored.
revised	Although the author does not claim to be writing a social study, his analysis does have social implications.

D47. tragic/tragically: Unnecessary use of either the adjective or the adverb constitutes overkill.

needs checking	Her husband, her child, and more than a hundred others died in a tragic plane crash in 1997.
revised	Her husband, her child, and more than a hundred others died in a plane crash in 1997.

D48. would like to take this opportunity to: *Would like.*

needs checking	I would like to take this opportunity to thank my cousin in Peoria.
revised	I am very grateful to my cousin in Peoria.
or	I would like to thank my cousin in Peoria.

⊙ Writing by Computer

No one born later than, say, 1950 needs to be convinced of the advantages of computers for writing. But many of us need to remind ourselves periodically of some of the pitfalls of word-processed writing. Some problems are readily avoided if one retains the habit of careful proofreading: the perils of spell-check, for example (see below), or the dangers of search and replace. It is all too easy to come to rely on the computer a little too heavily in such contexts—as you would find if you instructed your computer to replace all occurrences of *author* with the word *senior editor* in a book contract. Suddenly, you would find the absurdities *senior editorization* and *senior editority*. The computer would have no way of knowing where to stop searching and replacing.

Proofreading may check some of the bad cognitive habits that computers breed in many writers who work only on screen; it certainly will not eliminate them all. For some of us, computers can be wonderful facilitators of flow; many people find it easier to get a lot of ideas out of their heads and "on paper" by using a computer than by using a pen and paper. But the same habits of scrolling that can facilitate flow in writing and in reading can distort our ability to arrange ideas in an ordered fashion so as to best present an argument. Though researchers are far from understanding why, they have now assembled a considerable body of evidence suggesting that seeing a succession of printed pages enables one to combine and connect ideas in ways that are not always evident if one restricts oneself to scrolling on the screen. This is why it is vitally important to work with paper as well as on screen. It is ironic that the very means by which the re-ordering of blocks of text has become a matter of effortlessly keyboarding (rather than of laboriously retyping) also acts to dull the cognitive processes that are required for humans to re-order those blocks most effectively. But that is the reality all writers must come to terms with.

If computer technology may facilitate the sort of writing flow that is the best tonic for writer's block, the speed with which that technology changes may also sometimes give us an excuse not to write. It is all too easy to decide that it will be impossible to finish a thesis or complete a report unless and until one upgrades software, replaces that old hard drive, or acquires a faster machine. In almost all cases this is really just a way of trying to avoid the hard job of getting down to writing. We should all make it a firm rule not to let our fascination with technology get in the way of our writing.

O *Spell-check and Grammar-check*

Commonly used words are also commonly misspelled words—and not only because they occur frequently. Most of us have the sense when we use a word such as *surreptitiously* to check the spelling in a dictionary, or with the spell-check mechanism on our computer. But words such as *its* and *it's*, or *than* and *then*, or *compliment* and *complement* we tend to use without thinking—and no computer spell-check will tell us if we have had a mental lapse and used the wrong one. (Publishers often receive manuscripts that begin with a Forward rather than a Foreword.) It is worth remembering that no computer can be a substitute for careful proofreading.

Grammar-check programs can be useful in helping writers to catch slips in such areas as subject-verb agreement and dangling constructions. Even in cases such as these, however, grammar checkers are far from foolproof; you must still be able to make an informed judgement as to whether or not the words that the program draws to your attention do indeed need to be changed.

What is true for points of grammar is even more true for matters of style. Grammar checkers also offer advice on matters such as the length of sentences and the degree to which the passive voice is used. Such issues are by their nature not readily subject to precise formulations, and one should thus take advice of this sort from software programs with more than a grain of salt.

On the Web

There are several good grammar sites on the Internet; one of the best is *The Guide to Grammar and Writing*, sponsored by the Capital Community College Foundation. Its address is **http://www.ccc.commnet.edu/grammar/**.

O *The Internet*

In 1992 the media was full of references to the need to create an "electronic highway." But within a year almost everyone had realized that one had already been created. The Internet had originally been the product of the American Defense Department's desire to build diffuse lines of communication as a defense against attacks on the country's infrastructure. Made available for use by academics in the 1980s, it had quietly developed by the early 1990s into an extraordinarily efficient and inexpensive means of communication. And as Web technology has developed, its potential has continued to grow.

Technology that can be used in so many ways can of course also be misused in many ways. Given the pace of change—and the complexity of the topic—it would be unwise in a book of this size to attempt any comprehensive treatment of how to use the Internet as a resource tool for writing. But some general guidelines may be useful.

○ *Research Using the Internet*
   (See also Collaboration and Research, pages 69–82.)

The Internet may seem like a goldmine when it comes to research. But if so, the likeness is to a vein of ore that is not always sufficiently concentrated as to make the mining of it economic. Sometimes the most difficult thing is to decide when it is worth one's while to commit one's resources to the mining operation. Search engines are likely to turn up vast amounts of material on almost any topic. But often much of it will be unreliable—and it is extraordinarily difficult for the novice to tell what is likely to be reliable and what isn't.

At one end of the spectrum, most refereed scholarly journals are available online—and some are available only on the Internet. The best way to consult reference works that are constantly updated (such as the *Oxford English Dictionary*) is through the Internet. And some academic disciplines are now turning to publication via the Internet for new scholarly monographs. Rapid progress is also being made towards making previously published monographs available online.

At the other end of the spectrum are countless materials that have not been reviewed either by academic authorities or by publishers. How is one to gauge the reliability of such material? Should one just stick to established sources in the library? How is it possible to avoid spending a large amount of time merely to amass a large quantity of unreliable source material?

There are no easy answers to these questions, and the best strategies are likely to vary depending on the sort of research one is doing. The most important thing for the novice may be simply to consult one's instructor on the issue of what sources—whether in the library or on the Internet—may be most appropriate to use for a given assignment.

Some other research principles may be helpful. Think of the credentials of the author: is he or she an academic at a respected institution, and has he or she published widely on the topic? How new is the material? (Obviously some premium is to be placed on more recent research, though often the most important works on a topic will not be new.) Which works on a topic are cited most often by others? If a work is frequently cited by others, it will be one that should be taken into account. What is the point of view of the author? One key consideration in assembling the resources one will deal with is making sure that a variety of viewpoints are represented.

You should not feel obligated, though, to give equal weight to all points of view. Particularly where material on the Web is concerned, it will sometimes be the case that implausible or downright irresponsible points of view will be more widely represented than views that deserve greater respect. Such is obviously the case with websites promulgating racist or anti-Semitic views, but it may also be the case with certain scientific matters. By the late 1990s, for example, the vast majority of reputable scientific opinion was in broad agreement as to the dangers of global warming. Dissenting scientific voices comprised only a small minority among the community of reputable scientists—but for years their views received disproportionate space on the Web, where numerous sites were largely devoted to casting doubt on the consensus scientific view on global warming (and, not by coincidence, to preserving the status quo for the coal industry, the oil and gas industry, and so on). Where such ideologically charged issues as these are concerned, it is worth paying particularly close attention to accounts that run counter to the normal ideological stance of the publication. When the right-wing magazine *The Economist* accepted several years ago that the weight of evidence overwhelmingly supported the argument that global warming posed a real danger, or when the left-of-centre British newspaper *The Guardian* concluded that despite its socialist rhetoric the Mugabe government in Zimbabwe was denying its people both economic justice and basic human rights, such views deserve special respect.

With library sources, the publisher of a work is also a helpful clue for the researcher. The experienced researcher will take account of the publisher, but not put too much stock in its reputation; the university presses of Oxford, Cambridge, Harvard, and Princeton have published a few real clunkers as well as vast amounts of first-rate scholarship. And because librarians often have standing orders from such prestigious presses as these, a clunker from them is more likely to find its way onto the shelves of the university library than a clunker from, say, Wilfrid Laurier Press or Hackett Publishing. Nevertheless, there will always be a better-than-average chance of work published by a highly reputable organization being of high quality. This holds true for the Web as well. The beginning student will often not know which journals or which book publishers have a solid track record. But it will help to be wary of self-published material, whether in book form or on the Web, and it will help as well if the researcher pays attention to such matters, and is prepared to ask questions of instructors and of fellow students.

Perhaps above all, it is important to note each source you consult in writing an essay, report, or thesis. (Be sure as well to mark clearly any passages or phrases that are a direct quotation rather than a summary or your own commentary on what you have read, so as not to confuse your own ideas or phrasings with those of the authors you have consulted.) In the case of an Internet reference it may be more convenient to store the information on your hard drive or on a flash drive rather than on a card or piece of paper—but the principle of noting sources carefully remains the same.

If many of the principles are the same, the mechanisms of Web research are very different from the mechanisms of using the library, and are constantly changing. A number of good guidebooks devoted entirely to using Internet sources are now available, and are updated regularly. Referencing styles also change frequently. Some of the essential points of referencing Internet sources appear below in the chapter on referencing. The fullest and most up-to-date treatments of referencing according to particular styles, however, are to be found through the websites of the relevant organizations: the MLA, APA, and so on.

O *Observing Netiquette*

The word *netiquette* is a clever little pun that neatly encapsulates the notion that standards of courtesy and consideration are as important in cyberspace as they are in other areas of human existence—and that the Internet is sufficiently different from other forms of communication as to make some special guidelines advisable.

Anyone who has used e-mail has probably sensed that the medium lends itself to a higher degree of informality (for both sender and recipient) than does the sending of a letter printed on corporate or departmental letterhead. The combination of distance, informality, and invisibility that electronic communication embodies seems to encourage the spontaneous expression of emotion in ways that might otherwise not feel appropriate. It often seems to foster a breeziness that is as friendly as it is efficient. But it also seems to lend itself to the venting of certain sorts of anger, in ways that other means of communication do not. And sometimes it leads people to divulge personal information that on reflection they might rather have kept to themselves. These tendencies of e-mail—to foster sometimes unexpected degrees of intimacy, and to facilitate the unbridled expression of anger—argue for the wisdom of taking the time to edit and proof any electronic message, checking its tone quite as much as its grammar.

The ever-increasing use of electronic communication in a wide variety of contexts continues to raise issues of appropriate tone and of level of formality. For the most part, no one expects e-mails to conform to all the conventions of more formal communications; it would be foolish to worry about a typo or two in an e-mail dashed off to a friend—let alone in a text message! But any e-mail should be clear, unambiguous, and written in an appropriate tone; again, it is wise to edit and proofread carefully any message you send. And if you are using e-mail as a convenient way to convey a more formal document, that document should indeed conform to the conventions of standard usage. A proposal submitted electronically or a memo circulated electronically should be phrased, proofread, and presented as carefully as you would the same document in hard copy form. As with writing, faxing, or phoning, then, the context and the expectations of your audience are always important.

Privacy issues are at least as important with electronic communications as they are with other forms of communication. As a recipient, consider the feelings of the sender; unless it is obviously appropriate to forward a message, for example, ask the permission of the sender before you pass it on. And as a sender, it is worth remembering that electronic communication can often end up being less private than regular mail. Since recipients are not always as considerate as one might wish. And—particularly given that e-mails are often forwarded or copied by mistake to unintended recipients—it is wise to consider whether the potential recipients of a message may be a much larger group than intended—and word the message accordingly.

O *Point-form Netiquette*

- Keep messages clear and brief.
- Edit/proof all messages before sending—for tone as well as form.
- Use clear subject headings.
- Make the text as easy to read as possible; leave a line between paragraphs (rather than indent); use italics—or place an underscore mark before and after the relevant word(s) as a substitute for italics; use only well-known abbreviations.
- When quoting from a previous message, quote only the necessary passage(s).
- Address the message carefully.
- Attachments: be aware that some recipients may have difficulty downloading attachments, and be prepared to use alternative means in such circumstances.
- Visuals: remember that the recipient of your message may not have the same technology you do. Think twice, for

example, before sending a large file of graphic information that may take the recipient an inordinate amount of time to download—if indeed (s)he has the capacity to do so.

- Listservs/chatgroups/newsgroups/bulletin boards: There are a variety of Internet mechanisms for sharing information among many individuals with a common interest. Conventions may vary with each group; it makes sense to pay attention to the procedures followed and the tone adopted by established users before you start to play an active role yourself. If in any doubt as to appropriate procedures, ask the listowner/bulletin board organizer.

- Post only information that is likely to be of interest to others—and, as with e-mail, be as clear and as brief as possible.

- Be particularly sensitive to the demands you may be making on the time of others. If, for example, you are sending an "information-only" e-mail to a department head who may deal with a hundred e-mails a day, make it clear in the heading or at the beginning of the message that this is for information only, and that no reply is required.

- The overriding principle: always show consideration for your reader(s).

Plagiarism, Copyright, and the Web
(See also pages 76–78.)

Keeping careful track of your sources—and clearly indicating for your own reference what is a quotation and what is your own comment—not only saves time; it also prevents unintentional plagiarism. (For more on this subject see the first section of the book, on "The Writing Process," as well as the sections on "Documentation.")

Although the possibilities both for unintended and for intentional plagiarism are vastly greater with the Web than they were when hard-copy materials were the only resources, the mechanisms for detection have expanded as well; search engines can often confirm for an instructor in seconds that a particular string of words in a student essay has been lifted unacknowledged from another source.

Copyright rules for written materials apply to the Internet just as they do to books or articles; written work is under copyright protection for many years after it is published. Indeed, copyright restrictions have been extended in recent years in many jurisdictions. In the United States the 1998 Sonny Bono Copyright Amendment Act extended copyright protection by an additional twenty years; most written material published in 1923 or later will remain in copyright until at least 2019. In the UK and other European countries copyright restrictions were extended in the 1990s, such that work is now in copyright for seventy years after the death of the author (or translator); similar restrictions were imposed as of January 2005 in Australia. In Canada copyright restrictions are somewhat less severe; copyright protection extends for fifty years after the death of the author or translator.

There is now considerable feeling in many countries that, in extending copyright restrictions as far as they have been, governments have tilted the balance that such laws attempt to find (between the interests of authors and their heirs, and the interests of the general public) too much away from the public interest. Nevertheless, unless and until such laws are changed, a text such as T.S. Eliot's "The Hollow Men," first published in 1925, will be in

On the Web

Further information about copyright may be found on the Web at sites such as **www.accesscopyright.ca** (Canadian), **www.copyright.gov** (American), and **www.whatiscopyright.org**. Sites with a commitment to the public interest on copyright issues include **www.faircopyright.ca** (Canada), **www.creativecommons.org**, and **www.lessig.org**.

copyright in the United States until 2020, and in Europe (including Great Britain) and in Australia until 2035 (Eliot died in 1965). In Canada it will remain in copyright until 2015.

Except for quoting brief passages (with the proper acknowledgement), you may not reproduce copyright material, whether you have found it in a written publication or on the Web, without the permission of the copyright holder. Nor may you post copyrighted materials on the Web without permission from the copyright holders.

⊙ Business Writing

Tone may be the most important aspect of business writing. The adjective *businesslike* conjures up images of efficiency and professional distance, and certainly it is appropriate to convey those qualities in most business reports, memos, and correspondence. In a great deal of business writing, however, it is also desirable to convey a warm personal tone; striking the right balance between the personal and the professionally distanced is at the heart of the art of business writing. A few guidelines are offered here.

D49. **tone:** Perhaps the best guard against significant errors in tone is to consult your colleagues whenever you are uncertain. Circulate a draft of any important document to others and ask their opinion. Is the tone too cold and formal? Is it too gushy and enthusiastic? Is it too direct? Or not direct enough?

needs checking	Do you think it's fair to ask the accounts department to handle the extra work that would be entailed in moving to your new system? Get serious!
revised	If we adopted the proposed new plan, there would be questions of fairness involved that I think would need to be addressed. The accounts staff is seriously concerned that the proposed new plan

would entail significantly more work for them, while there appear to be no provisions for additional staff or compensation in the accounts area.

D50. **qualifications**: Bald statements are often not the most appropriate; it is better to qualify any generalizations you are making so as to be certain they are accurate. Be particularly careful about suggesting you are speaking for your entire organization; unless you are sure, you are well advised to qualify any extreme statements.

needs checking	Our organization always underprices every competitor.
revised	Our organization always tries to keep its prices lower than those of major competitors.
needs checking	There is no way our organization would ever cut back on research and development.
revised	As an organization we have a strong commitment to research and development.

D51. **courtesy and consideration**: Given that business communication usually operates within a hierarchical power structure, it is particularly important to foreground consideration in business, memos, letters, and e-mails. Avoid direct commands wherever possible; give credit to others when things go right; and take responsibility and apologize when things go wrong.

needs checking	Here is the material we spoke of. Send the report in by the end of the month to my attention.
revised	I enclose the material we spoke of. If you could send in the report by the end of the month to my attention, I'd be very grateful.
needs checking	I am writing in response to your complaint. We carry a large number of products with similar titles, and sometimes errors in shipping occur. Please in future specify the ISBN of the item you are ordering, as that will help keep errors to a minimum.

revised　　　Thank you for your letter—and my sincere apologies on behalf of our company for our mistake. As you may know, we carry a large number of products with similar titles, and (particularly in cases where our customer service department is not able to double-check against an ISBN) errors do sometimes occur. But that is an explanation rather than an excuse; I do apologize, and I have asked that the correct item be shipped to you immediately. Again, my sincere apologies—and my thanks to you for drawing this matter to my attention.

needs checking　　　It has come to my attention that you have not been filling in your expense forms in the proper fashion, or submitting them promptly. I refer you to Section C in the Staff Manual for instructions on how these forms are to be filled out, and I would remind you that all employees are to submit expense forms within one week of the end of the month in which the expenses were incurred. Thank you for your attention to this matter.

revised　　　Harry, you've been doing a great job these past few months—which is something I probably haven't mentioned enough! There is a small thing I want to draw to your attention, though, which I think can make things go even better. I know it makes a real difference to Carol and the others in accounts if they get the expense forms submitted promptly so that they can keep proper records month to month. If they have to keep going back into the records to make adjustments it can end up consuming an awful lot of their time. I know it can be a pain at the end of the month to fill in these forms, but it really does make a difference. Again, I appreciate the effort you've been putting in—as I know Carol does too.

D52. **memos**: The memo is a standard form of communication within an organization. In order to retain the attention of readers, memos are usually kept brief. (If a large volume of material is to be dealt with, it may be better to present the material in the form of a report, with a covering memo summarizing the key points or recommendations for action.)

Memos should follow a conventional format, whether on paper or in electronic form. See page 367 for a sample memo.

D53. **business letters**: It is now considered to be appropriate to send out business letters electronically. The advantage in speed is obvious; just as important is the time saved in printing, stuffing and addressing an envelope, stamping, and mailing.

Some business communication is still generally sent by mail. A personal thank-you to a business colleague is best sent by mail, as are contracts and any letters or other documents accompanying them. Remember that all letters sent by mail should be signed by hand above the sender's printed name.

As with letters, a conventional format should be followed with business letters. There should be room for considerable flexibility as to the details of format. Some prefer to use commas after the salutation, for example, while others don't. The main thing is to be consistent. See page 368 for a sample letter.

D54. **resumés and application letters**: A resumé is also sometimes referred as a CV—short for the Latin *curriculum vitae*, or, roughly, *the outline of a life*. In most circumstances these should be kept short—to one page, if possible—and the information should be allowed to speak for itself. The covering letter should also be kept brief, businesslike, and free of puffery. Resumés may be organized either chronologically (in reverse order, so that the most recent accomplishments or occupations are listed first) or thematically (Education; Employment; etc.). See page 369 for a sample covering letter and page 371 for a sample resumé.

Memo

To: All Those Involved in Academic Sales
From: Don LePan
Date: September 3, 2008

This is a cautionary note to all of us—myself perhaps
most of all, as I know I have traditionally tended to be
pretty generous in sending out complimentary copies
of our publications. As of the end of July expense for
complimentary copies was running at almost double
the level of last year, and the picture is almost as bad
at the end of August. Of course we knew we would be
publishing more books this year, but we had budgeted
for an increase in line with the increase projected in
sales—25–30%, in other words, not 70–80%!

As the figures have driven home to me, when complimentary copy expense goes way over budget,
one other category is sure to go way over budget as
well—the expense category of postage for promotional
purposes, which was running at more than double last
year's levels as of the end of July, and almost $30,000
above budget—with most of the difference attributable to more complimentary copies being sent out.

Please feel free to quote the above figures in situations
where you may find yourself explaining why this year
we can't afford to send out as many complimentary
copies as we would like! Thanks.

Prof. Elizabeth Jones
Department of English
Faculty of Arts & Social Sciences
Loyola University
Ames, Iowa 64223

Calgary: March 22, 2009

Dear Prof. Jones

Many thanks indeed for the proposal from you and Gary Collins for a new annotated edition of selected poems by Emily Dickinson.

As with all proposals for our Broadview Editions series, this one will go to outside reviewers before being brought to a meeting of our Humanities Editorial Board; the process typically takes two to three months before a formal decision is reached. I gather, however, that you are planning in the near future to apply for a grant to assist in research connected to this project. With that in mind I would like to say that we at Broadview have read through the proposal and find it extremely impressive. Certainly we are convinced that a market exists for a good edition of this sort, and I find it almost unimaginable that outside reviewers and Editorial Board members will not feel (as I do) that this is a very good proposal indeed. I fully expect as well as hope that it will move forward to publication with Broadview! With all best wishes,

Yours sincerely

Don LePan
Director, Special Projects

Ms. Dorothy Rosenberg
Personnel Dept.
Golden Mountain Resort
1212 James St.
Golden, BC V2R 4K5

Calgary: April 3, 2009

Dear Ms. Rosenberg

I am writing to apply for employment at the Golden
Mountain Resort this coming summer.

A resumé is enclosed; as you see, I have previous experience working outdoors as a guide, and I would certainly
be interested in something similar this summer. I am also
nearing completion of a university degree in English, and
I would be particularly interested in any work there that
might involve written communication.

My university classes are on Mondays, Wednesdays, and
Fridays; I could come to Golden for an interview on any
Tuesday or Thursday, and could probably make arrangements for another day if that were more convenient for
you.

I can be reached either at the above address and e-mail
address or by phone at (403) 283-8550; I will hope to hear
from you. With best wishes,

Yours sincerely

Joseph Alvarez
encl.

Resumé

Joseph Alvarez
316 7th St. NW
Calgary AB T2N 1N3
(403) 283-8550
joseph.alvarez@hotmail.com

Education: University of Calgary
                     two years completed towards a BA (Hons),
                         English Literature
                     John A. Macdonald Secondary School
                     Graduation Diploma, 2007
                     Irene Stitt Scholarship, 2006–07

Employment: Wintergreen Resort, Bragg Creek, AB
                     Nature Guide, summers 2007 and 2008
                     Ski Patrol, part-time, weekends, 2006–07

Other Activities: Sports Editor, UC News Campus Newspaper,
                         2008–09
                     Captain, Senior Basketball Team, John A.
                         Macdonald Secondary School, 2007
                     Member, Debating Team, John A.
                         Macdonald Secondary School, 2006

References: Prof. Sheila Goek
                     English Department
                     University of Calgary
                     Calgary AB T2N 1N4
                     (403) 244-6612 (w)
                     (403) 552-6988 (h)
                     sgoek@ucalgary.ca

                     Frederick Simpson
                     Manager, Wintergreen Resort
                     Bragg Creek AB T7K 3W2
                     (403) 669-7760 (w)
                     fsimpson@wintergreen.com

                     (additional references available on request)

⊙ Academic Writing: *Tense Situations*

As is discussed in the next chapter, all academic subject areas have their specialized vocabulary and writing conventions. One sort of convention that can take some getting used to is the way in which verb tenses are used. Many students find writing about literature particularly challenging in this respect; its conventions present fundamental problems for the student at the level of sentence structure.

D55. **verb tenses when writing about literature:** The past tense is, of course, normally used to name actions which happened in the past. But when one is writing about what happens in a work of literature, convention decrees that we use the simple *present* tense.

needs checking	Romeo fell in love with Juliet as soon as he saw her.
revised	Romeo falls in love with Juliet as soon as he sees her.
needs checking	In her short stories, Alice Munro explored both the outer and the inner worlds of small town life.
revised	In her short stories, Alice Munro explores both the outer and the inner worlds of small town life.

If literature in its historical context is being discussed, however, the simple past tense is usually the best choice:

needs checking	Shakespeare writes *Romeo and Juliet* when he was about thirty years of age.
revised	Shakespeare wrote *Romeo and Juliet* when he was about thirty years of age.
needs checking	Alice Munro wins the Governor General's Award for the first time in 1968, for her collection *Dance of the Happy Shades*.

revised	Alice Munro won the Governor General's Award for the first time in 1968, for her collection *Dance of the Happy Shades*.

In some circumstances either the past or the present tense may be possible in a sentence, depending on the context:

correct	In her early work Munro often explored themes relating to adolescence. (appropriate if the focus is on historical developments relating to the author)
also correct	In her early work Munro often explores themes relating to adolescence. (appropriate if the focus is on the work itself)

Notice that if the subject of a sentence is the work itself, the present tense is normally required:

needs checking	Munro's early work often explored themes relating to adolescence.
revised	Munro's early work often explores themes relating to adolescence.

Often in an essay about literature the context may require shifting back and forth between past and present tenses. In the following passage, for example, the present tense is used except for the sentence that recounts the historical fact of Eliot refusing permission:

> T.S. Eliot's most notorious expression of anti-Semitism is the opinion he expresses in *After Strange Gods* that in "the society that we desire," "any large number of free-thinking Jews" would be "undesirable" (64). Tellingly, Eliot never allowed *After Strange Gods* to be reprinted. But his anti-Semitism emerges repeatedly in his poetry as well. In "Gerontion," for example, he describes....

In such cases even experienced writers have to think carefully during the revision process about the most appropriate tense for each verb. Note in the following example the change in verb tense from *was* to *is*:

needs checking	In *The Two Gentlemen of Verona* Shakespeare exhibited a degree and a variety of technical accomplishment unprecedented in the English drama. He still had much to learn as a dramatist and as a poet; in its wit or its power to move us emotionally *The Two Gentlemen of Verona* was at an enormous remove from the great works of a few years later. But already, in 1592, Shakespeare had mastered all the basic techniques of plot construction that were to sustain the structures of the great plays.
revised	In *The Two Gentlemen of Verona* Shakespeare exhibits a degree and a variety of technical accomplishment unprecedented in the English drama. He still had much to learn as a dramatist and as a poet; in its wit or its power to move us emotionally *The Two Gentlemen of Verona* is at an enormous remove from the great works of a few years later. But already, in 1592, Shakespeare had mastered all the basic techniques of plot construction that were to sustain the structures of the great plays.

D56. **consistency in verb tense when integrating quotations:** If one is writing about literature the writing will usually be in the *present* tense, but the quotations one wishes to use are likely to be in the *past* tense. Often it is thus necessary, if you are incorporating a quotation into a sentence, to rephrase and/or adjust the length of the quotation in order to preserve grammatical consistency. If a quotation is set apart from the body of your own writing, on the other hand, you do not need to (and should not) rephrase.

needs checking   Emma Bovary lives largely through memory and fantasy. She daydreams frequently, and, as she reads, "the memory of the Vicomte kept her happy" (244). (The past tense *kept* is inconsistent with the present tense *reads* and *daydreams*.)

revised   Emma Bovary lives largely through memory and fantasy. She daydreams frequently, and, as she reads, the "memory of the Vicomte" (244) keeps her happy.

or   Emma Bovary lives largely through memory and fantasy. She daydreams frequently, and blends fact and fiction in her imaginings: "Always, as she read, the memory of the Vicomte kept her happy. She established a connection between him and the characters of her favourite fiction" (244).

On the Web

Exercises on choosing the correct tense when writing about literature and about other academic subjects may be found at **www.broadviewpress.com/writing**. Click on **Exercises** and go to **D55–56**.

D57. verb tenses when writing in other academic disciplines: To a large extent the same principles that are used in writing about literature apply too in other disciplines. In many other disciplines the present tense is the tense most commonly used. Indeed, if you are treating the ideas you are discussing as "live" ideas, it is wrong to use the past tense:

needs checking   In an important recent book, Nelly Ferguson surveyed the history of the decline of empires, and predicted that during the course of the twenty-first century China will replace the United States as the world's leading power.

revised	In an important recent book, Nelly Ferguson surveys the history of the decline of empires, and predicts that during the course of the twenty-first century China will replace the United States as the world's leading power.
needs checking	In their 2009 paper Smith and Johnson suggested that parental influence is more important than that of peers, even for adolescents. This essay will examine these claims and assess their validity.
revised	In their 2009 paper Smith and Johnson suggest that parental influence is more important than that of peers, even for adolescents. This essay will examine these claims and assess their validity.

In many disciplines, particularly in the sciences, it is also common to use the present perfect tense when discussing relevant recent research:

> Although research has often found the attitude-to-behaviour connection to be quite weak, the behaviour-to-attitude link has been shown to be quite strong. As Festinger (2008) and Kiesler, Nisbet, and Zanna (2006) have demonstrated, an asymmetry exists between the two possible directions. As Acheson (2009) has put it, "we are ... very good at finding reasons for what we do, but not very good at doing what we find reasons for" (25).

It is important to remember that the use of the present tense in academic writing is not dependent on how recently the ideas being discussed were first put forward; the key thing is whether or not you are discussing them as live ideas today. You may use the present tense when discussing a paper written six months ago—but you may also use the present tense when discussing a text dating from twenty-four centuries ago. Just as you may say when writing about literature that Shakespeare *explores* the potentially corrosive effects of ambition, so too you may say that Aristotle *approaches* ethical questions with a view as much to the virtue of the doer as to the rightness of the deed, and that Marx *values* highly the economic contribution of labour—even though Shakespeare and Aristotle and Marx are themselves long dead. As with the text of a story or poem, the writings of dead thinkers may be discussed as embodying live thoughts—ideas that may retain interest and relevance.

Conversely, if the ideas you are discussing are being considered historically, rather than as of current relevance, you should not use the present tense.

needs checking	In several articles the renowned astronomer Fred Hoyle advances arguments against the big bang theory of the origin of the universe. Hoyle suggests that the universe perpetually regenerates itself. (Hoyle's arguments have now been refuted.)
revised	In several articles the renowned astronomer Fred Hoyle advanced arguments against the big bang theory of the origin of the universe. Hoyle suggested that the universe perpetually regenerates itself.

As is the case with writing about literature, academic writing in disciplines such as history or philosophy or political science may often look at a text *both* from a historical perspective *and* from the perspective of the live ideas that are put forward within it. In such circumstances the writer needs to be prepared to shift verb tenses depending on the context:

purely historical	Darwin finally published his theory only after an article by Alfred Wallace advancing a similar theory had been published. The central element in Darwin's theory was the concept of natural selection. Unlike Wallace, Darwin had become convinced that....

historical context   Darwin finally published his theory only after an article by Alfred Wallace advancing a similar theory had been published. The central element in Darwin's theory is the concept of natural selection; according to Darwin's theory, all organisms are....

purely historical   Hobbes firmly believed that the tragic upheaval of the English civil war was caused by the spread of dangerous beliefs about humans and human society. Hobbes's view was that humans require a structure of government to enforce a structure of laws; otherwise, he felt, they would revert to a state of nature in which life would be "nasty, brutish, and short." Hobbes's opponents did not disagree with the substance of this notion. But because he had argued from first principles rooted in human realities rather than in any divine ordering, he was denounced by the authorities, accused of atheism, and threatened with prosecution....

historical context   Hobbes firmly believed that the tragic upheaval of the English civil war was caused by the spread of dangerous beliefs about humans and human society. Hobbes's view is that humans require a structure of government to enforce a structure of laws; otherwise they revert to a state of nature in which life will be "nasty, brutish, and short." That central notion still lies at the core of much political theory today....

⊙ Academic Writing:
Different Subjects, Different Styles

This section is designed to introduce the undergraduate student to some of the conventions of writing in a number of the main academic disciplines. The list of subjects covered is weighted towards those subjects that tend to place the greatest importance on writing (notably, the humanities and social sciences), though scientific writing is also covered.

Undergraduate students are often told that the conventions of writing vary between different disciplines, and that they should not expect that an approach to essay writing which works well in one discipline will work well in another. It is also the case that even *within* each discipline there can be more than one set of accepted practices when it comes to academic writing. What is entirely appropriate to an essay in the continental tradition of philosophy is not likely to suit the requirements of a course in epistemology taught entirely in the analytic tradition; an essay in the interpretivist tradition in sociology will be inappropriate for a course taught from a positivist perspective; and so on. This section attempts to give the student some sense of the divergent lines of approach in each discipline, and of the approach to academic writing in each case. Inevitably, the picture provided here in such a short space is a greatly simplified one. We hope that the information provided will nevertheless provide some guidance to those beginning the effort of reading and writing in a new academic subject.

Included with the discussions of writing practices of the disciplines are brief discipline-specific lists of useful websites and respected journals. Students are likely to benefit greatly from wide reading in general journals of news and opinion. Some of the most interesting, useful, and reliable of these are *The Atlantic Monthly*, *The Economist*, *Harper's Magazine*, *The New Yorker*, and *The New York Review of Books*. Some articles from these publications are available online, as are some materials from leading newspapers such as *The Australian, The Globe and Mail, The Guardian,* the London *Times,* the *Los Angeles Times, The New York Times, The Wall Street Journal,* and *The Washington Post.* As well, websites such as the Arts and Letters site (www.aldaily.com) provide access to a selection of the most interesting pieces from many of these and other sources.

Note: As this book is designed primarily for undergraduate use, professional faculties such as law and medicine are not included in the following list. Business and commerce are included, however, since at many institutions courses in these subjects are offered beginning at the first-year undergraduate level.

O *Anthropology*

Anthropology is unique among academic disciplines in the way it is configured. At many universities the department of anthropology includes four fields or subdivisions: cultural anthropology (the study of other cultures, or the study of one's own culture with a fresh eye); physical anthropology (the study of the physical evolution of humans, and connections to other primates); archeology (the study of the past through physical artifacts); and linguistics (the scientific study of human languages). In other universities archeology and linguistics may be separate departments on their own, with the anthropology department focusing on the study of physical and cultural anthropology. At still other institutions, the department of anthropology focuses exclusively on cultural anthropology—and in some cases, it is combined with sociology as one academic department. To complicate the picture further, what is known as "cultural anthropology" in the United States is referred to as "social anthropology" in Britain. (Both terms are understood and accepted in Canada and Australia, though the Canadians increasingly lean towards the American model.) Archeology, linguistics, and physical anthropology all tend towards a somewhat more scientific style of writing than does cultural anthropology. (For more on scientific styles of writing see below under "Biology" and "Psychology.") This section will focus on the most prevalent field within the discipline, cultural anthropology.

Until relatively recently the feature that most clearly distinguished cultural anthropology from sociology was that anthropology dealt with other cultures, sociology with our own culture. In the past generation, that distinction has very largely broken down, under both the pressure of a general realization among anthropologists of the degree to which perceptions of "otherness" were inherently problematic, and the practical pressures of greatly reduced funding for research in remote areas of the world. Cultural anthropologists are now at least as likely to focus on interesting and revealing aspects of cultures in the developed world as they are to focus on the kinship structures or belief systems of traditional societies in the Amazon basin or the forests of Papua, New Guinea. But whereas the sociologist is likely to search for statistical information about aggregations of people, the anthropologist is far more likely to rely on observation and interviews to collect information on the basis of which are put forward "explanatory generalizations." (The early twentieth-century anthropologist Franz Boas, who was probably more influential than any other single figure in giving shape to the discipline, used this phrase to describe what anthropology, as a "human science," could offer; in contrast, he suggested that the natural sciences offer "particular descriptions.") Here are two passages of anthropological writing, one concerning the Yanomamo of southern Venezuela and northern Brazil, and the other discussing RVers in North America:

> The soul aspect of the *noreshi* [a sort of spirit or portion of the soul], however, can leave the human body at will and wander. Sickness results when the *noreshi* has left the body; unless it is brought back soon, the person will die.... When sickness is deemed to be the result of soul loss, the people who are closely related to the sick person hunt for his *noreshi*. I participated in one of these soul hunts. Kaobawa's group had set up a temporary camp across the river from its main village site, as they suspected raiders would attack them. While they were camped

in their temporary village, one of the children became ill, and her malady was thought to be caused by soul loss.... (Napoleon Chagnon, *Yanomamo: The Fierce People*, New York, 1968, 49)

The people whose lifestyle we describe here challenge the stereotype of old age as a time of decline into senility, poverty, and illness. Their descriptions of their experiences, and their depictions of themselves and their fellow RVers defy the myths about elderly North Americans. They do not think of themselves as suffering the 'plight' of the elderly. The stereotype of seniors being lonely, isolated, ill, dependent, and suffering from the trauma of the 'empty nest' or meaningless retirement does not apply to them. They see themselves and their peers as adventurous, self-reliant, flexible, friendly, and 'gutsy.'... One of our correspondents, Tonia Thornson, describes the difference between RVing seniors and those living in a home for the elderly. She left RVing in 1993 at the age of 81 because, she says, of the 'bunch of crooks' who repair RVs. She now regrets her decision. (Dorothy and David Counts, *Over the Next Hill: An Ethnography of RVing Seniors in North America*, Peterborough, 2/e 2001, 50)

Much as the subject matter of these two passages may differ, we may notice that both advance generalizations about a culture or a subculture; that both couch these generalizations in the present tense; and that both support the generalizations they are making with evidence gleaned from personal interaction with members of the group being studied.

Not all cultural anthropology is characterized by an emphasis on the personal and the particular. As with other social sciences, postmodernist theory has exerted considerable influence within the discipline of cultural anthropology—and with it has come a writing style featuring long sentences, complex syntax, extremely high levels of abstraction, and a vocabulary quite different from that of traditional anthropology. That style is discussed extensively elsewhere in these pages (in particular, under "Art History," "English Studies," "History," and "Sociology").

• *Citation and Documentation*

The American Anthropology Association publishes its own brief Style Guide. In almost all particulars it follows the Chicago Style of parenthetical citation. It does, however, make some exceptions, most notably in using a colon (rather than a comma) to separate date and page number in a parenthetical citation:

> Evidence now suggests that the kinship system of the Pacaa Nova is extraordinarily complex (Von Graeve 2003: 24–35).

The AAA Style Guide may be downloaded from the AAA website.

• *Some Useful Websites*

- *American Anthropological Association*
  www.aaanet.org The official site of the AAA includes a range of useful information, as well as many useful links.
- *Anthropology Research on the Internet*
  www.archeodroit.net/anthro This site, with an emphasis on archaeology, includes links to a great deal of useful information.
- *JSTOR*
  www.jstor.org Founded in 1995 as a not-for-profit organization, this site is a leader in providing electronic access to a wide variety of scholarly journals online.

• *Some Respected Journals*

American Anthropologist The flagship journal of the American Anthropology Association.

American Ethnologist A respected journal published by the American Anthropological Association.

Annual Review of Anthropology Provides helpful reviews and syntheses of recent literature in the discipline.

Anthropologica The official journal of the Canadian Anthropological Society.

Anthropology Today A bimonthly, aimed at the general public as well as at anthropologists and students.

Australian Journal of Anthropology This respected journal is published by the Australian Anthropological Society.

Cultural Anthropology A leading journal published by the American Anthropological Association.

Journal of the Royal Anthropological Society (formerly *Man*) The most established British journal in the discipline.

O *Art History*

Scholarly writing in art history, like that in several other disciplines, alternates frequently between the past tense and the present tense, with the past tense used to discuss historical developments and the present tense employed when the appearance or present effect of a work is being discussed. Here is a sample:

> To trigger the process of elevation, many crucifixes were introduced as signposts to the pathway upwards. On the Copenhagen reliquary (Plate 6), for instance, the painting of Christ's death is transformed by the crystal and then exalted by the picture of Christ in heaven rendered on the reverse....
>
> Most often, medieval image makers deployed usual iconographic means to present Christ as both earthly and divine. For example, a manuscript in Stuttgart (Landesbibliothek, Brev. 128, fol. 9v) assimilates numerous texts and pictorial sources ... to establish the Lord's majesty; it incorporates personifications of light and dark and winter and summer to position Him in relation to the world. (Herbert L. Kessler, *Seeing Medieval Art*, Peterborough, 2004, 74–5)

The style of the above passage (by a leading historian of medieval art, writing both for fellow scholars and for general readers and students) is somewhat challenging conceptually, but relatively straightforward in the structure of its sentences. It employs concrete nouns (*crucifixes, pathway, manuscript*) more frequently than it does abstract nouns, and the abstract nouns that are used (*majesty, personifications*) tend to be readily comprehensible.

If this passage represents one pole in art history writing, another, quite different style finds expression in the following passage:

> Thus perhaps at stake has always been the murderous capacity of images, murderers of the real, murderers of their own model, as the Byzantine icons could murder the divine identity. To this murderous capacity is opposed the dialectical capacity of representations as a visible and intelligible mediation of the Real. All of Western faith was engaged in this wager on representation: That a sign could refer to the depth of meaning, that a sign could exchange for meaning, and that something could guarantee this exchange—God, of course. But what if God himself can be simulated, that is to say, reduced to the signs which attest his existence? Then the whole system becomes weightless, it is no longer anything but a gigantic simulacrum—not unreal, but a simulacrum, never again exchanging for what is real, but exchanging in itself, in an uninterrupted circuit without reference or circumference. (Jean Baudrillard. "The Evil Demon of Images and the Precession of Simulacra," in Thomas Docherty, ed., *Postmodernism: A Reader*, New York, 1993, 194)

This quotation (a translation from the French of a key passage by a leading postmodern theorist) is unlike the first passage in almost every respect. It aims to challenge the reader from every angle—in its style of writing as well as in the concepts themselves. It is extraordinarily dense, filled with abstract nouns (many of them specific to contemporary cultural theory), and lacking in concrete examples. It is syntactically complex, using devices such as the placing of phrases in apposition (*from the utopia of ..., from the radical negation of ..., from the sign as reversion and death sentence of ...*), which have the effect of continually recasting the thoughts being presented—as well as of lengthening the sentences. Writing such as this, in the style of certain sorts of theoretical schools commonly styled "postmodernist," is frequently used in several of the humanities and social sciences; it is discussed more fully below under the sections on English studies and history in particular. This style is frequently encountered in writing about art theory—contemporary theory in particular. The sorts of conventions that are followed in the Kessler passage, however, remain far more common in art history departments.

● *Citation and Documentation*

Art history and other disciplines in the fine arts generally use MLA Style. For a sample essay in art history see the second section of this book.

● *Some Useful Websites*

- *Association of Art Historians*
  www.aah.org The largest British association in this discipline maintains a helpful website.
- *College Art Association*
  www.collegeart.org This is the main site for America's unbrella association of art historians, curators, and other art professionals. It includes many helpful links.
- *The History of Art Virtual Library*
  www.chart.ac.uk/vlib/ This site provides a wide range of links and images.
- *Art Source*
  www.ilpi.com/artsource/welcome.html Selective but very useful site maintained by Mary Molinar of the University of Kentucky.
- *Image Collections and Online Art*
  www.umich.edu/%7Ehartspc/histart/mother/images.html Possibly the most comprehensive and helpful of all the online compendia of images and information about art history, this site has been developed at the University of Michigan.

● *Some Respected Journals*

Art and Australia This broadly based magazine is the leading Australian publication on the visual arts.

Art in America A broad-ranging monthly magazine, aimed at the general public and art dealers as well as art historians.

Art History This respected scholarly journal, published by the Association of Art Historians in the UK, is issued quarterly.

Art Journal This scholarly journal, founded in 1941, is the flagship publication of the College Art Association.

Artforum This monthly magazine provides good coverage of much of the contemporary art world.

Canadian Art This broadly based magazine is the leading Canadian publication on the visual arts.

O *Biology*

Academic writing about scientific subjects tends to be of two main sorts. The less common of these is the review article, in which the writer surveys and assesses evidence on a particular topic from various sources. Here is a passage from an abstract of a review article:

> Senescence is a complex, highly regulated, developmental phase in the life of a leaf that results in the co-ordinated degradation of macromolecules and the subsequent mobilization of components to other parts of the plant. The application of molecular biology techniques to the study of leaf senescence has, in the last few years, enabled the isolation and characterization of a large range of DNA clones representing genes that show increased expression in senescing leaves.... The analysis of these genes and identification of the function of the encoded proteins will allow a picture of the complex processes that take place during senescence to be assembled. To date, genes encoding degradative enzymes such as proteases and nucleases, enzymes involved in lipid and carbohydrate metabolism, and enzymes involved in nitrogen mobilization, have all been identified as

senescence-enhanced genes. A variety of other genes of no obvious senescence-related function have also been identified; their role in senescence may be less predictable and, possibly, more interesting. (V. Buchanan-Wollaston, "The Molecular Biology of Leaf Senescence," *Journal of Experimental Biology*, 1997, vol. 48, 181)

Notice here the variety of verb tenses used. When research is summarized the present perfect tense ("... *has enabled* the isolation ...," "... enzymes involved ... *have all been identified*") is used. The simple present tense is used when established scientific facts or ongoing realities are recounted ("Senescence *is* ...," "... genes that *show* ..."). The future tense is sometimes employed as well, when speculation as to the future direction of research is engaged in ("... *will allow* a picture ..."). One other aspect of this passage worth noting is that it makes no reference to other research. Whereas abstracts in the social sciences (and in a behavioural science such as psychology) tend always to place an article in the context of previous research, the abstracts of many papers in the pure sciences make little or no reference to previous research. Even in the introduction to a paper in biology, chemistry, or physics, there tends to be less by way of direct reference to previous research than is common in scientific papers in the social sciences.

The more common sort of scientific writing is the research paper, in which the writer reports on original research. Such papers follow a standardized format, with a precise **title**; an **abstract** summarizing the paper; an **introduction** outlining the nature of, rationale for, and background to the research; a section describing the **method** or procedures followed; a section presenting the **results**; a section providing a **discussion** of the results, their significance, and their implications; and a list of **references**. Here is a typical passage from a section setting out the method followed in an experiment:

Sperm samples were collected from adult males by penile electrostimulation, and sperm capacitation and IVF were done as described previously [20], with a few minor modifications [17]. Briefly, 10×10^6 washed sperm/ml were resuspended in 2 ml

TALP medium and incubated at $37°$ in 5% CO_2 in air for 1–10 h. Sperm were treated for 30–35 min with 1 mW each of dibutyryl cyclic AMP (dbcAMP) and caffeine to induce hyperactivation. Hyperactivated sperm (300,000/ml) were then coincubated with oocytes for 12–16 h in TALP medium containing 1mM each of dbcAMP and caffeine in microdrops under mineral oil at $37°$ in a humidified atmosphere of 5% CO_2 in air. Sperm and remaining cumulus cells were then removed manually by pipetting through a finely pulled glass pipette, and oocytes were examined for evidence of fertilization. (Ping Zheng et al., "The Primate Embryo Gene Expression Resource: A Novel Resource to Facilitate Rapid Analysis of Gene Expression in Non-Human Primate Oocytes and Preimplantation Stage Embryos," *Biology of Reproduction*, published online ahead of print 14 January 2004)

As this passage well illustrates, the convention generally followed when describing methods followed and results obtained is to present the information in as clear and concise a fashion as possible, using the simple past tense and the passive voice ("... samples *were collected* ...," "oocytes *were examined* ...").

It is often suggested that such descriptions should be written in the active voice. Under "Lab Reports for Biology" on the website for the Writing Centre of the respected liberal arts university Hamilton College, for example, appears the following advice: "writing that is predominantly in the passive voice is hard to read (e.g., *Acorns were eaten by the squirrels*), so use the active voice as much as possible (e.g., *The squirrels ate the acorns*). Remember: past tense, active voice." In fact, however, research papers or lab reports are one of the few academic contexts in which the passive voice is usually preferable to the active voice. In most writing situations conventional wisdom (that the active voice tends to be less wordy and more readable than the passive voice) is entirely correct. But all situations are not alike; the key consideration in choosing between the active and the passive voice is where the emphasis in a sentence should most appropriately lie. Look again at the above passage. Would any writer really prefer it to read

"*I collected* sperm samples ..., *we removed* sperm and remaining cumulus cells ..."? The reason for this universal feeling is not any squeamishness over the substances involved; it is rather a recognition that what matters to the research is not *who* collected the sperm, or spliced the genes, or placed the samples under direct sunlight, but rather that the sperm was collected, that the genes were spliced, that the samples were placed under direct sunlight. In all of these cases the passive voice places the emphasis where it is appropriate—on the subject of the experiment, not on the actions of the researcher.

While the equivalent of the review article in a university course is typically a term paper or research paper, the equivalent of the research paper is the lab report, in which the student writes up the results of an experiment performed in class.

● *Citation and Documentation*

The Council of Science Editors (CSE) style is followed in biology. See the section elsewhere in this book on "Documentation" for a full outline of CSE style.

● *Some Useful Websites*

- *Agricola*
  www.agricola.nal.usda.gov Provides a wide variety of materials relating to agriculture, animal science, and forestry.
- *Biology Online*
  www.biology-online.org A wide-ranging source of information, with links to hundreds of other sites.
- *Canada Institute for Scientific and Technical Information*
  www.cisti-icist.nrc-cnrc.gc.ca The collection includes technical reports and conference papers as well as journal articles.
- *Harvard BioLinks*
  www.mcb.harvard.edu/BioLinks.html This site is posted by Harvard University's Department of Molecular and Cell Biology; it provides quick links to many key sources of information.

- *Pubmed Central*
  www.pubmedcentral.nih.gov The US National Institutes of
  Health (NIH) free digital archive of biomedical and lifesci-
  ences journal literature.
- *Union of Concerned Scientists*
  www.ucsusa.org This site provides a wide of range of information regarding environmental problems and solutions.
- Virtual Library: Biosciences
  vlb.org/Biosciences This section of the Virtual Library includes a wide range of useful information and links.

● *Some Respected Journals*

Journal of Biological Chemistry Founded in 1905, this journal covers new
  developments in many areas of biochemistry.
Journal of Cell Biology Published every two weeks, this journal presents
  a wide range of new research in the field.
Journal of Bacteriology Published every two weeks; a leading journal for
  reporting research on genetics and molecular biology as well as on
  bacteria.
Nature Founded in 1869, this is one of the world's most prestigious
  scientific journals.
Quarterly Review of Biology Founded in 1923, this journal includes
  reviews of books and software as well as review articles; aimed at the
  discipline as a whole.

○ *Business and Commerce*

It is important, first of all, to be clear on the distinction between
business writing—the writing of business letters, memos, and so
on, which is covered in a separate chapter in this book—and academic writing about business and commerce (see pages 363–70).
Academic styles of writing in departments or faculties of business
or commerce fall into two broad categories. Much writing about
business is highly technical, and resembles academic writing about
economics (see below). Here is a sample:

A security market where the relative incidence of informed and uninformed trading determines liquidity may have more than one equilibrium. Equilibrium with high liquidity has a low bid-ask spread. This increases participation by traders who want to hedge risk exposure, as opposed to trading on private information, and justifies the small price impact of trades. Equilibrium with low liquidity has a high bid-ask spread. This deters some hedgers, increasing the relative incidence of informed trading, which justifies the larger spread. This analysis casts doubt on the relevance of comparative results in the existing literature relying on exogenous liquidity traders. (James Dow, "Is Liquidity Self-Fulfilling?" *Journal of Business*, 2004, vol. 77, no. 4, 78)

Notice that the discussion is largely couched in the present tense; the object of the study is to explore what *happens* as a general rule, not what happened in one particular case.

The other main style of academic writing about business is much less technical, and is in some respects unique to the study of business; this is the case study approach. Popularized by the Harvard Business School, this approach eschews abstract theoretical formulations and focuses instead on studies of real-world cases. Here is a sample:

Early in its development Nestlé established production facilities outside of Switzerland. By 1986, Nestlé had plants in 60 countries. In determining whether to set up production facilities in a particular country, the company considered several factors, including the availability of raw materials, the overall economic climate, and consumer tastes and purchasing power. (W.D. Dobson and Andrew Wilcox, *How Leading International Dairy Companies Adjusted to Changes in World Markets*, Babcock Institute, University of Wisconsin, 2002, 7)

Notice here that the sentence structures are relatively simple, and that abstract language is avoided. Business case studies are often written with a view to being accessible to business people as well as to academics, and to that end often include such features as point-form "executive summaries." As one would expect, business case studies tend to be couched largely in the simple past tense—though the present perfect may be used if the writer refers to a business practice that is still current at a particular company.

● Citation and Documentation

Although there is no universally accepted style of citation and documentation for business and commerce, APA style is very widely used. See the section on "Documentation" for a full outline of APA style.

● Some Useful Websites

- *Business.gov*
  www.business.gov This US government site provides a wide range of statistics on business activity.
- *Global Edge*
  www.globaledge.msu.edu/ibrd/ibrd.asp Provides a useful collection of information on international business.
- *JSTOR*
  www.jstor.org Founded in 1995 as a not-for-profit organization, this site is a leader in providing electronic access to a wide variety of scholarly journals online.
- *Virtual Library: Business and Economics*
  www.vlib.org/BusinessEconomics The business and economics section of the Virtual Library provides a wide variety of information and links.

● Some Respected Journals

The Academy of Management Journal This journal is respected for cutting-edge research.

Business Week Founded in 1929, this popular weekly magazine provides accessible news and analysis.

Fortune Founded in 1930, this respected twice-weekly magazine focuses on business and the economy.

The Journal of Business   Founded in 1928, this journal is published by the University of Chicago; it is perhaps the most prestigious academic journal in the discipline.

The Journal of Finance   This widely cited journal is the official publication of the American Finance Association.

O *Chemistry*

The conventions of writing followed in the pure sciences are broadly similar; they are discussed above under "Biology."

● *Citation and Documentation*

American Chemical Society. *American Chemical Society Style Guide: A Manual for Authors and Editors.* 2nd ed. Washington: American Chemical Society Publishing, 2/e/1997. A summary is available online at www.pubs.acs.org/books/references.html.

● *Some Useful Websites*

- *Links for Chemists*
  www.liv.ac.uk/chemistry/Links/links.html   Run by the University of Liverpool chemistry department, this site is the chemistry section of the WWW Virtual Library.
- *American Chemical Society*
  www.chemistry.org   The website of the American Chemical Society includes a wide variety of information, as well as links to other sites.
- *Cheminfo*
  www.indiana.edu/~cheminfo   A good general site run out of the University of Indiana.

● *Some Respected Journals*

Chemical Reviews   Founded in 1924, this journal publishes review articles on all areas of the discipline.

American Chemical Society Journal Founded in 1879, this journal is now published every two weeks; it is a key source for recent studies in all areas of the discipline.

Chemical Abstracts Founded in 1907, this journal is unrivalled for comprehensiveness in presenting abstracts of chemistry articles.

O *Economics*

Writing on economics has its roots in the long but elegantly balanced sentences of Adam Smith in the eighteenth century. There was no such thing as a "discipline" of economics when Smith was writing, and it would be very much an anachronism to describe him as an economist. As passages such as the following illustrate, Smith came to the topic of "the wealth of nations" as a moral philosopher rather than as a social scientist:

> People of the same trade seldom meet together, even for merriment and diversion, [without] the conversation end[ing] in a conspiracy against the public, or in some contrivance to raise prices. It is impossible indeed to prevent such meetings, by any law which either could be executed, or would be consistent with liberty and justice. But though the law cannot hinder people of the same trade from sometimes assembling together, it ought to do nothing to facilitate such assemblies, much less to render them necessary. (Adam Smith, *The Wealth of Nations*, Book One, Chapter 10)

Ties with the traditions of philosophical and historical writing were not abandoned as the academic discipline of economics developed in the late nineteenth and earlier twentieth centuries, and even into the 1930s the arguments of economists were put forward more frequently with words than with numbers or equations. In 1933 the journal *Econometrica* was founded, with the intent of countering an anti-mathematical bias in the discipline.

No such bias against numbers and equations exists in the discipline of economics today. Most economists now rely very largely on mathematics and statistics, and largely as well on very specialized vocabulary. Even aside from obviously technical terms (*Pareto-neutral*, *Phillips curve*, and so on) a number of everyday English words (e.g., *optimal*, *equilibrium*) are also used by economists with precise technical meanings particular to the discipline. The following passage, taken from the introduction to a paper on measuring the well-being of populations, gives something of the flavour:

> The dominance criteria of Atkins (1970) and Shorrocks (1983) have become well-known, and are now widely used for making welfare comparisons on the basis of income distribution data. These approaches, though, do not take into account the sort of non-income information—such as family size, age, type of housing—which is these days available in plenty in micro data-sets, and may be of welfare relevance. Hence the old results have begun to be viewed as of limited usefulness. One could not, for example, use the generalized Lorenz dominance approach to recommend as welfare-improving the transfer of income from single persons to families with children, or to those with special needs such as old age or infirmity.
>
> In response to this perceived shortcoming, Atkinson and Bourguignon (1987) developed their sequential generalized Lorenz dominance criterion, for the comparison of joint distributions of income and needs, the latter assumed to be an ordinal variable, and this criterion has been found broad enough for some operational purposes. There is now a flourishing literature on the sequential approach. One thinks for example of Atkinson's (1990) illustrative account, Jenkins's and Lambert's (1993) extension to allow for demographic change ... and the exploration of welfare fundamentals by Ok and Lambert (1999). (Peter J. Lambert and Xavi Ramos, "Welfare Comparisons: Sequential Procedures for Heterogeneous Populations," *Economica* Volume 69, No. 276, November 2002, 549–62)

The above is typical not only in its highly technical vocabulary, but also in the way it positions itself in the context of an extensive literature. Here, as in most economic writing, the verb tenses are quite straightforward, with the simple present tense and the present perfect tense the most widely used.

Economics, as it is practised today, is probably more homogenous in its approach than any of the other social science disciplines. It is far from being all of a piece, however; writing in subdisciplines such as economic history is often quite non-technical. The following passage, for example, could as easily have been written by a historian as an economist:

> Students of southern agriculture in the United States after the Civil War discovered a similar phenomenon. As the average size of farms began to shrink, small farmers had no choice but to grow cotton instead of corn. Although cotton production entailed much more risk, farmers could hope to survive only by adopting a strategy of buying corn in order to have more resources to devote to their cash crop (C. Wright 1978, 169). Consequently, higher corn prices would tend to work to the disadvantage of those farms that were too small to market grain. (Michael Perelman, *The Invention of Capitalism: Classical Political Economy and the Secret History of Primitive Accumulation.* Durham, NC, 2000, 298).

When one is dealing with economic history, of course, the past tense is the norm.

● *Citation and Documentation*

Although there is no universally accepted style of documentation for economics, APA (American Psychological Association) style is very widely used. See the section elsewhere in this book on "Documentation" for a full outline of APA style.

● *Some Useful Websites*

• *History of Economic Thought*
www.cepa.newschool.edu/net This site provides a range of reliable summaries of key ideas and movements in the history of economics.

- *EconLit*

  www.econlit.org This site, run through the American Economic Association, contains abstracts, indices, and links to articles in most major economic journals. It is available at libraries and on university websites throughout the world.
- *WebEc*

  www.helsinki.fi/webec WebEc (Worldwide Web Resources in Economics) provides links to a vast amount of free information in economics.

● *Some Respected Journals*

American Economic Review Founded in 1911, this is the flagship journal of the American Economic Association.

Econometrica An international journal of mathematical economics founded in 1933.

Economic Journal This British journal was founded in 1891, and remains influential.

Journal of Economic Literature This journal was created in 1969 by the American Economic Association in order to provide an annotated bibliography of publications in the discipline. It offers summaries of books and journal articles, and useful surveys of recent publications on particular topics within economics.

Journal of Economic History Founded in 1941, this journal has maintained a high reputation.

Journal of Political Economy Founded in 1892 at the University of Chicago, this journal has in the past generation been a leading venue for the expression of neoclassical and monetarist views.

O *English Studies*

In no academic discipline has the question of writing style been so vexed in the past generation as it has in English studies. For that reason—and because new styles of discourse that first took root in English studies have recently been spreading much more widely through other disciplines—more space will be devoted here to the writing conventions of this academic subject than to those of any other.

The study of English literature had by the late nineteenth century developed into a recognized academic subject, and for most of the twentieth century the discipline followed a broadly similar approach to writing about literature. While popular literary critics focused on evaluative judgements, academic critics moved substantially beyond the evaluative; the work of the scholar entailed pointing out aspects of a literary work that might not be obvious to the casual reader—whether they be points of style, of theme, of characterization, or of literary history—and clarifying those points for the reader. Irony, paradox, or contradiction were considered particularly fertile ground for the literary critic. Here is a sample:

> The prevailing literary mode in Nature poetry in the late eighteenth century (as derived from Edmund Burke) was the cult of the sublime and the picturesque, featuring views and inspirational scenery. In the first half of the nineteenth century this shifted to Wordsworthian Romanticism ... in which Nature was "good" and cities were "evil."...
>
> In *Roughing It in the Bush* [Susanna] Moodie's determination to preserve her Wordsworthian faith collides with the difficulty she has in doing so when Nature fails time and again to come through for her. The result is a markedly double-minded attitude towards Canada:
>
>> ... The aspect of Nature ever did, and I hope ever will, continue: "To shoot marvellous strength into my heart." As long as we remain true to the Divine Mother, so long will she remain faithful to her suffering children.
>>
>> All that period my love for Canada was a feeling very nearly allied to that which the condemned criminal entertains for his cell—his only hope of escape being through the portals of the grave.

These two emotions—faith in the Divine Mother and a feeling of hopeless imprisonment—follow each other on the page without break or explanation.... Moodie copes with the contradiction by dividing Nature herself in two, reserving the splendid adjectives and the Divine Mother attributes for the half that she approves of and failing to account for the hostile activities of the other half. (Margaret Atwood, *Survival: A Thematic Guide to Canadian Literature*, Toronto: 1972, 49-51)[1]

Notice here how the literary critic combines a discussion of historical change, for which the past tense is used, with a reading of a particular text—for which the present tense is used. Notice too the focus on an interesting paradox or contradiction.

The advent in the 1970s of several movements in literary theory that have come to be broadly termed postmodernist theory—structuralism, post-structuralism, deconstruction, and so on—called into question many of the fixed points of English studies' compass. Each of these approaches may be clearly distinguished from the others, but they have certain things in common, and together they brought an entirely fresh approach to the discipline in the 1980s and 1990s. They brought to it a more widespread awareness of the importance of the connections between politics and literature (the

---

1   Now long established as a core text in Canadian literature, *Survival* is an interesting case study in terms of audience and writing conventions. The book was written while Atwood was teaching Canadian literature at York University, and drew substantially on the academic research she had done as a graduate student in the English department at Harvard in the 1960s; given that background, it is not surprising that much of the book follows the conventions of academic writing within the discipline of English studies, very much in the manner of the passage quoted. But *Survival* was motivated less by a desire to communicate with scholars than by a desire on the part of Atwood to broaden awareness of certain traditions of Canadian literature and culture among the educated general public. In accordance with this aim (and with Atwood's range of talents as a writer), much of the book has a breeziness to its style that is rare in books of an academic nature.

politics of gender, of race, and of sexual orientation in particular). They shared a deep-seated scepticism of claims concerning any supposedly essential or immutable truths. They entirely distrusted the tenets of old-style evaluative criticism. And they challenged the vocabulary, the writing style, and the argumentative strategy of the discipline as a whole. The old approaches to the marshalling of evidence and the old striving for clarity of thought and expression came to be widely mistrusted, and indeed actively resisted. Too often, it came to be believed, such striving for clarity had contributed to overconfidence or naïve judgements. In what may be very loosely characterized as the postmodernist view, texts required problematizing more often than they required clarifying. Moreover, the use of difficult language and complicated syntax could in itself aid in what was an inherently valuable process of subversion. Here is how the noted theorist Judith Butler made the connection between writing style and social protest:

> Why are some of the most trenchant social criticisms often expressed through difficult and demanding language? No doubt scholars in the humanities should be able to clarify how their work informs and illuminates everyday life. Equally, however, such scholars are obliged to question common sense, interrogate its tacit presumptions, and provoke new ways of looking at a familiar world.... If common sense sometimes preserves the status quo, and that status quo sometimes treats unjust social hierarchies as natural, it makes good sense on such occasions to find ways of challenging common sense. Language that takes up this challenge can help point the way to a more socially just world. (Judith Butler, "A 'Bad Writer' Bites Back," *The New York Times*, 20 March 1999, A15)

Thus motivated, literary theorists evolved a new style of writing in English. The postmodern style, which drew on the often-labyrinthine texts of French philosophers such as Jacques Derrida and Julia Kristeva, is complex syntactically (often employing multiple phrases lined up in apposition), with challenging diction and a preponderance of abstract nouns. Free-flowing and given to bold assertions, at the same time it often embraces contradiction, and is resistant to absolute precision. Whereas the older tradition of writing in English studies had been to try to point out and analyse complexities, contradictions, or ironies in literary texts, postmodernist literary theory came to see itself in part as a vehicle for *embodying* complexities and even contradictions. Its role was less to argue towards any fixed conclusion or straightforward conclusion than to problematize, to lead the reader to see difficulty where before all had seemed clear. In its own way, indeed, theoretical and critical writing could also be a form of creative writing.

At its extreme the style approaches a purity of abstraction that presents enormous challenges to comprehension. The flavour of such writing may come as quite an eye-opener to the beginning student at university:

> To claim that this is what I *am* is to suggest a provisional totalization of this "I." But if the "I" can so determine itself, then that which it excludes in order to make that determination remains constitutive of the determination itself. In other words, such a statement presupposes that the "I" exceeds its determination, and even produces that very excess in and by the act which seeks to exhaust the semantic field of that "I." In the act which would disclose the full content of that "I," a certain radical *concealment* is thereby produced. (Judith Butler, "Imitation and Gender Insubordination," in *inside/out: Lesbian Theories, Gay Theories*, edited by Diana Fuss, London 1991, 15)

> In order to pass as material or empirical reality, the historical or social process must pass through an aesthetic alienation or privatization of its public visibility. The discourse of "the social" then finds its means of representation in a kind of *unconsciousness* that obscures the immediacy of meaning, darkens the public event with an unhomely glow. There is, I want to hazard, an incommunicability that shapes the public moment, a psychic obscurity that is formative for public memory.... (Homi K.

Bhabha, "The World and the Home," in *Dangerous Liaisons: Gender, Nation, and Postcolonial Perspectives*, edited by Anne McClintock et al., Minneapolis, 1997, 447)

It is worth pointing out here that the first of these two passages is by Judith Butler—the author of the very clearly worded defense of "difficult and demanding language" quoted above. The difference? In the first case Butler is addressing a broad audience (the readers of the op-ed pages of *The New York Times*), while in "Imitation and Gender Insubordination" she is addressing only her scholarly peers—and putting into practice her beliefs about difficult and demanding language.

The postmodernist approach does not always tend quite so overwhelmingly towards abstraction and opacity as do the above examples. Much as "pure" theory may be at the core of postmodernism, English studies has never ceased to look directly at literary texts. But when scholars with a strong background in deconstruction, for example, or in postcolonial theory, deal directly with textual evidence, they tend not to rely on a structure of "proof" buttressed by extensive quotation. The tendency is rather to focus on small, suggestive details—to work elliptically, as it were. Here is an example:

> The resonant details of the scene in which Brontë has Jane acquire her fortune mark Jane's financial and literary implication in colonialism as well. St. John announces Jane's accession to fortune by pulling the letter out of a "morocco pocket-book" (483), and he is able to identify Jane as the heiress because she has written her name, on a white sheet of paper, in "Indian ink" (486).
>
> In this way the novel implicates in colonialism not only Jane's finances (the leather of the wallet has a colonial provenance) but the act of writing itself, for the pigment in which Jane has absently traced her name, with its startlingly colonial appellation, has such a provenance as well.... Like imperialist trade itself, bringing home the spoils of other countries to become commodities in England, such as Indian ink, the use of the

racial "other" as a metaphor for class and gender struggles in England commodifies the dark-skinned people of the British empire as they exist in historical actuality and transforms them into East or West Indian ink with which to write a novel about ending injustices within England.

The eruption of the words "Indian ink" into the novel at this telling moment hints at Brontë's uneasiness about the East Indian ventures to which England was turning in 1848, as well as about the West Indian colonies that were by then clearly becoming unprofitable after the abolition of slavery....
(Susan Meyer, *Imperialism at Home: Race and Victorian Women's Fiction*, Ithaca, 1996, 93–94)

In some respects this passage may be likened to the passage by Margaret Atwood that we looked at initially above; comment about the text is couched in the present tense, and the writer is clearly interested in drawing connections among the text, the author, and the wide sweep of historical and literary developments. But where the one passage relies on extended quotation and carefully limits the conclusions drawn, in the other passage quotation is minimal and one small detail—the "Indian ink"—is made to serve a variety of purposes, suggest a range of connections.

That such a free-flowing approach to scholarly argument can forge interesting connections is now beyond doubt; scholars working through this sort of method have exerted an enduring impact on the discipline in the past generation. But in recent years many within the discipline have begun to feel that this more free-flowing approach to building arguments may bring its own set of difficulties—that it too often may run the risk of resting its conclusions on flimsy or unreliable foundations.

If some have raised questions as to the soundness of certain argumentative strategies associated with postmodernism, a much louder chorus has criticized the opacity that is often said to be characteristic of the postmodern style. Attacks on the alleged impenetrability of theoretical discourse in English departments were launched frequently through the 1980s and 1990s—but launched

almost exclusively by political conservatives in departments outside English studies. Given that most practitioners of such theory
were politically left-of-centre academics within English departments, it is not surprising that a mild form of trench warfare for
some time became the norm at many universities. By the turn of
the century, however, many politically progressive scholars within
the discipline of English studies (Terry Eagleton, who had done
more than any other individual to promote postmodernist theory
in the 1970s and 1980s, being the most prominent among them)
began to reject what they saw as the inherent elitism of a style
of communication so opaque as to impede communication more
often than it facilitated it.

In fairness, it should be noted that the trend towards an
opaque style of discourse was never so overwhelming in English
departments as either its critics or its proponents suggested at
the time. Throughout the last quarter of the twentieth century
many of the leading figures of English studies—Stephen Green-
blatt, Jerome McGann, Edward Said, and Elaine Showalter among
them—continued to make extended connections with individual
literary texts, and to write in styles accessible to the student and
to the educated general reader as much as to their fellow scholars.
They may not have enjoyed quite so large a public as did T.S. Eliot
and Lionel Trilling in an earlier generation, but it is simply not
the case that English studies became entirely a rarified scholarly
pursuit in the 1980s and 1990s.

In any event, the locus of academic conflict over styles of discourse has now very largely shifted. Much as English academics are
still widely derided for the supposed impenetrability of their prose
styles, the irony as the twenty-first century moves forward is that
the style that may be loosely characterized as postmodern is now
to be found with greater frequency in disciplines such as history or
anthropology than it is in English studies. There remains a variety
of styles of writing practised in English studies, but on the whole
the tide of postmodernism has receded in English departments
throughout the world. Above and beyond a permanently stretched
vocabulary, it has left behind two tendencies that seem likely to

remain fixtures in the landscape of the discipline for many years to come: a deep-seated scepticism when it comes to truth-claims, and a heightened awareness of the strength of the connections between politics and literature. In terms of writing style, however, the discipline as a whole now again embraces the idea of clear and comprehensible expression, and advocates building arguments by marshalling a body of textual evidence, including extensive direct quotation. Here is an extended example:

> By linking the request for a clear stage [i.e., free of gentleman spectators] to particularly spectacular productions such as *The Harlot's Progress* ... the notice also promised to compensate the stage spectator for the loss of his voyeuristic pleasure....
>
> When Sheridan presented his ban on stage seating, he did not repeat that bribe. In fact, by attaching his new policy to a production of *Aesop*, he sent the message that the gentlemen's pleasure was at best a matter of supreme indifference to him. Vanbrugh's prologue [to *Aesop*] begins by aggressively refusing to please the "gallants" in the audience:
>
>> Gallants; we never yet produced a Play
>> With greater fears than this we act to day.
>> Barren of all the Graces of the Stage,
>> Barren of all that entertains this Age.
>> No Hero, no Romance, no Plot, no Show,
>> No Rape, no Bawdy, no intrigue, no Beau:
>> There's nothing in't with which we use to please ye. (1–7)
>
> The play lives up to these low expectations; the plot is structured around a romance between the young and beautiful Euphronia and the young and handsome Oronces, but the bulk of the play consists of the old and ugly Aesop telling didactic fables. The only other significant female character is Doris, Euphronia's nurse.... (Susan Cannon Harris, "Clearing the Stage: Gender, Class, and the Freedom of the Scenes in Eighteenth-century Dublin," *PMLA*, October 2004, 1271)

As was the case with the 1972 passage we began with, we may notice here a transition between discussions of historical developments (in the past tense), and discussions of the text as a living literary entity, for which the present tense is used. The argument is built using extensive direct quotation from the text, with longer quotations indented. Elsewhere in this article we may find numerous indications of the degree to which the vocabulary of English studies has been broadened and enriched in the course of the developments of the past generation (*the eruption of that transgressive sexuality, the spectacle organized by the "technologies of objectification" that offered up the actresses' bodies to his gaze*). But, as with the passage by Margaret Atwood with which we began, clarity both of argument and of expression are here central goals of academic discourse.

● *Citation and Documentation*

MLA style is standard in the discipline. See the section elsewhere in this book on "Documentation" for a full outline of MLA style. Note that the sample essay that appears at the end of the book's first section uses the MLA system.

● *Some Useful Websites*

- *JSTOR*
  www.jstor.org Founded in 1995 as a not-for-profit organization, this site is a leader in providing electronic access to a wide variety of scholarly journals online.
- *Literary Resources on the Net*
  www.andromeda.rutgers.edu/~lynch/Lit Maintained by Jack Lynch of Rutgers University, this site provides access to a wide variety of reliable information.
- *Project Muse*
  www.muse.jhu.edu This site, founded in 1995 by the Johns Hopkins University Press, provides access to a wide range of scholarly journals, with a strong emphasis on literature and culture.

- *Project Gutenberg*
  www.gutenberg.org This site provides an extraordinarily wide-ranging collection of online texts in the public domain. Not all are reliably transcribed, but the site is nevertheless an invaluable resource.
- *Representative Poetry Online*
  www.eir.library.utoronto.ca/rpo/display/index.cfm Run out of the University of Toronto, this site provides reliable texts and excellent notes for many English poems.

● Some Respected Journals

American Literature Founded in 1929, this journal is the most established of those specializing in American literature.

Canadian Literature Founded in 1960, this journal is the leader among academic publications specializing in Canadian literature.

PMLA Founded in 1844, this is the flagship journal of the Modern Languages Association (the leading association in North America for academics specializing in English studies).

Review of English Studies Published by Oxford University Press, this leading journal emphasizes historical scholarship rather than interpretive criticism.

Studies in English Literature Published by Johns Hopkins University Press, this leading journal focuses on four fields of British literature: English Renaissance, Tudor and Stuart drama, Restoration and eighteenth century, and nineteenth century.

O History

Of the several styles of writing frequently practised by historians, the most established is much as one would expect—writing that tells a story. Even if one wished to question the prevailing academic orthodoxy, until relatively recently the accepted way of doing so was to tell the story again, from a different angle or with a different emphasis. One might pause periodically to analyse developments, discuss their causes, or address issues concerning the historical evidence, but the main mode of discussion would inevitably be narrative, using the simple past tense (or the past perfect tense when making reference in the course of a discussion of one set of historical events to something previous). Here is an example:

> The crisis of August 1939 which led to the Second World War was, ostensibly at any rate, a dispute over Danzig. This dispute was formulated in the last days of March, when Germany made demands concerning Danzig and the Corridor, and the Poles rejected them. From that moment, everyone expected Danzig to be the next great topic of international conflict. Yet, in strange contrast to earlier crises, there were no negotiations over Danzig, no attempts to discover a solution, not even attempts to screw up the tension....
>
> Both Hitler and the Poles held rigid positions in the war of nerves. After 26 March, Hitler did not again formulate demands concerning Danzig until the day before war broke out. This was not surprising; it was his usual method. So he had waited for offers from Schuschnigg over Austria; so he had waited for offers from Benes, from Chamberlain, finally from the conference at Munich over Czechoslovakia. Then he did not wait in vain. Did he appreciate that this time no offer would come from the Poles? It seemed so from the record. On 3 April he issued instructions that preparations for an attack on Poland "must be made in such a way that the operation can be carried out at any time as from 1 September 1939."[1] (A.J.P. Taylor, *The Origins of the Second World War*, London, 1961, 302–03)
>
> ---
>
> 1 Directive by Keitel, 3 April 1939. *German Foreign Policy*, Series D, VI, No. 149.

Though the narrative style is the most established approach to the writing of history, it is by no means the most widely practised by academic historians today. For much of the twentieth century, the trend in the academic discipline of history was toward a more scientific approach that emphasized social and economic forces rather than narratives involving individuals. This sort of historical writing, which remains widespread, is more likely to focus on numbers than on historical incidents. Again, the writing is typically in the past tense, but the tone is very different from that of a traditional historical narrative. Here is an example:

> Was there any special character to these neighbourhoods? Were they red-light districts or merely poor quarters? The most striking feature of these streets is how different they were from one another. Simnell Street contained common lodging houses inhabited by single dock labourers and families of hawkers. Koss Street, Southampton, while a "low" street and the scene of frequent drunken brawls, was the residence of skilled artisans living in nuclear families. 45 out of 70 households were nuclear (64.3 per cent); including subfamilies, 57 out of 77 (74.0 per cent) families were two-parent headed. Yet both Simnell and Koss streets had one or two houses characterized as brothels, where single women resided apart from their families. On the other hand, Plymouth's Granby and Central streets, which opened into the Octagon, the pub and entertainment centre of Plymouth, had nuclear families living in single tenement rooms, yet almost two of every three adults were women.[37]
>
> (J.R. Walkowitz and D.J. Walkowitz, "'We are not the beasts of the field': Prostitution and the Poor in Plymouth and Southampton under the Contagious Diseases Acts," in *Clio's Consciousness Raised: New Perspectives on the History of Women*, edited by M.S. Hartman and L. Banner, New York, 1974, 192–225, 199)

---

37 Census (1871), 1873, LXXI; part 1. Statistical data for the five streets discussed are based on the manuscript 1871 Census schedules. PRO, RG10/2120, RG10/1193, and RG10/1194.

Such historical writing as this aims to provide demonstrable proof (most of it empirical) of a particular line of argument; it is on this sort of approach that the claims of history to be as much one of the social sciences as one of the humanities rest.

Another broad approach to historical writing has been developed over the past generation. Influenced substantially by French cultural historians and theorists, this approach focuses largely on culture. Rather than attempt to prove a historical argument by assembling empirical evidence, cultural historians of the past generation have tended to operate as much by suggestion as by efforts to provide proof. Often sceptical of truth claims, they rely on suggestive anecdotes or pieces of information to provide insight into particular themes or aspects of historical reality. Often they approach topics from new and surprising angles—so, for example, Paul Edward Dutton inquires into what Charlemagne's mustache can tell us about eighth- and ninth-century Carolingian history and Robert Darnton explores various aspects of eighteenth-century life by discussing an attack in the 1730s by a group of printing apprentices on their masters' cats. Here is a sample:

> Cats as symbols conjured up sex as well as violence, a combination perfectly suited for an attack on the mistress. The narrative identified her with *La Grise, Her Chatte Favorite*. In killing it, the boys struck at her: "It was a matter of consequence, a murder, which had to be hidden."[1] The mistress reacted as if she had been assaulted: "They ravished from her a cat without an equal, a cat that she loved to madness." The text described her as lascivious and "impassioned for cats" as if she were a she-cat in heat during a wild cat's Sabbath of howling, killing, and rape. An explicit reference to rape would violate the proprieties that were generally observed in eighteenth-century writing. Indeed, the symbolism would work only if it remained veiled.... It was metonymic insult, the eighteenth-century equivalent of the modern schoolboy's taunt. But it was stronger, and more obscene. By assaulting her pet, the workers ravished the mistress symbolically. At the same time, they delivered the supreme insults to their master. (Robert Darnton, "Workers Revolt: The Great Cat Massacre of the Rue Saint-Séverin," from *The Great Cat Massacre and Other Essays in French Cultural History*, New York, 1984, 18.)

---

1 This and the following quotations come from Nicolas Contat's account of the cat massacre, *anecdotes typographiques*, pp. 48–56.

Those familiar with the styles of analysis and of writing that are common in English studies will note a number of similarities to the approach that Darnton takes here. Notice, though, that unlike literary scholars, cultural historians such as Darnton tend to use the past tense rather than the present tense when they are discussing texts.

Many historians in recent years have adopted far more of the style pioneered by continental theorists than has Darnton. The extreme here may be represented by the following passage from David Lloyd's *Ireland After History* on the need for a new approach to history:

> Constituted in simultaneity with, and different from, modern civil society, and representing in a certain sense the "constitutive other" of modernity, these spaces that are the objective of "new histories" are not, we have argued, to be conceived as alternative continuities, parallel to dominant narratives and only awaiting, in Gramsci's since, to attain hegemony in order to be completed. On the contrary, and at the risk of deliberate hypostatization, the apparent discontinuity of popular or non-elite history furnishes indications of alternative social formations, difficult as these may be to document and decipher for the disciplined historian; the same discontinuity as well as the formal grounds for the persistence in assimilability of non-elite formations to the state. (As quoted by David A. Wilson in *The Globe and Mail*, 28 December 2004, A–12).

These sentences—both nominated by Wilson as candidates for a Worst Sentence in the World Award—are not typical of historical writing today, but this sort of style, with its contorted syntax, extraordinary density of abstraction, and verbal tics that resist precision (*in a certain sense*), is becoming more common. Ironically, this is happening just as this sort of dense, opaque style is going very much out of fashion in English studies.

● *Citation and Documentation*

There is no universally accepted style of documentation for history. Many journals use some variety of Chicago Style; many use traditional footnotes or endnotes. For students the most important guideline is thus to follow whatever specifications each instructor may give you.

● *Some Useful Websites*

- *Historical Journals Online*
  www.tntech.edu/history/journals.html Provides links to a wide variety of historical journals.
- *JSTOR*
  www.jstor.org Founded in 1995 as a not-for-profit organization, this site is a leader in providing electronic access to a wide variety of scholarly journals online.
- *Labyrinth*
  www.georetown.edu/labyrinth This site provides access to a very wide range of materials on medieval history, including many primary sources.
- *Project Muse*
  www.muse.jhu.edu This site, founded in 1995 by the Johns Hopkins University Press, provides access to a wide range of scholarly journals. The strongest emphasis is on literature and culture, but many historical journals are included as well.
- *Virtual Library: History*
  www.vlib.org/History In this subject, as in others, the Virtual Library provides access to a great deal of useful information.

● *Some Respected Journals*

American Historical Review Founded in 1895, this is the flagship journal of the American Historical Association; it covers all historical fields, not just American history.

Canadian Historical Review Run by the Canadian Historical Association, this is the leading journal for articles on Canadian history.

English Historical Review Founded in 1886, this journal is the oldest journal of historical scholarship in the English-speaking world, and it remains one of the most prestigious. Published by Oxford University Press, the journal covers world as well as British history.

History and Theory Founded in 1960, this leading journal often features interdisciplinary articles.

O *Philosophy*

The academic discipline of philosophy as it has been practised in the English-speaking world in recent generations divides into two broad streams. By far the dominant stream is that of analytic philosophy. Perhaps above all, the tradition of analytic philosophy values clarity, and devotes very considerable effort to making fine distinctions that may help to clarify lines of thought. In doing so, it often employs hypothetical examples. Arguments are typically couched in the present tense, though the past tense is used if reference is being made to an argument from the past that is not being discussed as a live philosophical issue today. Thus, one would write "Hume *argued* ..." if discussing an argument of the eighteenth-century philosopher David Hume in the context of intellectual history, but "Hume *argues* ..." if analysing or discussing the argument itself. Analytic philosophers have a few verbal tics particular to their discipline (e.g., they tend to write "*on* Rawls's theory" where academics in other disciplines would write "*according to* Rawls's theory ..."), and they tend to employ a great many abstract nouns. Other than that, however, they prefer the clarity of sentences that are syntactically straightforward. Here is a sample:

> Deontological theories also capture our intuitions that certain things that have happened in the past are morally relevant. Consequentialist theories are strictly forward-looking moral theories. They look forward from the time of the decision at issue to see how we can bring about the best possible results in the future. Deontological theories allow that backward-look-

ing considerations can have moral significance. To take Ross's example, suppose that you have made a promise to someone. It now happens that you could produce 1,001 units of happiness if you break the promise, but only 1,000 units of happiness if you keep the promise. A strict consequentialist will look only at the number of units of happiness you can achieve in the future, all things considered, and may therefore tell you to break the promise. Intuitively, it seems seriously wrong to break a promise for such a frivolous reason. The fact that you have made a promise in the past cannot simply be dismissed because you want to bring about slightly better results you could achieve in the future by breaking it. Ross's theory holds that we have a prima facie duty to keep the promises we have made, and that this duty can be overridden only for serious reasons. Kant also holds that deceiving persons or making false promises to them constitutes using them as mere means to our own ends, and is therefore wrong. Likewise, deontological theories will not allow us to punish innocent persons even if we can promote general welfare in the future by doing so. Backward-looking considerations of desert are morally significant to the deontologist. It is simply wrong to punish someone who does not deserve the punishment, even if we could produce good consequences in the future by doing so. (Heimir Geirsson and Margaret Holmgren, *Ethical Theory*, Peterborough, 2000, 110–11)

The other stream of academic philosophy is commonly referred to as "continental philosophy." As the name suggests, it is heavily influenced by the writings of philosophers from continental Europe, from Nietzsche and Habermas to Heidegger and Foucault. Like analytic philosophers, those in the continental tradition tend to use a great many abstract nouns, but beyond that there are few similarities of style. Those in the continental tradition tend to be less interested in fine distinctions than in broad brushstrokes, and in many cases they embrace difficulty, even to the extent of cultivating a style that makes it difficult for the reader to decipher the meaning. Arguments are generally advanced in the present tense.

Here is a sample:

> Notice that, unlike Barthes, Gadamer insists on the re-identi-
> fication of one and the same text under plural, potentially infi-
> nite, interpretation and re-interpretation. The infinite openness
> of texts—in both an interpretive and historical sense (ultimately
> the same sense)—is ensured by the notion of reflexive applica-
> tion: the intentional import *of* a text essentially incorporates
> into *its* developing, endlessly reconstituted meaning but its
> recovery for our own historical experience and prejudice can
> make it out to be. Its meaning is heuristically schematized in
> the intersection between *our* present power of reading and what,
> from that evolving perspective, we posit as *its* collected past.
> In this regard, our logical proposal about interpretable texts is
> closer to Gadamer's usage than to Barthes's. (Joseph Margolis,
> "Reinterpreting Interpretation," *Journal of Aesthetics and of Criticism*
> 43, Summer 1989: 249)

If the styles of philosophy may be broadly divided into the analytic and the continental, the content of philosophy is also divided
into a variety of sub-disciplines, including aesthetics, ethics, epistemology, logic, and metaphysics. For the most part, conventions
of writing do not vary widely among these; an analytic philosopher
writing on a topic in aesthetics, for example, follows very much the
same conventions of writing as an analytic philosopher writing on
a topic in epistemology or ethics. The exception here is symbolic
logic, which uses its own language—or rather, its own variety of
symbolic languages.

● *Citation and Documentation*

There is no universally accepted style of documentation for philosophy. Many journals use some variety of Chicago Style; many
use traditional footnotes or endnotes. For students the most
important guideline is thus to follow whatever specifications each
instructor may give you.

● *Some Useful Websites*

- *JSTOR*
  www.jstor.org Founded in 1995 as a not-for-profit organization, this site is a leader in providing electronic access to a wide variety of scholarly journals.
- *Philosophy Pages*
  www.philosophypages.com A wide range of useful basic information in accessible form.
- *Project Muse*
  www.muse.jhu.edu This site, founded in 1995 by the Johns Hopkins University Press, provides access to a wide range of scholarly journals, with a strong emphasis on literature and culture, but a good representation of philosophy journals as well.
- *Virtual Library: Philosophy*
  www.vlib.org Click on Humanities and go to Philosophy. This section of the Virtual Library site is run through the University of Bristol.

● *Some Respected Journals*

Australian Journal of Philosophy A respected general journal.

Canadian Journal of Philosophy A respected general journal.

Ethics One of the leading journals for analytic articles on topics in ethics.

Journal of Philosophy The most prestigious general journal in the discipline.

Mind One of the leading journals for analytic articles on topics in the philosophy of mind.

Philosophy and Public Affairs This respected journal is aimed at the general reader as well as an academic audience.

O *Physics*

The conventions of writing followed in the pure sciences are broadly similar; they are discussed above under "Biology."

● *Citation and Documentation*

American Institute of Physics. *Style Manual for Guidance in the Preparation of Papers*. 4th ed. New York: American Inst. of Physics, 1990.

● *Some Useful Websites*

- *Net Advance of Physics*
  web.mit.edu/redingtn/www/netadv/welcome.html This site, supported by MIT, offers a wide range of information in an encyclopedic format.
- *Physics News*
  www.het.brown.edu/news/index.html This site provides information and links on all aspects of the subject.
- *Physics Today Online*
  www.physicstoday.org This site, run by the American Institute of Physics, offers information on recent research and provides links to databases, societies, and a variety of electronic publications.

● *Some Respected Journals*

Annals of Physics Publishes review articles intended to be accessible to a broad audience.

Physical Review The most established journal in the discipline is divided into five sections on different sub-disciplines.

Physics Letters This respected journal is divided into two sections—Part A on General, Atomic, and Solid Physics, and Part B on Nuclear, Elementary Particle, and High Energy Physics.

O *Politics*

The discipline that is variously styled "politics," "political studies," and "political science" borders on a considerable number of
other academic disciplines. At one end, it looks at political theory
historically (from Aristotle and Plato onwards), with interests
not dissimilar to those of philosophers. What is the nature of the
state? How may politics, morality, and the law best interact? And
so on. The study of politics also inevitably overlaps with the study
of history. And political science shares a border with sociology,
too—not only in the interest they share in social trends, but also
in their shared interest in ideology.

In most departments, the "science" in political science is a very
real presence, and frequent reference is made to empirical studies
as arguments are made concerning such things as the causes of
electoral victories and defeats, and of changes in public opinion.
Following are two examples:

> One important finding [of the World Values surveys] is that
> a very substantial proportion of people—some 22 per cent of
> respondents in 1981 and 16 per cent in 1990—were not willing
> to place themselves anywhere on the left/right scale. Another 36
> per cent of respondents in 1981 (and 39 per cent in 1990) occu-
> pied the middle ground of the left/right scale (Knutsen, 1993).
> In all, these "ideological indeterminants"—non-respondents
> and those in the "middle ground"—account for more than half
> of all publics surveyed in both 1981 (58 per cent) and 1990 (55
> per cent). In other words, somewhere between 42 to 45 per cent
> of these publics are clearly identifiable as willing and unequivo-
> cal occupants of left/right ideological space. (Neil Nevitte, *The
> Decline of Deference: Canadian Value Change in Cross-National Perspec-
> tive*, Peterborough, 1996, 235)

> The CBS News/*New York Times* poll of March 21 to 25 [1994]
> covers the four days after the Illinois primary, the days during

which news was disseminated about Hart's campaign controversies. There are enough interviews in this survey to divide it in half and treat each half of the survey independently. During the first half of this poll, the two days after the Illinois primary, when the commercials fracas was getting some publicity, Hart still led Mondale, 41 per cent to 38 per cent. In the second half of the survey, when the campaign news centred on Hart's embassy positions and his campaign management, Mondale jumped ahead 49 per cent to 29 per cent! This extraordinary turnaround is one more demonstration of how fragile the images and votes can be for candidates like Hart, or [George H.] Bush in 1980, or Carter in 1976, when voters are projecting future performance from campaign behaviour.[35] It reemphasizes the discussion in Chapter 3 of the logic of incumbents' attacking their challenger(s) instead of trying to change opinions about themselves. (Samuel L. Popkin, *The Reasoning Voter: Communication and Persuasion in Presidential Campaigns*, Chicago: 2/e 1994, 207)

---

35 Percentages from the March 5–8 CBS News/*New York Times* poll are based on 573 interviews: percentages from the second poll are based on 411 interviews, 235 on the first days and 176 on the last two days. Some of the interviews in the last two days are with people who were sampled but could not be reached on the first two days; eliminating these interviews makes no difference.

Notice in both of the above passages the shifts in verb tense. When Nevitte is referring to the carrying out of the surveys in 1981 and 1990 he uses the past tense ("*were* not willing"), whereas when he comments on what he sees as the ongoing relevance of the studies, he uses the present tense. Popkin also uses different verb tenses. When discussing the changes that occurred during the 1984 campaign, he uses the past tense ("Hart still *led*," "Mondale *jumped* ahead"), whereas when he comments on the ongoing relevance of these developments, he too switches to the present tense.

There are also interesting differences between the two passages. Nevitte uses far more of the jargon that has been developed by the academic discipline of political science—not only in the use of such phrases as *ideological space* but also in the use of *publics* in the plural. In contrast, Popkin adopts a less scholarly style, and for the most part relies on the vocabulary of everyday English. Notice too that Nevitte employs the APA style of parenthetical documentation, while Popkin employs the footnoting method that is traditional in history and several disciplines in the humanities. (Unlike many other disciplines, the study of politics has not developed its own documentation style; APA style and the Chicago Style of footnoting are the two most common approaches.)

Much as the "science" is a frequent presence in political science, there remains a good deal of writing within the discipline that analyses political realities and political trends with little or no reference to empirical data. Again, here is a sample:

> Besides its unique orientation to the prevailing ideological map, environmental politics also departs from the conventional framework of interest-group politics. The focus of environmental groups, that is, is concerned more with a broad public interest than with a narrow, particular interest. This point is implicit in the literature on "post-materialist" values; and environmentalism is central to discussions of the new social movements that challenge conventional politics. Those devoted to environmental politics are not typically seeking economic advantages. Instead, environmentalists see themselves generally as representing a universal human interest (including that of future generations), or as speaking for other species and especially threatened parts of non-human nature—indeed, more comprehensively, as working in the interests of the planet and its inhabitants as a whole. (Robert Paehlke and Douglas Torgerson, "Environmental Politics and the Administrative Estate," in Paehlke and Torgerson (eds.) *Managing Leviathan*, Peterborough, 1990, 291)

● *Citation and Documentation*

There is no universally accepted citation and documentation system in this discipline, but the *Chicago Manual of Style* is probably the most widely used.

● *Some Useful Websites*

- *Canadian Supreme Court Decisions*
  www.lexum.umontreal.ca/csc–scc/en   Canadian Supreme Court decisions may be accessed through this site.
- *Election Resources*
  www.electionresources.org This site provides a wealth of information on election results from nations around the world.
- *JSTOR*
  www.jstor.org Founded in 1995 as a not-for-profit organization, this site is a leader in providing electronic access to a wide variety of scholarly journals.
- *Virtual Library: International Affairs*
  www.vlib.org/internationalaffairs A wide range of useful information and links.
- *US Supreme Court*
  www.supremecourtus.gov US Supreme Court opinions may be accessed through the site.

● *Some Respected Journals*

Canadian Journal of Political Science The most respected political science journal in Canada.

Congressional Quarterly Focuses on American national politics.

The Economist The world's most authoritative weekly news magazine.

Foreign Affairs This quarterly journal publishes a wide range of articles on international affairs. Aimed at the general reader as well as the scholar.

Political Science Quarterly Founded in 1886, this journal remains one of the most respected.

Washington Monthly A magazine that appeals to the general public as well as to scholars.

O *Psychology*

Like others of the sciences and social sciences, psychology has many of its roots in philosophy; philosophers from Aristotle to John Locke and David Hume spent a good deal of time attempting to draw conclusions as to the workings of the human mind. It was not until the late nineteenth century that psychology began to be established as a scientific discipline—and even then writing on psychology tended more to resemble philosophical writing than the sort of writing we now associate with the academic discipline of psychology. William James, for example, whose classic work *The Principles of Psychology* helped to establish the discipline as a behavioural science, appeals in his writing to common experience in much the same way as had Locke or Hume in earlier centuries:

> When we have been exposed to an unusual stimulus for many minutes or hours, a nervous process is set up which results in the haunting of consciousness by the impression for a long time afterwards. The tactile and the muscular feelings of a day of skating or riding, after long disuse of the exercise, will come back to us all through the night. Images of the field of view of the microscope will annoy the observer for hours after an unusually long sitting at the instrument. (William James, *The Principles of Psychology*, 1890, Chapter 25)

At the same time as James was laying the foundations for the empirical study of psychology, another tradition of psychology was also beginning to take shape—psychoanalysis. Even more than had James, this tradition adopted a writing style that had little in common with scientific writing as we know it today. The writings of Freud, Jung, and English-speaking followers such as Havelock Ellis and Ernest Jones, while often elegant, relied on personal observation, anecdote, and often bold assertion, rather than empirical measurements.

By the middle of the twentieth century, however, the influence of the psychoanalytic tradition was starting to wane, while the growth of psychology as a scientific discipline was quickening. Nowadays the vast majority of writing in psychology relies on experimental evidence gathered according to standardized research methods. The typical article in psychology reports on an experiment, first summarizing the background of research against which the experiment has been conceived, then presenting method and results, before moving to a discussion of the results and a conclusion:

> Research on complex relational processes within families has revealed that parents' differential treatment of siblings is consistently linked with negative outcomes, such as children's poorer socio-emotional well-being (McGuire, Dunn, and Plomin, 1995; Stocker, 1995) and less positive sibling relationships (Brodie, Stoneman, and McCoy, 1992). However, what is not yet fully understood is how differential treatment relates to the quality of parent-child relationships. For example, do children or adolescents who feel they receive less-favoured treatment than a sibling develop feelings of resentment toward this parent, setting the stage for poorer parent-child relationships? Or do children understand and perhaps "forgive" unequal treatment as warranted for particular reasons? ...
>
> Method.
>
> The sample included mothers, fathers, and two adolescents from 74 maritally intact families. Participating families lived in one of two small adjoining Mid-western cities (combined population 120,000) or a suburban or rural area proximal to the two cities. Participating families were recruited using newspaper ads and through flyers distributed at local schools. Families were offered $15 for their participation. Families selected for inclusion in the study had a younger sibling between the ages of 11 and 13 years (M = 12.45, SD = 1.58) and an older sibling who was two to four years older (M = 15.58, SD = 1.87).... (Amanda K. Kowal, Jennifer L. Krull, and Laurie Kramer, "How the differential treatments

of siblings is linked with parent-child relationship quality," *Journal of Family Psychology*, Volume 18, No. 4, 2004, 658–59)

Not all psychological writing is devoted to presenting the results of experiments, of course. But when writing for their fellow academics, psychologists tend to maintain the same vocabulary and writing style that characterizes reports on experiments. It may be interesting in this connection to compare the following two passages. In the first, psychologist Judith Rich Harris is writing for other psychologists in an academic journal; in the second, she is expressing very much the same idea in a book aimed at the general reader as well as the psychologist:

> When group identity is not salient, differentiation is likely to predominate over assimilation. If siblings see themselves as separate individuals rather than as part of the family group, status hierarchies and social comparisons may increase the differences among them. Dominance hierarchies would tend to make older siblings dominant over younger ones, which happens as a matter of course in most societies and which North American parents try very hard, and not very successfully, to prevent (Whiting and Edwards, 1988). However, there is little or no resemblance between children's relationships with their siblings and their relationships with their peers (Abramovitch et al., 1986), which is consistent with the finding that birth order has no reliable effects on personality (Ernst and Angst, 1983; Reiss et al., 1994). (Judith Rich Harris, "Where is the child's environment? A group socialization theory of development," *Psychological Review*, Volume 102, No. 3, 1995, 332)

> Inevitably, children's relationships with their siblings are unequal. In most cases, the elder is the leader; the younger is the follower. The elder attempts to dominate, the younger to avoid domination. Peer relationships are different; peers are more equal, and often more compatible, than siblings. Among American children, conflict and hostility erupt far more frequently among siblings than among peers. (Judith Rich Harris, *The Nur-*

ture Assumption: Why Children Turn Out the Way They Do, New York, 1998, 61)

Not only are the parenthetical references to scholarship absent from the second passage above; the vocabulary is also far less abstract, and the syntax is much simpler. Like all disciplines, psychology has developed a special vocabulary involving not only terms specific to the discipline (e.g., *dominance hierarchies*) but also habits of using particular words with great frequency (*salience* is a word that psychologists and social scientists generally find very useful, for example). Psychologists also often use variants of common English words in ways peculiar to the discipline; they tend, for example, to use the plural form *behaviours*, whereas people outside the discipline of psychology tend to use *behaviour* only in its singular form.

Psychologists tend to use the past tense when reporting on the methods they have followed and the results they have obtained in an experiment. They use the present tense, however, when discussing what the evidence shows about human behaviour. They also often use the present perfect tense when reporting on the findings of other research (e.g., *Barclay and Jones have found that* ...).

● *Citation and Documentation*

Virtually all academic writing in psychology follows the principles set out in the APA Style manual.

● *Some Useful Websites*

- *American Psychological Association*
  www.apa.org The APA site provides access to a wide range of useful information.
- *Classics in the History of Psychology*
  www.psycclassicsals.yorku A useful archive of many key texts in the history of psychology.
- *Encyclopedia of Psychology*
  www.psychology.org A helpful and wide-ranging site.

- *PsychWeb*
  www.psywww.com An informal site with a range of useful links.
- *Social Psychology Network*
  www.socialpsychology.org Including a wide range of useful information, this site bills itself as "the largest social psychology database on the Internet."

● Some Respected Journals

American Journal of Psychology A leader in the discipline.

American Psychologist A broad-ranging monthly journal, founded in 1946.

Psychological Review A quarterly journal with an emphasis on psychology theory, founded in 1894.

Journal of Personality and Social Psychology Founded in 1965, this is the leading journal in the sub-discipline of social psychology.

○ Sociology

The discipline of sociology is often said to divide into two broad streams. One of these, the positivist tradition (with roots going back to the classic work of Emile Durkheim) emphasizes empirical studies and employs methods that have much in common with those of the natural sciences. The writing style favoured by most sociologists writing in this tradition tends to be purposefully dry in tone (no matter how striking or provocative the information presented may be), and to be written in syntactically straightforward sentences. Such writing employs the present tense where an ongoing social situation or structure is being described, but shifts to the past tense frequently when referring to how specific studies were conducted. Here is a sample:

> The surveys also show important differences in terms of the participation in paid and unpaid work on a given day. In 1986, 85 per cent of women and 52 per cent of men participated in

domestic activities (excluding childcare and shopping). Conversely, 54 per cent and 34 per cent of men and women participated in paid work activities on a given day (Harvey, Marshall, and Frederick 1991: 43, 50; Marshall 1990). Among married employed parents in 1986, the participation rate in household work was 63 per cent for men and 95.3 per cent for women (Haddad, 1996: 153).

In 1992, for parents with children under 19, with both spouses employed full-time, 95.9 per cent of women and 77.4 per cent of men participated in housework on a given day. In addition, for those who have children under 19, 63.7 per cent of women and 43.9 per cent of men participated in childcare (McFarlane, 1997: 73–77). Not only do employed men spend slightly less time in total productive activity than do employed women, but men's participation in unpaid work shows greater flexibility; they can more easily work around their paid work. This is probably a key factor underlying the higher stress experienced by women. (Rod Beaujot, *Earning and Caring*, Peterborough, 2000, 213)

The language of sociologists writing in this tradition is similar to that of those who employ empirical studies extensively in other social science disciplines; they often write of *controlling for various factors*, and of the *salience* of certain sorts of information. Particular to sociology is a frequent use of the noun *outcome*, including in the plural (e.g., *the study found several outcomes*).

In contrast, the interpretivist tradition of sociology, stemming largely from the classic works of Max Weber, tends to rely much less on empirical evidence—and, indeed, often to be sceptical of such evidence. It tends towards more free-flowing analyses, and makes reference far more frequently to theories and to broadly perceived social and cultural forces. In their writing style, interpretivist sociologists of the past generation have tended towards long sentences that are syntactically fairly complex, and towards abstract words that foreground their theoretical orientation. Here is a sample:

Social theory, and more specifically post-colonial social theory, must be able to make sense of such events, which testify among other things to the cultural dynamism of peoples living in oppressive conditions. To make sense of this, it is necessary to get past a blanket notion of incommensurability between cultures. An imbalance in social power, favouring the white stream, was integral to the traditions that produced the merging of previously foreign cultural elements. The fact remains that the merging happened, creating new cultural practices, in the Coast Salish case, practices strongly associated with aboriginality as a cultural and emancipatory project.

Should we conclude from this that *difference* loses its theoretic importance? Not exactly. What we see in the inter-cultural recognition portrayed here is not the kind of "unbiased communication" (as Habermas would say) that could found a renewed universalism. Communication between the two cultures is not easy; their codes are far from transparent to each other, and the power imbalances are enormous. Thus, there is a large gap between a belief in absolute incommensurability and a renewed universalism. (Claude Denis, *We Are Not You*, Peterborough, 1997, 157)

The author quoted above, like many (though by no means all) interpretivist sociologists of recent years, employs much of the vocabulary that theoretically oriented academic circles in the English speaking world imported from France in the 1970s and 1980s— the style that may be loosely characterized as postmodern.

● *Citation and Documentation*

The most widely accepted style of citation and documentation is that of the American Sociological Association (ASA style). This is in many ways similar to other styles of parenthetical citation. Note, however, that page numbers may be given in the citation, and that in that case they are preceded by a colon:

- What Wright terms "idealized capitalism" (2000: 959) relates to the neoclassical economic model.

References are provided at the end of an essay, alphabetically by author:

Pakulski, Jan and Malcolm Waters
1996 *The Death of Class*. London: Sage.

Wright, Erik Olin
2000 "Working-class power, capitalist class interests, and class compromise." *American Journal of Sociology* 105: 957–1002.

● *Some Useful Websites*

- *Auraria Library*
www.library.auraria.edu   Established as a shared library for three universities in Denver, Colorado, the Auraria Library includes useful subject guides that provide access to a wealth of information.
- *American Sociological Association*
www.asanet.org   This site provides a wide range of information about the discipline, together with useful links to other sites.
- *JSTOR*
www.jstor.org   Founded in 1995 as a not-for-profit organization, this site is a leader in providing electronic access to a wide variety of scholarly journals.

● *Some Respected Journals*

American Journal of Sociology   This highly respected journal is published by the University of Chicago Press; it was founded in 1895. Issues from recent years are available online at www.journals.uchicago.edu.

American Sociological Review   This wide-ranging and prestigious journal is published six times yearly; it is the flagship journal of the American Sociological Association. Available online through JSTOR.

Canadian Journal of Sociology   Published by the University of Toronto Press, this is the most highly respected of Canadian journals in the discipline.

Criminology   Probably the most highly respected journal in this important branch of sociology.

Social Forces   An influential interdisciplinary journal published by the University of North Carolina Press (also available through JSTOR).

Sociology   The flagship journal of the British Sociological Association.

Journal of Marriage and the Family   The leading North American journal in the area of the sociology of the family.

⊙ Bias-free Language

D58. **gender:** The healthy revolution in attitudes towards gender roles in recent generations has created some awkwardness in English usage—though not nearly so much as some have claimed. *Chair* is a simple non-sexist replacement for *chairman*, as is *business people* for *businessmen*. Nor is one forced into *garbageperson* or *police-person*; *police officer* and *garbage collector* are entirely unobjectionable even to the linguistic purist. Nor can the purist complain if *fisher* replaces *fisherman*; far from being a new or artificial coinage, *fisher* was linguistic currency when the King James version of the Bible was written in the early seventeenth century. Here again, there is no need for the *-person* suffix.

The use of *mankind* to mean *humanity*, and of *man* to mean *human being*, have for some years been rightly frowned upon. (Ironically enough, *man* originally had *human being* as its only meaning; in Old English a *werman* was a male adult human being, a *wifman* a female.) A remarkable number of adults still cling to sexist usages, however, and even still try to convince themselves that it is possible to use *man* in a gender-neutral fashion.

Among them are the editors of *The Economist*, who posed the question, "What is Man?" in the lead article of their September 14, 1996, issue. "To what extent are men's actions determined by their genes?" the article asked, and clearly did not intend the answer to apply to only one-half the human race.

Well, why can't *man* be gender neutral? To start with, because of the historical baggage such usage carries with it. Here, for example, is what the best-selling novelist Grant Allen had to say on the topic in a magazine called *Forum* in 1889:

> In man, I would confidently assert, as biological fact, the males are the race; the females are merely the sex told off to recruit and reproduce it. All that is distinctly human is man—the field, the ship, the mine, the workshop; all that is truly woman is merely reproductive—the home, the nursery, the schoolroom.

But the baggage is not merely historical; much of the problem remains embedded in the language today. A useful litmus test is how sex and gender differences are approached. Look, for example, at this sentence from the September 14, 1996 issue of *The Economist*:

- One of the most basic distinctions in human experience—that between men and women—is getting blurrier and blurrier.

Now let's try the same sentence using *man's* instead of *human*:

- One of the most basic distinctions in man's experience—that between men and women—is getting blurrier and blurrier.

In this sort of context we are all forced to sense that something is amiss. We have to realize when we see such examples that *man* and *he* and even *mankind* inevitably carry with them some whiff of maleness; they can never fully and fairly represent all of humanity. (If they didn't carry with them some scent of maleness it wouldn't be possible to make a joke about the difficulty of turning men into human beings.) Most contexts are of course more subtle than this, and it is thus often easy for humans—but especially for men—not to notice that the male terms always carry with them connotations that are not gender-neutral. *Humanity, humans, people*—these words are not in any way awkward or jargon-ridden; let's use them.

To replace *man* with *humanity* is not inherently awkward to even a slight degree. But the pronouns are more difficult. Clearly the consistent use of *he* to represent both sexes is unacceptable. Yet *he/she*, *s/he*, and *he or she* are undeniably awkward. *S/he* is quite functional on the printed page, but defies translation into oral English. Another solution is to avoid the singular pronoun as much as possible either by repeating nouns (*An architect should be aware of the architect's clients' budgets as well as the architect's grand schemes*) or by switching to the plural (*Architects should be aware of their clients' budgets as well as of their own grand schemes*). Of these two the second is obviously preferable. In longer works some prefer a third strategy that eliminates awkwardness entirely: to alternate between the masculine pronoun *he* and the feminine pronoun *she* when referring to a single, generic member of a group. Using *she* to refer to, say, an architect, or a professor, or a sports star, or a prime minister can have the salutary effect of reminding readers or listeners that there is nothing inherently male in these occupations. In a short piece of writing, however, it can be distracting to the reader if there are several bounces back and forth between female and male in the same paragraph. And a cautionary note should accompany this strategy even when it may conveniently be employed: be very careful not to assign *he* to all the professors, executives, or doctors; and *she* to all the students, secretaries, or nurses.

pronouns: Undoubtedly the most troublesome questions for those who are concerned both about gender equality and about good English arise over situations involving singular pronouns such as *everyone, anyone, anybody, somebody, someone, no one, each, either, neither*. It can be difficult enough to re-cast sentences involving such words so that everything agrees, even before the issue of gender enters the picture.

- Everybody felt that the film was better than any other they had seen that year.

According to the rules most of us have been taught, that sentence is wrong; *everybody* is singular, and *they* must therefore be changed:

- Everybody felt that the film was better than any other she had seen that year.
- Everybody felt that the film was better than any other he had seen that year.
- Everybody felt that the film was better than any other she or he had seen that year.

But, as Robertson Cochrane has pointed out ("Sex and the Single Pronoun," *The Globe and Mail*, May 1992), the insistence on the singularity of such pronouns is a relatively recent phenom-enon, dating from the codification of English grammar that took root in the eighteenth century. Before that time Chaucer, Shake-speare, Swift, and the rest had no qualms about using *they* or *their* to refer to *anyone* and *everyone*. Cochrane persuasively argues that returning to the ways of Chaucer and Shakespeare in this respect is better than constantly trying "to write around the pronoun prob-lem, and [it is] certainly less offensive than arrogantly and 'prop-erly' applying masculine labels to all of humankind."

inappropriate	Mankind cannot bear too much reality.
gender neutral	Humankind cannot bear too much reality.
inappropriate	Everyone will have a chance to express his views before the meeting is over.
gender neutral	Everyone will have a chance to express their views before the meeting is over.

Of course issues of gender are not confined to the right word choice. Consider the following descriptions of political candidates with essentially the same backgrounds:

- Carla Jenkins, a lawyer and a school board trustee, is also the mother of three lovely daughters.
- George Kaplan, a lawyer and a school board trustee, has a long record of public service in the region.
- George Kaplan, a lawyer and a school board trustee, is also the father of three lovely daughters.
- Carla Jenkins, a lawyer and a school board trustee, has a long record of public service in the region.

The impression left in many minds by such phrasings is that the person described as having a long record of public service is well suited to public office, while the person whose parenting is emphasized may be better suited to staying at home.

Some may feel that parenthood is relevant in such cases; if you do, be sure to mention it both for women and for men, and be sure to avoid unnecessary references to physical appearance. The general rule should be that parenting (and physical appearance) should not be mentioned unless you feel them relevant to the point(s) you are making.

Before leaving the issue of gender and language, it may be worth raising the issue of the attitude we bring with us when we read or write. It is often claimed that "political correctness" goes to ridiculous lengths to avoid giving offense—and that does indeed sometimes happen. Some of the euphemisms employed to describe the elderly or people with physical disabilities can come across as absurd—and indeed patronizing. And sometimes the speaker or writer is simply not thinking of the meaning of the words used. Such was the case a few years ago, for example, when a radio interviewer asked Nelson Mandela how it had felt when he became the first African American president of his country. And such too was the case with the academic who felt that we should replace the phrase *manual work* with *physical work*. (The word *manual* stems from *manus*, the Latin word for *hand*, and thus carries with it no connotation that such work is or should be the province only of men.)

In a great many cases, however, the complaints that are made as to the supposed excesses of political correctness are entirely spurious. Some writers seem to *prefer* to think of gender-neutral language as inherently awkward or absurd. Here's an example, taken from a widely adopted textbook:

Maintaining Objectivity

Avoiding discriminating language is important. Just as important, however, is avoiding a witch hunt. Taken to extremes, political correctness will weaken your writing. *Middleman*, for example, is a perfectly legitimate term, widely understood. There is no point in confusing readers by substituting *distributional intermediary* merely to avoid the suffix -*man*. Little is gained by referring to a stripper as an *ecdysiast* when most readers will not recognize the euphemism. And no one is going to take seriously a writer who calls short people *vertically challenged*. Remember, the point of considerate language is to be fair and polite, not to be obscure or silly. (Bonnie Carter & Craig Skates, *The Rinehart Guide to Grammar and Style*, Fort Worth: Rinehart, 4/e 1996)

Think about this for only a moment, and it may seem quite unexceptionable—entirely reasonable, even. Think again. The tip-off here is the way that the question of the word *middleman* has been approached: not as the occasion for an interesting, if possibly difficult, search for ways of expressing ourselves that will avoid both awkwardness and bias, but rather as a matter that will inevitably involve a choice between the two. The authors here seem more interested in finding reasons to ridicule the struggle for fairness than in joining in the effort to improve things.

Let's approach the word *middleman* in a different frame of mind. To start with, the fair comparison is not between *distributional intermediary* and *middleman* but between *intermediary* and *middleman*. Perhaps the former is more awkward, but it is not obviously so:

- One of the reasons for high prices in this industry is that there are too many middlemen.
- One of the reasons for high prices in this industry is that there are too many intermediaries.

Alternatives in different circumstances may include *wholesalers, distributors, go-betweens*—none of them obscure, confusing, or laughable. *Ecdysiast* is indeed a laughable euphemism, but not one that is needed to circumvent biased usages. (*He's a male stripper* suffers from the same defect as *He's a male nurse*, but *stripper* in itself is gender-neutral.) And, though there is indeed a societal bias against short people, no one seriously suggests euphemism as a solution.

For many years now "politically correct" has been used with quotation marks around it to mean esthetically distasteful and ethically wrong-headed—and we are often meant to be left with the suggestion that those who criticize the "politically correct" do not themselves have a political agenda; they are "maintaining objectivity." It is telling in this connection that the authors of *The*

Rinehart Guide couch the matter as an issue of etiquette rather than one of equity: "the point of considerate language is to be fair and polite." To be sure, it is a virtue to be polite and considerate. But unquestioning politeness to those in positions of power and privilege may sometimes entail an acceptance of terms of reference that are anything but fair. Sometimes one may have to choose between being fair and being polite. And the point of searching for bias-free ways of expressing oneself is in fact not to be polite, but to be fair. Sometimes it comes to a choice; language can be an instrument of positive change, or an instrument of repression. In that context we can probably never avoid being biased in one direction or the other, and we are wise to remember that complete objectivity is impossible.

Regrettably, the attitudes evident in the Carter and Skates passage quoted above are not disappearing quickly. And the prevailing tack taken by those fighting against bias-free language remains mockery rather than argument. Thus, for example, columnist Ron Haggart mocks efforts to replace the term *manhole cover* by suggesting as an alternative *circular utility access alternative facilitative infrastructure* (*The Globe And Mail*, "That Covers It," 19 March 2004). The most commonly proposed alternative to *manhole*, of course, is nothing so awkward or absurd. Moreover, *sewer hole* more accurately describes the object in question; someone new to English would surely never be able to guess the meaning of *manhole* from its component parts.

None of this should be taken to suggest that there are not awkwardnesses to struggle with in the search for bias-free coinages. (*Statesman* and *manned spaceflight*, for example, resist easy substitutions.) But these are surprisingly few. In most cases one need not resort to the oft-lampooned *-person* suffix. *Chair* and *flight attendant* felt a little odd at first (in language as in the rest of life it may take a while to get used to new things), but few are bothered by them now. *First-year student* still feels odd to many Americans, but not in Canada, where it has always been used. And the process continues. *Snowbody* is a wonderful word, but it will be years before *snowman* begins to sound as clunky as *stewardess*. Try it, though—and try to smile in fun rather than in derision (put the accent on the first syllable). This one may never catch on—but it's worth noting that there are few things more gender-neutral than a body made up of three spheres of snow.

D59. **race, culture, and sexual orientation**: Although gender is the most contentious issue in the struggle for bias-free language, it is not the only one. Almost everyone is aware that one should avoid various terms for particular racial or cultural groups (see the list below), and it is just as important to avoid language that conveys derogatory implications on the basis of sexual orientation. The most appropriate terms to use do not stay constant, however; everything hinges on connotation, and since connotations may change over time, so does appropriate usage. The best principle to follow here is to pay attention to how members of particular groups prefer to be described.

A few racial and cultural terms are so deeply encoded in the language that people may use them without being aware of their underlying meaning:

offensive	I'm convinced that the shopkeeper tried to gyp me. (*Gyp* originated in the prejudice that Roma were congenital cheats.)
bias-free	I'm convinced that the shopkeeper tried to cheat me.

Another example of a widely used expression that is strongly if more subtly coloured with bias is the expression *white trash*. The implications of the expression are brought forward in the following passage:

> The [Jerry Lee] Lewis and [Jimmy] Swaggart clans were, in the harsh modern parlance, white trash. They lived in the black part of town, and had close relations with blacks. Mr. Swaggart's preaching and Mr. Lewis's music were strongly influenced by black culture. "Jimmy Swaggart was as black as a white man can be," said black elders in Ferriday. (*The Economist*, 15 April 2000)

This passage brings out the implication of the expression; the "trashiness" that is the exception for white people is implicitly regarded as the norm for black people.

Given the generally high level of awareness in Western society of the evils of anti-Semitism, it is extraordinary that *jew* is still sometimes used in casual conversation as a verb in the same way that *gyp* is used. It is a use that should never be allowed to go unchallenged—and when such usages are challenged speakers will often realize they have been unthinkingly using a coinage learnt in childhood—and will change.

Less obviously offensive but still objectionable is the use of unnecessary racial or gender or religious identifiers. Mentioning a person's race or gender or religion in connection with occupation is a common habit, but one that reinforces stereotypes as to what sort of person one would naturally expect to be a lawyer or a doctor or a nurse. Unless race or gender or religion is in some way relevant to the conversation, there is no need to refer to someone as a male nurse, or a Jewish doctor, or a Native lawyer.

In one important respect the issue of bias-free usage differs from every other issue discussed in this book. Throughout, our focus has been on formal writing, and it has frequently been emphasized that many informal and colloquial usages that are inappropriate to formal writing may be quite unexceptional in other forms of writing, or in speech. The same cannot be said of the difference between biased and bias-free language. It is no less damaging to use sexist, racist, or homophobic language in speech than it is in writing; indeed, it may even be more so. The cumulative repetition in speech of colloquial expressions—including such "innocent" expressions as the contemptuous use of *that's so gay*—probably does considerably more to reinforce human prejudice than does the written word.

On the Web

Exercises on bias-free language may be found at **www.broadviewpress.com/writing**. Click on **Exercises** and go to **D58–59**.

O *Bias-free Vocabulary: A Short List*

actress	actor
alderman	councillor
anchorman	anchor/news anchor
Asiatic	Asian
bad guy	villain
bellboy	bellhop
bogeyman	bogey monster
businessman	businessperson, entrepreneur
caveman	cave-dweller
chairman	chair
clergyman	minister, member of the clergy
congressman	representative
con-man	con-artist
draftsman	drafter
Eskimo	Inuit

(Note: Some Alaskan groups still prefer *Eskimo*.)

farmer's wife	farmer
fireman	firefighter
fisherman	fisher
foreman	manager, supervisor
freshman	first-year student
garbageman	garbage collector
gunman	shooter
gyp	cheat, con
Gypsies	Roma

(Note: When a nomadic people of Hindu origin began to appear in Britain in the late medieval period, they were thought to have come from Egypt and termed *'gypcian*. Given that *Gypsies* has in the centuries since that time often been used in a derogatory way, many now regard *Roma* as preferable. Others argue that *Roma* names an ethnic group that is not precisely co-extensive with *Gypsies*, and feel that on balance the old term deserves to be retained.)

henchmen	thugs
Indian	Native, First Nations, Native American, Aboriginal

(Note: As with *Eskimo/Inuit* and *African American/black*, the key consideration is sensitivity to audience. If you do not belong to the group but you know that the people you are writing about prefer a particular designation, that is the one to use.)

infantryman	footsoldier
layman	layperson
longshoreman	shiploader, stevedore
maid	housekeeper
mailman	letter carrier, mail carrier
male nurse	nurse
man	humanity
man (an exhibit)	staff
man (a barricade)	fortify, occupy
man (a ship)	crew
manhandle	rough-up, maul
manhole	sewer hole, access hole
manhole cover	sewer cover
mankind	humankind, people, humanity, humans
manly	self-confident, courageous, straightforward
manmade	handmade, human-made, constructed
middleman	intermediary
negro	black, African American

(Note: In the United States *African American* is generally preferred; in Canada *black* is often the preferred term.)

niggardly	stingy

(Note: The word *niggardly* has no etymological connection with *nigger*. Since the one suggests the other to many minds, however, it is safer to avoid using it.)

Oriental	Asian, Middle Eastern

policeman	police officer
postman	letter carrier, mail carrier
salesman	salesperson
snowman	snowbody (rhymes with *nobody*)
sportsman	sportsperson
stewardess	flight attendant
unsportsmanlike	unsporting
waitress	server
weatherman	weather forecaster
womanly	warm, tender, nurturing, sympathetic
workman	worker, labourer

(Note: A much more complete guide is Rosalie Maggio's *Talking About People: A Guide to Fair and Accurate Language*, Oryx Press, 3/e 1997).

◎ "ESL": *For Those Whose Native Language Is Not English*

The fact that different languages have different grammatical and syntactical conventions creates particular problems for anyone learning a new language. That is a point that may seem obvious, but a large percentage of the population of North America, Britain, and Australia (a majority of whom are unilingual) remain unaware of it as a felt reality. (It is a measure of the degree to which English-speaking Americans and Canadians, in particular, are unaccustomed to learning other languages that the standard North American term is "ESL—English as a *Second* Language"; the notion that someone might already know more than one other language before learning English is in itself foreign.)

This section of *The Broadview Guide to Writing* focuses on some of the peculiarities of English that are most likely to present difficulties to those learning the language. More often than not, multilingual students who are not yet fully fluent in English have at least as good a grasp of the formal grammatical principles of the language as do those for whom English is their first language. If you are not familiar with these principles, however, the "Reference Guide to Basic Grammar" at the back of this book may be helpful.

Because of the differences in the ways that the structure of a student's own language may compare with English, students from different linguistic backgrounds are likely to want to focus on different aspects of English; what is particularly challenging for someone whose first language is Vietnamese may seem straightforward to someone whose first language is Spanish, and vice versa. For that reason the following guide may be helpful:

Many speakers of languages such as Chinese (in its various forms), Japanese, and Vietnamese are likely, as a result of the ways in which those languages differ structurally from English, to have particular difficulty with topics treated under the following headings in this book: articles (E1–2); plurals (E5);

infinitives (E12); conjugation of verbs, especially in the simple present tense (A2); word order (B1–10, E17–18).

Many speakers of languages such as Russian, Polish, and Bulgarian are likely, as a result of the ways in which those languages differ structurally from English, to have particular difficulty with topics treated under the following headings in this book: articles (E1–2); omission of the predicate (E3); double negatives (E9); the present perfect tense (A7); word order (B1–10, E17–18); possessives (E7); relative pronouns such as *who* and *which* (E6); countable and uncountable nouns and words such as *much*, *many*, *little*, and *few* (Please check index, E1).

Many speakers of languages such as French, Spanish, and Italian are likely, as a result of the ways in which those languages differ structurally from English, to have particular difficulty with topics treated under the following headings in this book: relative pronouns such as *who* and *which* (E6); double negatives (E9); comparatives and superlatives (E10); progressive (or continuous) verb tenses (A4, E14); word order (E17–18).

E1. **articles**: Articles are words used to introduce nouns. Unlike many other languages, English often requires the use of articles:

| *needs checking* | We are interested in house with garage. |
| *revised* | We are interested in a house with a garage. |

There are only three articles—*a*, *an*, and *the*. Articles show whether or not one is drawing attention to a particular person or thing. For example, we would say *I stood beside a house* if we did not want to draw attention to that particular house, but *I stood beside the house that the Taylors used to live in* if we wanted to draw attention to the particular house.

A (or *an* if the noun following begins with a vowel sound) is an indefinite article—used with singular nouns when you do not want to be definite or specific about which thing or person you are referring to. *The* is a definite article, used with singular or plural nouns when you *do* want to be definite or specific. Remember that, if you use *the*, you are suggesting that there can be only one or one group of what you are referring to.

In order to use articles properly in English it is important to understand the distinction English makes between nouns naming things that are countable (*houses, books, trees*, etc.) and nouns naming things that are not countable (*milk, confusion*, etc). *A* can be used with singular count nouns (*a radio*), *the* with singular and plural count nouns (*the carpet, the horses*). *The* should be used with a non-count noun when it is followed by a specifying phrase (*the furniture in my house*). Some non-count nouns name things that it does seem possible to count: *sugar, grass, furniture*, etc. In such cases counting must in English be done indirectly: *a grain of sugar, two grains of sugar, three blades of grass, four pieces of furniture*, and so on.

Distinguishing between count and non-count nouns is inevitably a challenge for those whose first language is not English. A dictionary such as *The Oxford Advanced Learner's Dictionary* can be very helpful; unlike most dictionaries it indicates whether or not each noun is a count noun.

needs checking	They bought a nice furniture.
revised	They bought a nice piece of furniture.

● *Frequently Used Non-count Nouns*

abstractions: advice, anger, beauty, confidence, courage, fun, happiness, hate, health, honesty, information, knowledge, love, poverty, truth, wealth, wisdom.

to eat and drink: bacon, beef, beer, bread, broccoli, butter, cabbage, candy, cauliflower, celery, cereal, cheese, chicken, chocolate, coffee, corn, cream, fish, flour, fruit, ice, ice cream, lettuce, margarine, meat, milk, oil, pasta, pepper, rice, salt, spinach, sugar, tea, water, wine, yogurt.

other substances: air, cement, clothing, coal, dirt, equipment, furniture, gas, gasoline, gold, grass, homework, jewelry, luggage, lumber, machinery, metal, mail, money, music, paper, petroleum, plastic, poetry, pollution, research, scenery, silver, snow, soap, steel, timber, traffic, transportation, violence, weather, wood, wool, work.

Note: The plural of many of these non-count nouns may be employed when you want to denote more than one type of the substance. *Breads*, for example, refers to different sorts of bread; *coffees* refers to different types of coffee, *grasses* to different types of grass, and so on.

E2. **dropping the article**: Articles are not used in English to the same extent that they are used in some other languages; nouns can frequently stand alone without their article, particularly when they are being used in a general, non-specific sense. When used in this way, non-count and plural-count nouns need no article.

needs checking	If the English is to be spoken correctly, the good grammar is important.
revised	If English is to be spoken correctly, good grammar is important.
needs checking	The freedom is something everyone values.
revised	Freedom is something everyone values.

In most cases no article is necessary before a noun that is capitalized:

needs checking	They were strolling through the Stanley Park.
revised	They were strolling through Stanley Park.

Unfortunately, there are many exceptions to this rule (e.g., *the Hebrides, the Netherlands, the Dominican Republic, the United Kingdom, the Soviet Union, the United States*). A dictionary such as

The Oxford Advanced Learner's Dictionary should be consulted in any case where you are uncertain if an article is needed.

E3. **omission of the subject or predicate**: Many languages allow the subject or the predicate to be assumed in certain situations, whereas (with the exception of imperative formations such as [*you*] *come here this instant!*) English requires that sentences include explicit subjects and predicates.

needs checking	Is very hot this afternoon.
revised	It is very hot this afternoon.
needs checking	She doctor and her husband carpenter. They both like their jobs.
revised	She is a doctor and her husband is a carpenter. They both like their jobs.
needs checking	Is not possible to finish the job this week.
revised	It is not possible to finish the job this week.
needs checking	Most authorities agree that malaria is a disease that could be targeted for eradication because would be feasible and relatively inexpensive to develop and distribute effective vaccines.
revised	Most authorities agree that malaria is a disease that could be targeted for eradication because it would be feasible and relatively inexpensive to develop and distribute effective vaccines.
needs checking	By the end of the century, were almost one million more people in Houston than there had been in 1980.
revised	By the end of the century, there were almost one million more people in Houston than there had been in 1980.

Note: In this sort of sentence construction English requires a "dummy" subject (such as *it* or *there*) before the verb *to be*; by contrast, languages such as Spanish allow the subject to be assumed in similar circumstances.

E4. repetition of the subject: Unlike many other languages, English does not permit the repetition of either the subject or the object within a single clause.

needs checking	The body of water outside the hotel it is called English Bay.
revised	The body of water outside the hotel is called English Bay.
needs checking	The members of the cast loved the play that they were acting in it.
revised	The members of the cast loved the play that they were acting in.

E5: plurals: Since many languages do not form plural nouns differently from nouns in the singular, it is easy if your background is in one of those languages to omit the *s* in plural formations in English.

needs checking	Many team play here every weekend.
revised	Many teams play here every weekend.

E6. gendered words/neutered words: In Romance languages such as French all nouns are masculine or feminine; for that reason many speakers of these languages use a masculine or feminine pronoun in English where the neuter pronoun is required.

needs checking	When I first saw the lake he was as smooth as glass.
revised	When I first saw the lake it was as smooth as glass.

Most Romance languages and Slavic languages do not differentiate things from people in their relative pronouns. For that reason it is easy to forget to use *who* or *whom* rather than *that* or *which* in English.

needs checking	I spent the weekend visiting my grandparents, which are both in their eighties.
revised	I spent the weekend visiting my grandparents, who are both in their eighties.

E7. **possessives**: Some languages make no distinction between possessive pronouns and possessive adjectives; in others possessive adjectives agree with what is possessed, not the possessor. In both cases English's different approach can cause difficulty.

needs checking	I told him that the book was my.
revised	I told him that the book was mine.
or	I told him that it was my book.
needs checking	As he sat in his office he looked out of her window at the moon.
revised	As he sat in his office he looked out of his window at the moon.

On the Web

Exercises specially designed for those whose native language is not English may be found at **www.broadviewpress.com/writing**. Click on **Exercises** and go to **E1–18**.

E8. **negatives**: Whereas English uses auxiliaries to form standard negatives, many languages use particles. As a result of this difference, the correct formation of negatives in English can present difficulties.

needs checking	In later life he not wanted to see his old friends.
revised	In later life he did not want to see his old friends.
or	In later life he never wanted to see his old friends.

E9. **double negatives**: Languages in both the Slavic and Romance groups permit double negatives, thus making it difficult for those whose first language is from one of those groups to become habituated to the English prohibition against double negatives—and to grasp that words such as *without* can function as negatives.

needs checking	I never not like to be away from home very long.
revised	I never like to be away from home for long.
or	I do not like to be away from home for long.
needs checking	No one can survive in this society without no money.
revised	No one can survive in this society without money.
or	No one can survive in this society with no money.
or	No one can survive in this society without any money.

E10. **comparatives and superlatives**: In many languages comparatives and superlatives must always include a word equivalent to *more* or *most*; there are no parallels for English formations such as *better, best* or *larger, largest*. Not surprisingly, many whose first language is not English find it difficult to get used to the English system of alternative forms of the comparative and superlative.

needs checking	I wanted to buy the more larger size.
revised	I wanted to buy the larger size.

E11. **compound verb formations**: English has many verb tenses, and many compound verb forms, including compound negative forms; these cause particular difficulty for those who are used to a less heavily conjugated system of verb tenses.

needs checking	I waited for some time, but he not come.
revised	I waited for some time, but he did not come.
needs checking	She always working hard to help her family.
revised	She is always working hard to help her family.

E12. infinitives: The infinitive form (*to go*, *to be*, *to do*, etc.) is not native to many languages, particularly many Far Eastern languages. For that reason it is sometimes given tense or person markers. In English the infinitive must always keep the same form.

needs checking	When she first met him she found it difficult to felt any sympathy for him.
revised	When she first met him she found it difficult to feel any sympathy for him.

E13. phrasal verbs: A phrasal verb occurs when a word that would normally function as a preposition instead becomes part of a two-word verb. *Break in, take off, put on, pick up, give up*—these are all examples of phrasal verbs. In such combinations an adverb cannot intercede between the two.

needs checking	He put hurriedly on his clothes.
revised	He put on his clothes hurriedly.

E14. continuous verb tenses (see also under "Verb Tenses" in "Writing Grammatically"): In English the continuous tenses are not normally used with many verbs having to do with feelings, emotions, or senses. Some of these verbs are *to see, to hear, to understand, to believe, to hope, to know, to think* (meaning *believe*), *to trust, to comprehend, to mean, to doubt, to suppose, to wish, to want, to love, to desire, to prefer, to dislike, to hate.*

needs checking	He is not understanding what I mean.
revised	He does not understand what I mean.
needs checking	At that time he was believing that everything on Earth was created within one week.
revised	At that time he believed that everything on Earth was created within one week.

E15. infinitives and gerunds: As discussed in the chapter on this topic earlier, there are no rules in English as to why some verbs must be followed by an infinitive and others by a gerund, while still others may take either. Some combinations are particularly odd from the point of view of anyone whose first language is not English. For example, *start to go* and *start going* may be used interchangeably in most circumstances, whereas *stop going* is the opposite of both; *stop to go* has a quite different meaning. Unfortunately, these combinations must be learned one by one. One helpful rule, however, is that an infinitive can never follow a preposition.

needs checking	They were planning for to go to New York for the holidays.
revised	They were planning to go to New York for the holidays.
or	They were planning on going to New York for the holidays.
or	They were planning a trip to New York for the holidays.

E16. **prepositions**: As discussed in the chapter on preposition problems earlier, there are no overarching logical principles governing the use of prepositions in English. We say *angry with someone* rather than *angry to someone* or *angry against someone* purely as a matter of convention. In some cases general guidelines may be offered, however. For example, where place and time are concerned, *in* is used for larger expanses of space and larger durations of time; *at* is used for specific times and specific addresses; and *on* is used for street names (without precise addresses) and days of the week or the month (without precise times). *She lives in England, she lives on Downing St., she lives at 10 Downing St; she will meet you at 1 p.m.; she will see you some time in December; she will see you on December 15.*

needs checking	I live in 316 7th St. NW.
revised	I live at 316 7th St. NW.
or	I live on 7th St. NW.
or	I live in the house at 316 7th St. NW.

E17. **word order (subject/verb/object):** The rules governing word order in English are much more rigid than those of many other languages. For one thing, the subject, verb, and object normally appear in that order. Many other languages permit far more freedom in the ordering of subject, object, and verb, and for that reason this basic structural element of English can be difficult to grasp.

> *needs checking*   Yoshiki opportunities always welcomes.
> *revised*   Yoshiki always welcomes opportunities.

(Note: Speakers of languages such as Japanese and Korean, in which the verb must always come last in a sentence, are particularly likely to experience this sort of difficulty with English.)

> *needs checking*   Opportunities welcomes Yevgeny always.
> *revised*   Yevgeny always welcomes opportunities.

(Note: Speakers of languages such as Russian, in which the object may appear before the subject, are particularly likely to experience this sort of difficulty with English.)

In most Romance languages object pronouns come before the verb. This often creates difficulties for native speakers of those languages with the word order required in English, where object pronouns normally follow the verb.

> *needs checking*   When we these give him, he will be very grateful.
> *revised*   When we give him these, he will be very grateful.

E18. **word order (adjectives and adverbs):** In English, adjectives generally precede the noun to which they refer, while adverbs generally follow the verb to which they refer. Moreover, there are rules governing the order of adjectives and adverbs—rules which native English speakers have absorbed unconsciously, but which otherwise must be learnt. Since it is common to use two or more adjectives to describe something, problems often arise.

The proper order of adjectives: determiners (*my, his, this, that,* etc.); adjectives concerning number or quantity (*first, many, some,* etc.); adjectives expressing a subjective opinion (*beautiful, sad, fascinating,* etc.); adjectives concerning size or shape (*large, small, straight, flat,* etc.); adjectives describing age or condition (*old, clean, sharp, wet,* etc.); adjectives describing colour (*red, mauve, blue,* etc.); adjectives naming substances and adjectives that may also be used as nouns (*metal, woolen, English,* etc.); the noun.

needs checking	They lived in a white lovely house near the sea.
revised	They lived in a lovely white house near the sea.

◉ PUNCTUATION, FORMAT, and SPELLING

◉ Punctuation

● *The Period*   .

The most important mark of punctuation is the full stop (or period), which is used to separate one sentence from another, and the most common punctuation mistakes involve the use of the period. The first of these is the run-on sentence: a sentence that continues running on and on instead of being broken up into two or more sentences. (Where a comma has been used instead of a period, the term *comma splice* is often used to denote a run-on sentence.) The second is the incomplete sentence (or sentence fragment): a group of words that has been written as if it were a full sentence, but that in fact needs something else to make it complete.

F1. **run-on sentence/comma splice**: The basic idea of a sentence is that it expresses one complete idea. Often, remembering this simple fact will be enough to keep run-on sentences at bay, particularly if one reads work over to oneself (aloud, if it's not too embarrassing) and notices where one pauses naturally.

needs checking	Early last Thursday we were walking in the woods it was a bright and clear morning.
revised	Early last Thursday we were walking in the woods. It was a bright and clear morning.

In the above example it should be quite clear that there are two separate ideas, and that these should be put into two separate sentences. Sometimes, though, it is not so simple. In particular, certain words may be used to join two clauses into one sentence, while other words should not be used in this way. We have already seen (in our survey of joining words) some examples of words that cause problems of this sort. Here is a review:

and: The appearance of more than one *and* in a sentence is often a sign that the ideas would be better rephrased.

needs checking	Beaverbrook effectively mobilized the resources of the country to serve the war effort overseas and he later was knighted and he is also well-known for creating a media empire.
revised	Beaverbrook effectively mobilized the resources of the country to serve the war effort—an accomplishment for which he later was knighted. He is also well-known for creating a media empire.
or	Beaverbrook, who had created a vast media empire before the war, then distinguished himself by effectively mobilizing the resources of the country to serve the war effort. It was in recognition of this service that he was knighted.
or	Beaverbrook, who had created a vast media empire before the war, then distinguished himself by effectively mobilizing the resources of the country to serve the war effort; it was in recognition of this service that he was knighted.

hence:

needs checking	With the exception of identical twins no two people have exactly the same genetic makeup hence it is impossible for two people to look exactly the same.
revised	With the exception of identical twins no two people have exactly the same genetic makeup. Hence, it is impossible for two people to look exactly the same.

however:

needs checking	During the rainy season more water flows over Victoria Falls than over any other falls in the world however several other falls are higher than Victoria.

revised	During the rainy season more water flows over Victoria Falls than over any other falls in the world. However, several other falls are higher than Victoria.
or	During the rainy season more water flows over Victoria Falls than over any other falls in the world; several other falls, however, are higher than Victoria.

ESL

More on run-on and incomplete sentences may be found in the chapter *ESL: For Those Whose Native Language Is Not English* and on the Web at **www.broadviewpress.com/writing**. Click on **Exercises** and go to **ESL**.

otherwise:

needs checking	You had better leave now otherwise we will call the police.
revised	You had better leave now. Otherwise, we will call the police.
or	You had better leave now; otherwise, we will call the police.

therefore:

needs checking	Money was tight and jobs were scarce, therefore she decided to stay in a job she did not like.
revised	Money was tight and jobs were scarce; therefore, she decided to stay in a job she did not like.

Notice in the above cases that one way to correct a comma splice is often to use a semicolon. Unlike a comma, a semicolon may be used as a connector between clauses. (The discussion of the semicolon below may be helpful in this connection.)

F2. then: An even more common cause of run-on sentences than any of the above is the word *then*. Unlike *when*, *then* should not be used to join two clauses together into one sentence. *And then* may be used, or a semicolon, or a new sentence may be begun.

needs checking	We applied the solution to the surface of the leaves then we made observations at half-hour intervals over the next twelve hours.
revised	We applied the solution to the surface of the leaves. Then we made observations at half-hour intervals over the next twelve hours.
or	We applied the solution to the surface of the leaves; then we made observations at half-hour intervals over the next twelve hours.
or	We applied the solution to the surface of the leaves, and then we made observations at half-hour intervals over the next twelve hours.
needs checking	On June 10, 1999, Yugoslav troops began withdrawing, then the NATO bombing was suspended and the war in Kosovo ended.
revised	On June 10, 1999, Yugoslav troops began withdrawing. Then the NATO bombing was suspended and the war in Kosovo ended.
needs checking	The Montreal Canadiens produced vital late-period goals then they wrapped their iron defense around the Calgary Flames to take an upper hand in the game.
revised	The Montreal Canadiens produced vital late-period goals and then wrapped their iron defense around the Calgary Flames to take an upper hand in the game.

F3. abbreviations: The period is also used to form abbreviations. If in any doubt about whether or not to use a period in an abbreviation, or where to put it, think of (or look up) the full form of what is being abbreviated.

needs checking	Jones, Smithers et. al. will be there in person.
revised	Jones, Smithers et al. will be there in person.

(*Et al.* is short for the Latin *et alia*, meaning *and others*.)

F4. **incomplete sentences**: A good writer always asks herself as she checks her work if each sentence is complete in itself; in this way the more obvious errors will almost always be caught. For example, if *When the meeting ends tomorrow* is in the rough draft as a complete sentence, re-reading will probably lead to the realization that the idea is not complete; the group of words needs another group of words to finish it (e.g., *When the meeting ends tomorrow we should have a comprehensive agreement*). Be particularly careful with longer sentences to make sure they are complete. For example, the group of words *Marina walked to the sea* is a complete sentence, but the following sentence is incomplete, even though it is much longer; it lacks a main clause that tells us what happened when she was walking:

needs checking	While Marina was walking to the sea and thinking of her father and the sound of a woodthrush.
revised	While Marina was walking to the sea she heard the sound of a woodthrush and thought of her father.
needs checking	Unemployment was a serious problem in Britain in the early 1990s. In fact, throughout the world.
revised	Unemployment was a serious problem in the early 1990s, both in North America and in Europe.
needs checking	So long as you have a place to live and enough to eat.
revised	So long as you have a place to live and enough to eat, you have some reason to be thankful.

The three words which most frequently lead students to write incomplete sentences are *and*, *because*, and *so*.

F5. **and**: Although there are certain cases in which it is possible to begin a sentence with *and*, these are extremely difficult to sense. It is usually better for all except professional writers not to begin sentences with *and* if they wish to avoid incomplete sentences.

worth checking	To make this crop grow well you should add Compound 'D' fertilizer to the soil. And you should add top dressing a few months later.
revised	To make this crop grow well you should add Compound 'D' fertilizer to the soil, and top dressing a few months later.

F6. **because**: In order to prevent young children who have difficulty in writing long sentences from writing incomplete sentences, many elementary school teachers wisely tell their pupils not to begin sentences with *because*. In fact it is not incorrect to begin with *because*, so long as the sentence is complete. The rule to remember is that any sentence with *because* in it must mention both the cause and the result. Whether the word *because* comes at the beginning or in the middle of the sentence does not matter; what is important is that the sentence has two parts.

needs checking	In the early 1980s Sandinista leaders told their people to be ready for war. Because the United States had been trying to destabilize Nicaragua.
revised	In the early 1980s Sandinista leaders told their people to be ready for war, because the United States had been trying to destabilize Nicaragua.
needs checking	Because of the cold and wet weather which affected the whole area. Many people were desperately trying to find more firewood.
revised	Because of the cold and wet weather which affected the whole area many people were desperately trying to find more firewood.

F7. **so**: This word is probably the biggest single cause of incomplete sentences. As is the case with *and*, there are certain situations in which professional writers manage to get away with beginning sentences with *so*, but normally this should not be attempted. *So* should be used to join ideas together into one sentence, not to separate them by starting a new sentence.

needs checking	I did not know what was happening. So my friends explained the procedure to me.
revised	I did not know what was happening, so my friends explained the procedure to me.
needs checking	The meat was too heavily spiced. So most of it had to be thrown away.
revised	The meat was too heavily spiced, so most of it had to be thrown away.

● *The Ellipsis* ...

Three dots are used to indicate the omission of one or more words needed to complete a sentence or other grammatical construction.

F8. **ellipsis**: Note that when used in quotation an ellipsis comes inside the quotation marks, and that when an ellipsis precedes a period the sentence should end with four dots (essentially the three-dot ellipsis followed by the period).

needs checking	Harris shows more than a trace of paranoia in her book; she speaks, for example, of "the elements trying to subvert the essence of liberal society, of tolerance, of goodwill ... They are all around us."
revised	Harris shows more than a trace of paranoia in her book; she speaks, for example, of "the elements trying to subvert the essence of liberal society, of tolerance, of goodwill.... They are all around us."

Ellipses may also be used to indicate the trailing off of speech: *Violet struggled for breath. "All my money," she gasped, "goes to...." Those were her last words.*

● *The Comma*   ,

Perhaps the most important function of the comma in modern English usage is to help the reader recognize the grammatical structure of a sentence. As a side benefit, commas also help those reading aloud to pause at places in a sentence where there are natural breaks in the grammatical structure. But commas should not be used simply to create pauses at any point in a long sentence where the writer thinks the reader might run out of breath.

It was not always thus. When commas began to appear in English prose (in the late sixteenth century), they were used simply as a way of suggesting pauses in speech. Given the extent to which people's natural speech patterns differ, it is no wonder that the placing of commas in seventeenth- and eighteenth-century usage seems to us haphazard. (In this respect eighteenth-century habits of punctuation resemble eighteenth-century habits of capitalization—see page 485.) A striking example is the Second Amendment to the American Constitution:

> A well regulated Militia, being necessary to the security of a free State, the right of the people to keep and bear Arms, shall not be infringed.

This is a sentence comprising two clauses, with a subordinate clause at the beginning providing context for the declaration made in the main clause. Though it is a long sentence, there is according to grammatical principles no good reason to include a comma anywhere except at the break between the two clauses:

> A well regulated Militia being necessary to the security of a free State, the right of the people to keep and bear Arms shall not be infringed.

In saying this sentence aloud some readers will undoubtedly pause slightly at points other than at the one marked by the comma. But it is at that point alone that there should be a comma (at least according to the conventions of modern English). The additional commas in early texts are in this case far more than a historical curiosity; they have fuelled endless debate and more than one court case over the constitutionality of twentieth- and twenty-first-century gun control measures in America.

The above should not be taken to imply that there is no room for individuality when it comes to the inclusion of "structural" commas; far from it. Many writers, for example, like to use a comma to set off an opening phrase from the sentence that follows. And that is perfectly acceptable; both the versions below of the sentence that opened the previous paragraph are correct, as are both versions of the other sample sentence below:

> In saying this sentence aloud some readers will undoubtedly pause slightly at points other than at the one marked by the comma.

> In saying this sentence aloud, some readers will undoubtedly pause slightly at points other than at the one marked by the comma.

> In the spring of 2008 she left her family and moved to Southampton.

> In the spring of 2008, she left her family and moved to Southampton.

Again, the key point is that if structural commas are to be included, they must come at points in the sentence where there are natural breaks in the grammatical structure.

Although the omission or wrong use of a comma sounds like a small mistake, it can be very important. The following group of words, for example, forms a sentence only if a comma is included:

needs checking	Because of the work that we had done before we were ready to hand in the assignment.
revised	Because of the work that we had done before, we were ready to hand in the assignment.

The omission or addition of a comma can also completely alter the meaning of a sentence—as it did in the Queen's University Alumni letter that spoke of the warm emotions still felt by alumni for *our friends, who are dead* (rather than *our friends who are dead*). The second would have been merely a polite remembrance of those alumni who have died; the first suggests that *all* the person's friends are dead.

F9. **omission of commas**: Commas very commonly come in pairs, and it is wrong to omit the second comma in a pair. Be particularly careful when putting commas around a name, or around an adjectival subordinate clause.

needs checking	My sister Caroline, has done very well this year in her studies.
revised	My sister, Caroline, has done very well this year in her studies.
needs checking	The snake which had been killed the day before, was already half-eaten by ants.
revised	The snake, which had been killed the day before, was already half-eaten by ants.

F10. **extra comma**: Writers often add a comma when they feel a sentence is getting long, regardless of whether one is needed or is appropriate.

needs checking	The ever-increasing gravitational pull of the global economy, is drawing almost every area of the earth into its orbit.
revised	The ever-increasing gravitational pull of the global economy is drawing almost every area of the earth into its orbit.

F11. **serial comma**: An important use of commas is to separate the entries in lists. Many authorities feel that a comma need not appear between the last and second-last entries in a list, since these are usually separated already by the word *and*. Omitting the last comma in a series will occasionally lead to ambiguity, though; when in doubt, include the serial comma. And when the list includes items that have commas within them, use a semicolon to separate the items in the list.

needs checking	This book is dedicated to my parents, Ayn Rand and God.
revised	This book is dedicated to my parents, Ayn Rand, and God.
needs checking	The three firms involved were McCarthy and Walters, Harris, Jones, and Engleby, and Cassells and Wirtz.
revised	The three firms involved were McCarthy and Walters; Harris, Jones, and Engleby; and Cassells and Wirtz.

On the Web

Exercises on punctuation may be found at
www.broadviewpress.com/writing.
Click on **Exercises** and go to **F1–F21**.

● *The Question Mark* ?

F12. **question mark**: Everyone knows that a question should be followed by a question mark, but it is easy to forget, particularly if one is writing quickly or if the question mark should appear within other punctuation.

needs checking   Would Britain benefit from closer ties with Europe. More than 30 years after the UK joined the EC, the question continues to bedevil British political life.

revised   Would Britain benefit from closer ties with Europe? More than 30 years after the UK joined the EC, the question continues to bedevil British political life.

It is easy to forget that sentences beginning with combinations such as *He asked if...* or *She wondered whether...* are statements, not questions. They may report a question in indirect speech, but they are not themselves questions, and should thus not end with a question mark.

needs checking   Many scholars have asked whether Truman was justified in dropping the atomic bomb in Japan, or whether he should have relied on conventional weapons?

revised   Many scholars have asked whether Truman was justified in dropping the atomic bomb in Japan, or whether he should have relied on conventional weapons.

or   Many scholars have asked the following question: was Truman justified in dropping the atomic bomb in Japan, or should he have relied on conventional weapons?

● *The Exclamation Mark*   **!**

This mark is used to give extremely strong emphasis to a statement. It should be used very sparingly, if at all, in formal written work; most good writers avoid it completely, since they realize that it does not lend any additional impact to what they are saying.

● *The Semicolon*   **;**

F13. This mark is used to separate independent clauses where the ideas are closely related to each other. In most cases a period could be used instead; the semicolon simply signals to the reader the close relationship between the two ideas. In the following example the second sentence reinforces the statement of the first; a semicolon is thus appropriate, although a period is also correct:

- This book is both exciting and profound. It is one of the best books I have read.
- This book is both exciting and profound; it is one of the best books I have read.

Similarly in the following example the second sentence gives evidence supporting the statement made in the first sentence. Again, a semicolon is appropriate:

- The team is not as good as it used to be. It has lost four of its past five games.
- The team is not as good as it used to be; it has lost four of its last five games.

The semicolon is also used occasionally to divide items in a series that includes other punctuation:

- The following were told to report to the coach after practice: Jackson, Form 2B; Marshall, Form 3A; Gladys, Form 1B.

A common notion is that the central distinction among punctuation marks such as the comma, semicolon, colon, and period is rooted simply in the length of the pause they ask the reader to make. Such indeed was the norm several centuries ago, when punctuation was designed less to indicate grammatical relationships than to mark pauses as an aid to the listener's understanding when the text was read aloud. Under that system, a period counted as four beats, a colon as three, a semicolon as two, and a comma as one. Ian Coutts, in an interesting article in *Quill and Quire* ("All About the Pause," February 2005, 7), uses a passage from the 1549 *Book of Common Prayer* as an example of how strangely such a system strikes the modern sensibility:

> Easter Day. The Collect.
> Almighty God, who through thine only begotten Son Jesus Christ hast overcome death, and opened unto us the gate of everlasting life; We humbly beseech thee, that, as by thy special grace preventing us thou dost put into our minds good desires, so by thy continual help we may bring the same to good effect; through Jesus Christ our Lord, who liveth and reigneth with thee and the Holy Ghost, ever one God, world without end.

Perhaps even stranger to modern eyes is the fashion in which the reading that follows is punctuated in sixteenth-century style:

> Mortify therefore your members which are upon the earth; fornication, uncleanness, inordinate affection, evil concupiscence, and covetousness, which is idolatry: For which things, sake the wrath of God cometh on the children of disobedience. In the which ye also walked some time, when ye lived in them.

It is not only the practice of punctuation here that is at odds with today's practice; so too are the principles of capitalization and of grammar considerably different. Here are the two passages again, set down according to modern practice:

> Almighty God, who through thine only begotten Son Jesus Christ hast overcome death, and opened unto us the gate of everlasting life, we humbly beseech thee that, as by thy special grace preventing us thou dost put into our minds good desires, so by thy continual help we may bring the same to good effect; through Jesus Christ our Lord, who liveth and reigneth with thee and the Holy Ghost, ever one God, world without end.

Mortify therefore your members which are upon the earth: fornication; uncleanness; inordinate affection; evil concupiscence; and covetousness, which is idolatry. For these things' sake the wrath of God cometh on the children of disobedience, in the which ye also walked some time, when ye lived in them.

Echoes of the ancient principles of punctuation are still to be found in surprising places. The section on punctuation in the fifteenth edition of *The Chicago Manual of Style* advises at one point that "the semicolon, stronger than a comma but weaker than a period, can assume either role." As Louis Menand fairly commented in discussing this passage in his review of the fifteenth edition, "What could the authors possibly have been thinking?" ("The End Matter," *The New Yorker*, 6 October 2003, 125). To retain elements of the old system of "pause punctuation" in the context of modern academic practice is simply to sow the seeds of confusion. In such a context, the semicolon has a set of precise grammatical functions; it is not to be used simply to indicate a longer-than-usual pause, any more than the comma is to be used to join independent clauses.

needs checking   The threat to the planet is constant and growing, it is to be found in the factories of Ohio; in the shrinking rain forests of Brazil; in the massive growth and massive pollution of China's cities; and in the coal-fired generation stations that still produce much of the world's electricity.

revised   The threat to the planet is constant and growing. It is to be found in the factories of Ohio, in the shrinking rain forests of Brazil, in the massive growth and massive pollution of China's cities, and in the coal-fired generation stations that still produce much of the world's electricity.

or   The threat to the planet is constant and growing; it is to be found in the factories of Ohio, in the shrinking rain forests of Brazil, in the massive growth and massive pollution of China's cities, and in the coal-fired generation stations that still produce much of the world's electricity.

● *The Colon*   **:**

F14. **colon:** This mark is often believed to be virtually the same as the semicolon in the way it is used. In fact, there are some important differences. The most common uses of the colon are as follows:

- in headings, to announce that more is to follow, or that the writer is about to list a series of things.
- to introduce a quotation.
- between two clauses, to indicate that the second one provides an explanation of what was stated in the first.

This last (the least common way in which the colon is used) is very similar to the main use of the semicolon. The subtle differences are that the semicolon can be used in such situations when the ideas are not quite so closely related, and the colon asks the reader to pause for a slightly longer period. Some authorities, it should be noted, feel it is inappropriate to use a colon in this way; if in any doubt as to the appropriateness of using a colon to separate two independent clauses, the student is well advised to use a semicolon instead.

- *Unquiet Union: A Study of the Federation of Rhodesia and Nyasaland.*
- In the last four weeks he has visited five countries: Mexico, Venezuela, Panama, Haiti, and Belize.
- The theory of the Communists may be summed up in a single phrase: abolition of private property.

Be sure to use a colon (rather than a comma or a semicolon) to introduce a list.

needs checking	The operation in Toronto has supplied Mr. Bomersbach with four luxury cars, two Cadillacs, a Mercedes, and a Jaguar.
revised	The operation in Toronto has supplied Mr. Bomersbach with four luxury cars: two Cadillacs, a Mercedes, and a Jaguar.

● *The Hyphen*

F15. **hyphen**: This mark may be used to separate two parts of a compound word (e.g., *tax-free*, *hand-operated*). Notice that many such word combinations are hyphenated only if the combination acts as an adjective:

- No change is planned for the short term.
  (*Term* acts here as a noun, with the adjective *short* modifying it.)
- This is only a short-term plan.
  (Here the compound *short-term* acts as a single adjective, modifying the noun *plan.*)
- George Eliot is one of the major figures in the literature of the nineteenth century.
  (*Century* acts here as a noun, with the adjective *nineteenth* modifying it.)
- George Eliot is one of the major figures of nineteenth-century literature.
  (Here the compound *nineteeth-century* acts as a single adjective, modifying the noun *literature.*)

Hyphens are also used to break a word at the end of a line if there is not enough space. A hyphen should never be used to break up proper nouns, and should be used to break up other words only when it is placed between syllables. Any noun beginning with a capital letter (e.g., *Halifax*, *Blair*, *January*, *Harriet*) is a proper noun.

Whenever one is uncertain about whether or not to use a hyphen, the easy solution is to put the entire word on the next line.

● *The Dash* ⸻

F16. **dash**: Dashes are often used in much the same way as parentheses, to set off an idea within a sentence. Dashes, however, call attention to the set-off idea in a way that parentheses do not:

- Peterborough (home of Broadview Press's distribution facility) is a pleasant city of 70,000.
- Peterborough—home of Broadview Press's distribution facility—is a pleasant city of 70,000.

A dash may also be used in place of a colon to set off a word or phrase at the end of a sentence:

- He fainted when he heard how much he had won: one million dollars.
- He fainted when he heard how much he had won—one million dollars.

Em dashes and en dashes: The above applies to what is known as the em dash—so-called because in most typefaces it is about the same length as the letter *m*. There is also a slightly shortened form of dash—known as the en dash—which fulfils a different function.

On the Web

Exercises on punctuation may be found at **www.broadviewpress.com/writing**. Click on **Exercises** and go to **F1-F21**.

Whereas an em dash is used to separate groups of words, an en dash is used to separate numbers, as in these examples:

- Paul Newman (1925–2008) was both a philanthropist and a noted actor.
- The street numbers are as follows: in the first block west of Main Street, 1–100; in the second block, 100–200; and so on.

Although it is standard to use the en dash in such circumstances in published work, the en dash does not appear on most keyboards, and the hyphen is usually used in its stead in everyday work. In most word processing programs an em dash may be formed by typing two hyphens (--). Note that no spaces should be left either before or after the dash. In some word processing programs a dash may be chosen from the menu symbols.

needs checking	Taipei 101-at the time the tallest building in the world-was completed in 2004. Towers in Shanghai and Dubai have since surpassed it.
revised	Taipei 101—at the time the tallest building in the world—was completed in 2004. Towers in Shanghai and Dubai have since surpassed it.

● *Parentheses* ( )

F17. **parentheses:** Parentheses are used to set off an interruption in the middle of a sentence, or to make a point which is not part of the main flow of the sentence. They are frequently used to give examples, or to express something in other words using the abbreviation i.e. Example:

- Several world leaders of the 1980s (Deng in China, Reagan in the US, etc.) were very old men.

● *Square Brackets*   [ ]

F18. **square brackets:** Square brackets are used for parentheses within parentheses, or to show that the words within the parentheses are added by another person.

- Lentricchia claims that "in reading James's Preface [to *What Maisie Knew*] one is struck as much by what is omitted as by what is revealed."
- Smith writes that as the end of the trial approached, "Sacco and Vanzetti had a good idea of what there [sic] fate would be."
  (Here the Latin *sic*, meaning *thus*, is used to indicate that the error is reproduced just as it appears in the original quotation.)

● *The Apostrophe*   ʼ

apostrophe: The two main uses of the apostrophe are to show possession (e.g., *Peter's book*) and to shorten certain common word combinations. The shortened forms (e.g., *can't, shouldn't, he's*) are known as contractions.

F19. **contractions:** Contractions are used frequently in this book, which is relatively informal in its style. Contractions, however, should not be used in more formal written work. Use *cannot*, not *can't*; *do not*, not *don't*; and so on.

informal	The experiment wasn't a success because we'd heated the solution to too high a temperature.
more formal	The experiment was not a success because we had heated the solution to too high a temperature.

F20. **possession**: The correct placing of the apostrophe to show possession can be a tricky matter. When the noun is singular and does not already end with an *s*, an *s* at the end of the word, preceded by an apostrophe, shows possession (e.g., *Peter's*, *George's*, *Canada's*). When the noun is plural and ends in an *s* already, the apostrophe should be added after the *s*.

needs checking	We have been asked to dinner by Harriets mother.
revised	We have been asked to dinner by Harriet's mother.
needs checking	His parent's house is filled with antiques.
revised	His parents' house is filled with antiques.
needs checking	All three groups of parents attended their infant's one-month pediatric checkup, and observations were made of father's interactions with their infants.
revised	All three groups of parents attended their infants' one-month pediatric checkup, and observations were made of fathers' interactions with their infants.

Authorities differ on how one should show possession with singular nouns that already end in s. The MLA recommends that an *s* always be added at the end of such nouns, even where they are multi-syllabic and pronunciation with an additional *s* is ungainly:

- Dickens's next novel was *Bleak House*.
- The riding was a stronghold for Duplessis's Union Nationale party.
- Ulysses's voyage was a long one.
- Socrates's method of communicating his ideas has been as influential as the ideas themselves.

The Chicago Manual of Style, on the other hand, recommends adding just the apostrophe (with no additional *s*) where a singular noun ending in *s* is already more than one syllable. This approach has the great advantage of avoiding amusing but distracting tongue twisters:

- Dickens' next novel was *Bleak House*.
- The riding was a stronghold for Duplessis' Union Nationale party.
- Ulysses' voyage was a long one.
- Socrates' method of communicating his ideas has been as influential as the ideas themselves.

Whichever convention a writer chooses, he should be consistent. And be sure in such cases not to put an apostrophe before the first *s* in a noun ending with *s*.

needs checking	Shield's novel is finely, yet delicately constructed. (concerning novelist Carol Shields)
revised	Shields's novel is finely, yet delicately constructed.

Where possession is joint, an *s* should be added to the last mentioned noun:

- Bob and Carol's view is that this can be settled amicably.
- Woodward and Bernstein's persistence eventually paid off.

One important exception to the convention of using an apostrophe to show possession is the possessive *its*. In that case the form *it's* is used as a contraction of *it is*, and no apostrophe is included in the possessive *its*. If you are ever uncertain as to whether or not you are making the correct choice between *it's* and *its*, ask yourself if the sentence would make sense if you substituted *it is*. If it would, *it's* is the one you want; if not, you should be using *its*.

Apostrophes are used by some writers to form the plurals of letters and numbers:

- That sort of music was popular in the 1990's.
- She received straight A's in high school.

Since apostrophes are not otherwise used to show plurality, most authorities now prefer to omit the apostrophe:

- That sort of music was popular in the 1990s.
- She received straight As in high school.

● *Quotation Marks* " "

The main use of quotation marks is to show that the words are repeated exactly as they were originally spoken or written. For a discussion of difficulties associated with this use see the chapter on direct and indirect speech immediately following.

According to different conventions, words that are being mentioned in a grammatical sense, rather than used to convey meaning, may be set off by quotation marks, single quotation marks, or italics:

- The words "except" and "accept" are sometimes confused.
- The words 'except' and 'accept' are sometimes confused.
- The words *except* and *accept* are sometimes confused.

Quotation marks (or single quotation marks) are sometimes used to indicate that the writer does not endorse the quoted statement, claim, or description. Quotation marks are usually used in this way only with a word or a brief phrase. When they are so used they have the connotation of *supposed* or *so-called*; they suggest that the quoted word or phrase is either euphemistic or downright false:

- After a violent workout the weightlifters would each consume a "snack" of a steak sandwich, a half-dozen eggs, several pieces of bread and butter, and a quart of tomato juice.

In the following two versions of the same report, the more sparing use of quotation marks in the second version signals clearly to the reader the writer's scepticism as to the honesty of the quoted claim, and may be taken to imply that the former Russian president indulged his legendary fondness for alcohol during the flight.

- President Yeltsin appeared to stagger as he left the plane. "The president is feeling tired and emotional," his press secretary later reported.
- A "tired and emotional" President Yeltsin appeared to stagger as he left the plane.

F21. **misuse of quotation marks to indicate emphasis:** Quotation marks (unlike italics, bold letters, capital letters, or underlining) should never be used to try to lend emphasis to a particular word or phrase. Because quotation marks may be used to convey the sense *supposed* or *so-called* (see above), the common misuse of quotation marks to try to lend emphasis often creates ludicrous effects.

needs checking	All our bagels are served "fresh" daily.
	(The unintended suggestion here is that the claim of freshness is a dubious one.)
revised	All our bagels are served fresh daily.
or	All our bagels are served *fresh* daily.
	(if emphasis is required in an advertisement)
needs checking	Dogs must be "leashed." (BC ferries sign)
revised	Dogs must be leashed.

( )

● *Single Quotation Marks*

In North America the main use of single quotation marks is to mark quotations within quotations:

- According to Obama's press secretary, "When the president said, 'I will bring change to Washington,' he meant it."

Depending on convention, single quotation marks may also be used to show that a word or phrase is being mentioned rather than used (see above).

In the United Kingdom and some other countries, quotation marks and single quotation marks are used for direct speech in precisely the opposite way that North Americans use them; single quotation marks (or inverted commas, as they are sometimes called) are used for direct speech, and double marks are used for quotations within quotations. Here is the correct British version of the above sentence:

- According to Obama's press secretary, 'When the president said, "I will bring change to Washington", he meant it.'

Note here that UK usage also places the comma outside the quotation mark.

⊙ Direct and Indirect Speech

● *Direct Speech*

Direct speech is a written record of the exact words used by the person speaking. The main rules for writing direct speech in English are as follows:

- The exact words spoken—and no other words—must be surrounded by quotation marks.
- A comma should precede a quotation, but according to American convention other punctuation should be placed inside the quotation marks. Examples:

  - He said, "I think I can help you."
    (The period after *you* comes before the quotation marks.)
  - "Drive slowly," she said, "and be very careful."
    (The comma after *slowly* and period after *careful* both come inside the quotation marks.)

On the Web

Exercises on direct and indirect speech may be found at **www.broadviewpress.com/writing**. Click on **Exercises** and go to **F22-FA27**.

With each change in speaker a new paragraph should begin. Example:

> "Let's go fishing this weekend," Mary suggested. "It should be nice and cool by the water."
>
> "Good idea," agreed Faith. "I'll meet you by the store early Saturday morning."

British convention, however, places the punctuation outside the quotation marks:

- 'An iron curtain is descending across Europe', declared Winston Churchill in 1946.

Canadian usage demands that all punctuation go inside the quotation marks in quotations that are stand-alone sentences. At the same time, it allows writers either to follow the American convention or to make an exception when the punctuation clearly pertains only to the structure of the surrounding sentence and not to the quoted word or phrase:

- "An iron curtain is descending across Europe," declared Winston Churchill in 1946.
- Was it Churchill who described the post-war divide between newly Communist Eastern Europe and the West as "an iron curtain"?

The most common difficulties experienced when recording direct speech are as follows:

F22. omission of quotation marks: This happens particularly frequently at the end of a quotation.

needs checking	She said, "I will try to come to see you tomorrow. Then she left.
revised	She said, "I will try to come to see you tomorrow." Then she left.

F23. placing punctuation outside the quotation marks:

needs checking	He shouted, "The house is on fire"!
revised	He shouted, "The house is on fire!"

F24. including the word *that* before direct speech: *That* is used before passages of indirect speech, not before passages of direct speech.

needs checking	My brother said that, "I think I have acted stupidly."
revised	My brother said, "I think I have acted stupidly."
or	My brother said that he thought he had acted stupidly.
needs checking	The official indicated that, "we are not prepared to allow galloping inflation."
revised	The official said, "We are not prepared to allow galloping inflation."
or	The official indicated that his government was not prepared to allow galloping inflation.

F25. when to indent: In a formal essay, any quotation longer than four lines[*] should normally be single-spaced and indented to set it off from the body of the text. Any quotation of more than three lines from a poem should also be single-spaced and indented.

---

[*] This is what the MLA recommends; *The Chicago Manual of Style* specifies forty words.

Quotations set off from the body of the text in this way should not be preceded or followed by quotation marks.

needs checking   Larkin's "Days" opens with childlike simplicity: "What are days for? / Days are where we live. / They come, they wake us / Time and time over." But with Larkin, the shadow of mortality is never far distant.

revised   Larkin's "Days" opens with childlike simplicity:
> What are days for?
> Days are where we live.
> They come, they wake us
> Time and time over.

But with Larkin, the shadow of mortality is never far distant.

● Indirect Speech

Indirect speech reports what was said without using the same words that were used by the speaker. The rules for writing indirect speech are as follows:

- Do not use quotation marks.
- Introduce statements with the word *that*, and do not put a comma after *that*. Questions should be introduced with the appropriate question word (*what, why, whether, if, how, when,* etc.).
- First-person pronouns and adjectives (e.g., *I, me, we, us, my, our*) must often be changed to third person (*he, she, they, him, her, them* etc.) if the subject of the main clause is in third person.

correct   "I am not happy with our team's performance," said Paul.

also correct   Paul said that he was not happy with his team's performance.

correct	I said, "I want my money back."
also correct	I said that I wanted my money back.
	(Here the subject, *I*, is first person.)

- Second-person pronouns must also sometimes be changed.
- Change the tenses of the verbs to agree with the main verb of the sentence. Usually this involves moving the verbs one step back into the past from the tenses used by the speaker in direct speech. Notice in the first example above, for instance, that the present tense *am* has been changed to the past tense *was* in indirect speech. Here are other examples:

correct	"We will do everything we can," he assured me.
correct	He assured me that they would do everything they could.
	(*Will* and *can* change to *would* and *could*.)
correct	"You went to school near Brandon, didn't you?" he asked me.
correct	He asked me if I had gone to school near Brandon.
	(*Went* changes to *had gone*.)

- Change expressions having to do with time. This is made necessary by the changes in verbs discussed above. For example, *today* in direct speech normally becomes *on that day* in indirect speech, *yesterday* becomes *on the day before*, *tomorrow* becomes *the next day*, and so on.

The most common problems experienced when indirect speech is being used are as follows:

F26. **confusion of pronouns**: Many writers do not remember to change all the necessary pronouns when shifting from direct to indirect speech.

- When I met him he said, "You have cheated me." (direct)

| *needs checking* | When I met him he said that you had cheated me. |
| *revised* | When I met him he said that I had cheated him. |

• He will probably say to you, "I am poor. I need money."

| *needs checking* | He will probably tell you that he is poor and that I need money. |
| *revised* | He will probably tell you that he is poor and that he needs money. |

F27. **verb tenses**: Remember to shift the tenses of the verbs one step back into the past when changing something into indirect speech.

• She said, "I will check my tires tomorrow."

| *needs checking* | She said that she will check her tires the next day. |
| *revised* | She said that she would check her tires the next day. |

• "Can I go with you later this afternoon?" he asked.

| *needs checking* | He asked if he can go with us later that afternoon. |
| *revised* | He asked if he could go with us later that afternoon. |

⊙ Format and Spelling

● *Capitalization*

F28. **capitalization**: Conventions concerning capitalization have been anything but fixed in the history of the English language. It was not until the late medieval period that capital letters began to be used consistently to begin sentences and proper names. From there the use of capitals became more and more common, until, during the eighteenth century, a great many common nouns were often capitalized. In particular, common nouns naming abstract qualities were capitalized frequently, but many writers would also capitalize without any great degree of consistency any noun or pronoun that they felt to be important. Here is a sample: ... *you may be Mine in the manner you now are for a much longer time, yet I at last may lose you, and one unlucky Moment destroy the Constancy of Ages.*

In the past ten years there has been a substantial resurgence of this eighteenth-century practice. Students and other writers—many of whom have not been taught at school the difference between a proper and a common noun—are reverting more and more frequently to the eighteenth-century practice of simply making a stab at what words should begin with a capital letter, without much sense of any rules governing the practice. The basis of those rules is very simple, but there are also a good many subtleties and gray areas.

needs checking	In this Company we want to hire Managers who convey a strong sense of Authority.
revised	In this company we want to hire managers who convey a strong sense of authority.

In English the fundamental principle on which the rules of capitalization are based is that proper nouns (naming specific persons, places, or things) should always be capitalized. Proper adjectives (adjectives formed from these proper nouns) are also always capitalized. Common nouns, however, are not normally capitalized. *Marx*, *California*, and *Spain*, are all proper nouns. *Marxist*, *Californian*, and *Spanish* are all proper adjectives. The nouns *sinker*, *state*, and *nation*, on the other hand, are all common nouns; they do not name *specific* persons, places, or things. Here are a number of other examples of proper and common nouns:

Proper	Common
June	summer
Parliament of Canada	in parliament
Mother (used as a name)	my mother
Remembrance Day	in remembrance
Memorial Day	as a memorial
National Gallery	a gallery
Director	a director
Professor	a professor
the Enlightenment	the eighteenth century
the Restoration	the restoration
(historical period in England)	(other uses of the word)
the Renaissance	renaissance
(historical period)	(a revival)
God	a god
Catholic	catholic
(belonging to that particular church)	(meaning *wide-ranging* or *universal*)
a Liberal	a liberal
(belonging to the Liberal Party)	(holding liberal ideas)
a Democrat	a democrat
(belonging to the Democratic Party)	(believing in democratic ideals)

Some categories frequently cause difficulty over the issue of capitalization. When should one write *professor* and when *Professor*, for example? Following are some more detailed guidelines.

Names of People

Margaret Atwood, Professor Smith, Samantha.

Names of Places
Cleveland, Asia, the North Pole, the White House, Parliament Hill. Note here that all nouns in a name should be capitalized (*Central Park, the Statue of Liberty*).

Names of Days of the Week, Months, and Holidays
Monday, January, Boxing Day, Yom Kippur. Note that the names of seasons are not capitalized.

F29. **Academic names:** All nouns in a formal name should be capitalized: *the University of Chicago, Camosun College, Philosophy 150, Economics 205.* Note that, when not describing a specific course, the names of academic subjects are not capitalized unless they are names of languages. In formal use, capitalize *the Physics Department, the Department of History,* etc.

needs checking	Most offices in the Philosophy department are located in the Arts Tower.
revised	Most offices in the Philosophy Department are located in the Arts Tower.
needs checking	She is studying Philosophy at the University of Michigan.
revised	She is studying philosophy at the University of Michigan.

On the Web
Exercises on capitalization may be found at **www.broadviewpress.com/writing**. Click on **Exercises** and go to **F28–32**.

F30. **institutional names:** All nouns in these names should be capitalized (*the University of San Diego, the Audit Committee, the Board of Directors, the Golden Financial Corporation, the Department of Justice*). Note that where a specific body is not being named, capitals should not be used.

needs checking	Every large company must have an Audit Committee.
revised	Every large company must have an audit committee.

F31. **occupational names:** When a title is used before a person's name, it must be capitalized: *Reverend Philips*; *President Carter*; *Professor Said*; *Claude Johnson, minister of justice,* or *Justice Minister Claude Johnson.* When the title appears as a substitute for the name, capitalizing the title is optional. As always in such cases, be sure to be consistent.

worth checking	The Prime Minister will deliver a speech this afternoon, and the president of Shell Oil will be speaking this evening.
revised	The Prime Minister will deliver a speech this afternoon, and the President of Shell Oil will be speaking this evening.
or	The prime minister will deliver a speech this afternoon, and the president of Shell Oil will be speaking this evening.

When titles follow a name, capitalization of the title is optional.

Sandra Mbeki, professor of German
or Sandra Mbeki, Professor of German
Frank Gibbs, president of Acme Tools
or Frank Gibbs, President of Acme Tools

Names of Major Historical Events, Movements, or Periods
It is not surprising that students and other writers often become confused over whether or not to capitalize historical references of this sort, since the names of centuries, decades, and so on are not normally capitalized. It is thus correct to refer to *the eighteenth century* in lower case, but *the Enlightenment* with a capital; to *the medieval period*, but to *the Middle Ages* with capitals; *the thirties*, to refer to the 1930s, but *the Depression* to refer to the economic

condition that dominated the period. If we speak of the study of *Romantic literature* we are speaking of the study of the Romantic period (i.e., the late eighteenth and early nineteenth centuries), whereas if we speak of studying romantic literature we are referring to the study of any literary works with romantic themes. Here are a few more examples of major historical events, movements, or periods that are normally capitalized: *the Thirty Years War, the Great Fire of London, World War II, the Big Bang, the Impressionists.*

Names of Religions, Deities, Religious Persons, Terms, or Texts

Nouns or adjectives of this sort are normally capitalized: *Buddhism, a Buddhist, Islam, a Muslim, Christian, Jewish, Holy Ghost, the Bible, the Koran.*

Names of Races, Groups, Nationalities, and Their Languages

Nouns or adjectives of this sort should be capitalized: *Mexican, Hispanic, the Yoruba, Nova Scotians, a Native American, First Nations, a European professor, Chinese, students learning Mandarin or French.* Note that capitalization when referring to colour is optional. It is more common to use lower case, however (e.g., *In South Africa blacks and whites are on far better terms than was the case twenty years ago*).

Names of Geographical Areas

Depending on context, certain geographical words may denote either a direction or an area—or, indeed, more than one area. If, for example, we say *keep travelling west, and you will reach the sea*, the word *west* is a direction and should not be capitalized. If, however, we write that *in the West, American voters tend to be fiscally conservative*, when referring to the western portion of the United States, it is normal to capitalize *West*. In a different context we might write *in the West, capitalism took root in the seventeenth and eighteenth centuries*. In that context *the West* is a synonym for *the Western World*. Similar multiple meanings may attach to the words *south, north,* and *east* and *South, North,* and *East*.

F32. **literary titles:** Major words in titles should be capitalized. Articles, short prepositions, and conjunctions are normally not capitalized in titles.

needs checking	Robert Boardman discusses *The Bridge On The River Kwai* extensively in his book.
revised	Robert Boardman discusses *The Bridge on the River Kwai* extensively in his book.

Names of Teams or Clubs

Where a specific name is given it should be capitalized (*the Toronto Maple Leafs, Team USA, Manchester United*). Where a specific team or club is mentioned but not given its formal name, no capitals should be used (*the national team, our bridge club*).

Names of Abstract Qualities

As in the eighteenth century, writers today are often inclined to capitalize the names of abstract qualities in order to signal their importance. These are common nouns, however, and should in almost all cases not be capitalized. An exception occurs if in the context the abstract quality is personified; in that case the noun may be regarded as a proper name (*if Chance is often blind, it is also often a powerful friend*).

needs checking	Keats shared with writers of the Romantic period a strong interest in notions of Truth and Beauty.
revised	Keats shared with writers of the Romantic period a strong interest in notions of truth and beauty.

Capitalization Following a Colon

Some style guides recommend capitalizing independent clauses that begin after a colon. Somewhat oddly, they do not similarly recommend capitalizing independent clauses that begin after a semicolon. In view of this inconsistency—and in view as well of the fact that the colon is often used for purposes other than separating independent clauses—it is probably wisest for students to refrain from any use of capitals following a colon.

● *Abbreviations*

Abbreviations are a convenient way of presenting information in a smaller amount of space. This section discusses conventions for using abbreviations in formal writing.

Titles
Titles are normally abbreviated when used immediately before or after a person's full name.

Mr. Isaiah Thomas *Dr. Jane Phelps*

Sammy Davis Jr. *Marcia Gibbs, MD*

When using a title together with the last name only, the full title should be written out.

Prof. Marc Ereshefsky *Professor Ereshefsky*

Sen. Keith Davey *Senator Davey*

Academic and Business Terms
Common abbreviations are acceptable in formal writing so long as they are likely to be readily understood. Otherwise, the full name should be written out when first used and the abbreviation given in parentheses. Thereafter, the abbreviation may be used on its own, as shown in these examples:

- The Atomic Energy Commission (AEC) has broad-ranging regulatory authority.
- The American Philosophical Association (APA) holds three large regional meetings annually.

Latin abbreviations

Several abbreviations of Latin terms are common in formal academic writing:

cf.	*compare* (Latin *confer*)
e.g.	*for example* (Latin *exempli gratia*)
et al.	*and others* (Latin *et alia*)
etc.	*and so on* (Latin *et cetera*: *and the rest*)
ibid.	*in the same book or passage* (Latin *ibidem*: *in the same place*)
i.e.	*that is to say* (Latin *id est*)
NB	*note well* (Latin *nota bene*)

F33. **numbers:** Numbers of one or two words should be written out. Use figures for all other numbers.

needs checking	The building is 72 storeys tall.
revised	The building is seventy-two storeys tall.

The same principle applies for dollar figures (or figures in other currencies).

needs checking	She lent her brother 10 dollars.
revised	She lent her brother ten dollars.

It is acceptable to combine figures and words for very large numbers:

- The government is projecting a $200 billion deficit.

In general, figures should be used in addresses, in dates, to give percentages, and to report scores or statistics.

needs checking	In the third game of the tournament, Canada and the Czech Republic tied three three.
revised	In the third game of the tournament, Canada and the Czech Republic tied 3–3.

F34. **italics**: Italics serve several different functions. While short stories, poems, and other works are set off by quotation marks, longer works and the names of newspapers, magazines, and so on should appear in italics:

"The Dead"	*Dubliners*
"Burnt Norton"	*Four Quartets*
"Budget Controversy Continues"	*The Economist*
"Smells Like Teen Spirit"	*Nevermind*

Italics are also used for the names of paintings and sculptures, television series, and software. In addition, italics are used for words or phrases from other languages in written English.

needs checking	The play ends with an appearance of a deus ex machina.
revised	The play ends with an appearance of a *deus ex machina.*

Either italics or quotation marks may be used to indicate that words are mentioned rather than used (see above, under "Quotation Marks"). Finally, italics are often used to provide special emphasis that is not otherwise clear from the context or the structure of the sentence.

⊙ Spelling

● *Spelling and Sound*

The wittiest example of the illogic of English spelling remains Bernard Shaw's famous spelling of *fish* as *ghoti*. The *gh* sounds like the *gh* in *enough*; the *o* sounds like the *o* in *women* (once spelled *wimmen*, incidentally); and the *ti* sounds like the *ti* in *nation* or *station*. Shaw passionately advocated a rationalization of English spelling; it still has not happened, and probably never will. Perhaps the best way to learn correct spelling is to be tested by someone else, or to test yourself every week or so on a different group of words. For example, you might learn the words from the list below beginning with *a* and *b* one week, the words beginning with *c* and *d* the next week, and so on.

spell-check: No computer can be a substitute for careful proofreading. Spell-check is wonderful, but it cannot tell if it is your friend or your fiend, or if you have signed off a letter with best wishes or beast wishes.

F35. **spelling and sound—a/an**: Authorities agree that an *n* should be added to the indefinite article when the following word begins with a vowel sound. This is a "rule," it should be noted, that is based entirely on euphony; the reason that *a egg* is not "good English" is simply that it is awkward to say. Thus it is that we use *an* not only before words that begin with a vowel, but also before words that are pronounced as if they began with a vowel (*an hour, an f-word*).

Something of a gray area exists with a small group of words that have a *his-* sound at the beginning, and in which the second syllable is stressed. No one would think of writing *an hiccup* or *an hellish day*, and nor are most people ever tempted to write *an history* or *an hysterectomy*. Many people, though, think that *an hysterical outburst* sounds better than *a hysterical outburst*, and that *an historical introduction* sounds better than *a historical introduction*. As the first sound in an unstressed syllable, the *h* in such words is softer than the *h* in such words as *history*, where a strong stress is placed on the first syllable. Some authorities ridicule this common practice; we sound the *h* in such words, goes the argument, and therefore we should use *a* rather than *an*. But what is the rationale for this "rule" in the first place? Again, purely what sounds better. And the fact is that many people find it easier to say *an historical introduction* than *a historical introduction*. So why the fuss? We may reasonably disagree as to which sounds better, but there is surely no justification for terming one correct and the other incorrect.

F36. **spelling and sound**: Many spelling mistakes result from similarities in the pronunciation of words with very different meanings. These are covered in the list below. Other words that cause spelling difficulties are listed separately.

absent (adjective)	absence (noun)
absorb	absorption
accept	except
access (*entry*)	excess (*too much*)
advice (noun)	advise (verb)
affect (verb)	effect (noun)
allowed (*permitted*)	aloud
alter (*change*)	altar (*in a church*)
appraise (*value*)	apprise (*inform*)
bitten	beaten
base (*foundation*)	bass (*in music*)
bath (noun)	bathe (verb)
berry (*fruit*)	bury (*the dead*)
beside (*by the side of*)	besides (*as well as*)
birth	berth (*bed*)
bizarre (*strange*)	bazaar (*market*)
bloc (political grouping)	block
breath (noun)	breathe (verb)
buoy (*in the water*)	boy
buy (*purchase*)	by
cash	cache (*hiding place*)
casual (*informal*)	causal (*to do with causes*)
cause	case
ceased (*stopped*)	seized (*grabbed*)
ceiling (*above you*)	sealing
chick	cheek/chic (*stylish*; pronounced *sheek*)
chose (past tense)	choose (present tense)
cite (*make reference to*)	sight/site
climatic (*climate*)	climactic (*climax*)
cloths (*fabric*)	clothes
colonel (*officer*)	colonial (*of colonies*)

coma (*unconscious*)	comma (*punctuation*)
compliment (*praise*)	complement (*make complete*)
conscious (*aware*)	conscience (*sense of right*)
contract	construct
conventional (*usual*)	convectional (*transfer of heat*)
conversation	conservation/concentration
cord (*rope*)	chord (*music*)
convinced	convicted (*of a crime*)
council (*group*)	counsel (*advice*)
course	coarse (*rough*)
credible (*believable*)	creditable (*deserving credit*)
critic (*one who criticizes*)	critique (*piece of criticism*)
defer (*show respect*)	differ
deference (*respect*)	difference
deprecate (*criticize*)	depreciate (*reduce in value*)
desert (*dry place;* also *what is deserved*)	dessert (*sweet*)
device (*thing*)	devise (*to plan*)
died/had died	dead/was dead/dyed (*coloured*)
dissent (*protest*)	descent (*downward motion*)
distant (adjective)	distance (noun)
edition (*of a book*, etc.)	addition (*something added*)
emigrant	immigrant
entomology (*study of insects*)	etymology (*study of words*)
envelop (verb)	envelope (noun)
exercise	exorcise (*remove*)
except	expect
fear	fair/fare (*payment*)
feeling	filling
fell	feel/fill
flaunt (*display*)	flout (*disobey*)
formally	formerly (*previously*)
forth (*forward*)	fourth (*after third*)
forward	foreword (*in a book*)
foul	fowl (*birds*)
future	feature

genus (*biological type*)	genius (*creative intelligence*)
greet	great/grate (*scrape*)
guerrillas	gorillas
guided (*led*)	guarded (*protected*)
had	heard/head
heat	heart/hate
heir (*inheritor*)	air
human	humane (*kind*)
illicit (*not permitted*)	elicit (*bring forth*)
illusion (*unreal image*)	allusion (*reference*)
immigrate	emigrate
independent (adjective)	independence (noun)
inhabit (*live in*)	inhibit (*retard*)
instance (*occurrence*)	instants (*moments*)
intense (*concentrating*)	intents (*purposes*)
isle (*island*)	aisle (*to walk in*)
know	no/now
kernel	colonel
lack	lake
later	latter/letter
lath (*piece of wood*)	lathe (*machine*)
lead (*heavy element*)	led (*guided*)
leave	leaf
leave	live
leaving	living
lessen (*reduce*)	lesson
let	late
lightning (*from clouds*)	lightening (*becoming lighter*)
lose (*be unable to find*)	loose (*not tight*)
mad (*insane*)	maid (*servant*)
man	men
martial (*to do with fighting*)	marshal
mental	metal
merry	marry
met	meet/mate
minor (*underage*, or *lesser*)	miner (*underground*)

mist (*light fog*)	missed
moral (*ethical*)	morale (*spirit*)
mourning (*after death*)	morning
new	knew
of	off
on	own
ones	once
ordinance (*decree*)	ordnance (*guns*)
pain	pane (*of glass*)
patients (*sick people*)	patience (*ability to wait*)
peer (*look closely*)	pier (*wharf*)
perpetrate (*be guilty of*)	perpetuate (*cause to continue*)
perquisite (*privilege*)	prerequisite (*requirement*)
personal (*private*)	personnel (*employees*)
perspective (*vision*)	prospective (*anticipated*)
peruse (*study*)	pursue (*follow*)
poor	pour (*liquid*)/pore
precede (*go before*)	proceed (*continue*)
precedent	president
price (*cost*)	prize (*reward*)
prostate (*gland*)	prostrate (*lying down*)
quay (*wharf;* pronounced *key*)	key
quite	quiet (*not noisy*)
rein (*to control animals*)	rain/reign
release (*let go*)	realize (*discover*)
relieve (verb)	relief (noun)
residence (*place*)	residents (*people*)
response (noun)	responds (verb)
rid	ride
ridden	written
rise	rice
rite (*ritual*)	right/write
rod	rode/reared
rote (*repetition*)	wrote
saved	served
scene (*location*)	seen

saw	seen
saw	so/sew
seam (*in clothes*)	seem (*appear*)
secret	sacred (*holy*)
sell (verb)	sail (*boat*)/sale
senses	census (*population count*)
shed	shade
shone	shown
shot	short
sit	sat/set
smell	smile
snake	snack (*small meal*)
soar	sore (*hurt*)
sole (*single, a fish*, or *an undersurface*)	soul (*spirit*)
sort (*type or kind*)	sought (*looked for*)
steal (present tense)	stole (past tense)
straight (*not crooked*)	strait (*of water*)
striped (e.g., *a zebra*)	stripped (*uncovered*)
suite (*rooms* or *music*)	suit/sweet
super	supper (*meal*)
suppose	supposed to
sympathies (noun)	sympathize (verb)
tale (*story*)	tail
talk	took
tap	tape
than	then
they	there/their
thing	think
this	these
throw	threw (past tense)
tied	tired
urban (*in cities*)	urbane (*sophisticated*)
vanish (*disappear*)	varnish
vein (*to carry blood*)	vain
vicious (*brutal*)	viscous (*sticky*)

whole (*complete*)	hole (*empty space*)
waist (*your middle*)	waste
wait	weight (*heaviness*)
waive (*give up*)	wave
wants	once
weak (*not strong*)	week
weather (*sunny, wet,* etc.)	whether (*or not*)
wedding	weeding
were	where
wholly (*completely*)	holy (*sacred*)/holly
woman	women
won	worn
yoke (*for animals*)	yolk (*of an egg*)

F37. **English language spelling variations:** A number of words that cause spelling difficulties are spelled differently in different countries. In most cases Australians prefer British spellings. Either British or American is correct in Canada, so long as the writer is consistent.

American	British
behavior	behaviour
center	centre
color	colour
defense	defence
favor	favour
favorite	favourite
fiber	fibre
fulfill	fulfil
gray	grey
humor	humour
likable	likeable
maneuver	manoeuvre
marvelous	marvellous
meter (*measurement*)	metre
neighbor	neighbour

omelet	omelette
program	programme
Shakespearian	Shakespearean
skillful	skilful
skeptical	sceptical
theater	theatre
traveling	travelling

On the Web

Exercises on spelling may be found at
www.broadviewpress.com/writing.
Click on **Exercises** and go to **F35-F38**.

F38. **commonly misspelled words**: Following is a list of some other commonly misspelled words:

abbreviation	affidavit	anti-Semitic
absence	aficionado	anxious
accelerator	ambulance	apocalypse
accident	ameba (also	apparatus
accidentally	*amoeba*)	apparently
accommodation	among	appreciate
achieve	ammonia	approach
acknowledge	amortize	architect
acquire	amount	arguable
acquisition	anachronism	argument
acquit	analogous	arsonist
acre	analysis	arteriosclerosis
across	anchor	artillery
address	androgynous	asinine
adjacent	annihilate	atheist
advertisement	antecedent	author

auxiliary
awful
awesome
bacteria
basically
battery
beautiful
beginning
believe
boast
boastful
bouillon
breakfast
bulletin
burglar
burial
buried
business
candidate
capillary
cappuccino
Caribbean
carpentry
cautious
ceiling
chaise longue (or
    chaise lounge)
changeable
character
chilblain
chlorophyll
choir
cholesterol
chrome
chromosome
chronological

chrysalis
chrysanthemum
coincidence
colleague
colonel
colossal
column
commitment
committee
comparative
competition
competitor
complexion
conceive
condemn
conjunction
connoisseur
consensus
consistent
controller
convenience
cooperation
cooperative
courteous
courtesy
creator
creature
criticism
cyst
decisive
definite
delicious
description
desirable
despair
despise

destroy
develop
diesel
different
dilemma
dining
disappear
disappoint
disastrous
discrimination
disease
disintegrate
dissatisfied
dominate
dormitory
double
doubtful
drunkard
drunkenness
duchess
due
dyeing
dying
eclipse
eczema
effective
efficient
eighth
embarrass
employee
encourage
enemy
enmity
enormous
entertain
enthusiasm

entitle
entrepreneur
environment
enzyme
epidermis
epididymis
erroneous
esophagus
especially
espresso
essential
exaggerate
excessive
excite
exercise
exhilaration
existence
existent
experience
extraordinary
Fahrenheit
faithful
faithfully
farinaceous
fault
February
financial
foreigner
foretell
forty
fourth
gauge
gamete
germination
government
grammar

grateful
gruesome
guarantee
guerrillas
guilty
happened
happiest
harass
hatred
hectare
helpful
hyena
hypothesis
ichthyology
idiosyncratic
imaginary
imagine
immigration
immersible
impeccable
importance
impresario
inchoate
incomprehensible
indigenous
independent
indestructible
indispensable
ineffable
infinitesimal
inoculate
insufferable
intention,
    intentional
interrupt
irrelevant

irresponsible
isosceles
isthmus
itinerary
jealous
jeopardy
journalist
junction
kneel
knowledge
knowledgeable
laboratories
laboratory
language
lazy, laziness
ledger
leisure
liaise
liberation
library
license
lieutenant
liquid, liquefy
literature
lying
medicine
medieval
membrane
memento
merciful
mermaid
millennia
millennium
millionaire
mischief
mischievous

modern
naked
naughty
necessary
necessity
noticeable
nuclear
nucleus
obscene
obsolescent
obsolete
occasion
occasional
occupy
occur
occurred
occurrence
omit
ophthalmology
ourselves
paid
parallel
parliament
parliamentary
party
permissible
permission
perpendicular
perseverance
photosynthesis
playful
possess
possession
poultry
predictable
pregnancy

pregnant
prerogative
prescription
privilege
properly
psychiatric
psychological
punctuation
pursue
questionnaire
really
receipt
recommend
referee
reference
regret
repeat
repetition
replies
reply
residence (*place*)
residents (*people*)
restaurant
restaurateur
revolutionary
rheumatism
rhododendron
rhombus
rhubarb
rhyme
rhythm
saddest
sandals
scene
schedule
schizophrenic

science
scintillate
scissors
scream
scrumptious
search
seize
sense
separate
shining
shotgun
sigh
significant
simultaneous
sincerely
ski, skis, skied,
    skiing
slippery
slogan
smart
solemn
spaghetti
speech
spongy
sponsor
stale
stingy
stomach
stubborn
studious
studying
stupefy
stupid
subordinate
subpoena
substitute

subtle, subtlety
suburbs
succeed
success,
   successful
sue, suing
summary
supersede
surprised
surreptitious
surrounded
survive
synthesis
symbol
talkative

tarred
television
temperature
tendency
theoretical
theory
title
tough
tragedy
trophy
truly
unique
until
vacancy
vacillate

valuable
vegetable
vehicle
vicious
visitor
volume
voluntary
Wednesday
welcome
whisper
writer
writing
written
yield
zucchini

◎ DOCUMENTATION—*MLA Style*

There are two chief concerns when it comes to citing and documenting material: accuracy and consistency. Whatever system of citation is used, a research writer must follow it closely and consistently. Four of the most commonly used systems of citation are summarized in these pages: MLA style, APA style, Chicago style, and CSE style. Further information about styles of writing as well as of citation and reference in various academic disciplines appears on pages 378–430. It may also be helpful to consult exemplary essays. (A selection of these may be found on the Broadview Press website in the pages providing adjunct material to this and other Broadview writing texts; go to www.broadviewpress.com, and click on links.)

G1. **citation and plagiarism**: To take the words or ideas of another without properly acknowledging them is to commit plagiarism—a serious form of dishonesty. Plagiarism is subject to serious penalties at all academic institutions; these may range from a failing grade being assigned for the relevant course to outright expulsion from the institution.

The avoidance of plagiarism begins with careful research so as to remove any chance of your confusing someone else's words for your own during the writing process. Judgement of the crime of plagiarism, incidentally, makes no provision for malice aforethought; whether or not a writer is wilfully deceptive makes no difference. Therefore, competent writers are extremely careful. As discussed in the section on the writing process at the beginning of this book, careful writers will keep thorough and well-organized notes while reading and researching—notes that clearly indicate where each idea comes from and when the exact words used by another writer are being jotted down.

If you summarize or paraphrase someone else's work without using the exact words that they use, you do not need to use quotation marks—but you must still cite the work.

- Researchers have shown that the model of genetic mapping first advanced by Crick and Watson leaves many questions unanswered (Commoner 42).

Do you need a citation for everything? No. Obviously citations are not needed when you are putting forward your own original ideas. Nor are they necessary when you are touching on common knowledge. If you refer to the population of China or the date when the North American Free Trade Agreement was signed, you do not need to provide any citation, since such information is generally available and widely known.

G2. **signal phrases**: If you quote the exact words of a source, rather than summarize or paraphrase, it is important to integrate the quotation into the body of your writing. You must not drop quoted phrases or sentences in amongst your own; instead, you must signal to the reader where the quoted material comes from and how it connects to your own argument. To this end, phrases such as the following are very useful:

- As Smith and Jones have demonstrated, "...
- In the words of one researcher, "...
- In his most recent book McGann advances the view that, as he puts it, "...
- As Nussbaum observes, "...
- Kendal suggests that "...
- Murphy and other scholars have rejected these claims, arguing that "...
- Morgan has emphasized this point in her recent research: "...
- As Sayeed puts it, "...
- To be sure, Mtele allows that "...
- In his later novels Hardy takes a bleaker view, frequently suggesting that "...

Phrases such as those above are known as signal phrases: they signal to the reader that the research of another is being referred to.

Here is a fuller list of words and expressions that may be useful in signal phrases:

according to _____, "...	endorses
acknowledges	finds
adds	grants
admits	illustrates
advances	implies
agrees	in the view of _____, "...
allows	in the words of _____, "...
argues	insists
asserts	intimates
attests	notes
believes	observes
claims	points out
comments	puts it
compares	reasons
concludes	refutes
confirms	rejects
contends	reports
declares	responds
demonstrates	suggests
denies	takes issue with
disputes	thinks
emphasizes	writes

needs checking   Many critics and theorists of the past generation have been in no doubt as to the perniciousness of Conrad's attitudes. "Conrad was a bloody racist" (Achebe 788). But others have taken a more nuanced view.

>   (Here the Achebe quotation has been dropped into the text.)

revised   Many critics and theorists of the past generation have been in no doubt as to the perniciousness of Conrad's attitudes. Achebe's influential 1977 article is perhaps the most unequivocal statement of this view: "Conrad was a bloody racist" (788), Achebe asserts. But others have taken a more nuanced view.
(Here the same quotation has been integrated into the surrounding text.)

In academic writing prose quotations of more than four lines and verse quotations of more than three lines should be indented, without surrounding quotations marks. Longer quotations also need signals; they need to be introduced in a way that integrates them into the text of your essay. Normally this is done with a sentence ending with a colon.

Edward Said sets Conrad's fiction in the context of its original readers:

> Conrad's readers of the time were not expected to ask about or concern themselves with what became of the natives. What mattered to them was how Marlow makes sense of everything.... This is a short step away from King Leopold's account of his International Congo Association "rendering lasting and disinterested services" to the cause of progress. (200)

Yet Conrad himself unequivocally described the activities Leopold sponsored as "the vilest scramble for loot that ever disfigured the history of human conscience" ("Geography" 17).

The lines of long verse quotations should be arranged just as they are in the original.

The ending of Margaret Avison's "September Street" moves from the decaying, discordant city toward a glimpse of an outer/inner infinitude:

> On the yellow porch
> one sits, not reading headlines; the old eyes
> read far out into the mild
> air, runes.
>
> See. There: a stray sea-gull. (lines 20-24)

In short verse quotations, lines should be separated from one another by a forward slash with a space on either side of it.

> Pope's "Epistle II. To a Lady," in its vivid portrayal of wasted lives, sharply criticizes the social values that render older women superfluous objects of contempt: "Still round and round the Ghosts of Beauty glide, / And haunt the places where their Honour dy'd" (lines 241-42).

More information on integrating quotations is provided in section D56 of the chapter "Academic Writing: Tense Situations."

⊙ MLA Style

A complete sample essay using MLA style appears at the end of the first part of this book. Additional sample essays using MLA style appear on the Broadview website. Key points about parenthetical referencing and "Works Cited" lists presented according to the MLA style guidelines appear below. *The MLA Handbook for Writers of Research Papers* (7th edition 2009) should be consulted for more detailed questions—or they may be answerable at the website of the MLA, www.mla.org, where updates and answers to frequently asked questions are posted.

● *Summary List: Parenthetical Referencing*

● *Summary List: Works Cited*

O *About Parenthetical Referencing*

G3. **parenthetical referencing**: Under the MLA system a quotation or specific reference to another work is followed by a parenthetical page reference:

- Bonnycastle refers to "the true and lively spirit of opposition" with which Marxist literary criticism invigorates the discipline (204).

The work is then listed under "Works Cited" at the end of the essay:

- Bonnycastle, Stephen. *In Search of Authority: An Introductory Guide to Literary Theory*. 2nd ed. Peterborough: Broadview, 1996. Print.

(See below for information about the "Works Cited" list.)

G4. **titles: italics/quotation marks**: Notice in the above example that both the title and the subtitle are in italics. Italicize the titles of works that are not part of other works (that is, that are published or offered as "stand alone" works). Examples include titles of books (*Oryx and Crake*), magazines (*The New Yorker*), newspapers (*The Guardian*), journals (*The American Poetry Review*), websites (*The Camelot Project*), films (*Memento*), television shows (*The X-Files*), and compact discs, audiocassettes, or record albums (*Dark Side of the Moon*).

Don't italicize but do put into double quotation marks the titles of works that are part of other, longer works. Examples include chapters in books ("The Autist Artist" in *The Man Who Mistook His Wife for a Hat and Other Clinical Tales*), encyclopedia articles ("Existentialism"), essays in books ("Salvation in the Garden: Daoism and Ecology" in *Daoism and Ecology: Ways within a Cosmic Landscape*), short stories ("Young Goodman Brown"), poems ("Daddy"), pages on websites ("The Fisher King" from *The Camelot Project*), episodes of television shows ("Small Potatoes" from *The X-Files*), and songs ("Eclipse" from *Dark Side of the Moon*). Put the titles of public lectures in double quotation marks as well ("Walls in the *Epic of Gilgamesh*").

Notice that the last example features a book title within a lecture title, and that the book title is in italics, according to the convention outlined above. If the title of a stand-alone work contains the title of a work that is not independent, the latter is put in double quotation marks, and the entire title is put in italics (*"Self-Reliance" and Other Essays*). If the title of a stand-alone work appears within the title of another independent work, MLA recommends that the former be put in italics and the latter not (*Chaucer's House of Fame: The Poetics of Skeptical Fideism*). If the title of a non-independent work is embedded in another title of the same kind, put the inner title into single quotation marks and the outer title in double quotation marks ("The Drama of Donne's 'The Indifferent'").

G5. **placing of parenthetical references**: Place parenthetical references at the ends of clauses or sentences in order to keep disruption of your writing to a minimum. The parenthetical reference comes before the period or comma in the surrounding sentence. (If the quotation ends with punctuation other than a period or comma, then this should precede the end of the quotation, and a period or comma should still follow the parenthetical reference.)

- Ricks refuted this point early on (16), but the claim has continued to be made in recent years.
- In "The Windhover," on the other hand, Hopkins bubbles over; "the mastery of the thing!" (8), he enthuses when he thinks of a bird, and he exclaims shortly thereafter, "O my chevalier!" (10).

When a cited quotation is set off from the text, however, the parenthetical reference should be placed after the concluding punctuation.

- Muriel Jaeger draws on the following anecdote in discussing the resistance of many wealthy Victorians to the idea of widespread education for the poor:

    In a mischievous mood, Henry Brougham once told [some well-off acquaintances who were] showing perturbation about the likely results of educating the "lower orders" that they could maintain their superiority by working harder themselves. (105)

G6. **parenthetical reference when text is in parentheses**: If a parenthetical reference occurs within text in parentheses, square brackets are used for the reference.

- The development of a mass literary culture (or a "print culture," to use Williams's expression [88]) took several hundred years in Britain.

G7. no signal phrase (or author not named in signal phrase): If the context does not make it clear who the author is, that information must be added to the parenthetical reference. Note that no comma separates the name of the author from the page number.

- Even in recent years some have continued to believe that Marxist literary criticism invigorates the discipline with a "true and lively spirit of opposition" (Bonnycastle 204).

G8. page number unavailable: Many Internet sources lack page numbers. In that case you should not rely on the page number of a printout on your printer, as page breaks may differ with different printers. Instead, provide a section or paragraph number if possible.

- Bhabha clearly implies that he finds such an approach objectionable (par. 7).
- In a recent Web posting a leading critic has clearly implied that he finds such an approach objectionable (Bhabha, par. 7).
- In "The American Scholar" Emerson asserts that America's "long apprenticeship to the learning of other lands" is drawing to a close (par. 1).

Notice that (unlike with page numbers), MLA style requires a comma between author and paragraph number in a citation.

G9. one page or less: If a source is one page long or less, it is advisable to still provide the page number (though MLA does not require this).

- In an article in the online edition of *The Chicago Tribune*, Bosley says that he finds the writing of the novel "excruciating" (1).

G10. page, section, or paragraph numbers all unavailable: In some cases a source may be more than one page long but neither section nor paragraph numbers may be available. If so, it may be best to lead into the quotation without using a signal phrase; the citation in that case will provide only the author's name.

- In a manifesto issued in 2001, the artist advances a radically different approach (Mbeki).

G11. **multiple authors**: If there are two or three authors, all authors should be named either in the signal phrase or in the parenthetical reference.

- Chambliss and Best argue that the importance of this novel is primarily historical (233).
- Two distinguished scholars have recently argued that the importance of this novel is primarily historical (Chambliss and Best 233).

four authors/more authors: In the parenthetical reference, you have two options, but whichever you choose should match the format of the corresponding entry in Works Cited. You may use only the first author's name, followed by *et al.*, short for the Latin *et alia*, meaning *and others* (Fromkin et al. 34–36), or you may list the last names of all the authors in the order in which they appear in the original work (Fromkin, Rodman, Hultin, and Logan 34–36).

G12. **author unknown/corporate author**: Be sure to refer to the relevant organization and/or the title of the piece so as to make the reference clear. Shorten a long title to avoid awkwardness, but be sure that the shortened version begins with the same word as the corresponding entry in "Works Cited" so that readers a can move easily from the citation to the bibliographic information. For example, *Comparative Indo-European Linguistics: An Introduction* should be shortened to *Comparative Indo-European* rather than *Indo-European Linguistics*. The first two examples below cite unsigned newspaper or encyclopedia articles; the last is a corporate author parenthetical citation.

- As *The New York Times* reported in one of its several December 2 articles on the Florida recount, Vice-President Gore looked tired and strained as he answered questions (Gore Press Conference A16).
- According to the *Columbia Encyclopedia*, in the 1990s Sao Paulo began to rapidly overtake Mexico City as the world's most polluted city ("Air Pollution" 21).
- There are a number of organizations mandated "to foster the production and enjoyment of the arts in Canada" (Canada Council for the Arts 2).

G13. electronic source—author not given: If the author of the electronic source is not given, it may be identified in the parenthetical reference by a short form of the title (see the advice on shortening titles in G12 above).

- During the campaign the party's electronic newsletter mentioned the candidate's leading role in the recent protests ("Globalization," par. 4).

G14. more than one work by the same author cited: If you include more than one work by the same author in your list of works cited, you must make clear which work is being cited each time. This may be done either by mentioning the work in a signal phrase or by including in the citation a short version of the title.

- In *The House of Mirth*, for example, Wharton writes of love as keeping Lily and Selden "from atrophy and extinction" (282).
- Wharton sees love as possessing the power to keep humans "from atrophy and extinction" (*House of Mirth* 282).

G15. multi-volume works: Note, by number, the volume you are referring to, followed by a colon, before noting the page number. Use the abbreviation "vol." when citing an entire volume.

- Towards the end of *In Darkest Africa* Stanley refers to the Victoria Falls (2:387).
- Metatextuality is a dominant feature in the later scenes of the graphic novel *Maus* (Spiegelman, vol. 2).

G16. **two or more authors with the same last name:** If the Works Cited list includes two or more authors with the same last name, the parenthetical reference should supply both first initials and last names, or, if the first initials are also the same, the full first and last names:

- One of the leading economists of the time advocated wage and price controls (Harry Johnston 197).

G17. **indirect quotations:** When an original source is not available but is referred to by another source, the parenthetical reference includes *qtd. in* (an abbreviation of *quoted in*) and a reference to the second source. In the example below, Casewell is quoted by Bouvier; the parenthetical reference directs readers to an entry in Works Cited for the Bouvier work.

- Casewell considers Lambert's position to be "outrageously arrogant" (qtd. in Bouvier 59).

● *Literary Works*

The underlying principle of the parenthetical reference system is the same regardless of the type of work one is citing—to make it as easy as possible for your reader to find the reference.

G18. **short poems:** For short poems, cite line numbers rather than page numbers.

- In "Dover Beach" Arnold hears the pebbles in the waves bring the "eternal note of sadness in" (line 14).

If you are citing the same poem repeatedly, use just the numbers for subsequent references.

- The world, in Arnold's view, has "really neither joy, nor love, nor light" (33).

G19. **longer poems:** For longer poems with parts, cite the part (or section, or "book") as well as the line (where available). Use Arabic numerals, and use a period for separation.

- In "Ode: Intimations of Immortality" Wordsworth calls human birth "but a sleep and a forgetting" (5.1).

G20. **novels or short stories:** When a work of prose fiction has chapters or numbered divisions the citation should include first the page number, and then book, chapter, and section numbers as applicable. (These can be very useful in helping readers of a different edition to locate the passage you are citing.) Arabic numerals should be used. A semicolon should be used to separate the page number from the other information.

- When Joseph and Fanny are by themselves, they immediately express their affection for each other, or, as Fielding puts it, "solace themselves" with "amorous discourse" (151; ch. 26).
- In *Tender Is the Night* Dick's ambition does not quite crowd out the desire for love: "He wanted to be loved too, if he could fit it in" (133; bk. 2, ch. 4).

G21. **plays:** Almost all plays are divided into acts and/or scenes. For plays that do not include line numbering throughout, cite the page number in the edition you have been using, followed by act and/or scene numbers as applicable:

- As Angie and Joyce begin drinking together Angie pronounces the occasion "better than Christmas" (72; act 3).
- Near the conclusion of Inchbald's *Wives as They Were* Bronzely declares that he has been "made to think with reverence on the matrimonial compact" (62; act 5, sc. 4).

For plays written entirely or largely in verse, where line numbers are typically provided throughout, you should omit the reference to page number in the citation. Instead, cite the act, scene, and line numbers, using Arabic numerals. For a Shakespeare play, if the title isn't clear from the introduction to a quotation, an abbreviation of the title may also be used. The parenthetical reference below is for Shakespeare's *The Merchant of Venice*, Act 2, Scene 3, lines 2–4:

> Jessica clearly has some fondness for Launcelot: "Our house is hell, and thou, a merry devil, / Dost rob it of some taste of tediousness. / But fare thee well; there is a ducat for thee" (*MV* 2.3 2–4).

G22. **literary texts cited from the Web**: If you are citing literary texts where you have consulted editions on the Web, the principles are exactly the same, except that you need not cite page numbers. For example, if the online Gutenberg edition of Fielding's *Joseph Andrews* were being cited, the citation would be as follows:

- When Joseph and Fanny are by themselves, they immediately express their affection for each other, or, as Fielding puts it, "solace themselves" with "amorous discourse" (ch. 26).

Students should be cautioned that online editions of literary texts are often unreliable. Typically there are far more typos and other errors in online versions of literary texts than there are in print versions, and such things as the layout of poems are also often unreliable. It is often possible to exercise judgement about such matters, however. If, for example, you are not required to base your essay on a particular copy of a Thomas Hardy poem but may find your own, you will be far better off using the text you will find on the Representative Poetry Online site run out of the University of Toronto than you will using a text you might find on a "World's Finest Love Poems" site.

G23. **sacred texts**: The Bible and other sacred texts that are available in many editions should be cited in a way that enables the reader to check the reference in any edition. For the Bible, book, chapter, and verse should all be cited, using periods for separation. The reference below is to Genesis, chapter 2, verse 1.

- According to the Christian myth of creation, at the end of the sixth day "the heavens and the earth were finished" (Gen. 2.1).

G24. **works in an anthology or book of readings**: In the parenthetical reference for a work in an anthology, use the name of the author of the work, not that of the editor of the anthology. The page number, however, should be that found in the anthology. The following citation refers to an article by Frederic W. Gleach in an anthology edited by Jennifer Brown and Elizabeth Vibert.

- One of the essays in Brown and Vibert's collection argues that we should rethink the Pocahontas myth (Gleach 48).

In your list of Works Cited, this work should be alphabetized under Gleach, the author of the piece you have consulted, not under Brown. If you cite another work by a different author from the same anthology or book of readings, that should appear as a separate entry in your list of Works Cited—again, alphabetized under the author's name.

O *About Works Cited*

The Works Cited list in MLA style is an alphabetized list at the end of the essay, article, or book. It should include information about all the works you have cited. Unlike a Bibliography, however, a Works Cited list should not include works that you consulted but did not cite in the body of your text. The basic publication information of each entry in the list must include the work's publication medium (i.e., whether it appears in print, on the Web, on a CD, and so on).

G25. **single author**: In most cases the Works Cited list is alphabetized by author last name. For a work with one author the entry should begin with the last name, followed by a comma, and then the author's first name or initials (use whatever appears on the work's title page), followed by a period. Entries for books then include the book's title, a period, and the publication information as it appears on the book's title and copyright pages; include the city of publication, a colon, the basic publisher's name (omit "Press," "Inc.," "Publisher," etc.), the copyright date, a period, and the publication medium. End every entry with a period.

> Frankfurt, Harry G. *The Importance of What We Care About: Philosophical Essays*. New York: Cambridge UP, 1988. Print.

G26. **two or three authors**: Only the first author's name should be reversed. Note also that the authors' names should appear in the order they are listed; sometimes this is not alphabetical.

> Eagles, Munro, James P. Bickerton, and Alain Gagnon. *The Almanac of Canadian Politics*. Peterborough: Broadview, 1991. Print.

G27. **four or more authors**: Either include all the authors' names or name only the first author followed by a comma and *et al.* (the abbreviation of the Latin *et alia*, meaning *and others*).

> Blais, Andre, et al. *Anatomy of a Liberal Victory*. Peterborough: Broadview, 2002. Print.
> Fromkin, Victoria, Robert Rodman, Neil Hultin, and Harry Logan. *An Introduction to Language*. 1st Canadian ed. Toronto: Harcourt, 1997. Print.

G28. **corporate author**: If a work has been issued by a government body, a corporation, or some other organization and no author is identified, the entry should be listed by the name of the group even if the group is also the publisher. Note that corporate author entries for government documents begin with the name of the government; the various departments or agency subdivisions then follow (e.g., Canada. Department of Communications. Arts and Culture Branch.)

Broadview Press. "Questions and Answers about Book Pricing." *Broadview Press.* Broadview, 2008. Web. 17 Feb. 2005.

Broadview Press. *2007 Annual Report.* Calgary: Broadview, 2008. Print.

Commonwealth of Massachusetts. "History of the Arms and Great Seal of the Commonwealth of Massachusetts." Public Records Division. Commonwealth of Massachusetts, n.d. Web. 6 Oct. 2008.

Ontario. Ministry of Natural Resources. *Keeping the Land: A Draft Land Use Strategy for the Whitefeather Forest and Adjacent Areas.* Toronto: Queen's Printer for Ontario, 2005. Print.

G29. **works with no author**: Works with no author should be alphabetized by title.

Sir Gawain and the Green Knight. Trans. James Winny. Peterborough: Broadview, 1992. Print.

G30. **two or more works by the same author**: The author's name should appear for the first entry only; for subsequent entries substitute three hyphens for the name of the author.

Menand, Louis. "Bad Comma: Lynne Truss's Strange Grammar." Rev. of *Eats, Shoots and Leaves*, by Lynne Truss. *The New Yorker* *28 June 2004*: n. pag. Web. 18 Feb. 2005.

---. *The Metaphysical Club: A Story of Ideas in America.* New York: Knopf, 2002. Print.

G31. **edited works**: If you are citing the parts of a work written by an editor or editors, the entry should begin with the names of the editor(s) and include the abbreviation *ed.* or *eds.*, as follows:

Rosengarten, Herbert, and Amanda Goldrick Jones, eds. *The Broadview Anthology of Poetry.* Peterborough: Broadview, 1992. Print.

When referring to an edited version of a work written by another author or authors, list the editor after the title and use the abbreviation "Ed." for "Edited by":

> More, Thomas. *Utopia*. Ed. Paul Turner. London: Penguin, 2003. Print.

G32. works in translation: Entries for works in translation include the translator's name after the abbreviation *trans.*, as follows:

> Calvino, Italo. *Cosmicomics*. 1965. Trans. William Weaver. San Diego: Harvest-Harcourt, 1968. Print.

G33. selections from anthologies or collections of readings: A selection from a collection of readings or an anthology should be listed as follows below. If they are available, be sure to add the selection's inclusive page numbers after the anthology's publication date; if there are no page numbers (as in many online sites), write *n. pag.* for *no pagination*.

> Crawford, Isabella Valancy. "The Canoe." *Representative Poetry Online*. Ed. Ian Lancashire. n. pag. U of Toronto, Oct. 2002. Web. 17 Feb. 2005.
> Gleach, Frederic W. "Controlled Speculation: Interpreting the Saga of Pocahontas and Captain John Smith." *Reading Beyond Words: Contexts for Native History*. Eds. Jennifer S. H. Brown and Elizabeth Vibert. Peterborough: Broadview, 1996. 21–42. Print.
> Mahfouz, Naguib. "Half a Day." *The Picador Book of African Stories*. Ed. Stephen Gray. Basingstoke: Picador, 2001. 3–6. Print.

If you are listing two or more items from the same collection or anthology, create a full entry for the collection or anthology, then list each cited item in its own entry. Arrange the entries alphabetically by author, and use a short form for the collection or anthology, as in the following example:

> Brown, Jennifer S. H., and Elizabeth Vibert, eds. *Reading Beyond Words: Contexts for Native History*. Peterborough: Broadview,

1996. Print.

Cruikshank, Julie. "Discovery of Gold on the Klondike: Perspectives from Oral Tradition." Brown and Vibert 433–59.

Gleach, Frederic W. "Controlled Speculation: Interpreting the Saga of Pocahontas and Captain John Smith." Brown and Vibert 21–42.

G34. multi-volume works: If you are citing two or more volumes of a multi-volume work, the entry should note the total number of volumes. If you cite only one of the volumes, list the volume cited after the title. If you wish, you may add the total number of volumes at the end of the entry, though MLA does not require this.

Jeeves, Julie, ed. *A Reference Guide to Spanish Architecture*. 3 vols. Indianapolis: Hackett, 2005. Print.

Mercer, Bobby, ed. *A Reference Guide to French Architecture*. Vol. 1. Indianapolis: Hackett, 2002. Print. 3 vols.

G35. different editions: The edition should be specified whenever it is not the first edition. Include whatever the title page indicates about the particular edition, and use abbreviations (e.g., *rev. ed.* for *revised edition*, *2nd ed.* for *second edition*, and so on). Sometimes it may be helpful to specify editions more than once in a single entry—as, for example, with the second example below.

Fowles, John. *The Magus*. Rev. ed. London: Jonathan Cape, 1977. Print.

Shelley, Mary. *Frankenstein*. 1818 ed. Ed. Lorne Macdonald and Kathleen Scherf. 2nd Broadview ed. Peterborough: Broadview, 1999. Print.

G36. reference work entries: List by the author of the entry, if known; otherwise, list by the entry itself. The citation of a well-known reference work (because such works are frequently updated) should not have full publication details; provide the edition number, date, and medium of publication only. Don't include page numbers for works that arrange their entries alphabetically.

> "Artificial." *Oxford English Dictionary.* 2nd ed. 1989. Print.
> Marsh, James. "Canoe, Birchbark." *The Canadian Encyclopedia.* 2000 ed. McClelland & Stewart, 1999. Print.
> "Saint Lawrence Seaway." *The Columbia Encyclopedia.* 6th ed. *Bartleby.com.* Bartleby, 2001. Web. 17 Feb. 2005.

G37. works with a title in the title: The entries below follow the formatting guidelines specified in section G4.

> Bettelheim, Bruno. "'The Goose Girl': Achieving Autonomy." *The Uses of Enchantment: The Meaning and Importance of Fairy Tales.* 1976. Vintage Books ed. New York: Vintage-Random House, 1989. 136-43. Print.
> Morelli, Stefan. *Stoppard's* Arcadia *and Modern Drama.* London: Ashgate, 2004. Print.
> Wimsatt, C.W. *"Fern Hill" and British Poetry in the 1950s.* Toronto: ECW, 2004. Print.

G38. material from prefaces, introductions, etc.: If you refer to something from a work's preface, introduction, or foreword, the reference under Works Cited should begin with the name of the author of that preface, introduction, or foreword. Add inclusive page numbers after the date of publication.

> Warkentin, Germaine. Introduction. *Set in Authority.* By Sara Jeannette Duncan. Peterborough: Broadview, 1996. 9–51. Print.

G39. films, programs, interviews, performances, music, art: Films, radio or television programs, interviews, dramatic performances, musical recordings, and works of visual art should be listed as in the examples below.

● *Films, Television, Radio, Performances*

> *Corner Gas.* CTV, 14 Feb. 2005. Television.
> *A Doll's House.* By Henrik Ibsen. Dir. Anthony Page. Perf. Janet McTeer and Owen Teale. Belasco, New York. 22 May 1997. Performance.
> Bob Dylan. Concert. Wings Stadium, Kalamazoo. 8 Nov. 2008.
> "Family Farm vs. Factory Farm." *Country Canada.* CBC, 21 Nov. 2003. Radio. *CBC Archives.* Web. 17 Feb. 2005.
> *Wag the Dog.* Dir. Barry Levinson. Perf. Robert DeNiro and Dustin Hoffman. Alliance, 1997. Film.

● *Interviews*

> Bellow, Saul. Interview. *Books in Canada* Sept. 1996: 2–6. Print.
> Counts, Dorothy Ayers, and David R. Counts. Interview. Pamela Wallin Live. CBC Newsworld. 26 Nov. 1997. Television.
> Rosengarten, Herbert. Personal interview. 21 Jan. 2005.

● *Recorded Music*

> Williams, Lucinda. "Real Love." *Little Honey.* Lost Highway, 2008. CD.

● *Works of Visual Art*

> Housser, Yvonne McKague. *Cobalt.* Oil on canvas. 1931. National Gallery of Canada, Ottawa.

G40. **magazine articles:** The title of the article should appear in quotation marks, the title of the magazine in italics. Note that no punctuation separates the magazine name and the date of its publication, while a colon is used to separate the date of publication from the page reference. If no author is identified, the title of the article should appear first.

MacRitchie, Lynn. "Ofili's Glittering Icons." *Art in America* Jan.
    2000: 44–56. Print.
"Shifting Sands." *The Economist* 12–18 Feb. 2005: 46–47. Print.

If you accessed the article online yourself, you should include
the date you accessed the source after the medium of publication
(*Web*). If the website is hosted by a body other than the magazine
itself, include the site name, sponsor, and date of posting (use *n.d.*
if no date is listed) before the publication medium.

Gladwell, Malcolm. "The Art of Failure: Why Some People Choke
    and Others Panic." *The New Yorker* 21 Aug. 2000: n. pag. Web.
    18 Feb. 2009.
MacRitchie, Lynn. "Ofili's Glittering Icons." *Art in America* Jan.
    2000: n. pag. *Find Articles at BNET*. BNET. Web. 16 Feb.
    2009.

G41. **newspaper articles:** The basic principles to follow with newspaper articles or editorials are the same as with magazine articles
(see above). Note, however, that when the newspaper's sections
are paginated separately, section as well as page numbers are often
required. If an article is not printed on consecutive pages, include
only the first page number followed by a plus sign. In the following
reference the article begins on page 12 of the first section:

Glanz, James. "Iraq's Shiite Alliance Wins Slim Majority in New
    Assembly." *New York Times* 17 Feb. 2005, sec. 1: 12+. Print.

If you are citing an online version of a newspaper article you
should include the date you accessed the site as well as the site
name.

Glanz, James. "Iraq's Shiite Alliance Wins Slim Majority in New
    Assembly." *New York Times* 17 Feb. 2005: n. pag. Web. 18 Feb.
    2005.

G42. **journal articles:** The basic principles are the same as with magazine articles, but entries for journal articles include the volume and issue numbers separated by a period.

> Roy, Indrani. "Irony and Derision in Congreve's *The Way of the World.*" *PMLA* 120.6 (2005): 60–72. Print.

If you are citing an online version of a journal article you should include the date you accessed the site as well as the site name. If the document is not paginated, write *n. pag.*(*not paginated*) in place of inclusive page numbers. Because printers don't always divide documents into the same number of pages, don't rely on the pagination of a printed hardcopy of the article as a guide.

> Sohmer, Steve. "12 June 1599: Opening Day at Shakespeare's Globe." *Early Modern Literary Studies* 3.1 (1997): n. pag. Web. 26 June 2008.

G43. **book reviews:** The name of the reviewer (if it has been provided) should come first, followed by the title of the review (if there is one), and the information on the book itself, as follows:

> O'Hagan, Andrew. "In His Hot Head." Rev. of *Robert Louis Stevenson: A Biography*, by Claire Harman. *London Review of Books* 17 Feb. 2005: n. pag. *Arts and Letters Daily*. Chronicle of Higher Education, 2005. Web. 18 Feb. 2009.
> "Our Fathers." Rev. of *Please Don't Come Back from the Moon*, by Dean Bakopoulos. *The Economist* 1–18 Feb. 2005: 83. Print.
> Schuessler, Jennifer. "Family Values." Rev. of *The Love Wife*, by Gish Jen. *New York Review of Books* 13 Jan. 2005: 16–17. Print.

G44. **periodical publications in online databases:** Full newspaper, magazine, and journal articles are now often available in online databases subscribed to by the libraries of academic institutions. Begin the entries for such sources as you would if they were print publications, but omit the word *print*. If there is no pagination, use the abbreviation *n. pag.* in place of inclusive page numbers. End by providing the name of the database (in italics), *Web*, and the date of access.

> Citron, Paula. "A Journey into 'the Human Side of Dance.'" *Globe and Mail* 24 Sept. 2008: R4. *Canadian Newsstand*. Web. 6 Oct. 2008.
>
> Hill, Katherine C. "Virginia Woolf and Leslie Stephen: History and Literary Revolution." *PMLA* 96.3 (1981): 351-62. *JSTOR*. Web. 6 Oct. 2008.
>
> Pope, Charles. "Interior Bill Includes Funding for Arts, despite GOP Efforts to Avoid Controversial Issue." *CQ Weekly* 27 June 1998: 1771. *Academic Search Premier*. Web. 6 Oct. 2008.

G45. **online projects:** In the case of large projects involving many contributors the name of the project should come first, not the name of the general editor:

> *Victorian Women Writers Project*. Ed. Perry Willett. Indiana U, May 2000. Web. 26 June 2002.

G46. **online books:** As with all online references, you should provide date of access along with information as to author, publisher or hosting website, date of posting (if available), and so on. If the book also appears in a print version, it may be helpful to include the print publication information. For older works, the date alone is sufficient.

> Emerson, Ralph Waldo. *The American Scholar*. 1837. *Literary Works of American Transcendentalism*. Ed. Ann Woodlief. Virginia Commonwealth U, 1999. Web. 16 Mar. 2001.
>
> Herman, Jonathan R. *I and Tao: Martin Buber's Encounter with Chuang Tzu*. Albany: State U of New York P, 1996. *NetLibrary*. Web. 5 Oct. 2008.

Rinehart, Mary Roberts. *Tish*. 1916. Etext produced by Lynn Hill. *Project Gutenberg*. Project Gutenberg, 16 Feb. 2005. Web. 18 Feb. 2005.

G47. information databases: You should provide date of access as well as information about the source.

"Profile of Book Publishing and Exclusive Agency, for English Language Firms." Chart. *Statistics Canada, 3 Mar. 2004. Web.* 18 Feb. 2005.

G48. publication on a CD-ROM or DVD-ROM: Cite a work on CD-ROM or DVD-ROM as you would a printed book, but omit *print* and add a description of the medium of publication.

Beam, Kathryn L., and Traianos Gagos, eds. *The Evolution of the English Bible: From Papyri to King James*. Ann Arbor: U of Michigan P, 1997. CD-ROM.

G49. posting to a discussion list: The date of the posting as well as the date of access should be given.

Merrian, Joanne. "Spinoff: Monsterpiece Theatre." Online posting. 30 Apr. 1994. *Shaksper: The Global Electronic Shakespeare Conference*. Ed. Hardy M. Cook. Shaksper, 2007. Web. 23 Sept. 2008.

G50. electronic sources—other information: In the above pages information about electronic sources has been presented in an integrated fashion, with information about referencing hard copies of journal articles presented alongside information about referencing online versions, and so on. In general, begin an entry for an electronic source as you would an entry for a print publication, but leave out the designation *print*. Continue with the title of the website or database (in italics), the site publisher or sponsor, a comma, the date of posting (if there is no date listed, write *n. d.*), the medium of publication (*Web*), and the date on which you accessed the source. MLA does not require listing the site's URL, but if you feel that your readers would find your source more easily with the help of its electronic address, or if your instructor asks that it be included, put the Web address at the end of the entry in angle brackets, and follow it with a period. If your word processor automatically converts the address into a hyperlink, remove the hyperlink. An example of an entry that includes a URL is shown below. Notice that if a URL has to be divided, it must be broken only after a slash, with no hyphen to indicate the break.

> Annis, Matthew. "The Fisher King." *Project Camelot*. U of Rochester, 2007. Web. 6 Oct. 2008. <http://www.lib.rochester.edu/camelot/Fisherking/fkessay.htm>.

O *MLA Style Sample*

Following is a sample of text with citations in MLA style. Note that the sample essay reproduced at the end of the first section of this book (pages 85–106) is also in MLA style.

Urban renewal is as much a matter of psychology as it is of bricks and mortar. As Paul Goldberger has described, there have been many plans to revitalize Havana (50–61). But both that city and the community of Cuban exiles in Florida remain haunted by a sense of absence and separation. As Lourdes Casal reminds us, "Exile / is living where there is no house whatever / in which we were ever children" (lines 1–3).

The psychology of outsiders also makes a difference. Part of the reason Americans have not much noticed the dire plight of their fifth-largest city is that it does not stir the national imagination (Rybczynski 12). Conversely, there has been far more concern over the state of cities such as New Orleans and Quebec, whose history and architecture excite the romantic imagination. As Nora Phelps has discussed, the past is in itself a key trigger for romantic notions, and cities whose history is particularly visible will engender passionate attachments. And as Stephanie Wright and Carole King have detailed, almost all French-speaking Quebecers feel their heritage to be bound up with that of Quebec City (2: 171–74). (Richard Ford's character Frank Bascombe has suggested that "New Orleans defeats itself" by longing for "a mystery it doesn't have and never will, if it ever did" [48; ch. 3] but this remains a minority view.) Georgiana Gibson is also among those who have investigated the interplay between urban psychology and urban reality (*Cities* 64–89). Gibson's personal website now includes a working model she is developing in an attempt to represent the effects of various psychological schemata on the landscape.

The above references connect to Works Cited as follows:

Works Cited

Casal, Lourdes. "Definition." Trans. Elizabeth Macklin. *The New Yorker* 26 Jan. 1998: 79. Print.

Ford, Richard. *The Sportswriter*. 1986. 2nd Vintage ed. New York: Vintage-Random House, 1995. Print.

Gibson, Georgiana. *Cities in the Twentieth Century*. Boston: Beacon, 2004. Print.

---. Homepage. *Geography. Brigham Young University*. Brigham Young U, 10 July 1999. Web. 30 June 2008.

Goldberger, Paul. "Annals of Preservation: Bringing Back Havana." *The New Republic* 26 Jan. 2005: 50–62. Print.

Phelps, Nora. "Pastness and the Foundations of Romanticism." *Romanticism on the Net* 11.3 (2007): n. pag. Web. 6 July 2008.

Rybczynski, Witold. "The Fifth City." Rev. of *A Prayer for the City*, by Buzz Bissinger. *The New York Review of Books* 5 Feb. 1998: 12–14. Print.

Wright, Stephanie, and Carole King. *Quebec: A History*. 2 vols. Montreal: McGill-Queen's UP, 2003. Print.

Among the details to notice here:

- All important words in titles are capitalized.
- Dates appear in Works Cited only.
- When a work has appeared in an edited collection, information on the editors must be included in the reference.
- Only the first author's first and last names are reversed in the list of Works Cited.
- If a book review or film review has a title, that should appear under Works Cited, which should also indicate the title of the book or film being reviewed.
- Translators should be included in Works Cited.
- Publisher as well as city of publication should be given.
- UP is the abbreviation used for University Press.
- Online citations include the date of publication or of last revision as well as the date of access.
- Where two or more works by the same author are included in Works Cited, second and subsequent entries substitute three hyphens and a period for the author name.

⊚ DOCUMENTATION: *APA, Chicago, CSE*

⊙ APA Style

There are two chief concerns when it comes to citing and documenting material: accuracy and consistency. Whatever system of citation is used, a research writer must follow it closely and consistently. Four of the most commonly used systems of citation are summarized in these pages—MLA style (see the previous chapter), APA style, Chicago style, and CSE style. The American Psychological Association (APA) style is used in many behavioural and social sciences.

Further information about styles of writing as well as of citation and reference in various academic disciplines appears elsewhere in this book in the section on "Style." It may also be helpful to consult exemplary essays. (A selection of these may be found on the Broadview Press website in the pages providing adjunct material to this and other Broadview writing texts; go to www.broadviewpress. com, and click on links.)

To understand more of the basic principles and workings of academic citation and documentation, students are advised to consult G1 "Citation and Plagiarism" and G2 "Signal Phrases" at the beginning of the previous chapter.

O *About In-text Citations*

H1. **in-text citation**: The APA system emphasizes the date of publication, which must appear within an in-text citation. Whenever a quotation is given, the page number must also be provided:

- Bonnycastle (2007) refers to "the true and lively spirit of opposition" (p. 204) with which Marxist literary criticism invigorates the discipline.

It is common to mention the names of authors you are citing in the body of your text, as is done in the example above. If author names are not mentioned in the body of the text, however, they must be provided within the in-text citation:

- One overview of literary theory (Bonnycastle, 2007) has praised "the true and lively spirit of opposition" (p. 204) with which Marxist literary criticism invigorates the discipline.

If the reference does not involve a quotation (as it commonly does not in social science papers), only the date need be given as an in-text citation, providing that the author's name appears in the signal phrase:

- Bonnycastle (2007) argues that the oppositional tone of Marxist literary criticism invigorates the discipline.

A citation such as this connects to a list of references at the end of the paper. In this case the entry under "References" at the end of the paper would be as follows:

- Bonnycastle, S. (2007). *In search of authority: A guide to literary theory* (3rd ed.). Peterborough, ON: Broadview Press.

Notice here that the date of publication is again foregrounded, appearing immediately following the author's name. Notice too that all words in a title except the first word in the title, the first in the subtitle, and any proper nouns appear in lower case.

H2. **titles: italics/underlining/quotation marks**: Notice in the above example that both the title and the subtitle are in italics. The APA allows either italics or underlining for titles. Most writers now seem to feel that italic type has a more attractive appearance than underlining does; that italics is the form used in published work (meaning that if you have used underlining and your work is then published, all that underlining has to be converted to italics); and that italics is just as easy as underlining to produce with word processing systems. For all those reasons, we use italics rather than underlining for titles in these pages.

H3. **titles of short works**: The titles of works are not usually used in the body of the text. Titles of short works (such as articles, lyric poems, and short stories) should be put in quotation marks if they appear in the body of the text or in an in-text citation, with key words capitalized. (In the list of references, however, such works should *not* be put in quotation marks or italicized, and no words should be capitalized except the first word in the title and the first in the subtitle, if any.)

H4. **placing of in-text citations**: The in-text citation comes directly after the name of the author or after the end quotation mark. Often, the citation comes just before the period or comma in the surrounding sentence. (If a quotation ends with punctuation other than a period or comma, then this should precede the end of the quotation, and a period or comma should still follow the parenthetical reference, if this is grammatically appropriate.)

- The claim has been convincingly refuted by Ricks (2001), but it nevertheless continues to be put forward (Dendel, 2008).
- One of Berra's favourite coaching tips was that "ninety per cent of the game is half mental" (Adelman, 2007, p. 98).
- Berra at one point said to his players, "You can observe a lot by watching!" (Adelman, 2007, p. 98).
- Garner (2005) associates statistics and pleasure.

H5. **parenthetical reference when text is in parentheses**: If a parenthetical reference occurs within text in parentheses, commas are used to set off elements of the reference.

- (See Figure 6.1 of Harrison, 2006, for data on transplant waiting lists.)

H6. no signal phrase (or author not named in signal phrase): If the context does not make it clear who the author is, that information must be added to the in-text citation. Note that commas separate the name of the author, the date, and the page number (where this is given):

- Even in recent years some have continued to believe that Marxist literary criticism invigorates the discipline with a "true and lively spirit of opposition" (Bonnycastle, 2005, p. 4).

H7. electronic source—page number unavailable: If a Web document cited is in PDF format, the page numbers are stable and may be cited as one would the pages of a printed source. Many Web page numbers are unstable, however, and many more lack page numbers. In such cases you should provide a section or paragraph number if a reference is needed. For paragraphs APA suggests using either the abbreviation "para." or the symbol ¶. (Remember that with APA style you need only provide information as to author and date if you are not quoting directly.)

- In a recent Web posting a leading theorist has clearly stated that he finds such an approach "thoroughly objectionable" (Bhabha, 2005, para. 7).
- In a recent Web posting a leading theorist has clearly stated that he finds such an approach "thoroughly objectionable" (Bhabha, 2005, ¶ 7).
- Bhabha (2005) has clearly stated his opposition to this approach.
- Carter and Zhaba (2005) describe this approach as "more reliable than that adopted by Perkins" (Method section, para. 2).

If you are citing longer texts from electronic versions, chapter references may be more appropriate. For example, if the online Gutenberg edition of Darwin's *On the Origin of the Species* were being cited, the citation would be as follows:

- Darwin refers to the core of his theory as an "ineluctable principle" (1856, chap. 26).

Students should be cautioned that online editions of older or classic works are often unreliable; typically there are far more typos and other errors in such versions than there are in print versions.

H8. **two or more dates for a work**: If you have consulted a re-issue of a work (whether in printed or electronic form), you should provide both the original date of publication and the date of the re-issue (the date of the version you are using).

- Emerson (1837/1909) asserted that America's "long apprentice-ship to the learning of other lands" was "drawing to a close" (para. 1).

The relevant entry in the list of references would look like this:

- Emerson, R. W. (1909). *Essays and English Traits*. New York: P. F. Collier & Son. (Original work published 1837)

If you are citing work in a form that has been revised by the author, however, you should cite the date of the revised publication, not the original.

- In a preface to the latest edition of his classic work (2004), Watson discusses its genesis.

H9. **multiple authors**: If there are two or three authors, all authors should be named either in the signal phrase or in the in-text citation. Use *and* in the signal phrase but *&* in parentheses.

- Chambliss and Best (2005) have argued that the nature of this research is practical as well as theoretical.
- Two distinguished scholars have argued that the nature of this research is practical as well as theoretical (Chambliss & Best, 2005).

three to five authors: In the body of the text list the names of all authors the first time the work is referred to; for subsequent references use only the first author's name, followed by "et al." (short for the Latin *et alia*: *and others*).

- Chambliss, Best, Didby, and Jones (2005) have argued that the nature of this research is practical as well as theoretical.
- Four distinguished scholars have argued that the nature of this research is practical as well as theoretical (Chambliss, Best, Didby, & Jones, 2005).

more than five authors: Use only the first author's name, followed by "et al." (short for the Latin *et alia*: *and others*).

- Chambliss et al. (2005) have argued that the nature of this research is practical as well as theoretical.
- Six distinguished scholars have argued that the nature of this research is practical as well as theoretical (Chambliss et al., 2005).

H10. **author unknown/corporate author**: Be sure to refer to the relevant organization and/or the title of the piece so as to make the reference clear. For organizations, recommended practice is to provide the full name on the first occasion, followed by an abbreviation, and then to use the abbreviation for subsequent references:

- Blindness has decreased markedly but at an uneven pace since the late 1800s (National Institute for the Blind [NIB], 2002).

H11. **electronic source—author not given**: If the author of the electronic source is not given, it may be identified in the parenthetical reference by a short form of the title.

- The party's electronic newsletter said the candidate mentioned his role in the protests ("Globalization," 2004).

H12. **electronic source—date not given**. Some electronic sources do not provide a date of publication. Where this is the case, use the abbreviation *n.d.* for *no date*.

- Some still claim that evidence of global warming is difficult to come by (Sanders, n.d.; Zimmerman, 2005).

H13. **order of authors' names**: Works should appear in in-text citations in the same order they do in the list of references, i.e., alphabetically by author's last name and then by publication date.

- Various studies have established a psychological link between fear and sexual arousal (Aikens, Cox, & Bartlett, 1998; Looby, 1999a, 1999b, 2003; Looby & Cairns, 2008, in press).
- Various studies appear to have established a psychological link between fear and sexual arousal (Looby & Cairns, 1999, 2002, 2005).

H14. **two or more authors with the same last name**: If the "References" list includes two or more authors with the same last name, the in-text citation should supply an initial:

- One of the leading economists of the time advocated wage and price controls (H. Johnston, 1977).

H15. **works in a collection of readings or anthology**: In the in-text citation for a work in an anthology or collection of readings, use the name of the author of the work, not that of the editor of the anthology. If the work was first published in the collection you have consulted, there is only the one date to cite. But if the work is reprinted in that collection after having first been published elsewhere, cite the date of the original publication and the date of the collection you have consulted, separating these dates with a slash. The following citation refers to an article by Frederic W. Gleach that was first published in a collection of readings edited by Jennifer Brown and Elizabeth Vibert.

- One of the essays in Brown and Vibert's collection argues that we should rethink the Pocahontas myth (Gleach, 1996).

In your list of references, this work should be alphabetized under Gleach, the author of the piece you have consulted, not under Brown.

The next example is a lecture by George Simmel first published in 1903, which a student consulted in an edited collection by Roberta Garner that was published in 2001.

- Simmel (1903/2001) argues that the "deepest problems of modern life derive from the claim of the individual to preserve the autonomy and individuality of his existence" (p. 141).

The reference list entry would look like this:

Simmel, G. (2001). The metropolis and mental life. In R. garner (Ed.), *Social theory–Continuity and confrontation: A reader* (pp. 141–153). Peterborough, ON: Broadview Press. (Original work published in 1903)

As you can see, in your reference list these works are listed under the authors of the pieces (Gleach or Simmel), not under the compilers, editors, or translators of the collection (Brown & Vibert or Garner). If you cite another work by a different author from the same anthology or book of readings, that should appear as a separate entry in your list of works cited—again, alphabetized under the author's name.

H16. **indirect source:** If you are citing a source from a reference other than the source itself, you should use the phrase "as cited in" (or a variation thereof) in your in-text citation.

- In de Beauvoir's famous phrase, "one is not born a woman, one becomes one" (as cited in Levey, 2001, para. 3).

In this case, the entry in your reference list would be for Levey, not de Beauvoir.

O *About References*

The list of references in APA style is an alphabetized list at the end of the essay, article, or book. Usually, it includes all the information necessary to identify and retrieve each of the sources you have cited, and only the works you have cited. In this case the list is entitled *References*. If the list includes all works you have consulted, regardless of whether or not you have cited them, it should be entitled *Bibliography*.

H17. **single author**: In most cases the references list is alphabetized by author last name. For a work with one author the entry should begin with the last name, followed by a comma, and then the author's initials as applicable, followed by the date of publication in parentheses. Note that initials are generally used rather than first names, even when authors are identified by first name in the work itself.

> Eliot, G. (2004). *Middlemarch: A study of provincial life* (G. Maertz, Ed.). Peterborough, ON: Broadview. (Original work published 1872)

H18. **two or three authors**: Last names should in all cases come first, followed by initials. Up to six authors may be listed in this way. Use an ampersand rather than *and* before the last author. Note that the authors' names should appear in the order they are listed; sometimes this is not alphabetical.

> Eagles, M., Bickerton, J. P., & Gagnon, A. (1991). *The almanac of Canadian politics*. Peterborough, ON: Broadview.

H19. **more than six authors**: Rather than name all authors, name the first six and then use *et al.*

> Allain, P., Verny, C., Aubin, G., Pinon, K., Bonneau, D., Dubas, F., et al. (2005). Arithmetic word-problem-solving in Huntington's disease. *Brain and Cognition, 57*(1), 1–3.

H20. **corporate author**: If a work has been issued by a government body, a corporation, or some other organization and no author is identified, the entry should be listed by the name of the group.

> Broadview Press. (2005). *Annual report*. Calgary, AB: Author.
> Broadview Press. (n.d.). Questions and answers about book pricing. Broadview Press Web Site. Retrieved from www.broadviewpress.com/bookpricing.asp?inc=bookpricing
> City of Toronto, City Planning Division. (2000, June). *Toronto at the crossroads: Shaping our future*. Toronto: Author.

H21. **works with no author**: Works with no author should be alphabetized by title.

> *Columbia encyclopedia* (6th ed.) (2001). New York: Columbia University Press.

If you have referred to only one entry in an encyclopedia or dictionary, however, the entry in your list of references should be by the title of that entry (see below).

H22. **two or more works by the same author**: The author's name should appear for all entries. Entries should be ordered by year of publication.

> Menand, L. (2002). *The metaphysical club: A story of ideas in America*. New York: Knopf.
> Menand, L. (2004, June 28). Bad comma: Lynne Truss's strange grammar. [Review of the book *Eats, shoots & leaves*]. *The New Yorker*. Retrieved from http://www.newyorker.com

If two or more cited works by the same author have been published in the same year, arrange these alphabetically and use letters to distinguish among them (2005a), (2005b), and so on.

H23. **edited works**: Entries for edited works include the abbreviation *ed.* or *eds.*, as follows:

Gross, B., Field, D., & Pinker, L. (Eds.). (2002). *New approaches to the history of psychoanalysis.* New York: Duckworth.

H24. selections from anthologies or collections of readings: A selection from a collection of readings or an anthology should be listed as follows:

Rosengarten, H. (2002). Fleiss's nose and Freud's mind: A new perspective. In B. Gross, D. Field, & L. Pinker (Eds.), *New approaches to the history of psychoanalysis* (pp. 232–243). New York: Duckworth.

Crawford, I. V. (n.d.). The canoe. *Representative poetry online.* Retrieved February 17, 2005, from http://www.eir.library.utoronto.ca/rpo/display/poem596

Gleach, F. W. (1996). Controlled speculation: Interpreting the saga of Pocahontas and Captain John Smith. In J. Brown & E. Vibert (Eds.), *Reading beyond words: Contexts for Native history* (pp. 21–42). Peterborough, ON: Broadview.

H25. works available in both printed and electronic versions: If a work is available both online and in a printed journal, you are not required to provide the URL; if you have consulted the electronic version, however, that should be noted as follows.

Earn, B., & Towson, S. (2005). Shyness and aggression: A new study. *Journal of Personality and Social Psychology, 44*(3), 144–153. DOI: 10.1006/jpsp.2005.0722

H26. reference work entries: List by the author of the entry, if known; otherwise, list by the entry itself.

Marsh, J. (1999). "Canoe, birchbark." *The Canadian encyclopedia* (Year 2000 ed.). Toronto: McClelland & Stewart.

Saint Lawrence Seaway. (2001). *The Columbia encyclopedia* (6th ed.). Retrieved from http://www.bartleby.com/65/st/STLawrSwy.html

H27. **films, programs, interviews, performances, music, art**: Films, radio or television programs, interviews, dramatic performances, musical recordings, and paintings should be listed as follows:

● *Films, Television, Radio*

> Levinson, B. (Director). (1997). *Wag the dog*. [Motion picture]. Los Angeles: MGM.
>
> Family farm vs. factory farm. (2003, November 23). *Country Canada*. Toronto: CBC. *CBC Archives*. Retrieved from http://www.archivescbc.ca/IDC-I-73-1239-6930/pig_INDUSTRY/CLIP2

● *Interviews*

> Bellow, S. Interview. *Books in Canada*. Sept. 1996: 2–6.
>
> Counts, D. A., & Counts, D. R. (1997, November 26). [Interview with Pamela Wallin]. *Pamela Wallin Live*. CBC Newsworld.
>
> Rosengarten, H. (2005, January 21). [Personal interview].

H28. **magazine articles**: Note that neither quotation marks nor italics are used for the titles of articles. If no author is identified, the title of the article should appear first. If you are citing a printed version, you should give the page reference for the article.

> Gladwell, M. (2000, August 21). The art of failure: Why some people choke and others panic. *The New Yorker*. Retrieved from http://http://www.gladwell.com/2000_08_21_a_choking.htm
>
> MacRitchie, L. (2000, January). Ofili's glittering icons. *Art in America*. Retrieved from http://www.findarticles.com.ofili.j672.jn.htm
>
> Shifting sands. (2005, February 12–18). *The Economist*, 46–47.

H29. newspaper articles: The basic principles to follow with newspaper articles or editorials are the same as with magazine articles (see above). Note that APA requires that all page numbers for print versions be provided when articles do not continue on consecutive pages.

> Clash over Nobel cash. (1998, February 11). *The Washington Post*, A14.
> Glanz, J. (2005, February 17). Iraq's Shiite alliance wins slim majority in new assembly. *The New York Times*, pp. A1, A12.

If you are citing an online version of a newspaper article you have retrieved through a search of its website, you should provide the URL for the site, not for the exact location.

> Glanz, J. (2005, February 17). Iraq's Shiite alliance wins slim majority in new assembly. *The New York Times*. Retrieved from http://www.nytimes.com

H30. journal articles: The basic principles are the same as with magazine articles. Volume number is considered part of the journal's title and should be italicized; issue number is given in brackets for journals that are paginated by issue. For online versions you should include the digital object identifier (DOI) where available, as well as volume and issue number. If no DOI is available, you should cite a URL for the article (or for the home page of the journal if the URL is very lengthy or if the article is available by subscription only).

> Barker, P. (2004). The impact of class size on the classroom behaviour of special needs students: A longitudinal study. *Educational Quarterly, 25*(4), 87–99.
> Hurka, T. M. (1996). Improving on perfectionism. *Philosophical Review, 99*, 462–473.
> Roy, I. (2005). Irony as a psychological concept. *American Psychologist, 58*, 244–256. DOI: 10.1006/ap.2005.0680

Sohmer, S. (1999). Ways of perceiving maps and globes. *Current Research in Spatial Psychology, 46*(3). Retrieved from http://www.shu.ac.uk/emls/03-1/sohmjuli.html

Surtees, P. (2008). The psychology of the children's crusade of 1212. *Studies in Medieval History and Society, 3*(4), 279–325. DOI: 10.1008/smhs.2008.0581

H31. book reviews: The name of the reviewer (if it has been provided) should come first, followed by the date and title of the review, and the information on the book itself, as follows:

O'Hagan, A. (2005, February 18). Fossil fuels. [Review of the book *Underground Energy*]. *London Review of Books.* Retrieved from http://www.lrb.co.uk/v27/n04/ohago1_.html

Our fathers. (2005, February 11–18). [Review of the book *Parenting: The other half*]. 83.

H32. other Web references: In the case of online sources not covered by the above, the same principles apply. Where an author or editor is indicated, list by author. If the source is undated or its content likely to change, you should include the date on which you accessed the material.

Brown University. (2006, May). Brown University. Women writers project. Retrieved February 28, 2009, from http://www.brown.edu/

LePan, D. (n.d.) *The psychology of skyscrapers.* Retrieved February 20, 2009, from http://donlepan.com

Profile of book publishing and exclusive agency, for English language firms [Chart]. (2002). *Statistics Canada.* Retrieved from http://www.statcan.ca/english/pgdb/arts02.htm

H33. electronic sources—other information: In the above pages information about electronic sources has been presented in an integrated fashion, with information about referencing hard copies of journal articles presented alongside information about referencing online versions, and so on.

O *APA Style Sample*

Following is a sample of text with citations in APA style. Note that a sample essay in APA style appears on the adjunct website associated with this book.

Urban renewal is as much a matter of psychology as it is of bricks and mortar. As Goldberger (2005) has described, there have been many plans to revitalize Havana. But both that city and the community of Cuban exiles in Florida remain haunted by a sense of absence and separation. As Lourdes Casal (1998) reminds us,

> Exile
>
> is living where there is no house whatever
>
> in which we were ever children; (1. 1–3)

The psychology of outsiders also makes a difference. Part of the reason Americans have not much noticed the dire plight of their fifth-largest city is that it does not "stir the national imagination" (Rybczynski, 1998, p. 12). Conversely, there has been far more concern over the state of cities such as New Orleans and Quebec, whose history and architecture excite the romantic imagination. As Nora Phelps (1998) has discussed, the past is in itself a key trigger for romantic notions, and it is no doubt inevitable that cities whose history is particularly visible will engender passionate attachments. And as Stephanie Wright and Carole King (2003) have detailed in an important case study, almost all French-speaking Quebecers feel their heritage to be bound up with that of Quebec City. (Richard Ford's character Frank Bascombe has suggested that "New Orleans defeats itself" by longing "for a mystery it doesn't have and never will, if it ever did" [Ford, 1995, 48] but this remains a minority view.)

Georgiana Gibson (2004a) is also among those who have investigated the interplay between urban psychology and urban reality. Gibson's personal website (2004b) now includes the first of a set of working models she is developing in an attempt to represent the effects of psychological schemata on the landscape.

The in-text citations above would connect to References as follows:

References

Casal, L. (1998, January 26). Definition. (E. Macklin, Trans.). *The New Yorker*, 79.

Ford, R. (1995). *The sportswriter* (2nd ed.). New York: Random House.

Gibson, G. (2004a). *Cities in the twentieth century*. Boston: Beacon.

Gibson, G. (2004b, June 10). Homepage. Retrieved from http:www.geography. byu.edu/GIBSON/personal.htm

Goldberger, P. (2005, January 26). Annals of preservation: Bringing back Havana. *The New Yorker*, 50–62. Retrieved from http://www.newyorker. com

Phelps, N. (1998). Pastness and the foundations of romanticism. *Romanticism on the Net, 11*. DOI: 10.1008/rotn.1998.4611

Rybczynski, W. (1998, February 5). The fifth city. [Review of the book *A prayer for the city*]. *The New York Review of Books*, 12–14.

Wright, S., & King, C. (2003). *Quebec: A history* (Vols. 1–2). Montreal: McGill-Queen's University Press.

Among the details to notice in this reference system:

- Where two or more works by the same author are included in References, they are ordered by date of publication.
- APA style prefers author initials rather than first names.
- Only the first words of titles and subtitles are capitalized, except for proper nouns.
- The date appears in parentheses near at the beginning of each entry in References.
- The in-text citation comes directly after the name of the author or after the end quotation mark. Often, these citations fall just before the period or comma in the surrounding sentence.
- If an in-text citation occurs within text in parentheses, commas are used to set off elements of the reference.
- When a work has appeared in an edited collection, information on the editors must be included in the reference.
- Authors' first and last names are reversed; note the use of the ampersand (&) between author names.
- Translators should be included under References.
- Publisher as well as city of publication should be given.
- Months and publisher names are not abbreviated; the day of the month follows the name of the month.
- Online references include the date of publication or of last revision in parentheses immediately after the author's name, and the date of access, which appears within a phrase near the end of the entry, e.g., "Retrieved July 6, 2006, from http://www.broadviewpress.com": note that, if a URL ends a reference entry, there is no period at the end of the entry.

⊙ Chicago Style

There are two chief concerns when it comes to citing and documenting material: accuracy and consistency. Whatever system of citation is used, a research writer must follow it closely and consistently. Four of the most commonly used systems of citation are summarized in these pages—MLA style (see the previous chapter), APA style, Chicago style, and CSE style.

Further information about styles of writing as well as of citation and reference in various academic disciplines appears elsewhere in this book in the section on "Style." It may also be helpful to consult exemplary essays. (A selection of these may be found on the Broadview Press website in the pages providing adjunct material to this and other Broadview writing texts; go to www.broadviewpress.com, and click on links.)

To understand more of the basic principles and workings of academic citation and documentation, students are advised to consult G1 "Citation and Plagiarism" and G2 "Signal Phrases" at the beginning of the previous chapter.

The massively comprehensive *Chicago Manual of Style* provides full information both on an author-date system of citation that is similar to APA style, and to a traditional footnoting system. The latter is outlined below. A fuller outline is available in Kate Turabian's *A Manual for Writers of Term Papers, Theses, and Dissertations*.

The Chicago Manual of Style now deals extensively with the citation of electronic materials; sensibly, it recognizes that practices in such areas are likely to remain to some extent "under construction," and the editors emphasize that rules "are meant for the average case, and must be applied with a certain degree of elasticity."

footnoting: The basic principle of Chicago style is to create a footnote each time one cites a source:

- Bonnycastle refers to "the true and lively spirit of opposition" with which Marxist literary criticism invigorates the discipline.[1]

The superscript number [1] here is linked to the information provided where the same number appears at the foot of the page:

1. Stephen Bonnycastle, *In Search of Authority: An Introductory Guide to Literary Theory*, 2nd ed. (Peterborough: Broadview Press, 1996), 204.

In addition, all works cited (and works that have been consulted but are not cited in the body of your essay) must be included in a Bibliography that appears at the end of the essay. The reference under Bibliography at the end of the paper would in this case be as follows:

Bonnycastle, Stephen. *In Search of Authority: An Introductory Guide to Literary Theory*. 2nd ed. Peterborough: Broadview Press, 1996.

Notice in the above examples that the author's full first name is provided (not an initial). In a footnote, publication information is placed in parentheses, a page number for the quotation is provided, and the note is indented. In the entry in the Bibliography no parentheses are placed around the publication information, and the entry is out-dented.

titles: italics/underlining/quotation marks: Notice in the above example that both the title and the subtitle are in italics. Titles of short works (such as articles, poems, and short stories) should be put in quotation marks. In all titles key words should be capitalized.

H34. **when to include a citation**: Any quotation should include a reference, as should factual information that is not general knowledge. Here is an example:

- At the time of the rebellion per capita income is estimated to have been less than $500,[1] and tens of thousands of children had already starved to death.[2]

The superscript numbers in the above text connect to footnotes as follows:

1. Sean Carver, "The Economic Foundations for Unrest in East Timor, 1970–1995," *Journal of Economic History* 21, no. 2 (2004): 103.
2. Jennifer Riley, "East Timor in the Pre-Independence Years," *Asian History Online* 11, no. 4 (2003): par. 18, http://www.aho.ubc.edu/prs/text-only/issue.45/16.3jr.txt.

Note that where page numbers are unavailable it is recommended that other available information (such as paragraph or section references) be provided.

H35. **square brackets:** If you need to include words of your own within a quotation, square brackets may be used for this purpose. Single quotation marks should be used for quotations within a quotation:

- As Smith has pointed out, "it was [Raymond] Williams who first outlined the development in Britain of a 'print culture,' in his influential 1960s book *The Long Revolution*."[1]

If a quotation includes an error, or something the reader might assume to be an error, the word *sic* (Latin for *thus*) should be inserted in square brackets:

- The secretary has written that "America, in it's [sic] wisdom, can be counted on to come to the assistance of those suffering under tyrannous regimes."[1]

H36. **multiple references to the same work:** For later references to an already-cited source, use the author's last name, title, and page number only. (Note that the use of *op. cit.* is no longer accepted practice.)

1. Bonnycastle, *In Search of Authority*, 28.

If successive references are to the same work, use *ibid.* (an abbreviation of the Latin *ibidem*, meaning *in the same place*).

1. Sean Carver, "The Economic Foundations for Unrest in East Timor, 1970–1995," *Journal of Economic History* 21, no. 2 (2004): 103.
2. Ibid., 109.
3. Ibid., 111.
4. Jennifer Riley, "East Timor in the Pre-Independence Years," *Asian History Online* 11, no. 4 (2003): par. 18, http://www.aho.ubc.edu/prs/text-only/issue.45/16.3jr.txt.
5. Ibid., par. 24.

H37. **page number unavailable**: If an Internet document cited is in PDF format, the page numbers are stable and may be cited in the same way that one would the pages of a printed book or journal article. Many Internet page numbers are unstable, however, and many more lack page numbers. Instead, provide a section number, paragraph number, or other identifier if available. Note that Chicago style now recommends (though it does not require) that date accessed be included for electronic sources.

2. Hanif Bhabha, "Family Life in 1840s Virginia," *Southern History Web Archives* (2003): par. 14. http://shweb.ut.edu/history/american.nineteenthc/bhabha.html (accessed March 3, 2009).

If you are citing longer texts from electronic versions, and counting paragraph numbers is impracticable, chapter references may be more appropriate. For example, if the online Gutenberg edition of Darwin's *On the Origin of the Species* were being cited, the citation would be as follows:

- Darwin refers to the core of his theory as an "ineluctable principle."[1]

> 1. Charles Darwin, *On the Origin of the Species* (1856; Project Gutenberg, 2001), chap. 26, http://www.gutenberg.darwin.origin.frrp.ch26.html (accessed March 2, 2009).

Students should be cautioned that online editions of older or classic works are often unreliable; typically there are far more typos and other errors in online versions of literary texts than there are in print versions.

H38. two or more dates for a work: Note that in the above example both the date of the original publication and the date of the modern edition are provided. If you are citing work in a form that has been revised by the author, however, you should cite the date of the revised publication, not the original.

> 1. Eric Foner, *Free Soil, Free Labor, Free Men: A Study of Antebellum America*, rev. ed. (New York: Oxford University Press, 1999), 178.

H39. multiple authors: If there are two or three authors, they should be identified as follows in the footnote and in the Bibliography:

> 4. Eric Alderman and Mark Green, *Tony Blair and the Rise of New Labour* (London: Cassell, 2002), 180.

> Alderman, Eric, and Mark Green. *Tony Blair and the Rise of New Labour*. London: Cassell, 2002.

Four or more authors: In the footnote name only the first author, and use the phrase *and others* (preferred to the Latin *et al.*); in the bibliography name all authors, as below:

> 11. Richard Johnston and others, *Letting the People Decide: Dynamics of a Canadian Election* (Montreal: McGill-Queen's University Press, 1992), 232.

> Johnston, Richard, Andre Blais, Henry E. Brady, and Jean Crete. *Letting the People Decide: Dynamics of a Canadian Election*. Montreal: McGill-Queen's University Press, 1992.

H40. **author unknown/corporate author/government document**: Identify by the corporate author if known, and otherwise by the title of the work. Unsigned newspaper articles or dictionary and encyclopedia entries are usually not listed in the bibliography. In notes, unsigned dictionary or encyclopedia entries are identified by the title of the reference work, e.g., *Columbia Encyclopedia*, and unsigned newspaper articles are listed by the title of the article in footnotes but by the title of the newspaper in the bibliography. Ignore initial articles (the, a, an) when alphabetizing.

6. *National Hockey League Guide, 1966–67* (Toronto: National Hockey League, 1966), 77.

7. "Globalization's Effects Felt in Rural Ecuador," *New York Times*, September 12, 2004, A14.

8. Broadview Press, "Questions and Answers about Book Pricing," Broadview Press, http://www.broadviewpress.com/book pricing.asp?inc=bookpricing (accessed March 5, 2009).

9. Commonwealth of Massachusetts, *Records of the Transportation Inquiry, 2004* (Boston: Massachusetts Publishing Office, 2005), 488.

10. Columbia Encyclopedia, "Ecuador," http://bartleby.com. columbia.txt.acc.html (accessed March 4, 2009).

11. House Committee on Ways and Means. Subcommittee on Trade, *Free Trade Area of the Americas: Hearings*, 105th Cong., 1st sess., July 22, 1997, Hearing Print 105-32, 160, http://www. waysandmeans.house.gov/hearings.asp (accessed July 22, 2009).

Following are the bibliography entries for the preceding notes:

Broadview Press. "Questions and Answers about Book Pricing." Broadview Press. http://www.broadviewpress.com/bookpricing. asp?inc=bookpricing (accessed March 5, 2009).

Commonwealth of Massachusetts. *Records of the Transportation Inquiry, 2004.* Boston: Massachusetts Publishing Office, 2005.

National Hockey League Guide, 1966-67. Toronto: National Hockey League, 1966.

New York Times. "Globalization's Effects Felt in Rural Ecuador," September 12, 2004, A14.

U.S. Congress. House Committee on Ways and Means. Subcommittee on Trade. *Free Trade Area of the Americas: Hearing before the Subcommittee on Trade.* 105th Cong., 1st sess., July 22, 1997. Hearing Print 105-32. http://www.waysandmeans.house. gov/hearings.asp (accessed March 5, 2009).

H41. **works from a collection of readings or anthology:** In the citation for a work in an anthology or collection of essays, use the name of the author of the work you are citing. If the work is reprinted in one source but was first published elsewhere, include the details of the original publication in the bibliography.

6. Eric Hobsbawm, "Peasant Land Occupations," in *Uncommon People: Resistance and Rebellion* (London: Weidenfeld & Nicolson, 1998), 167.

7. Frederic W. Gleach, "Controlled Speculation: Interpreting the Saga of Pocahontas and Captain John Smith," in *Reading Beyond Words: Contexts for Native History,* 2nd ed., ed. Jennifer Brown and Elizabeth Vibert (Peterborough: Broadview Press, 2003), 43.

Gleach, Frederic W. "Controlled Speculation: Interpreting the Saga of Pocahontas and Captain John Smith." In *Reading Beyond Words: Contexts for Native History,* 2nd ed., edited by Jennifer Brown and Elizabeth Vibert, 39–74 (Peterborough: Broadview Press, 2003).

Hobsbawm, Eric. "Peasant Land Occupations." In *Uncommon People: Resistance and Rebellion* (London: Weidenfeld & Nicolson, 1998), 166–190. Originally published in *Past and Present* 62 (1974): 120–52.

H42. **indirect source:** If you are citing a source from a reference other than the source itself, you should include information about both sources, supplying as much information as you are able to about the original source.

- In de Beauvoir's famous phrase, "one is not born a woman, one becomes one."[1]

1. Simone de Beauvoir, *The Second Sex* (London: Heinemann, 1966), 44, quoted in Ann Levey, "Feminist Philosophy Today," *Philosophy Now*, par. 8, http://www.ucalgary.ca.philosophy.now site675.html (March 4, 2005).

de Beauvoir, Simone. *The Second Sex*. London: Heinemann, 1966. Quoted in Ann Levey, "Feminist Philosophy Today," *Philosophy Now*, http://www.ucalgary.ca.philosophy.nowsite675.html (accessed March 4, 2005).

H43. two or more works by the same author: After the first entry in the bibliography, use three hyphens for subsequent entries of works by the same author (rather than repeat the author's name). Entries for multiple works by the same author are normally arranged alphabetically by title.

Menand, Louis. *The Metaphysical Club: A Story of Ideas in America*. New York: Knopf, 2002.
---. "Bad Comma: Lynne Truss's Strange Grammar." *The New Yorker*, June 28, 2004. http://www.Newyorker.com/critics/books/?040628crbo_books1 (accessed March 5, 2009).

H44. edited works: Entries for edited works include the abbreviation *ed.* or *eds*. Note that when *ed.* appears after a title, it means "edited by."

5. Brian Gross, ed., *New Approaches to Environmental Politics: A Survey* (New York: Duckworth, 2004), 177.
6. Mary Shelley, *Frankenstein*, 2nd ed., ed. Lorne Macdonald and Kathleen Scherf, Broadview Edition (1818; Peterborough: Broadview Press, 2001), 89.

Gross, Brian, ed. *New Approaches to Environmental Politics: A Survey.* New York: Duckworth, 2004.

Shelley, Mary. *Frankenstein.* 2nd ed. Edited by Lorne Macdonald and Kathleen Scherf. Broadview Edition. Peterborough: Broadview, 2001. First published in 1818.

H45. **magazine articles**: The titles of articles appear in quotation marks. The page range should appear in the bibliography if it is known. (This will not always be possible if the source is an electronic version.) If no authorship is attributed, list the title of the article as the "author" in the footnote, and the magazine title as the "author" in the bibliography.

> 2. Lynn MacRitchie, "Ofili's Glittering Icons," *Art in America*, January 2000, par. 14, http://www.findarticles.com.ofili.j672.jn.htm (accessed March 4, 2009).
>
> 3. "Shifting Sands," *Economist*, February 12-18, 2005, 47.
>
> 4. Malcolm Gladwell, "The Art of Failure: Why Some People Choke and Others Panic," *The New Yorker,* August 21, 2000, par 8, http://www.gladwell.com/2000_08_21_a_choking.html (accessed March 5, 2005).

> *Economist.* "Shifting Sands." February 12–18, 2005, 46–47.
>
> Gladwell, Malcolm. "The Art of Failure: Why Some People Choke and Others Panic." *The New Yorker,* August 21, 2000. http://www.gladwell.com/2000_08_21_a_choking.html (accessed March 5, 2009).
>
> MacRitchie, Lynn. "Ofili's Glittering Icons." *Art in America*, January 2000, 75–84. http://www.findarticles.com.ofili.j672.jn.htm. (accessed March 4, 2005).

H46. **newspaper articles**: The basic principles to follow with newspaper articles or editorials are the same as with magazine articles (see above). Page numbers should be given if your source is a hard copy or microfilm rather than an electronic version.

> 1. "Clash over Nobel Cash," *Washington Post*, February 11, 1998, A14.

2. Glanz, Jane, "Iraq's Shiite Alliance Wins Slim Majority in New Assembly," *New York Times*, February 17, 2005, http://www.nytimes.com/2005/02/17/international/middleeast/17cnd-iraq.html (accessed March 4, 2005).

Glanz, Jane. "Iraq's Shiite Alliance Wins Slim Majority in New Assembly." *New York Times*, February 17, 2005. http://www.nytimes.com/2005/02/17/international/middleeast/17cnd-iraq.html (accessed March 4, 2005).
Washington Post. "Clash over Nobel Cash." February 11, 1998, A14.

H47. **journal articles**: The basic principles are the same as with magazine articles. Volume number should not be italicized; issue number as well as page number should be provided where available.

1. Paul Barker, "The Impact of Class Size on the Classroom Behavior of Special Needs Students: A Longitudinal Study," *Educational Quarterly* 25, no. 4 (2004): 88.
2. Thomas Hurka, "Improving on Perfectionism," *Philosophical Review* 99 (1996): 472.
3. Peter Raedts, "The Children's Crusade of 1212," *Journal of Medieval History* 3, no. 4 (1994): 303.
4. Sally Sohmer, "Ways of Perceiving Maps and Globes," *Psychology and History* 3, no. 4 (2004): par. 7, http://www.shu.ac.uk/emls/03-1/sohmjuli.html (accessed March 5, 2005).

Barker, Paul. "The Impact of Class Size on the Classroom Behavior of Special Needs Students: A Longitudinal Study." *Educational Quarterly* 25, no. 4 (2004): 87–99.
Hurka, Thomas M. "Improving on Perfectionism." *Philosophical Review* 99 (1996): 462–73.
Raedts, Peter. "The Children's Crusade of 1212." *Journal of Medieval History* 3, no. 4 (1994): 279–304.
Sohmer, Sally. "Ways of Perceiving Maps and Globes." *Psychology and History* 3, no. 4 (2004). http://www.shu.ac.uk/emls/03-1/sohmjuli.html (accessed March 5, 2005).

H48. **films, programs, interviews, performances, music, art**: Films, radio or television programs, interviews, dramatic performances, musical recordings, and paintings should be listed as follows:

● *Films, Television, Radio*

1. *Wag the Dog*, directed by Barry Levinson (Los Angeles: MGM, 1997).
2. "Family Farm vs. Factory Farm," *Country Canada*, CBC Television, November 23, 2003, http://www.archivescbc.ca/IDC-I-73-1239-6930/pig_INDUSTRY/CLIP2 (accessed March 5, 2005).
3. Charles White, *Dr. Rock*, Radio York, July 2, 2006.

"Family Farm vs. Factory Farm." *Country Canada*. CBC Television, November 23, 2003. http://www.archivescbc.ca/IDC-I-73-1239-6930/pig_INDUSTRY/CLIP2 (accessed March 5, 2005).
Wag the Dog. Directed by Barry Levinson. Los Angeles: MGM, 1997.
White, Charles. Dr. Rock. *Radio York*, July 2, 2006.

● *Interviews*

1. Saul Bellow, interview by Jim Smith, *Books in Canada*, September 1996, 3.
2. Dorothy Counts and David Counts, interview by Pamela Wallin, *Pamela Wallin Live*, CBC Television, November 26, 2002.
3. Herbert Rosengarten, telephone interview by author, January 21, 2005.

Bellow, Saul. Interviewed by Jim Smith. *Books in Canada*, September 1996, 2–6.
Counts, Dorothy and David Counts. Interview by Pamela Wallin. *Pamela Wallin Live*. CBC Television, November 26, 2002.

Note that unpublished interviews and unattributed interviews are usually not included in the bibliography.

H49. **book reviews:** The name of the reviewer (if it has been provided) should come first, as shown below:

1. Andrew O'Hagan, "Fossil Fuels," review of *Underground Energy*, by Phyllis Jackson, *London Review of Books*, February 18, 2005, http://www.lrb.co.uk/v27/n04/ohag01_.html (accessed March 5, 2009).

O'Hagan, Andrew. "Fossil Fuels." Review of *Underground Energy*, by Phyllis Jackson. *London Review of Books*, February 18, 2005. http://www.lrb.co.uk/v27/n04/ohag01_.html (accessed March 5, 2009).

H50. **other Web references:** In the case of online sources not covered by the above, the same principles apply. Where an author or editor is indicated, list by author.

Brown University. *Women Writers Project*. http://www.brown.edu/~letrs/html (accessed March 5, 2009).
"Profile of book publishing and exclusive agency, for English language firms, 2004." *Statistics Canada*. http://www40.statcan.ca/101/cst01/arts02.htm (accessed March 6, 2009).

H51. **electronic sources—other information:** In the above pages information about electronic sources has been presented in an integrated fashion, with information about referencing hard copies of journal articles presented alongside information about referencing online versions, and so on. Note that (unlike MLA Style), Chicago style does not put angle brackets around URLs.

O *Chicago Style Sample*

A sample of text with citations in Chicago style appears on the following page. Note that a sample essay in Chicago style appears on the adjunct website associated with this book.

Urban renewal is as much a matter of psychology as it is of bricks and mortar. As Paul Goldberger has described, there have been many plans to revitalize Havana.[1] But both that city and the community of Cuban exiles in Florida remain haunted by a sense of absence and separation. As Lourdes Casal reminds us,

> Exile
>
> is living where there is no house whatever
>
> in which we were ever children;[2]

The psychology of outsiders also makes a difference. Part of the reason Americans have not much noticed the dire plight of their fifth-largest city is that it does not "stir the national imagination."[3] Conversely, there has been far more concern over the state of cities such as New Orleans and Quebec, whose history and architecture excite the romantic imagination. As Nora Phelps has discussed, the past is in itself a key trigger for romantic notions, and it is no doubt inevitable that cities whose history is particularly visible will engender passionate attachments. And as Stephanie Wright and Carole King have detailed in an important case study, almost all French-speaking Quebecers feel their heritage to be bound up with that of Quebec City. (Richard Ford's character Frank Bascombe has suggested that "New Orleans defeats itself" by longing "for a mystery it doesn't have and never will, if it ever did,"[4] but this remains a minority view.)

Georgiana Gibson is also among those who have investigated the interplay between urban psychology and urban reality. Gibson's personal website now includes the first of a set of working models she is developing in an attempt to represent the effects of psychological schemata on the landscape.

---

1 Paul Goldberger, "Annals of Preservation: Bringing Back Havana," *The New Republic*, January 2005, 54.
2 Lourdes Casal, "Definition," trans. Elizabeth Macklin, *New Yorker*, January 26, 1998, 79.
3 Witold Rybczynski, "The Fifth City," review of *A Prayer for the City*, by Buzz Bissinger, *New York Review of Books*, February 5, 1998, 13.
4 Richard Ford, *The Sportswriter*, 2nd ed. (New York: Random House, 1995), 48.

The bibliography relating to the above text would be as follows:

Bibliography

Casal, Lourdes. "Definition." Translated by Elizabeth Macklin. *New Yorker*, January 26, 1998, 79.

Ford, Richard. *The Sportswriter*. 2nd ed. New York: Random House, 1995.

Gibson, Georgiana. *Cities in the Twentieth Century*. Boston: Beacon, 2004.

---. Homepage. http:www.geography.by/u.edu/GIBSON/personal.htm (accessed March 4, 2009).

Goldberger, Paul. "Annals of Preservation: Bringing Back Havana." *New Yorker*, January 26, 2005, 50–62. http://www.findarticles.com.goldberg.p65. jn.htm (accessed March 4, 2009).

Phelps, Nora. "Pastness and the Foundations of Romanticism." *Romanticism on the Net* 11 (May 2001). http://users.ox.ac.uk/~scato385/phelpsmws.htm (accessed March 4, 2009).

Rybczynski, Witold. "The Fifth City." Review of *A Prayer for the City*, by D.B. Smith. *New York Review of Books*, February 5, 1998, 12-14.

Wright, Stephanie, and Carole King. *Quebec: A History*. 2 vols. Montreal: McGill-Queen's University Press, 2003.

Among the details to notice in this reference system:

- Where two or more works by the same author are included in the bibliography, they are normally arranged alphabetically by title.
- All major words in titles and subtitles are capitalized.
- Date of publication must appear, where known. Provision of your date of access to electronic materials may be helpful, but is not required.
- Commas are used to separate elements within a footnote, and, in many circumstances, periods separate these same elements in the bibliographic entry.
- When a work has appeared in an edited collection, information on the editors must be included in the reference.
- First authors' first and last names are reversed in the bibliography.
- Translators must be noted both in footnotes and in the bibliography.
- Publisher as well as city of publication should be given.
- Months and publisher names are not abbreviated.
- The day of the month comes after the name of the month.
- Online references should *not* include the revision date but may include the date on which you visited the site (access date).

⊙ CSE Style

There are two chief concerns when it comes to citing and documenting material: accuracy and consistency. Whatever system of citation is used, a research writer must follow it closely and consistently. Four of the most commonly used systems of citation are summarized in these pages—MLA style (see the previous chapter), APA style, Chicago style, and CSE (Council of Science Editors) style.

Further information about styles of writing as well as of citation and reference in various academic disciplines appears elsewhere in this book in the section on "Style." It may also be helpful to consult exemplary essays. (A selection of these may be found on the Broadview Press website in the pages providing adjunct material to this and other Broadview writing texts; go to www.broadviewpress. com, and click on links.)

To understand more of the basic principles and workings of academic citation and documentation, students are advised to consult G1 "Citation and Plagiarism" and G2 "Signal Phrases" at the beginning of the previous chapter.

The Council of Science Editors (CSE) style of documentation is commonly used in the natural sciences and the physical sciences. Guidelines are set out in *The CSE Manual for Authors, Editors, and Publishers*, 7th ed. (2006).

H52. **in-text citation**: Citations in CSE style may follow three alternative formats: a citation-name format, a citation-sequence format, or a name-year format.

1. In the citation-name format, a reference list is compiled and arranged alphabetically by author. Each reference is then assigned a number in sequence, with the first alphabetical entry receiving the number 1, the second the number 2, and so on. Whenever you refer in your text to the reference labelled with number 3, for example, you use either a superscript number 3 (in one variation) or the same number in parentheses (in another).

- The difficulties first encountered in this experiment have been accounted for, according to Zelinsky[3]. However, the variables still have not been sufficiently well controlled for this type of experiment, argues Gibson[1].
- The difficulties first encountered in this experiment have been accounted for, according to Zelinsky (3). However, the variables still have not been sufficiently well controlled for this type of experiment, argues Gibson (1).

2. In the citation-sequence format, superscript numbers (or numbers in parentheses) are inserted after the mention of any source. The first source mentioned receives number 1, the second number 2, and so on.

- The difficulties first encountered in this experiment have been accounted for, according to Zelinsky[1]. However, the variables still have not been sufficiently well controlled for this type of experiment, argues Gibson[2].
- The difficulties first encountered in this experiment have been accounted for, according to Zelinsky (1). However, the variables still have not been sufficiently well controlled for this type of experiment, argues Gibson (2).

Reuse the number you first assign to a source whenever you refer to it again.

3. In the name-year format, you cite the author name and year of publication in parentheses:

- The key contributions to the study of variables in the 1990s (Gibson et al. 1998; Soames 1999; Zelinsky 1997) have been strongly challenged in recent years.

H53. **list of references:** Citations in CSE style must correspond to items in a list of References. In the citation-name format, entries are arranged alphabetically and assigned a number.

1. Gibson DL, Lampman GM, Kriz FR, Taylor DM. Introduction to statistical techniques in the sciences. 2nd ed. New York: MacQuarrie Learning; 1998. 1254 p.
2. Soames G. Variables in large database experiments. J Nat Hist. 1999;82: 1811–41.
3. Zelinsky KL. The study of variables: an overview. New York: Academic; 1997. 216 p.

In the citation-sequence format, the references are listed in the sequence in which they have been cited in the text.

1. Zelinsky KL. The study of variables: an overview. New York: Academic; 1997. 216 p.
2. Gibson DL, Lampman GM, Kriz FR, Taylor DM. Introduction to statistical techniques in the sciences. 2nd ed. New York: MacQuarrie Learning; 1998. 1254 p.
3. Soames G. Variables in large database experiments. J Nat Hist. 1999;82: 1811–41.

In the name-year format, the references are listed alphabetically, and the year of publication is given prominence.

Gibson DL, Lampman GM, Kriz FR, Taylor DM. 1998. Introduction to statistical techniques in the sciences. 2nd ed. New York: MacQuarrie Learning. 1254 p.

Soames G. 1999. Variables in large database experiments. J Nat Hist. 82: 1811–41.

Zelinsky KL. 1997. The study of variables: an overview. New York: Academic. 216 p.

The basic principles of the system are the same regardless of whether one is citing a book, an article in a journal or magazine, a newspaper article, or an electronic document.

O *CSE Style Sample*

Over the centuries scientific study has evolved into several distinct disciplines. Physics, chemistry, and biology were established early on; in the nineteenth and twentieth centuries they were joined by others, such as geology and ecology. Much as the disciplines have their separate spheres, the sphere of each overlaps those of others. This may be most obvious in the case of ecology, which some have claimed to be a discipline that makes a holistic approach to science respectable[1]. In the case of geology, as soon as it became clear in the nineteenth century that the fossil record of geological life would be central to the future of geology, the importance of connecting with the work of biologists became recognized[2]. Nowadays it is not surprising to have geological research conducted jointly by biologists and geologists (e.g., the work of Newton, Trewman, and Elser[3]). And, with the acceptance of "continental drift" theories in the 1960s and 1970s, physics came to be increasingly relied on for input into discussions of such topics as collision tectonics (e.g., Pfiffton, Earn, and Brome[4]).

The growth of the subdiscipline of biochemistry at the point of overlap between biology and chemistry is well-known, but many are unaware that the scope of biological physics is almost as broad; Frauenfrommer[5] provides a helpful survey. Nowadays it is not uncommon, indeed, to see research such as the recent study by Corel, Marks, and Hutner[6], or that by Balmberg, Passano, and Proule[7], both of which draw on biology, chemistry, and physics simultaneously.

Interdisciplinary scientific exploration has also been spurred by the growth of connections between the pure sciences and applied sciences such as meteorology, as even a glance in the direction of recent research into such topics as precipitation[8] or crating[9] confirms. But to the extent that science is driven by the applied, will it inextricably become more and more driven by commercial concerns? Christopher Haupt-Lehmann[10] thinks not.

The citations above would connect to References as follows:

References

1. Branmer A. Ecology in the twentieth century: a history. New Haven: Yale UP; 2004. 320 p.

2. Lyell C. Principles of geology. London: John Murray; 1830. 588 p.

3. Newton MJ, Trewman NH, Elser S. A new jawless invertebrate from the Middle Devonian. Paleontology 2004; 44 (1):43–52. http://www.onlinejournals.paleontology.44/html (accessed March 5, 2005).

4. Pfiffton QA, Earn PK, Brome C. Collision tectonics and dynamic modelling. Tectonics 2000;19(6):1065–94.

5. Frauenfrommer H. Introduction. Frauenfrommer H, Hum G, Glazer RG, editors. Biological physics third international symposium; 1998 Mar 8–9; Santa Fe, NM [Melville, NY]: American Institute of Physics. 386 p.

6. Corel B, Marks VJ, Hutner H. The modelling effect of Elpasolites. Chemical Sciences 2005;55(10):935–38.

7. Balmberg NJ, Passano C, Proule AB. The Lorenz-Fermi-Pasta-Ulam experiment. Physica D: Nonlinear phenomena [serial online] 2005; 138(1):1–43. Available at http://www.elseviere.com/locate/phys (accessed March 21, 2001).

8. Caine JS, Gross SM, Baldwin G. Melting effect as a factor in precipitation-type forecasting. Weather and Forecasting 2000;15(6):700–14.

9. Pendleton AJ. Gawler cration. Regional Geology 2001;11:999–1016.

10. Haupt-Lehmann C. Money and science: the latest word. New York Times 2001 Mar 23; Sect. D:22(col 1).

Among the details to notice in the citation-sequence format of the CSE style:

- The entries in References are listed in the order they first appear in the text.
- Unpunctuated initials rather than first names are used in References.
- The date appears near the end of the reference, before any page reference.
- Only the first words of titles are capitalized (except for proper nouns and the abbreviated titles of journals).
- When a work has appeared in an edited collection the names of the editor(s) as well as the author(s) must appear in the reference.
- *and* is used for in-text citations of works with more than one author—but not in the corresponding reference.
- Publisher as well as city of publication should be given.
- Months and journal names are generally abbreviated.
- References to electronic publications include the date of access as well as date of publication or latest revision.
- Names of articles appear with no surrounding quotation marks; names of books and journal titles appear with no italics.

Here is the same passage with the CSE name-year format used:

Over the centuries scientific study has evolved into several distinct disciplines. Physics, chemistry, and biology were established early on; in the nineteenth and twentieth centuries, they were joined by others, such as geology and ecology. Much as the disciplines have their separate spheres, the sphere of each overlaps those of others. This may be most obvious in the case of ecology, which some have claimed to be a discipline that makes a holistic approach to science respectable (Branmer 2004). In the case of geology, as soon as it became clear in the nineteenth century that the fossil record of geological life would be central to the future of geology, the importance of connecting with the work of biologists became recognized (Lyell 1830). Nowadays it is not surprising to have geological research conducted jointly by biologists and geologists (e.g., Newton, Trewman, and Elser 2001). And, with the acceptance of "continental drift" theories in the 1960s and 1970s, physics came to be increasingly relied on for input into discussions of such topics as collision tectonics (e.g., Pfiffton, Earn, and Brome 2000).

The growth of the subdiscipline of biochemistry at the point of overlap between biology and chemistry is well-known, but many are unaware that the scope of biological physics is almost as broad; Frauenfrommer (1998) provides a helpful survey. Nowadays it is not uncommon, indeed, to see research such as the recent study by Corel, Marks, and Hutner (2005) or that by Balmberg, Passano, and Proule (2005), both of which draw on biology, chemistry, and physics simultaneously.

Interdisciplinary scientific exploration has also been spurred by the growth of connections between the pure sciences and applied sciences such as meteorology, as even a glance in the direction of recent research into such topics as precipitation (Caine, Gross, and Baldwin 2000) or crating (Pendleton 2001) confirms. But to the extent that science is driven by the applied, will it inextricably become more and more driven by commercial concerns? Christopher Haupt-Lehmann (2001) thinks not.

The citations above would connect to References as follows:

References

Branmer A. 2004. Ecology in the twentieth century: a history. New Haven: Yale UP. 320 p.

Balmberg NJ, Passano C, Proule AB. 2005. The Lorenz-Fermi-Pasta-Ulam experiment. Physica D: Nonlinear phenomena [serial online]. 138(1): 1–43. Available at the Elsevier Journals website via the Internet (http://www.elseviere.com/locate/phys).

Caine JS, Gross SM, Baldwin G. 2000. Melting effect as a factor in precipitation-type forecasting. Weather and Forecasting. 15(6):700–14.

Corel B, Marks VJ, Hutner H. 2005. The modelling effect of Elpasolites. Chem Sci. 55(10):935–38.

Frauenfrommer H. Introduction. Frauenfrommer H, Hum G, Glazer RG, editors. 1998 Mar 8-9. Biological physics third international symposium. Santa Fe, NM. [Melville, NY]: American Institute of Physics. 386 p.

Haupt-Lehmann C. 2001 Mar 23. Money and science: the latest word. New York Times; Sect D:22 (col 2).

Lyell C. 1830. Principles of geology. London: John Murray. 588 p.

Newton MJ, Trewman NH, Elser S. 2001. A new jawless invertebrate from the Middle Devonian. Paleontology. 44 (1):43–52. Available from the Online journals site via the Internet (http://www.onlinejournals. paleontology.44/html).

Pendleton AJ. 2001. Gawler cration. Reg Geol; 11:999–1016.

Pfiffton QA, Earn PK, Brome C. 2000. Collision tectonics and dynamic modelling. Tectonics. 19(6):1065–94.

Among the details to notice in this reference system:

- The entries in References are listed in alphabetical order by author.
- Unpunctuated initials rather than first names are used in References.
- The date appears immediately after the author name(s) at the beginning of the reference, before any page reference.
- The in-text citation comes before the period or comma in the surrounding sentence.
- Only the first words of titles are capitalized (except for proper nouns and the abbreviated titles of journals).
- When a work has appeared in an edited collection the names of the editor(s) as well as the author(s) must appear in the reference.
- *and* is used for in-text citations of works with more than one author—but not in the corresponding reference list entry.
- Publisher as well as city of publication should be given.
- Months and journal names are generally abbreviated.
- References to electronic publications include the date of publication or latest revision.
- Names of articles appear with no surrounding quotation marks; names of books, journals, etc. appear with no italics.

◉ APPENDIX 1: *A Reference Guide to Basic Grammar*

◉ Parts of Speech

● *Nouns*

Nouns are words that name people, things, places, or qualities. Some examples follow:

- names of people: *boy, John, parent*
- names of things: *hat, spaghetti, fish*
- names of places: *Saskatoon, Zambia, New York*
- names of qualities: *silence, intelligence, anger*

Nouns can be used to fill the gaps in sentences like these:

- I saw _____ at the market yesterday.
- He dropped the _____ into the gutter.
- Has she lost a lot of _____ ?
- Hamilton is a _____ with several hundred thousand people living in it.

Some nouns (e.g., *sugar, milk, confusion*) are uncountable—that is, we cannot say *a sugar, two sugars,* or *three sugars.*

● *Pronouns*

Pronouns replace or stand for nouns. For example, instead of saying, *The man slipped on a banana peel* or *George slipped on a banana peel,* we can replace the noun *man* (or the noun *George*) with the pronoun *he* and say *He slipped on a banana peel.*

definite and indefinite pronouns: Whereas a pronoun such as *he* refers to a definite person, the words *each, every, either, neither, one, another*, and *much* are indefinite. They may be used as pronouns or as adjectives; in either case, a singular verb is needed.

- Each player wants to do his best.
    (Here the word *each* is an adjective, describing the noun *player*.)
- Each wants to do his best.
    (Here the word *each* is a pronoun, acting as the subject of the sentence.)
- Each of the players wants to do his best.
    (The word *each* is still a pronoun, this time followed by the phrase *of the players*. But it is the pronoun *each* that is the subject of the sentence; the verb must be the singular *wants*.)

possessive pronouns and adjectives: See under "Adjectives" below.

relative pronouns: These pronouns relate back to a noun that has been used earlier in the same sentence. Look at how repetitious these sentences sound:

- I talked to the man. The man wore a red hat.

We could of course replace the second *man* with *he*. Even better, though, is to relate or connect the second idea to the first by using a relative pronoun:

- I talked to the man who wore a red hat.
- I found the pencil. I had lost the pencil.
- I found the pencil that I had lost.

The following are all relative pronouns:

- who whose (has other uses too)
- which that (has other uses too)
- whom

Try replacing the second noun in these pairs of sentences with a relative pronoun, so as to make only one sentence out of each pair:

- I polished the table. I had built the table.
- Premier Calvert is vacationing this week in Quebec's Eastern Townships. The premier cancelled a planned holiday last fall.
- The word *other* is often used by literary theorists when speaking of a sense of strangeness in the presence of cultural difference. *Other* is usually preceded by the definite article when so used.

pronouns acting as subject and as object: We use different personal pronouns depending on whether we are using them as the subject or the object and whether they are singular or plural.

	singular	*plural*
Subject	I	we
Pronouns	you	you
	he/she/it	they
	who, what, which	who, what, which (interrogative)

	singular	*plural*
Object	me	us
Pronouns	you	you
	him/her/it	them
	whom, what, which	whom, what, which (interrogative)

- He shot the sheriff.
  (Here the pronoun *he* is the subject of the sentence.)
- The sheriff shot him.
  (Here the word *him* is the object; *the sheriff* is the subject.)
- That's the man who shot the sheriff.
  (Here the pronoun *who* is the subject of the clause *who shot the sheriff*.)
- That's the man whom the sheriff shot.
  (Here the pronoun *whom* is the object of the verb *shot*; *the sheriff* is the subject of the clause *whom the sheriff shot*.)

The distinctions between *I* and *me* and between *who* and *whom* are treated more fully under Pronouns, pages 174–87.

● *Articles*

Articles (determiners often classed as a form of adjective) are words used to introduce nouns. There are only three of them: *a, an,* and *the.* Articles show whether or not one is drawing attention to a particular person or thing.

For example, we would say *I stood beside a house* if we did not want to draw attention to that particular house, but *I stood beside the house that the Taylors used to live in* if we did want to draw attention to the particular house. *A* (or *an* if the noun following begins with a vowel sound) is an indefinite article—used when you do not wish to be definite or specific about which thing or person you are referring to. *The* is a definite article, used when you do wish to call attention to the particular thing or person. Remember that if you use *the*, you are suggesting that there can be only one or one group of what you are referring to.

Choose the appropriate article (*a, an,* or *the*):
- _____ moon shone brightly last night.
- She had _____ long conversation with _____ friend.
- Have you ever driven _____ car?
- Have you driven _____ car that your wife bought on Monday?

● *Adjectives*

Adjectives are words used to tell us more about (describe or modify) nouns or pronouns. Here are some examples of adjectives:

big	good	heavy
small	bad	expensive
pretty	careful	fat
quick	slow	thin

- The fat man lifted the heavy table.
  (Here the adjective *fat* describes or tells us more about the noun *man*, and the adjective *heavy* describes the noun *table*.)
- The fast runner finished ahead of the slow one.
  (*Fast* describes *runner* and *slow* describes *one*.)

Notice that adjectives usually come before the nouns that they describe. This is not always the case, however; when the verb *to be* is used, adjectives often come after the noun or pronoun, and after the verb:

- That woman is particularly careful about her finances.
  (*Careful* describes *woman*.)
- It is too difficult for me to do.
  (*Difficult* describes *it*.)

Adjectives can be used to fill the gaps in sentences like these:

- This _____ sweater was knitted by hand.
- As soon as we entered the _____ house we heard a clap of _____thunder.
- Those shoes are very _____.
- Derrida's argument could fairly be described as _____.

Some words can be either adjectives or pronouns, depending on how they are used. That is the case with the indefinite pronouns (see above), and also with certain possessives (words that show possession):

	singular	*plural*
Possessive	my	our
Adjectives	your	your
	his/her	their
	whose	whose

	singular	*plural*
Possessive	mine	ours
Pronouns	yours	yours
	his/hers	theirs
	whose	whose

- I have my cup, and he has his.

     (Here the word *his* is a pronoun, used in place of the noun *cup*.)
- He has his cup.

     (Here the word *his* is an adjective, describing the noun *cup*.)
- Whose book is this?

     (Here the word *whose* is an adjective, describing the noun *book*.)
- Whose is this?

     (Here the word *whose* is a pronoun, acting as the subject of the sentence.)

● *Verbs*

Verbs are words that express actions or states of affairs. Most verbs can be conveniently thought of as "doing" words (e.g., *open, feel, do, carry, see, think, combine, send*), but a few verbs do not fit into this category. Indeed, the most common verb of all—*be*—expresses a state of affairs, not a particular action that is done. Verbs are used to fill gaps in sentences like these:

- I _____ very quickly, but I _____ not _____ up with my brother.
- She usually _____ to sleep at 9:30.
- Stephen _____ his breakfast very quickly.
- They _____ a large farm near Newcastle.
- There _____ many different languages that people _____ in India.

One thing that makes verbs different from other parts of speech is that verbs have tenses; in other words, they change their form depending on the time you are talking about. For example, the present tense of the verb *to be* is *I am, you are, he is*, etc., while the past tense is *I was, you were, he was*, etc. If unsure whether or not a particular word is a verb, one way to check is to ask if it has different tenses. For example, if one thought that perhaps the word *football* might be a verb, one need only ask oneself if it would be correct to say, *I footballed, I am footballing, I will football*, and so on. Obviously it would not be, so one knows that *football* is the noun that names the game, not a verb that expresses an action. See the first chapter in this book for a discussion of verb tenses.

● *Adverbs*

These words are usually used to tell us more about (describe or modify) verbs, although they can also be used to tell us more about adjectives or about other adverbs. They answer questions like *How ...?, When ...?*, and *To what extent ...?*, and often they end with the letters *ly*. Here are a few examples, with some adjectives also listed for comparison:

Adjective	Adverb
careful	carefully
beautiful	beautifully
thorough	thoroughly
sudden	suddenly
slow	slowly
easy	easily
good	well

- He walked carefully.
  (The adverb *carefully* tells us how he walked; it describes the verb *walked*.)
- He is a careful boy.
  (The adjective *careful* describes the noun *boy*.)

- My grandfather died suddenly last week.
    (The adverb *suddenly* tells how he died; it describes the verb *died*.)
- We were upset by the sudden death of my grandfather.
    (The adjective *sudden* describes the noun *death*.)
- She plays the game very well.
    (The adverb *well* tells us how she plays; it describes the verb *plays*. The adverb *very* describes the adverb *well*.)
- She played a good game this afternoon.
    (The adjective *good* describes the noun *game*.)
- She played a very good game.
    (The adverb *very* describes the adjective *good*, telling us how good it was.)
- According to his press secretary, Bush will meet Putin soon.
    (The adverb *soon* describes the verb *will meet*, telling when the action will happen.)

Choose adverbs to fill the gaps in these sentences:

- Ralph writes very _____.
- The judge spoke _____ to Milken after he had been convicted on six counts of stock manipulation and fraud.
- They were _____ late for the meeting this morning.

● *Prepositions*

Prepositions are joining words, normally used before nouns or pronouns. Some of the most common prepositions are as follows:

about	after	across
at	before	for
from	in	into
of	on	off
over	to	until
with		

Choose prepositions to fill the gaps in these sentences:

- I will tell you _____ it _____ the morning.
- Please try to arrive _____ eight o'clock.
- He did not come back _____ Toronto _____ yesterday.
- I received a letter _____ my sister.

● *Conjunctions*

Conjunctions are normally used to join groups of words together, and in particular join clauses together. Some examples:

because	unless	after
although	until	if
and	since	or
as	before	that

- They stopped playing because they were tired.
     (The conjunction *because* joins the group of words *they were tired* to the group of words *They stopped playing*.)
- I will give her your message if I see her.
     (The conjunction *if* introduces the second group of words and joins it to the first.)

Many conjunctions can also act as other parts of speech, depending on how they are used. Notice the difference in each of these pairs of sentences:

- He will not do anything about it until the morning.
     (Here *until* is a preposition joining the noun *morning* to the rest of the sentence.)
- He will not do anything about it until he has discussed it with his wife.
     (Here *until* is a conjunction introducing the clause *until he has discussed it with his wife*.)

- I slept for half an hour after dinner.

   (Here *after* is a preposition joining the noun *dinner* to the rest of the sentence.)
- I slept for half an hour after they had gone home.

   (Here *after* is a conjunction introducing the clause *after they had gone home.*)
- She wants to buy that dress.

   (Here *that* is an adjective describing the noun *dress*: "*Which dress?*" "*That dress!*")
- George said that he was unhappy.

   (Here *that* is a conjunction introducing the clause *that he was unhappy.*)

Choose conjunctions to fill the gaps in the following sentences:

- We believed _____ we would win.
- They sat down in the shade _____ it was hot.
- My father did not speak to me _____ he left.

⊙ Parts of Sentences

● *Subject*

The subject is the thing, person, or quality about which something is said in a clause. The subject is usually a noun or pronoun.

- The man went to town.

   (The sentence is about the man, not about the town; thus the noun *man* is the subject.)
- Groundnuts are an important crop in Nigeria.

   (The sentence is about groundnuts, not about crops or about Nigeria; thus the noun *groundnuts* is the subject.)
- Nigeria is the most populous country in Africa.

   (The sentence is about Nigeria, not about countries or about Africa; thus the noun *Nigeria* is the subject.)

- He followed me up the stairs.
    - (The pronoun *He* is the subject.)

core subject: The core subject is the single noun or pronoun that forms the subject.

complete subject: The complete subject is the subject together with any adjectives or adjectival phrases modifying it:

- The lady in the huge hat went to the market to buy groceries.
    - (The core subject is the noun *lady* and the complete subject is *the lady in the huge hat*.)

● Object

An object is something or someone towards which an action or feeling is directed. In grammar an object is the thing, person, or quality affected by the action of the verb. (To put it another way, it receives the action of the verb.) Like a subject, an object normally is made up of a noun or pronoun.

direct object: The direct object is the thing, person, or quality directly affected by the action of the verb. A direct object usually answers the question *What?* or *Who?* Notice that direct objects are not introduced by prepositions.

indirect object: The indirect object is the thing, person, or quality that is indirectly affected by the action of the verb. All indirect objects could be expressed differently by making them the objects of the prepositions *to* or *for*. Instead, the prepositions have been omitted. Indirect objects answer the questions *To whom?* and *For whom?*

- McGriff hit the ball a long way.
    - (What did he hit? The ball. *The ball* is the direct object of the verb *hit*.)

- She threw me her hat.
    (What did she throw? Her hat. *Her hat* is the direct object. To whom did she throw it? To me. *Me* is the indirect object. Note that the sentence could be rephrased: *She threw her hat to me.*)
- They gave their father a watch for Christmas.
    (The direct object is *watch*, and the indirect object is *father*.)

● *Predicate*

The predicate is everything that is said about the subject. In the example under "Subject," *went to the market to buy groceries* is the predicate. A predicate always includes a verb.

● *Clause*

A distinct group of words that includes both a subject and a predicate. Thus a clause always includes a verb.

● *Phrase*

A distinct group of words that does not include both a subject and a verb. Examples:

Clauses	*Phrases*
because he is strong	because of his strength (no verb)
before she comes home	before the meeting (no verb)
the professor likes me	from Halifax
a tree fell down	at lunch
who came to dinner	in the evening

● *Types of Clauses*

main clause: A main clause is a group of words that is, or could be, a sentence on its own.

subordinate clause: A subordinate clause is a clause that could not form a complete sentence on its own.

Except for the coordinating conjunctions (*and, but, or, nor, for, yet,* and *so*), conjunctions do not introduce main clauses, so if a clause begins with a word such as *because, although,* or *if,* you can be confident it is a subordinate clause. Similarly, relative pronouns introduce subordinate clauses—never main clauses.

- She lives near Pittsburgh.
    > (One main clause forming a complete sentence. The pronoun *She* is the subject, *lives* is the verb, and the preposition *near* and the noun *Pittsburgh* together form a phrase.)
- He danced in the street because he was feeling happy.
    > main clause: He danced in the street
    > subject: _____
    > predicate: _____
    > subordinate clause: because he was feeling happy
    > subject: _____
    > predicate: _____
- Mavis has married a man who is older than her father.
    > main clause: Mavis has married a man
    > subject: _____
    > predicate: _____
    > subordinate clause: who is older than her father
    > subject: _____
    > predicate: _____

● *Types of Subordinate Clauses*

adjectival subordinate clause: a subordinate clause that tells us more about a noun or pronoun. Adjectival clauses begin with relative pronouns such as *who, whom, whose, which,* and *that.*

adverbial subordinate clause: a subordinate clause that tells us more about the action of the verb—telling *how, when, why,* or *where* the action occurred.

noun subordinate clause: a clause that acts like a noun to form the subject or object of a sentence.

Examples:

- He talked at length to his cousin, who quickly became bored.
  > (*Who quickly became bored* is an adjectival subordinate clause, telling us more about the noun *cousin*.)
  > subject of subordinate clause: the pronoun *who*
  > verb in subordinate clause: _____
  > subject of main clause: the pronoun *He*
  > verb in main clause: _____

- My husband did not like the gift that I gave him.
  > (*That I gave him* is an adjectival subordinate clause telling us more about the noun *gift*.)
  > subject of subordinate clause: the pronoun *I*
  > verb in subordinate clause: _____
  > subject of main clause: _____
  > verb in main clause: _____

- The boy whom she wants to marry is very poor.
  > (*Whom she wants to marry* is an adjectival subordinate clause telling us more about the noun *boy*. Notice that here the subordinate clause appears in the middle of the main clause, *The boy is very poor.*)
  > subject of subordinate clause: _____
  > verb in subordinate clause: _____
  > subject of main clause: _____
  > verb in main clause: _____

- I felt worse after I had been to the doctor.
  > (*After I had been to the doctor* is an adverbial subordinate clause telling you when I felt worse.)

- He could not attend because he had broken his leg.
  > (*Because he had broken his leg* is an adverbial subordinate clause telling you why he could not attend.)

- She jumped as if an alarm had sounded.
  > (*As if an alarm had sounded* is an adverbial subordinate clause telling you how she jumped.)

- What he said was very interesting.
    > (*What he said* is a noun clause acting as the subject of the sentence, in the same way that the noun *conversation* acts as the subject in *The conversation was very interesting.*)
- Sue-Ellen told me that she wanted to become a lawyer.
    > (*That she wanted to become a lawyer* is a noun clause acting as the object, in the same way that the noun *plans* acts as the object in *Sue-Ellen told me her plans.*)

● *Types of Phrases*

adjectival phrase: a phrase that tells us more about a noun or pronoun.

adverbial phrase: a phrase that tells us more about the action of a verb, answering questions such as *When ...?*, *Where ...?*, *How ...?*, and *Why ...?*

- The boy in the new jacket got into the car.
    > (*In the new jacket* is an adjectival phrase telling us more about the noun *boy.*)
- I drank from the cup with a broken handle.
    > (*With a broken handle* is a phrase telling us more about the noun *cup.*)
- We went to the park.
    > (*To the park* is an adverbial phrase telling where we went.)
- They arrived after breakfast.
    > (*After breakfast* is an adverbial phrase telling when they arrived.)

● *Phrases and Clauses*

- They were late because of the weather.
    > (*Because of the weather* is an adverbial phrase telling us why they were late. It has no verb.)

- They were late because the weather was bad.
    (*Because the weather was bad* is an adverbial clause telling us why they were late.)
    subject: _____
    verb: _____
- The man at the corner appeared to be drunk.
    (*At the corner* is an adjectival phrase telling us more about the noun *man*.)
- The man who stood at the corner appeared to be drunk.
    (*Who stood at the corner* is an adjectival clause telling us more about the noun *man*.)
    subject: _____
    verb: _____

● Parts of Speech and Parts of the Sentence

- After the generous man with the big ears has bought presents, he will quickly give them to his friends.

Parts of speech:

after: *conjunction* the: *article*

generous: _____ man: _____

with: _____ the: _____

big: _____ ears: _____

has bought: _____ presents: _____

he: _____ will give: _____

quickly: _____ them: _____

to: _____ his: _____

friends: _____

Parts of the sentence:

main clause: He will quickly give them to his friends.

subject: _____

predicate: _____

verb: _____

direct object: _____

indirect object: _____

subordinate clause: After the generous man with the big ears has bought presents,

> (Is this an adjectival or an adverbial subordinate clause?)
> core subject: the noun _____
> complete subject: _____
> adjectival phrase: with the big ears
> this phrase tells us more about the noun: _____
> predicate: _____
> direct object: _____

◎ APPENDIX 2: *Some National Variations*

The following list of variants from some nations in which English is a primary first language does not include slang or idioms.

Australia	Canada
announcer/host/presenter	announcer/host
attic/loft	attic
autumn	fall/autumn
award rate	minimum wage
baby carriage/pram	baby carriage
backyard	backyard/garden
back bacon	back bacon
baked potato/jacket potato	baked potato
bangs (hair)	bangs
bank note	bill
bathers/cozzy	bathing suit/swimsuit
beanie	toque
billion	billion
biscuit	cookie
bitumen road	paved road
block of land	plot of land
bowser	gas pump
brew (tea)	steep
bus/coach (inter-city)	bus
cake (layer)	cake (layer)
can/tin (of food)	can/tin
car (rail passenger)	car
chemist	drugstore/pharmacy
chips (potato)/crisps	chips
Cludo	Clue (board game)
coloured pencil	pencil crayon
concrete block	concrete block
constituency	riding/constituency
(House of Representatives)	(House of Commons)
contraceptive	condom/safe/rubber
cornstarch/corn flour	cornstarch
dam (human-made)	pond/lake/dugout
dessert/pudding	dessert
diaper/nappy	diaper
different from/to	different from
drapes	curtains/drapes

England	United States
presenter/host	host/announcer
loft	attic
autumn	fall/autumn
minimum wage	minimum wage
pram	baby carriage
back garden	backyard
back bacon	Canadian bacon
jacket potato	baked potato
fringe	bangs
bank note	bill
swimming costume	swimsuit
woolly hat	wool hat
thousand million	billion
biscuit	cookie
metalled road	paved road
plot of land	plot of land
petrol pump	gas pump
brew	steep
coach	bus
gateau	cake (layer)
tin	can
carriage	car
chemist	drugstore
crisps	chips
Cludo	Clue
pencil crayon	colored pencil
breeze block/concrete block	concrete block
constituency	district
(House of Commons)	(House of Representatives)
condom/rubber	condom/safe
corn flour	cornstarch
pond/lake	pond/lake
sweet/pudding	dessert
nappy	diaper
different from/to	different from/than
curtains	drapes/curtains

Australia	Canada
dumpster	dumpster
eggplant/aubergine	eggplant
electrical cord/flex	electrical cord
elevator/lift	elevator
engaged (phone)	busy
eraser	rubber/eraser
escalator/moving staircase	escalator
extension cord/lead	extension cord
fire plug	fire hydrant
first-year student	first-year student
fish fingers	fish sticks
fizzy drink	soft drink/pop
flashlight/torch	flashlight
frankfurt	hotdog/wiener
freeway/motorway	expressway/freeway
gas/petrol (for a car)	gas
general store	grocery store
generator/dynamo	generator
get a rise (in pay)	get a raise
give (someone) a bell	a call/ring
globe (light)	bulb
grazier	farmer
green beans	green beans
gum boots	rubber boots
hamburger (prepared)/mince	hamburger/ground beef
half-mast (flag)	half-mast
hang up/ring off	hang up
hood/bonnet (of a car)	hood
hot-water service	hot water heater
house for sale	house for sale
house for let	house for rent
icing (cake)	icing
in the post	in the mail/by post
intersection	intersection
invigilate (exam)	invigilate
kerosene/paraffin	kerosene
latex paint/emulsion	paint latex paint
lima beans/broad beans	lima beans
locked/shut tight	locked/shut tight
lollies	candies
match/game	game
Mother's Day	Mother's Day
(Father's Day is the same in all cases)	
moving company	movers
muffler/silencer (of a car)	muffler
nature strip	shoulder

England	United States
rubbish skip	dumpster
aubergine	eggplant
flex	electrical cord
lift	elevator
engaged	busy
eraser	rubber
moving staircase	escalator
lead	extension cord
fire hydrant	fire hydrant
first-year student	freshman
fish fingers	fish sticks
fizzy drink	soda
torch	flashlight
frankfurter	frank/wiener/hotdog
dual carriageway/motorway	freeway/thruway
petrol	gas
grocer	grocery store
dynamo	generator
get a rise	get a raise
a ring	a call
bulb	bulb
farmer	farmer
runner beans	green beans
wellingtons	rubber boots/rainboots
beefburger/mince	hamburger
half-mast	half-staff
ring off	hang up
bonnet	hood
immersion heater	hot water heater
house under offer	house for sale
house for let	house for rent
frosting	icing
in the post/by the post	in the mail/by mail
junction	intersection
proctor	invigilate
paraffin	kerosene
emulsion paint	latex paint
broad beans	lima beans
made fast/locked	locked/shut tight
sweets	candies
fixture/match	game
Mothering Sunday	Mother's Day
removals	van line
silencer	muffler
verge	shoulder

Australia	Canada
odometer/milometer	odometer
outbuildings (at a farm)	outbuildings
outside toilet	outhouse
oval/sports field	sports field
pacifier	pacifier/soother
paddock	field
parka	rain jacket/windbreaker/raincoat/parka
pie/flan	pie
post box	post box/mailbox
prawns	shrimps
prospectus (university)	calendar
public holiday	public holiday
car hire/rental	car rental
ring off (phone)	hang up
rowboat	rowboat
rubbish tin	wastebasket/garbage can
rubbish tip/tip	garbage dump
runners	track shoes/runners/sneakers
sailboat/sailing boat	sailboat
sand shoes	running shoes/canvas shoes
scrapyard/car breaker	scrapyard (car)
second floor	second floor
semi-(trailer)	semi-/transport trailer
(road train—more than one trailer)	
shallots	green onions/spring onions/scallions
skirting board	baseboard
skivvy	turtleneck
sleepers (railway)	ties
standings (sports)	standings
station (sheep or cattle)	ranch/farm
sticky tape	scotch tape
stockyard	stockyard
stretcher	cot
stroller	stroller
study/revise (for a test)	study
subway/underground	subway
sun bake	sunbathe
surgery	doctor's office
sweater/jumper	sweater
take away (food)	take-out
taxi-truck	rent-a-truck
traffic circle	traffic circle
trailer/caravan	trailer/camper
trousers	pants/trousers/slacks
truck/lorry	truck
ute (utility vehicle)	pick-up truck

England	United States
milometer/trip meter	odometer
outhouses	outbuildings
outdoor privy	outhouse
pitch/sports field	sports field
dummy	pacifier/soother
field	field
anorak/mac	windbreaker/rainjacket
flan	pie
pillar box	mailbox
prawns	shrimps
prospectus	catalog
bank holiday	public holiday
car hire	car rental
ring off	hang up
rowing boat	rowboat
wastepaper basket	wastebasket
rubbish tip/refuse tip/tip	garbage dump
trainers	track shoes
sailing boat	sailboat
plimsolls	sneakers/tennis shoes
car breaker	scrapyard
third floor	second floor
articulated lorry	eighteen-wheeler
spring onions	green onions
skirting board	baseboard
polo-neck top	turtleneck shirt
sleepers	ties
tables	standings
farm	ranch
sellotape	scotch tape
cattle pen	stockyard
camp bed	cot
push chair/pusher	stroller
revise (for a test)	study
underground/tube	subway
sunbathe	sunbathe
surgery	doctor's office
jumper	sweater
take away	take out
van hire service	rent-a-truck
roundabout	traffic circle
caravan	trailer
trousers	slacks/pants
lorry	truck
pick-up	truck

Australia	Canada
trucks (railway)	freight cars
trunk/boot (of a car)	trunk
turf/sods	turf
underground walkway	underground walkway
vacuum/hoover	vacuum
vest	vest/waistcoat
wait on	wait for
wake up (someone else)	wake up
washcloth/flannel	washcloth
washing-up liquid	dish detergent
winery	vineyard
woolgrower	sheepfarmer

England

trucks
boot
sods
subway/underpass
hoover
waistcoat
wait for
knock up/wake up
flannel
washing-up liquid
vineyard
sheepfarmer

United States

freight cars
trunk
turf
underground walkway
vacuum
vest
wait for
wake up
washcloth
dish detergent
vineyard
sheepfarmer

◎ APPENDIX 3: *Correction Key*

Ab	Faulty abbreviation
Adj	Improper use of adjective
Adv	Improper use of adverb
Agr	Faulty agreement
Amb	Ambiguous
Awk	Awkward expression or construction
Cap	Faulty capitalization
D	Faulty diction
Dgl	Dangling construction
Frag	Fragment
lc	Use lowercase
Num	Error in use of numbers
||	Lack of parallelism
P	Faulty punctuation
Ref	Unclear pronoun reference
Rep	Unnecessary repetition
R-O	Run-on
sp	Error in spelling
ss	Faulty sentence structure
T	Wrong tense of verb
↶↷	Transpose elements
V	Wrong verb form
Wdy	Wordy
⌄̇	Add apostrophe or single quotation mark
⌣	Close up
⌄̂	Add comma
℮	Delete
∧	Insert
¶	Begin a new paragraph
No ¶	Do not begin a new paragraph
⊙	Add a period
⌄̈ ⌄̈	Double quotation marks
#	Add space

◎ APPENDIX 4: *Essay Checklist*

_____ Does this piece of writing have a clear purpose? Have I made that purpose clear to the reader?

_____ What audience is this written for? Is the tone suited to the intended audience?

_____ Of what am I trying to persuade my audience? Is this made completely clear near the beginning (whether in a formal thesis statement or otherwise)? Is it again made clear near the conclusion?

_____ Does the essay follow a clear path? Are there too many digressions? Is there extraneous material that should be cut, or transferred out of the body of the text and into a note?

_____ Is the structure of the argument signalled by the paragraphing? Does the paragraph remain the unit of composition throughout?

_____ Does the point I am making remain clear in every paragraph? In every sentence?

_____ Is there some variety in sentence structure? Have I avoided awkward sentence constructions? And run-on sentences?

_____ Are most verbs in the active voice?

_____ Do the verbs always agree with the subjects?

_____ Do I use concrete and specific language wherever possible?

_____ Do I avoid excessive use of jargon or unnecessarily obscure language?

_____ Am I careful in my use of qualifiers, avoiding statements that are too bald or extreme, but not qualifying all the strength or interest out of my argument?

_____ Is my writing ever wordy? Where could I still trim? Did I revise (from hard copy) and rewrite the essay thoroughly? Did I proofread after I revised?

_____ Have I checked the punctuation carefully throughout?

_____ Have I proofread as well as used a computer spell-check?

_____ Have I used the correct system of documentation? Do the references follow this system consistently throughout?

_____ Have I given appropriate acknowledgement to all the sources I used? Is there any point at which I might have been guilty of plagiarism by paraphrasing without acknowledgement?

_____ Does the format (spacing, margins, etc.) follow specifications?

_____ Have I answered all the above questions honestly?

◎ INDEX

Entries in **bold** are to words, not topics.

Using 4,608 lb of Rolland Opaque 30 instead of virgin fibres paper reduces your ecological footprint of:

Tree(s): 12
Solid waste: 747 lb
Water: 7,047 gal
Suspended particles in the water: 4.7 lb
Ai emissions: 2,083 lb
Natural gas: 5,696 ft^3